STUDIES IN INTERDISCIPLINARY HISTORY
Edited by ROBERT I. ROTBERG and THEODORE K. RABB

British Capitalism and Caribbean Slavery

Fernando

GFG

287
0672

British Capitalism and Caribbean Slavery

The Legacy of Eric Williams

BARBARA L. SOLOW
Harvard University

STANLEY L. ENGERMAN
University of Rochester

The right of the
University of Cambridge
to print and sell
all manner of books
was granted by
Henry VIII in 1534.
The University has printed
and published continuously
since 1584.

CAMBRIDGE UNIVERSITY PRESS

CAMBRIDGE

NEW YORK   NEW ROCHELLE   MELBOURNE   SYDNEY

PUBLISHED BY THE PRESS SYNDICATE OF THE UNIVERSITY OF CAMBRIDGE
The Pitt Building, Trumpington Street, Cambridge, United Kingdom

CAMBRIDGE UNIVERSITY PRESS

The Edinburgh Building, Cambridge CB2 2RU, UK
40 West 20th Street, New York NY 10011–4211, USA
477 Williamstown Road, Port Melbourne, VIC 3207, Australia
Ruiz de Alarcón 13, 28014 Madrid, Spain
Dock House, The Waterfront, Cape Town 8001, South Africa

http://www.cambridge.org

First published 1987
First paperback edition 2004

A catalogue record for this book is available from the British Library

Library of Congress Cataloguing-in-Publication Data
British capitalism and Caribbean slavery.
Papers originally presented at the Rockefeller Study
and Conference Center at Bellagio, Italy, May 21–25,
1984.
1. Slave trade—West Indies, British—History—Congresses. 2. Slave trade—Great Britain—History—Congresses. 3. Great Britain—Economic conditions—1760-
1860—Congresses. 4. Williams, Eric Eustace, 1911–
—Congresses I. Solow, Barbara L. (Barbara Lewis)
II. Engerman, Stanley L.
HT1092.B75 1987 306´. 362´09729 86–31771

ISBN 0 521 33478 0 hardback
ISBN 0 521 53320 1 paperback

Contents

Contributors

Hilary McD. Beckles, Department of History, University of the West Indies, Bridgetown, Barbados

Selwyn H. H. Carrington, Department of History, University of the West Indies, St. Augustine, Trinidad

Michael Craton, Department of History, University of Waterloo, Waterloo, Ontario

David Brion Davis, Department of History, Yale University, New Haven, Connecticut

Seymour Drescher, Department of History, University of Pittsburgh, Pittsburgh, Pennsylvania

Richard S. Dunn, Department of History, University of Pennsylvania, Philadelphia, Pennsylvania

Stanley L. Engerman, Departments of Economics and History, University of Rochester, Rochester, New York

William A. Green, Department of History, College of the Holy Cross, Worcester, Massachusetts

Joseph E. Inikori, Department of History, Ahmadu Bello University, Zaria, Nigeria

David Richardson, Department of Economic and Social History, University of Hull, Yorkshire, England

Richard B. Sheridan, Department of Economics, University of Kansas, Lawrence, Kansas

Barbara L. Solow, W. E. B. DuBois Institute for Afro-American Research, Harvard University, Cambridge, Massachusetts

Howard Temperley, School of English and American Studies, University of East Anglia, Norwich, England

Gavin Wright, Department of Economics, Stanford University, Stanford, California

Preface

Eric Williams's *Capitalism and Slavery* (1944) defined the study of Caribbean history, and its writing affected the course of Caribbean history. He initiated modern scholarship on the historical relation between the British West Indies and Great Britain. The themes of *Capitalism and Slavery* remain the themes of Caribbean history, and current controversies are being debated in the terms in which Williams posed them. Scholars may agree or disagree with his ideas, but they remain the starting point of discussion. Henry Steele Commager's verdict of 1944—that *Capitalism and Slavery* is "one of the most learned, most penetrating and most significant [books] that has appeared in this field of history"—is still true today.

Any conference on British capitalism and Caribbean slavery is a conference on the work of Eric Williams. This volume consists of papers originally presented at the Rockefeller Study and Conference Center at Bellagio, Italy, on May 21–25, 1984. It honors Eric Williams in the way he would have liked best: by subjecting to the best modern scholarship from America, Europe, Africa, and the Caribbean the ideas that he advanced nearly half a century ago.

We would like to thank the following participants in the conference for their valuable contributions in discussion and comment: Roy Augier, Bridget Brereton, William A. Darity, Jr., David Eltis, Alastair Hennessy, Herbert S. Klein, Patrick O'Brien, Orlando Patterson, Robert I. Rotberg, and Paul Sutton.

We would also like to thank the Rockefeller Foundation and the staff at the Center at Bellagio for making this facility available. We are grateful for financial assistance to the Amoco Foundation; the Alfred P. Sloan Foundation; and, in Trinidad and Tobago, to the government of Trinidad and Tobago, Honorable George Chambers, Prime Minister; Butler's Limited; National Commercial Bank; National Energy Corporation; National Flour Mills; National Petroleum; Trinidad Tesoro Petroleum Company, Ltd.; and Yorke Structures Limited. Much of the editing was completed while Engerman was a Fellow at the Center for Advanced Study in the Behavioral Sciences at Stanford, California, with financial support from the Andrew W. Mellon Foundation as well as support from the National Science Foundation and the University of Rochester, and Solow was a Research Associate at the W. E. B. DuBois Institute for Afro-American Research of Harvard University. The papers by Barbara L. Solow, Joseph E. Inikori, David Richardson, Selwyn H. H. Carrington, Richard S. Dunn, and Gavin Wright appeared as a special issue of *The Journal of Interdisciplinary History* (Volume XVII, Number 4, Spring 1987). We would like to thank the editors of the Journal, Robert I. Rotberg and Theodore K. Rabb, and the Managing Editor, Rhoda Fischer, for their editorial advice and assistance.

Barbara L. Solow
Stanley L. Engerman

Barbara L. Solow and Stanley L. Engerman

British Capitalism and Caribbean Slavery: The Legacy of Eric Williams: An

Introduction   Eric Williams, in *Capitalism and Slavery*, presented four important themes: (1) slavery was an economic phenomenon; and thus racism was a consequence, not the cause, of slavery; (2) the slave economies of the British West Indies caused (the strong version) or contributed greatly (the weaker version) to the British Industrial Revolution; (3) after the American Revolutionary War the slave economies declined in profitability and/or importance to England; and (4) abolition of the slave trade and emancipation of the slaves in the British West Indies were driven not by philanthropy or humanitarianism but by economic motives within England. While all of these themes have been debated, it is the second and fourth that have had the most impact upon subsequent scholarship, and each has become a "Williams thesis."

I. SLAVERY AS AN ECONOMIC PHENOMENON   To Eric Williams, modern slavery in the Americas was not racial in origin, nor the result of color, inherent inferiority, or climate. Rather, it was a matter of economic profitability: "a specific question of time, place, labor and soil."[1] Williams's explanation derives from the economic arguments presented in the nineteenth century by Wakefield, Merivale, and Cairnes. In a new colony, with simple agricultural technology and where land is abundant and therefore cheap, there will be no voluntary supply of labor, because "the

---

1   Eric Williams, *Capitalism and Slavery* (New York, 1966), b. All subsequent page references in the text of this essay are to this edition, published by Capricorn Books.

   Williams restricts his analysis of slavery to the modern period and to slavery in the colonies of European powers. Thus he omits discussion of the very long history of slavery and of its wide distribution. Given, however, the unique characteristics of New World slavery, Williams's issues remain of importance.

laborer [will] exercise his natural inclination to work his own land and toil on his own account" (p. 5). In these circumstances, if there is to be a labor supply, it must be coerced.

The British had colonial possessions in America reflecting both outcomes of the availability of abundant land. In the North the "mere earth-scratcher" was "practicing . . . intensive agriculture and wringing by the sweat of his brow niggardly returns from a grudging soil" (pp. 4–5). In the South and the Caribbean, slave labor was engaged in large-scale production of staple crops for export. Following Cairnes and Merivale, Williams argued that economies of scale and gang labor in certain crops—sugar, cotton, and tobacco—determined the adoption of slavery. To Williams, stories of racial inferiority, the " 'subhuman' characteristics so widely pleaded, were only the later rationalizations to justify a simple economic fact: that the colonies needed labor and resorted to Negro labor because it was the cheapest and the best" (p. 20).[2]

> Negro slavery therefore was only a solution, in certain historical circumstances, of the Caribbean labor problem. Sugar meant labor—at times that labor has been slave, at other times nominally free; at times black, at other times white or brown or yellow. Slavery in no way implied, in any scientific sense, the inferiority of the Negro. Without it the great development of the Caribbean sugar plantations, between 1650 and 1850, would have been impossible. (P. 29)

In his chapter "Race and Slavery: Considerations on the Williams Thesis," William A. Green points out that Williams turns the tables on those who see blacks as "weak and backward" and in need of a "civilizing mission." Rather, he presents them as a productive source of wealth for England and as victims of economic exploitation past and present. Green's chapter discusses the debate on racial versus economic theories of slavery with respect to Virginia and Barbados.

In the literature on Virginia, the Williams position that rac-

---

2 Williams omits discussion of the prior history of the enslavement of blacks in the Middle East and in southern Europe. While earlier slavery could have lead to a predisposition to treat blacks and whites differently, legally and culturally, it could have been that it was only after the establishment of large-scale black slavery that racism became reinforced and magnified into its modern form.

ism was a consequence and not a cause of slavery gained support in the 1950's from such influential scholars as the Handlins, Stampp, and Myrdal. But Degler's response did weaken this position, and by the early 1970's the theory of the prior origins of racism appeared to have conquered the field. This was buttressed in particular by Jordan, who saw racism as a complex psycho-historical problem, and argued against the view that slavery was a choice of labor supply alone, based on relative cheapness. While he recognized that once in place slavery could exacerbate racial attitudes, Jordan pointed to an earlier presence of racism. Hoetink and Degler denied that slavery had a primary role in explaining race prejudice, while Craven doubted the existence of a relationship between economic forces and black slavery in colonial Virginia.

"By the early 1970's then," Green writes, "the Williams-Handlin-Stampp position was in full retreat. The origin of black slavery in the American mainland colonies was being interpreted primarily as a function of race, not economic necessity." But the eclipse was only temporary. The appearance of Morgan's influential *American Slavery—American Freedom* offered new political and economic explanations for the adoption of slavery, arguing that racism had been deliberately fostered by the planter class as a means of severing any possible bond between white and black laborers. The pendulum thus swung back toward the Williams view. Breen and Innes and Evans, from a wide reading of historical evidence, further supported the idea that there is nothing inherent in blacks which accounts for discrimination and that race relations are the result of economic and political power relationships.[3]

Clearly, Williams's position against the consensus of prewar scholars continues to command widespread support. His economic theory of slavery was not original, but was his own blend of the mercantilists and early classical economists. But by 1944 these views had either been discredited or forgotten, and slavery was being explained by race, climate, and geography. Nearly a century of silence on the economic analysis of slavery separates Cairnes from Conrad and Meyer. The reintroduction of eco-

---

3 *Inherent* refers to genetic factors, as contrasted with cultural perceptions that led to a differential attitude toward whites and blacks.

nomic analysis into the analysis of slavery caused a furor in the history profession. Thus, Williams's insistence on treating slavery as a supply of labor, with certain productivity and costs, whose adoption was determined by considerations of profit-maximization, was prophetic and has remained indispensable.

Williams devoted only a few pages to support his dictum that racism was a consequence and not a cause of slavery. His evidence was the case of white indentured servants who coexisted with black slaves: he argued that discrimination followed and did not precede the widespread substitution of black slavery in the labor force.[4] He made no attempt to trace the subsequent path that led to racism or to investigate the power relationships and alienation associated with the institution. The conclusions of Morgan, Breen and Innes, and Evans are in broad agreement with Williams, although the recent literature displays a sophistication and deeper understanding of colonial history than Williams possessed. Green concludes that "if [he] seemed vindicated in the 1980's it was the direction of his thinking, not the credibility of his argument, that gained scholarly endorsement."

II. CARIBBEAN SLAVERY AND THE INDUSTRIAL REVOLUTION. Solow's chapter follows Williams's economic explanation of slavery and extends it in time and space. She identifies a pattern of export-oriented colonial tropical agriculture producing (mainly) sugar with slave labor, a pattern which had its roots in the Italian colonies of the Mediterranean in the late Middle Ages and spread to the Atlantic islands, the islands off Africa, and finally to the Western Hemisphere. She sees the slave-sugar complex as the economic institution that formed the main bridge from the Old World to the New, and the economic relation with the Third World that endured longest and contributed most to European economic development. Following Williams, she agrees that this complex is not an accidental development but the solution to Europe's problem of how to exploit underpopulated colonial conquests quickly.[5] The solution is seen as capitalistic in organization

4 In regard to the literature on the choice between white indentured labor and black slave labor there have been several noteworthy recent works emphasizing the economic aspects of this choice. See, for example, the work of Menard, Galenson, and, for the Barbados case, Beckles.

5 Note that Williams does not discuss the epidemiological consequences of the interaction of European and native American populations.

from the first, combining European capital, African slave labor, and cheap land, to maximize profits by growing and processing a commercial crop and marketing it on a Europe-wide scale.

Through slavery, Europe gained greater investment opportunities, furthered her commercial institutions, and exchanged some of her manufactures for colonial primary products. Solow argues that these flows of factors and commodities become quantitatively important for the economic growth of eighteenth-century Britain, which was developing for domestic reasons and therefore able to take advantage of the opportunities offered by the plantation sector.

This is certainly one of Williams's main themes: "The West Indian islands became the hub of the British Empire, of immense importance to the grandeur and prosperity of England. It was the Negro slaves who made these sugar colonies the most precious colonies ever recorded in the whole annals of imperialism" (p. 52). Quoting Postlethwayt, Williams calls the eighteenth-century empire "a magnificent superstructure of American commerce and naval power on an African foundation." The trade gave a triple stimulus to British industry, sending British manufactures to Africa in return for slaves; to the West Indies in return for tropical products; and to New England and Newfoundland in return for foreign exchange they had earned by exporting agricultural products and fish to the West Indies. Quoting another eighteenth-century writer, Gee, Williams claims that "By 1750 there was hardly a trading or a manufacturing town in England which was not in some way connected with the triangular or direct colonial trade." "The profits obtained," Williams continues, "provided one of the main streams of that accumulation of capital in England which financed the Industrial Revolution" (p. 52). He then goes on to cite specific industries whose growth was associated with the triangular trade and to give examples of the investment of plantation profits into banking, insurance, shipping, and, most importantly, the industrial development of the early Industrial Revolution.

Three lines of criticism have been levelled at these arguments. When Sheridan presented quantitative estimates showing sizable returns on British investment in the West Indies, Thomas countered by criticizing both Sheridan's methods and numerical estimates. He concluded that, if properly measured, the colonies' contribution to the mother country was negative: British income would have been greater without them.[6] Second, Engerman argued that even a deliberately overstated estimate of the profits of the slave trade was too small to have greatly affected British investment and income. Third, critics were quick to point out that no great surge in investment was associated with the onset of the Industrial Revolution: most new industries had modest capital requirements and were financed by personal savings of family or friends. The conclusions of Thomas and Engerman have been disputed by Solow, and the three chapters on this subject all lend support to Eric Williams's original contention. While there are important differences among them, Inikori, Richardson, and Solow all agree in attributing an important role to the plantation economies in explaining the spurt in British industrial output of the late eighteenth century.

For Inikori, this case is an example of a more general thesis that foreign trade was the principal impetus leading from subsistence agrarian economies to developed industrial economies within Europe. According to him, the Atlantic trading system saved England from the fate suffered by the Mediterranean countries in the seventeenth century. Combining African slaves with New World land, England was able to reap great advantages from her Atlantic empire. It constituted a large common market containing diversified economies: in this setting, mercantilist policies assisted her development, in contrast with their deleterious effects in the Iberian countries. Inikori sees the Atlantic system in the seventeenth century as providing England with commodities for re-export and thereby strengthening her mercantile sector. In the eighteenth century he finds the Atlantic trade propelling her toward industrialization by contributing to the growth of trade, transport, and manufacturing.

Richardson's chapter focuses on developments in a specific time period. He argues that the increase in British trade in the third quarter of the eighteenth century was associated with the Atlantic economy (Africa, the Caribbean, and the North Ameri-

6 It should be noted that Thomas's response raises an important analytical issue for further consideration in this debate—the extent to which England, at this time, can be considered to be an economy with relatively full employment of its productive factors, or rather if the opportunity costs of employment within the slave nexus were low or zero in many cases.

can colonies); that the principal roots of this trade lay in the response of the slave economies to increased demand for sugar in Britain; and (since the counterpart of British sugar imports was British manufactured exports) that the growth of this trade assisted significantly in shifting the British economy away from nonindustrial production and toward industrial production at this time.[7] Thus British industrial growth in the third quarter of the century is seen to depend not exclusively but importantly on the Atlantic trade, and Caribbean sugar is the key to this trade: "exports to Africa and America in particular proved to be at least a very capable handmaiden in promoting further expansion in England's emerging industrial regions before 1776."

Richardson's statistical estimates of the British slave trade to the Caribbean show the greatest expansion coming in the third quarter of the eighteenth century. He speculates that this growth was accounted for by buoyant demand for sugar in England, due to changes in taste, to price-induced shifts in consumption patterns, and to increased incomes in London and the newly industrializing areas, such as Lancashire. At this time the British economy was probably experiencing decreasing rates of growth of total output; industrial output, however, was rising faster that at any previous time in the century. There was thus a sharp divergence between the growth of the industrial and nonindustrial sectors, signaling substantial structural change. It is in this context that the link to Caribbean developments is found.

The acceleration in new industrial growth based on exports depended to a considerable extent on purchasing power generated by the British West Indies. Tentative calculations suggest that the African, Caribbean, and North American demands ultimately generated by the sugar colonies may have raised British

---

7 Note that Richardson's argument here resembles that of Deane and Cole, in that the increased demand from the New World colonies for British goods is not exogenous, but represents an endogenous response to higher demands for colonial products emanating from Great Britain. The exogenous factor is the institution of slavery which, by providing an elastic supply of cheap productive labor, allows for the continuing production of sugar.

Another important issue that remains when "expansion" is used as a measure of the value of the slave colonies is that since trade, both before and after the American Revolution, was carried on under a protectionist commercial policy, expansion may merely indicate more and more misallocation of resources. This argument was familiar in eighteenth-century England, among influential politicians as well as others.

total exports "by almost £1.6 million per annum between the late 1740's and the early 1770's." These colonies may be responsible for more than half of the growth of English domestically produced exports in the third quarter of the century, and about 8.5 percent of the growth in English industrial output during that time.

The slave-sugar complex and the trade and capital flows it engendered were important to British economic growth in the late eighteenth century.[8] This is the conclusion of Solow, Inikori, and Richardson, and was the broad consensus of the conference. To this extent Williams was correct. But slavery did not contribute by sending a vast stream of capital investment to finance technological change in cotton and iron in late eighteenth-century England. There was no such sudden large increase in investment. To this extent Williams was wrong. However, drawing on Solow, Inikori, and Richardson, one can formulate a different causal explanation to support his thesis.

Instead of West Indian profits leading to increased investment in England, it is likelier that there was an abundance of saving and a lack of investment opportunities. This is consistent with the falling interest rates in England. Once an elastic supply of productive labor was added to the cheap land of the Caribbean and the American South, such an investment outlet was in place. Colonial investment followed slavery. West Indian mortgages constituted a relatively large share of the London market. If we accept Sheridan's estimate of the total value of investments in the Caribbean of about £37 million and Price's estimate for the American South of about £5 million (both for the period just prior to the Revolution), we can see that the institution of slavery had an important effect in increasing investment in the Empire, and that the return on this investment increased income in England.

Such investment was dependent on slavery, and was not merely a diversion of funds from potential domestic investment. It increased British income *whatever the recipients of the income chose to do with it:* whether they spent it on land or coaches or wine— or on textile machinery. It did not have to be invested in order

---

8 It can be argued that it was the slave colonies that benefited Great Britain by providing a market for British industrial exports when domestic sources of growth were weak, and that they mattered less to her as the Industrial Revolution quickened its pace.

for there to be a relation between colonial slave production and British income—any positive return on investment does that. If some of the returns were saved, there was a greater ultimate increase in income than if they were all consumed. But the income recipients did not themselves have to invest in order to establish a relation between colonial sugar production and British industrial production. Eric Williams was wrong about that relation. His was a misunderstanding of elementary macroeconomics.

But the increased British income associated with colonial investment is not the whole story. Richardson's paper makes this clear. The pounds spent for sugar by British consumers cover not only the profits but also the costs of producing the sugar. These latter pounds were earned by slave traders, shippers, and insurers, and by the suppliers of fish, flour, horses, timber, and other commodities to the plantations. The after-profit pounds paid by British sugar consumers appear in the incomes of the people in England, in Africa, in the West Indies, and in the North American colonies, whose economic activity constituted the costs of producing the sugar. A substantial part of these pounds was spent on importing British goods. In particular, some counterpart of British expenditures on sugar became British exports to the North American colonies and the West Indies, the exports to North America probably exceeding those to the islands.

This colonial trade changed the direction and content of British foreign trade in the eighteenth century as well as its magnitude: on this Solow, Inikori, and Richardson are in agreement. Previously Britain traded wool textiles to Europe for primary products; the continent to a large degree produced its own manufactures. By the eighteenth century France, Germany, and Austria began to supply their own woolen textile needs, and traditional British export markets faltered. Here the colonial trade became important: not only did it provide new markets for increased exports, but it provided a new pattern of trade. For the trade was of British manufactures for foodstuffs, not of woolens for raw materials. The North American colonies were important customers for British manufacturers; population there increased tenfold from 1700 to 1774, and their total income rose even faster. They spent the greater part of their foreign exchange earnings—most of it earned either in the British West Indies or from the production within their own slave sector—on British manufactures: silk, linen, wool, hats, glass, cordage, gunpowder, and above all a wide range of small metalwares, like buttons, nails, cutlery, watches, and jewelry.

The value of British manufacturing exports more than doubled between 1699–1701 and 1772–74. Between those dates the share of manufacturing exports going to Europe fell from 82 percent to 42 percent, while the share going to America and Africa rose from 12 percent to 43 percent. Thus, it was the widening of the market through the earnings of the colonies from the production of slave-grown commodities that provided Britain with new markets when the old ones were drying up. Second, the new export demand was for manufactures and encouraged the development of the nonagricultural sector of the home country. Neither Solow nor Richardson claims that all the increased industrial production or all the increased exports were due to exogenous colonial demand. Both—but not Inikori—find the roots of the increased colonial demands in the domestic economy. But all three agree that the increased demand for British manufactured exports played an important role in the expansion of the British industrial sector.[9] Behind this increased colonial demand was the slave labor of the Caribbean and the American South, without whose work colonial production could never have reached such levels.

Williams's story of plantation profits being invested to produce the technological changes we call the Industrial Revolution does not hold up. But if the technical change of the Industrial Revolution is put into the context of an increasingly rich, commercial, manufacturing society, then the connection holds. For slavery helped make eighteenth-century England more rich, more commercial, and more industrial. Where investment is sluggish and technical change is slow, external stimulus through market-widening will be an important means to stimulate growth. In Britain these forces were added to those in the domestic economy pushing toward industrialization. It would be hard to claim that they were either necessary or sufficient for an Industrial Revolution, and equally hard to deny that they affected its magnitude and timing.

9 If there were unemployed resources in Britain, foreign demand would have further expanded British incomes through the multiplier process; i.e., by the respending of the incomes initially earned through the export market.

Writing as he did before Deane and Cole, Davis, Crafts, Crouzet, and Feinstein, and with no economic analysis beyond that of the early nineteenth century, it is surprising how well Eric Williams's general position has withstood the test of time. He was right in his intuition but excessive in his claims and incorrect in some of his arguments. His originality lay in identifying neither exports nor colonialism but slavery as an active force contributing to British growth. He anticipates subsequent scholars in stressing the productivity and economic importance of slave economies. Had all emigration to the Western Hemisphere been voluntary and none coerced, the British economy and its North American colonies would have developed more slowly.

III. THE DECLINE OF THE BRITISH WEST INDIES   Scholars like Drescher, Eltis, and Temperley go beyond Williams in describing the contribution made by slavery to the British economy. They maintain that this contribution never diminished as a result of economic conditions, but was strangled by the legislative acts of abolition and emancipation passed in contradiction to British economic interests. They hold that the British inflicted severe economic loss on themselves by adopting antislavery measures; the idea is well captured by Drescher's neologism for the effects of the ending of the British slave trade—*econocide*. For Williams the slave-based plantation economies contributed to the British Industrial Revolution and a different kind of British economy, but after the American Revolution the slave system made, at best, a negligible or, at worst, a negative contribution. To him British antislavery policy was dictated by British metropolitan interests, and there was nothing paradoxical about it and nothing that justified any self-congratulation.[10]

The "decline" of the British West Indies can only be discussed if we are clear about precisely what it was that did or did not decline. Since we are interested in the relation between the colonies and the metropolis we must specify the mechanism of that relation before we can evaluate its changes. If one accepts the link posited by Williams between West Indian profits and British industrial investment, then the relevant decline could be

---

10   As Williams discusses both the origins of slavery in the British West Indies and then its endings, it can be seen that the British only ended what they themselves had begun— another ground for denying them a self-congratulatory reaction.

in rates of return on sugar plantations. If one accepts the importance of the role of trade patterns, the relevant decline would be in the functioning of the entire multilateral trading system. And if one argues the view that the demand from the plantation colonies led to a new industrial economy in Britain, the relevant measure would be the colonies as a source of economic growth and structural change within England.

Drescher has vigorously attacked the whole idea of decline. He asserts that there was no decline in the value of the slave system to the metropolis, that West Indian slavery was expanding until its growth was terminated by the abolition of the slave trade. Further, there was no critical change in the colonial system after the American Revolution and no dramatic change in British imperial policy in regard to colonial trade until after emancipation. Carrington's chapter, following Williams and an older tradition going back to Pitman, argues that American independence dealt the Old Colonial System a blow from which it never recovered.

Carrington argues that the British North American colonies were an essential ingredient in the West Indies' value to Britain. The entire system—capital exports from Britain; slave exports from Africa; sugar imports into Britain; North American exports of supplies to the West Indies; British manufacturing exports to North America, Africa, and the West Indies; and North American imports of rum and minor staples—he sees as an interdependent whole, impossible to function without the economic involvement of the North American colonies. He argues that the American Revolution had a devastating impact on the West Indian colonies and initiated an uninterrupted decline in their importance. As evidence he cites severe shortages in food and lumber; increased freight and insurance costs; uncertain, irregular, and diminished shipping; declining sugar prices; and disappearing markets. After the war only Jamaica continued to increase its import of slaves; Barbados, Antigua, and Dominica showed declines in the numbers of slaves imported, and French Saint-Domingue and Spanish Cuba were taking an increasing share of the slaves brought to the West Indies. According to Carrington, British West Indian exports to, and merchandise imports from, Britain declined after 1779.

Drescher, following what he regards as Williams's key variable, measures the value of the colonies by their share in the value of British long-distance trade. He argues that this percentage was consistently higher after 1776 than before. According to him the British West Indies were as valuable to Britain in 1828–32 as in the mid-eighteenth century. The subsequent decline of West Indian importance was due, first, to the abolition of the slave trade and, a quarter-century later, to the emancipation of the slaves. Drescher rejects the argument that any downturns in West Indian production, slave imports, and their share of British trade during some years within the period 1783–1807 can be taken as evidence of permanent secular decline. He argues that those declines that occurred were mainly a short-run phenomenon, and that the slave plantations in the colonies were operating with undiminished profit rates until 1820. Drescher also maintains that long-run decline in sugar production in the older islands is not incompatible with expansion of the system as a whole; indeed, it was the expansion of the new areas that lowered profitability and production in the old islands. Drescher's final verdict is that Williams was wrong to claim a permanent diminution in the value of the colonies after the Revolutionary War, and also wrong to see the triumph of antislavery as a victory for nascent capitalist classes over the old mercantile class, but that Williams was correct in recognizing that it was new classes thrown up by the Industrial Revolution that propelled the antislavery forces to their ultimate success. His disagreement with Williams concerns the question of which of the new classes was instrumental in raising and resolving the antislavery issue.

On the decline issue the conference came to no clear-cut consensus. By positing a direct link between an alleged decline in the economic importance of the West Indian colonies and the success of the antislavery movement, Eric Williams perhaps muddied the issue more than he clarified it. In fact there are two quite separable issues: (1) what are the simple economic facts about the contribution of the West Indies to British growth, how do we measure it, and how does it change over time; (2) what role, if any, do these simple economic facts play in explaining the success of the antislavery movement?

Carrington's argument is that the West Indies' importance depended on the functioning of the whole network of trade flows that characterized the Old Colonial System and that the functioning of this system changed drastically after American independence. His chapter mainly addresses the period 1775–91. The questions of timing still remain. It was not until after the War of 1812, for example, that the share of the United States in the growth of British exports began to fall sharply. The United States then began to develop domestically and became less dependent on Britain for manufactures and less dependent on the West Indies for the foreign exchange with which to buy them. Southern cotton exports began to take care of that. A simple measure like the share of British trade going to the West Indies will alone not capture the implications of the changed role of the United States in making the West Indian colonies valuable to the mother country. It was the American market that had translated as much as half of the West Indian sugar earnings into British exports at the end of the eighteenth century; this now changed as the United States developed economically and turned from deficit toward surplus on merchandise account.

It can be argued that changing conditions in England diminished the colonial contribution in the nineteenth as compared with the eighteenth century. The Old Colonial System can be seen as an important means of stimulating industrial development by encouraging exports through market-widening, when investment is sluggish and technical change is slow. This characterized England during the late eighteenth century: in the last two decades of the eighteenth century nearly 60 percent of additional industrial output was exported. British export growth rates declined after 1802 and remained slow until midcentury. The ratio of export growth to national product growth, which Crouzet calculates as 40 percent in 1783–1801, became negative in 1801–11 and does not become large again until the 1840's. The leading role of exports did not survive the eighteenth century. The nineteenth-century home market was expanding faster than was foreign demand, and domestic consumption and investment and technical change increased relative to exports as sources of growth. It was only in the last two decades of the eighteenth century that exports played a role in leading industrial output. The United States accounted for a major portion of this export spurt, but after the War of 1812 this changed drastically. Within the (diminished) export sector, India, Australia, and Latin America increasingly supplanted the areas of the Old Colonial System as Britain's best customers. The diminished role of exports in British growth and the further diminished importance of the Old Colonial System both antedate abolition and emancipation, according to this argument, and cannot be accounted for by them. The implication is that an end to slavery in the 1770's would have severely diminished the demand for English manufactures but that an end to slavery after the 1820's had an imperceptible effect on the British economy.[11]

In the conference discussion David Eltis argued that the comparison should be with how the British economy would have benefited had slavery not been ended. He contended that by abolishing slavery while the Empire was expanding into underpopulated tropical areas—for whose products demand remained high—the British missed a great opportunity. Had they abolished their own slave trade but refrained from interfering with that of others; or had they allowed intercolonial slave trade from the old areas to Trinidad and Demerara; or had they repealed the abolition altogether and reopened the slave trade, they would have been better off than by pursuing the course they took. The same elastic supply of cheap productive labor that helped the British economy before 1807 would have continued to do so after 1807 if it had been allowed: cheaper British West Indian sugar and other plantation produce, more employment at home, more British exports, a higher standard of living, and better relations between capital and labor would have been the consequence.

The decline issue thus continues to be in dispute. None of the conferees followed Eric Williams in seeing the West Indian slave system as an obstacle to British growth—although at times Williams appeared to have equated British trade protection with slavery, which is quite a different story. But his portrayal of a concerted conspiratorial step-by-step attack by capitalists on the slave trade, slavery, and the sugar duties drew no support.[12] It was felt to have reflected an outdated view of British politics.

---

11 Note that this measure of decline is relative to the overall growth of the British economy. It does not argue that the profitability of slavery in the West Indies had fallen, nor that the West Indies had become responsible for a smaller share of British foreign trade. Rather it indicates that the role of the West Indies, and of exports in general, had become less critical to the British economy relative to the importance of the home market. Thus the West Indian slave system had become more dispensable to the British—however profitable and productive it might have continued to be.

12 Williams's conspiratorial view is perhaps best seen from a long-run vantage; he further attributed the specific timing of the successful accomplishment of the first two to the same cause—overproduction of sugar.

Yet problems remain with each of the views that were put forth at the conference. The discussion was marked by a failure to distinguish the causes and effects of abolition in 1807 from those of emancipation (1833), and by a tendency to lump them together as antislavery. Of course they are related. But the agitation for one began in the 1780's and for the other in the 1820's; they occurred in quite different economic environments; the generation between them saw changes in both the British and the colonial economies; they can be expected to have had different causes as well as effects; and the respective campaigns were organized by different people, with different techniques, in different political circumstances.

The conference thus left many unresolved problems related to the topic of the economic decline of the West Indies and (to the extent that one occurred) its consequences. Were the conditions pointed to by Carrington for the period 1775–91 continued or reversed? If Drescher is correct that the colonies were at peak value in 1828–32, what does that imply about the effects of abolition? Eltis disagrees about the role of trade and exports in the British economy, arguing that exports earned a high percentage of national income and international trade became an increasing factor in British growth between 1800 and 1850. Eltis's argument raises the question of how much difference it would have made in a free-trade world if Britain had imported sugar, coffee, and cotton from Trinidad and Demerara rather than from Cuba, Brazil, and the United States. These are only examples of the range of issues still under discussion.

Finally, with a single exception, not much was said about internal developments in the West Indian islands in assessing their economic decline. The one major area of Caribbean history to which Eric Williams did not contribute is demographic analysis: its development is recent but very important. Dunn's chapter makes a major contribution here, as did the earlier work by Barry Higman on the economic implications of Jamaican demographic decline after abolition.

Dunn discusses the work experience of the slave labor force of a Jamaica plantation for which continuous data are available from 1762 to 1831. He discusses demographic development, work patterns, sex roles, health, and miscegenation. Among many interesting findings, those on the changing slave sex ratios may have implications for the decline issue. The female/male ratio, which was low in the 1760's, turned to a female majority by 1810. This shift, Dunn finds, was a general phenomenon in Jamaica. His data show that 95 percent of female adult slaves became prime field hands, compared with only 65 percent of males. Females were excluded from jobs as craftsmen and drivers and from miscellaneous other skilled occupations. They thus came to outnumber men in the field gang, with probably adverse effects on their health and reproductive capacity. Even so, females lasted longer in prime field work than did males, and they lived longer. His work raises the question of the possible effects of a lowered productivity in sugar production from a more female labor force in planting and harvesting, not only in Jamaica, but elsewhere in the British West Indies as well. These demographic developments, with their possible significant effects on plantation profitability, appear to antedate the abolition of the slave trade. Dunn's findings raise the question to what extent profitability of slave plantations may have been changing for internal reasons.

IV. THE BASIS OF ABOLITION AND EMANCIPATION   The connection between economic decline in the British West Indies and the British antislavery movement has generally been discussed in the terms set by *Capitalism and Slavery*. Against the idea that the abolition and emancipation exemplified disinterested, philanthropic altruism, Eric Williams opposed an explanation based on the narrow economic motives of the British industrial capitalist class. This has given rise to some heated, but often unfruitful, debates about humanitarian versus economic motives, but the conference discussion did not proceed along these oversimplified lines. Yet there were strongly contrasting opinions. To those who denied that the West Indies declined in importance, antislavery legislation presented a paradox. Why, asked Temperley, was a thriving useful capitalist system of agriculture dismantled by the legislative arm of a capitalist society? For Eric Williams and for David Brion Davis, and for Drescher, Eltis, and Temperley as well, the West Indian slave system was destroyed by a capitalist society: to its advantage in the first case; to its economic detriment in the second.

The discussion did not portray the antislavery movement as a simple clash among abolitionists, planters, and capitalists, but set it in a broader context of changes occurring within the slave economies on the one hand and English society on the other. The question addressed was not *whether* ideology or economic forces affected the movement but *how* they affected it.

Drescher argues against the notion that the antislavery movement came when the colonies diminished in importance to the British economy. Having denied such diminution, he denies any simple role for economic motivation in the antislavery movement. He is also skeptical about ideology as a motivating force. He views the "historians of ideology"—among whom he includes Temperley and Davis—as relying on a convergence of humanitarian ideals and capitalist ideology, and he finds their explanation of how this combination functions obscure. Neither the philanthropy of the Saints, nor the ideology of the capitalists, nor the economic analysis of Adam Smith alone explains the rise of abolitionism, according to Drescher.

Instead, "the diffuse and often ambivalent ideology of antislavery became rooted as a national social movement at the cutting edge of the Industrial Revolution. It was British public opinion that launched the great 'takeoff' of abolitionism in the winter of 1787–88. And it was the abolitionists of the booming, industrializing North of England, who, quite independently of the London Saints, made the mass abolition petition the principal new weapon of abolitionism." Manchester, a hard-nosed manufacturing town, not London, the home of an isolated sect with a tender conscience, drove the movement. Abolitionism was engrafted into the everyday practices of commercial capitalism and consumer capitalism, Drescher maintains. For him, as for Eric Williams, Manchester brought down slavery. For Williams, Manchester stands for a new kind of industrial economy which slavery and mercantilism brought about and which then outgrew its need for both of them. For Drescher, however, Manchester represents the emergence of a new social movement of entrepreneurs, artisans, and skilled laborers that used mass petitions to attack slavery.

It may be asked, however, why, if the slave colonies were pouring undiminished wealth into Britain, was Manchester signing these petitions? This is the question that Temperley and others have seen as critical to those who would put economic motives out of court. As Davis asks, why were so many Britons of different rank and background concerned about Negro slavery, an institution thousands of miles away?

Davis addresses a narrower question than Drescher: how did abolitionist sentiment gain widespread acceptance in the era of reactionary politics from the late 1790's to the early 1820's? Not only does Davis shrink from offering a global explanation, he raises serious questions about the value of such attempts. The context of antislavery movements differed enormously from country to country, and continuities are exaggerated within countries as well. For his own question, Davis argues that, although abolitionist thought served conflicting ideological functions, in the end it helped reinforce a hegemony of capitalist values. The argument is subtle and complex and far from the crude notion that somehow capitalists used abolitionism to deflect working-class antagonisms from themselves.

By defining slavery in a particular way, as a legal status where persons can be bought and sold and owned as property, abolitionist discourse also defined slavery's opposite, "freedom," in a particular way. Wilberforce and the elder Stephen could sharply contrast the colonies with England and her celebrated free institutions: slavery affected people of a different color in foreign lands. Not being a slave meant one was free to sell one's labor in the marketplace. Buying and selling and *owning* people was wrong; buying and selling and *renting* labor was not only morally acceptable but positively desirable. This formulation can be made to fit perfectly into the rhetoric of laissez-faire capitalism. If property rights are clearly defined and confirmed, then when individuals pursue their own self-interest, the invisible hand of the unfettered market will ensure an optimal result for society. Economic as well as moral problems ensue when one's labor is someone else's property. Adam Smith's attack on slavery converts it to a principal agent problem, and Temperley has elaborated on this without using the term.

The terms of abolitionist discourse then permitted ruling elites to join with reformers in a nonthreatening way. Landlords, merchants, and manufacturers could affirm moral standards while containing debates about morality and oppression within limits that served to reinforce the legitimacy of the existing social order. Of course they could not monopolize the use of abolitionist terms and techniques, and slavery in other hands became a powerful metaphor in radical British ideology. But for the most part, "governing elites could tolerate and even encourage reforms that redeemed the national character and enhanced their own authority."

Davis is not concerned with the issue of the economic decline of the West Indies and mentions Eric Williams only in terms of his "cynical reductionism." The importance of decline to Williams is that, just for that reason, abolition and emancipation offered ruling elites an attractive opportunity to demonstrate their commitment to morality and justice, without cost, and possibly even with great benefit, to themselves. Williams's decline explanation can be used to explain the timing of the antislavery movement. At the very least, the decline story fits well with the hegemony story in locating the British antislavery movement in a middle ground between crude economic determinism and simple ideological determinism. Together they take account of the realities of economic and class power.

Others argued that while the economy had undergone important social and economic changes in the years from the 1780's to the 1820's—in urbanization, industrialization, religion, and squire-tenant relations—the old eighteenth-century polity of unreformed Parliament, Church, merchants, and landed aristocracy remained in control of political power. The West Indian planters were part of this establishment. The people associated with the changing economic and social structure pressed for political power commensurate with their emergent numbers and importance. They were the Outs just starting to attack the Ins—not just cotton capitalists or the bourgeoisie of Marxian literature, but elite skilled workers, clerks, shopkeepers, even disaffected rural people. Their target was the political hegemony of the eighteenth-century establishment, and they supported antislavery because it was an effective ideological weapon against that establishment. Neither economic determinist nor ideological, this argument has a different flavor, derived perhaps from Victorian historians like Kitson Clark, and would be compatible with Davis's hegemony story in a certain sense. The antislavery campaigns are thus seen as part of the entire movement for reform, free trade, religious toleration, and penal reform that began in the 1820's but had its roots in the prewar era before the reaction to the French Revolution set in.

Another important set of issues concerning the process of abolition lies in the effect of the petitions of the 1780's, emphasized by Drescher, on the unreformed Parliaments of George III. Was Pitt's accession to abolition influenced more by petitions than by his friendship with Wilberforce and his attraction to the doctrines of Adam Smith? In the structure of eighteenth-century politics, how many petitions were worth one Pitt to the antislavery camp? Did petitions turn Castlereagh and the Duke of Wellington away from the West Indian interests or had they simply ceased to believe in their crucial importance?

Craton's chapter explores the reciprocal relation between slave revolts in the islands and the antislavery movement in England. His chapter highlights the difference between the two generations of antislavery agitation. In the reactionary era, when Creole Christian slaves revolted in Barbados in 1816, Wilberforce's antislavery arguments were undercut, and the planters were able to embarrass the movement by blaming them for the revolt. In the era of the Tory Liberalism of Canning and Huskisson, when Wilberforce ceased to be active and Buxton and Brougham led the movement, slave revolt could be presented as a response to planter resistance to ameliorist policies, and a gulf could be opened between the ruling class in the islands and that in the metropolis.

V. *CAPITALISM AND SLAVERY* IN HISTORICAL PERSPECTIVE

Wright's contribution compares the American slave experience with that of the British colonies. The basic difference between investment in slaves and investment in land and capital, he observes, is that slaves are movable while land and capital are not. This distinction helps explain differences between slave and free societies in population growth, public and private investment, exploration for mineral wealth, and political development. Northern perceptions that the antebellum South was poor and backward arose because Northerners mistook the absence of Northern forms of wealth for poverty. Like nomads, Southerners held their wealth in movable form. Nevertheless, Southerners were less expansionist geographically than Northerners: Southern expansion was slower, "reflecting a collective interest in high slave prices," and westward expansion meant increased competition for the planters of the Old South.

Despite their many differences, Wright finds that American and Caribbean slave societies shared many characteristics. Slavery fostered no strong tie between planter and land in both; the profits derived from slavery helped finance early industrialization elsewhere in both economies; planters were reluctant to open new slave territories in both. The islands exhibited a life-cycle trajectory, with high initial growth followed by subsequent retardation. This occurred because of low investment incentives for land and capital. Over time the economic interests of both came to lie in abolishing the slave trade to protect the value of their stocks.

Wright concludes that neither abolition nor emancipation hurt the British domestic economy. In preindustrial societies economic growth is more dependent on expansion of trade and commerce, while in industrial societies technical change and investment are more important sources of growth. The movement by which Britain successively abolished the slave trade and emancipated the slaves marched in parallel with this change in economic interests: if the British did not actually "do well by doing good," they did themselves little harm.

From Wright's analysis one can draw a picture that would be compatible in certain respects with a Williams thesis (although this is not Wright's intention): early prosperity and value to Britain, followed by decline and a reluctance to expand, followed by an end to the slave system without serious harm to the British economy. This does not quite correspond to Wright's picture of the Southern economy where per capita income (including slaves) grew as fast as or faster than the national average, and per capita income of free Southerners was about equal to that of Northerners. The average wealth of adult free male Southerners was nearly double that of their Northern counterparts. This is not the picture of a declining life cycle: Wright contends that "by no conventional measure of performance was the South stagnating or declining, nor was slavery unviable economically." The contrast with the Caribbean remains to be explained. Questions were also raised about the relation between Wright's basic point that the hallmark of slave societies is the mobility of their assets with his later point that slave societies are recalcitrant to expansion.

The papers presented at the final session of the conference placed *Capitalism and Slavery* and its author in historical perspective. Beckles discussed the relation between Williams's work and the modern plantation school of political economy in the West Indies. The contemporary theorists acknowledge Williams as a seminal thinker and have extended some of his views to the postslavery period.

The conference closed with papers by Paul Sutton, W. A. Darity, Jr., and Richard B. Sheridan. The former two are not published in this volume. Darity saw *Capitalism and Slavery* as Marxist analysis, but in some respects flawed Marxist analysis. He further suggested that some of what appear to be inconsistencies in the work can be made to disappear when the Marxist framework is better understood and articulated. Sutton's paper considered Eric Williams as economic historian, development economist, political theorist, social critic, and educator. Sheridan's paper traced the history of Williams's work since its appearance and discussed its critics, its supporters, and its overall influence and status. His comprehensive and judicious assessment was an appropriate conclusion to the proceedings.

Part I. Slavery as an Economic Phenomenon

William A. Green

Race and Slavery: Considerations on the Williams Thesis

No history is timeless. Works inspired by the exigencies of contemporary politics are least likely to enjoy enduring acclaim. Eric Williams's *Capitalism and Slavery* is a politically inspired book, and it has, at long last, begun to exhibit advancing age. But one dare not write its obituary. Whenever in the past Williams's work has appeared irreparably discredited, some new academic physician has breathed fresh life into the old pages.

How do we account for its durability? That it embraces the salient issues which have gripped much of the historical profession in recent decades—racism, slavery, the origins of industrialization, and the evolution of a world order deeply divided between rich and poor—is a partial but insufficient explanation. In treating these questions, Williams challenges our collective self-esteem. He repudiates Anglo-Saxon heroes, renders ascribed nobility ignoble, and raises doubts whether the most honored economic achievements of the North Atlantic nations are, in reality, the reward of superior energy, organization, and inventiveness. Although his text is laden with moral purpose, it rigorously, almost ostentatiously, rejects moral sentimentality. He proffers no diatribe, just the systematic application of a stringent intellectual chemical—the doctrine of economic necessity—to our most cherished notions. An iconoclast, not a Marxist, he challenged the Anglo-American historical establishment on its own philosophical turf: Smith, Wakefield, and Merivale, not Marx, were his esteemed theoretical forebears. His unusual ability to identify patterns and establish linkages between wide-ranging and seemingly divergent historical developments has rendered his text both absorbing and persuasive. Even where he is outrageous, it has been difficult to prove him so.

Capitalism and Slavery was conceived, researched, and drafted during a time of intense West Indian demand for self-government. Since Britain promised self-government whenever the colonies were ready, West Indian intellectuals in the 1930's were determined to demonstrate their readiness. C. L. R. James, fellow Trinidadian and intellectual inspiration for the young Eric Williams, assured Britons that Caribbean colonists, being Western in social customs, religion, education, and outlook, were amply prepared for political responsibility.[1] Williams affirmed West Indian competency and ridiculed Britain's "civilizing mission,"[2] asserting that England's relationship with her Caribbean colonies had always been governed by self-interest, never by self-sacrifice.

Having won the lone island scholarship for university study in England, Williams achieved a first in modern history at Oxford and advanced in 1936 to doctoral research under Vincent Harlow. Harlow worked in the shadow of Sir Reginald Coupland, Professor of Colonial History, whom Williams deeply distrusted for his admixture of history and imperial apologetics. Coupland's biography of Wilberforce (1923) emphasized "the power of pure idealism" to achieve a moral revolution over materialism in the colonial empire. He endorsed Lecky's contention that British abolitionism provided "among the three or four perfectly virtuous pages" in history, and he enshrined the principle of humanitarian trusteeship in nineteenth-century imperial historiography. Britain, Coupland urged, enjoyed a special tradition of responsibility toward "weak and backward black peoples. . . ."[3] Colonists in the modern Empire could rest assured that Britain would afford them justice and opportunity. After all, Britons of the 1930's were the "heirs and guardians of a great tradition."[4]

Such humanitarian sentimentality was abhorrent to Williams. It patronized him. It denied him and his Afro-Caribbean forebears any significant responsibility for working out their own destinies. Moreover, it collided with his perception of reality in colonial Trinidad. Nevertheless, Coupland's approach dominated

---

1 C. L. R. James, *The Case for West-Indian Self Government* (London, 1933), pp. 5–6.
2 Eric Williams, *Inward Hunger: The Education of a Prime Minister* (London, 1969), p. 21.
3 For an extended critique by Williams of Coupland's historical orientation, see his *British Historians and the West Indies* (New York, 1966), pp. 197–207.
4 Quotation from Coupland is in Williams, *Inward Hunger*, p. 50.

Anglo-American historical writing on abolitionism.[5] His cardinal sin, Williams thought, was not his emphasis upon moral force; it was his self-serving use of history to justify contemporary practices in the beleaguered Empire. This, Williams thought, was a political abuse of history. Responding to his own political agenda, he set out to deny contemporary overlords of the British Empire a "great tradition" to be the "heirs and guardians of." by exposing the sentimental pretense in Coupland's legitimizing historical morality.

The question of race was fundamental. The whole edifice of British imperial power rested upon deeply held convictions of superiority—the superior governing capabilities of the British, the superior culture of the metropolitan country. Britain's vaunted "civilizing mission" was but one expression of a profound and pervasive, though often subtle, sense of racial superiority. It had long been assumed that a causal link existed between the inferior heritage of Africans and their inferior status as slaves. Williams denied it. Racism, he declared, was a product of slavery. It was contrived by Europeans to justify acts of greed and brutality, and it continued to serve the modern British Empire as a legitimizing device.[6] By separating race from slavery, Williams hoped to undermine imperial legitimacy and discredit the historical support system that sustained contemporary race prejudice. Since the debasement of blacks was a consequence of slavery, an institution long since abolished and abominated, it was high time, he argued, to reject its bitterest fruit.

5 In America, Frank Klingberg's work strongly emphasized British altruism, and even the distinguished economic historian Lowell Ragatz offered an idealistic interpretation of abolition. See Frank J. Klingberg, *The Anti-Slavery Movement in England* (New Haven, 1924). This work was followed by others emphasizing the trusteeship mission: "The Lady Micro Charity Schools [for emancipated slaves] in the British West Indies, 1835–1842," *Journal of Negro History*, XXIV (1939), pp. 291–344; *Codrington Chronicle: An Experiment in Anglican Altruism on a Barbados Plantation 1716–1834* (Berkeley, 1949). See also Lowell Joseph Ragatz, *The Fall of the Planter Class in the British Caribbean 1763–1833* (New York, 1928).

6 Williams repeatedly objected to the use of racism to justify colonialism, and he consistently ridiculed that position by focusing upon the achievements of non-European peoples. See, for example, his 1955 public lectures delivered in Port-of-Spain, San Fernando, and Tobago, reprinted in part in Paul K. Sutton's compilation of Williams's speeches under the title *Forged from the Love of Liberty* (Trinidad, 1981), pp. 205–210; also, Eric Williams, "The Blackest Thing in Slavery Was Not The Black Man," *Revista Interamericana Review*, III (1973), pp. 1–23.

In Williams's view, Afro-American slavery was an economic institution. It had nothing to do with race, geography, or climate. Its origins could be expressed in three words: "in the Caribbean, Sugar; on the mainland, Tobacco and Cotton."[7] Had a choice existed between free labor and slave, free labor would have prevailed. But there was no choice. Free laborers were not sufficiently abundant to permit the large-scale production of American staples. Although at some point all racial groups would be subjected to coerced labor in the New World, the onus of plantation slavery fell upon Africans because Indian labor was inadequate, Asian labor too distant, and indentured Europeans too costly and vexatious. Durable, docile, and plentiful, African slaves provided a highly efficient and relatively inexpensive means of meeting the demands of agricultural industries that could benefit from economies of scale.[8]

In probing the relationship between race prejudice and slavery, Williams concentrated exclusively on the English experience in the New World, notably upon island and mainland colonies that received the largest early importations of African labor, Barbados and Virginia. Both colonies began as tobacco producers, but their careers quickly diverged. Within twenty-five years of settlement, Barbados had become a thriving sugar island. Slavery emerged quickly in Barbados, more gradually in Virginia. Each of these colonies has provided special credence to one aspect of Williams's argument. His contention that highly capitalized plantation agriculture gave rise to black slavery has received strongest academic affirmation in the context of Barbados. The other side of the same argument—that racism was a product of slavery— has garnered greatest support in studies of Virginia. This paper examines the Virginia and Barbados experiences in turn, assess-

7 Eric Williams, *Capitalism and Slavery* (New York, 1966), p. 23.
8 Williams dismissed any presumption that Africans were especially despised, observing that European bondsmen were kidnapped, abused, and transported under conditions as disgusting as those of the slave trade. In the colonies, they suffered worse treatment than African slaves. Any connection between African race and American slavery was a myth contrived by whites to excuse the degradation of blacks: "The features of the man, his hair, color and dentifrice, his 'subhuman' characteristics so widely pleaded, were only later rationalizations to justify a simple economic fact: that the colonies needed labor and resorted to Negro labor because it was cheapest and best." Williams, *Capitalism and Slavery*, pp. 17, 20.

ing the durability of Williams's views in light of recent historical scholarship.

For his analysis of Virginia, Williams made little use of documentary evidence, relying instead on the North American historians James Ballagh and Thomas Wertenbaker. The former determined that blacks retained the legal status of servants until the first slave act of 1661;[9] Wertenbaker explained that the slave trade to Virginia became significant only after the large expansion of tobacco exports in the 1680's.[10] Combining these positions, Williams concluded that a heightened demand for tobacco generated the need to transform the colonial labor system. Large-scale plantation agriculture, he contended, could only achieve efficiency under a slave labor regime. In effect, economic necessity, not race, occasioned the debasement of blacks in Virginia.[11]

Williams's reading of Ballagh and Wertenbaker was all too selective. He ignored other literature that dated the *de facto* enslavement of blacks much earlier than 1661,[12] and he failed to account for the gap in dates between the first slave act and the period after 1680 when, in Wertenbaker's view, slave imports assumed "fairly large numbers."[13] Why would English colonists have enslaved blacks who, in 1650, may have numbered only 300 in a population of 15,000, unless the colony was undergoing a major social or economic change? The American historians whom Williams read as well as those whom he did not read were explicit on the matter: the compelling reason, they contended, was race prejudice.[14]

---

9   James Curtis Ballagh, *A History of Slavery in Virginia* (Baltimore, 1902).
10   Thomas J. Wertenbaker, *The Planters of Colonial Virginia* (Princeton, 1922).
11   Williams, *Capitalism and Slavery*, p. 26.
12   Writing in 1913, John H. Russell declared that slavery was becoming established in practice, if not law, during the two decades after 1640. See his *The Free Negro in Virginia, 1619–1865* (Baltimore, 1913). An earlier date for genuine enslavement was proposed in Susie Ames's *Studies of the Virginia Eastern Shore in the Seventeenth Century* (Richmond, 1940). James M. Wright's *The Free Negro in Maryland, 1634–1860* (New York, 1921) declared that Africans were enslaved almost from the beginning of their experience in that colony.
13   Wertenbaker held that "only in the years from 1700 to 1720" did slavery accomplish the "overthrow of the old system of labor. . . ." *Planters of Colonial Virginia*, p. 126.
14   Ballagh declared, "The philosophic basis of slavery rests historically either upon race or creed or both. . . . If explanation for slavery is sought beyond the unquestioned exigencies of the actual situation it is to be found in race prejudice, a principle which has

The race/slavery question acquired new urgency in the United States after World War II, and as a result, the Williams position gained important, if not unqualified, support. In a celebrated 1950 article, Oscar and Mary Handlin rejected the findings of earlier American writers, insisting that the first blacks to arrive in Virginia (as well as in Barbados) were maintained and treated like their unfree white counterparts. What ultimately divided white servants from black, in the Handlins' view, was something other than racism. It was the psychological need of European immigrants, separated from the "security of home and isolated in an immense wilderness," to seek out the company of people most like themselves. The condition of servitude for blacks deteriorated for a simple practical reason. They were the only servants whose treatment, good or ill, could not influence the future immigration of badly needed bondservants to the Chesapeake.[15]

Kenneth Stampp uncritically accepted the Handlins' position, and his principal work, *The Peculiar Institution* (1956), constituted the historical centerpiece for an academic reorientation to studies on race and slavery initiated by the Myrdal group a decade earlier.[16] This new scholarship consciously reinforced important claims of the civil rights movement. Slavery was neither necessary nor inevitable. Racism, its insidious product, was an acquired, not an inborn, prejudice. Blacks were victims of a downspiraling cycle of oppression and debasement in which slavery and prejudice had become mutually reinforcing. If white colo-

---

constantly worked to reduce to subjection the inferior and weaker race, where two peoples have been brought into close contact." *Slavery in Virginia*, p. 45.

Wertenbaker's text is decidedly racist; he deeply lamented the passing of the white yeomanry in Virginia in favor of a "Black Tide" born "in savagery": "It was one of the great crimes of history, this undermining of the yeoman class by the importation of slaves." Although he explained the changeover to slavery in economic terms, he viewed the process more in terms of criminally bad judgment than of inexorable economic logic. *Planters of Colonial Virginia*, pp. iii, 127, 134.

15 At first, Irish and other less desirable whites received longer terms of bondage than Englishmen in Virginia, but the compelling need of the colonists to encourage the immigration of all types of Europeans prevented discrimination in the conditions of white indenture. Reductions in the length of service of blacks could only produce loss for the masters. Oscar and Mary F. Handlin, "Origins of the Southern Labor System," *The William and Mary Quarterly*, 3rd series, VII (1950), pp. 210–211.

16 This work, launched under the initiative of the Carnegie Foundation, included Gunnar Myrdal, *An American Dilemma* (New York, 1944); Melville Herskovits, *The Myth of the Negro Past* (New York, 1941); Charles S. Johnson, *Patterns of Negro Segregation* (New York, 1943); and Richard Steiner, *The Negro's Share* (New York, 1943).

nists had deliberately imposed this burden on blacks "little by little, step by step, choice by choice,"[17] their descendants, exercising good will and sound reason, could just as deliberately remove it.

This optimistic line of argument, echoing the sentiments of Eric Williams, suffered formidable challenge in 1959 by Carl Degler. Employing the same type of evidence used by the Handlins (early statutes, judicial decisions, fragmentary demographic data and personal memoranda), Degler drew a contrary conclusion: the African had been considered "inferior to the white man, servant or free" from the moment he arrived in North America.[18] In effect, Anglo-American racism was a more complex psychohistorical problem than either the Handlins or Stampp had allowed, and its eradication would require substantially more than the exercise of good will. Degler's work was persuasively argued, but it only stalemated the historical question. For at least four generations, a stream of reputable scholars had inferred sharply different conclusions from fragmentary colonial evidence and from the logic of evolving historical circumstances. It was time to acknowledge that the meager documentary record of the early Chesapeake settlements offered no certain proof one way or the other whether blacks were treated in a manner substantially different from white bondsmen.[19] The debate had reached an impasse, an impasse that could only be broken by a creative new approach to the problem.

Winthrop Jordan provided it. His *White over Black* (1968) shifted attention away from the Chesapeake and focused it on the attitudinal properties that English settlers carried with them to

17 Kenneth M. Stampp, *The Peculiar Institution* (New York, 1956), p. 6. Although Stampp affirmed Williams's position concerning the nonracial origins of slavery, neither he nor the Handlins made reference to *Capitalism and Slavery* and together they dismissed any notion that slavery in the Chesapeake resulted from the inexorable operation of powerful economic forces associated with the cultivation of tobacco.

18 Carl N. Degler, "Slavery and the Generation of American Race Prejudice," *Comparative Studies in Society and History*, II (1959–1960), pp. 48–66. Like the Handlins and Stampp, Degler made no reference to Williams. He identified Tocqueville as champion of the view that slavery was the source of American prejudice against the Negro.

19 This point is repeatedly made in the literature of the 1960's and 1970's. See, for example, Winthrop Jordan, "Modern Tensions and the Origins of American Slavery," *The Journal of Southern History*, XXVIII (1962), p. 22; and Paul C. Palmer, "Servant into Slave: The Evolution of the Legal Status of the Negro Laborer in Colonial Virginia," *The South Atlantic Quarterly*, LXV (1966), p. 369.

the New World. Beginning with the Englishman's concept of blackness ("loaded with intense meaning") and continuing with his Christian cosmology, his attitude toward savagery, his physiognomic preferences, and his perception of African libidinousness, Jordan declared that Englishmen discriminated fundamentally between themselves and blacks. Moreover, the ancient practice of villeinage as well as Tudor literature on law, divinity, and relations with alien societies had equipped English colonists with a view of slavery for which the African qualified on all counts.[20] The enslavement of blacks in Virginia was not a matter of deliberate choice, as Stampp had argued. It was an "unthinking decision," a steady process of debasement whereby a deep-seated, largely irrational race prejudice had combined with persistent labor shortages to produce a predictable result among people well endowed with the concept, if not the legalities, of perpetual servitude.

For a time, historians seemed content to applaud, punctuate, or extend Jordan's findings.[21] Emphasis upon the fundamental importance of somatic properties was echoed in Hoetinck's and Degler's comparative studies of race relations in the hemisphere.[22] In another vein, Wesley Frank Craven cast doubt on the causal relationship between economic forces and the origins of black slavery in colonial Virginia. Through a study of headrights, Craven determined that at least half of the 80,000 Englishmen who entered the colony between 1630 and 1700 arrived in the third quarter of the century, whereas Africans trickled in at a rate of only 56 per year between 1660 and 1690.[23] Such figures,

---

20 Winthrop D. Jordan, *White Over Black: American Attitudes Toward the Negro, 1550–1812* (Chapel Hill, 1968), p. 97.

21 Eldred D. Jones, *The Elizabethan Image of Africa* (Charlottesville, 1971). For colonial Virginia, see for example Alden T. Vaughan, "Blacks in Virginia: A Note on the First Decade" *The William and Mary Quarterly*, 3rd series, XXIX (1972), pp. 469–478; and Warren M. Billings, "The Cases of Fernando and Elizabeth Key: A Note on the Status of Blacks in Seventeenth-Century Virginia," *The William and Mary Quarterly*, 3rd series, XXX (1973), pp. 467–474.

22 H. Hoetinck, *Caribbean Race Relations: A Study of Two Variants* (Oxford, 1967); and Carl N. Degler, *Neither Black Nor White: Slavery and Race Relations in Brazil and the United States* (New York, 1971). Dismantling the major components of Frank Tannenbaum's *Slave and Citizen* (New York, 1947), they rejected the notion that slavery, or any particular form of slavery, was the primary factor in shaping race relations.

23 The average rose to 184 in the 1690's. Wesley Frank Craven, *White, Red, and Black: The Seventeenth-Century Virginian* (Charlottesville, 1971), p. 86.

if reliable,[24] would suggest that until late in the century "the typical slaveholder possessed only a few Negroes" and that before the mid-1690's slavery and the slave trade probably had limited effect on the expansion of tobacco production—or vice versa.[25] By the early 1970's then, the Williams-Handlin-Stampp position appeared in full retreat. The origin of black slavery in the American mainland colonies was being interpreted primarily as a function of race, not economic necessity.[26]

With the publication of Edmund Morgan's *American Slavery—American Freedom* (1975), the interpretive pendulum began to swing in reverse. Morgan agreed that race was a factor in the inception of slavery in Virginia, but he resisted Jordan's complex psychological explanation and he was attracted by the Handlins' pragmatic gradualism. Slavery was established not by "unthinking decision," he thought, but by non-decision. Virginians had no need to enslave blacks. They had only to buy people whose servile status had been established by others. As long as mortality rates were exceptionally high for unseasoned immigrants, both black and white, planters could reap no advantage by acquiring slaves for life rather than bondservants for several years, particularly when the cost of slaves was double that of indentures. When around 1660, however, a decline occurred in the mortality rate for newcomers, slaves became economically more advantageous than servants.[27] By dating the economic desirability of black enslavement at precisely the time when colonial statutes formalized

24 The use of headrights to measure the number of slaves and servants conveyed to Virginia has been criticized as unreliable. See Edmund S. Morgan, "Headrights and Head Counts: A Review Article," *Virginia Magazine of History and Biography*, LXXX (1972), pp. 361–371; and Russell R. Menard, "Immigration to the Chesapeake Colonies in the Seventeenth Century: A Review Essay," *Maryland Historical Magazine*, LXVIII (1973), pp. 323–329.

25 Craven, *White, Red, and Black*, p. 96.

26 It is important to note that in this, as in most academic controversies, interpretive differences were more a matter of emphasis and shadings than of absolutes. If race had become the foremost explanatory factor, no reputable historian could ignore the persistent economic problem of labor shortage in the colonies. Jordan made the point best of all: "The concept of Negro slavery [in the tobacco colonies] was neither borrowed from foreigners, nor extracted from books, nor invented out of whole cloth, nor extrapolated from servitude, nor generated by English reaction to Negroes as such, nor necessitated by the exigencies of the New World. Not any one of these made the Negro a slave, but all." *White Over Black*, p. 72.

27 Edmund S. Morgan, *American Slavery, American Freedom: The Ordeal of Colonial Virginia* (New York, 1975), pp. 297–299.

it, Morgan was able to draw important distinctions between slavery and racism. Slavery could be explained essentially, though not wholly, in terms of economic advantage. Racism—contempt of whites for blacks—was, on the other hand, deliberately fostered by "the men who ran Virginia" in order to divide lower-class whites from blacks, Morgan declared.[28]

Although Morgan did not refute Jordan directly, his studies, particularly those of the Eastern Shore, provided too much evidence of social integration and black assertiveness to permit his acceptance of prevailing academic notions about the hostile predisposition of whites toward blacks. His views acquired explicit theoretical formulation in 1980 by Breen and Innes, who accused earlier writers of succumbing to a teleological trap. In attempting to discover the roots of the modern race problem in scanty colonial documents, researchers had seized upon every conceivable hint of discriminatory behavior, exaggerating, distorting, and misrepresenting the social reality of colonial Virginia. A less purposeful examination of those documents, Breen and Innes argue, would enable us to conclude that much of the early legislation presumed to be discriminatory had neither the intent nor the impact we may have thought.[29] Twentieth-century historians, obsessed by contemporary race problems, have attributed race prejudice to seventeenth-century settlers for whom discrimination was unimportant and essentially benign.

Climaxing this revisionary trend, William McKee Evans traced the "Sons of Ham" legend over two millennia, showing that slave

28 When the slave population was small, Morgan observed, it was difficult to distinguish race prejudice from class prejudice. But as slave numbers grew (Morgan made an upward adjustment of Craven's figures for slave imports), fear of servile insurrection arose, and planters hastened to instill race hatred among the lower orders. *Ibid.*, pp. 330–331.

29 These authors note, for example, that cases of racially differentiated punishments accorded to black and white runaways, routinely considered unimpeachable evidence of racial distinctions, give as much indication of racial cooperation among the lowly as of racial discrimination among the elite. Breen and Innes provide an analysis of interaction between a small group of free blacks and their white fellow colonists, concluding that in some spheres their relationships were governed by economic status, in others by race, but that in no case was conflict between blacks and whites inevitable. If the free black lost his place in Virginia, so did the poor white. The reason was not race (or at least not primarily race): small planters could not compete with great planters when prices fell and the latter achieved increased efficiency and higher productivity on their large holdings. T. H. Breen and Stephen Innes, *"Myne Owne Ground": Race and Freedom on Virginia's Eastern Shore, 1640–1676* (New York, 1980), pp. 112–114.

masters of all cultures have expressed the same stereotypical views of bondsmen whatever their race. In language highly reminiscent of Williams, Evans concluded that "race relations and prejudice are determined by power relationships."[30] The intense prejudice deliberately aroused by self-serving colonial capitalists had deceived Jordan, Degler, and others into mistaking a discrete historical phenomenon for an abiding psychological condition.

By 1980, then, the debate had come full circle. Once again, the tide was running with Williams. Evans's widely read article was probably the most explicit and emphatic statement since *Capitalism and Slavery* of the proposition that racism was a product, not a cause, of Afro-American slavery. In reality, however, Williams's work on Virginia had not been well-informed. If it seemed vindicated in the 1980's it was the direction of his thinking, not the credibility of his argument, that had earned scholarly endorsement.

Even in the direction of thinking, the Williams orientation to Virginia continues to present perplexing problems. If race prejudice was not deliberately incited by self-serving capitalists until the later decades of the seventeenth century, as Morgan and Evans have argued, how do we account for the inescapable fact that between 1640 and 1660 blacks suffered a progressive degradation in status? Morgan and Evans have contended that the swing to slavery was a rational economic choice occasioned by falling mortality rates. Evans makes the point without regard to time; Morgan declares that the lower mortality rate of blacks manifested itself around 1660.

Their arguments are highly problematical. Although Morgan makes no distinction between the seasoning mortality of whites and blacks, Galenson has shown that a parallel decline in the seasoning mortality of both races would have produced no appreciable change in the relative value of either group to the planters.[31] In a compatible statement, Bean and Thomas have calculated

---

30   William McKee Evans, "From the Land of Canaan to the Land of Guinea: The Strange Odyssey of the Sons of Ham," *The American Historical Review*, 85 (1980), p. 43. For a comprehensive evaluation of the power relationship and alienation, see Orlando Patterson, *Slavery and Social Death: A Comparative Study* (Cambridge, Mass., 1982).

31   Among those who died in seasoning, it is reasonable to assume that servants, being more easily trained by virtue of their language and cultural identity with planters, would generally have produced more value per time elapsed in the colony than slaves. Since Europeans outnumbered Africans in the Chesapeake, the disease environment would

that life expectancies would have to have shifted dramatically to produce significant impact on the planters' profit calculation. In view of the prevailing discount rate, they argue, a one-third fall in seasoning mortality coupled with a one-third rise in life expectancy for seasoned immigrants would have produced only a 10-percent increase in the relative value of slaves over bondservants.[32] Even if Morgan was correct about the relative economic desirability of blacks over whites after 1660, any significant increase in the ratio of black labor to white did not occur in Virginia for another two decades.

Is there any firm evidence that after 1660 the Chesapeake planters actually preferred slave labor? No, argues Russell Menard. Referring to relative price data, Menard contends that tobacco planters preferred servants to slaves even when the labor force began to shift from white to black.[33] It was the declining supply of servant labor after the mid-1660's, not the desirability of slave labor, that altered the character of the Chesapeake laboring population. After 1665, the number of householders in Maryland and Virginia who demanded servant labor rose steadily while the flow of European servants subsided. The reasons for declining servant immigration are manifold, including a decrease in British population growth beginning around 1640, rising English wage rates, lower availability of land for time-expired servants, and growing competition from Pennsylvania and Carolina for the available supply of European migrants. In the final third of the century, Chesapeake planters confronted a deepening labor shortage, but only after considerable lag time did they begin to satisfy their labor needs through a steady importation of African slaves. If the shift to black labor constituted a rational economic choice, it was not, as Williams, Morgan, and Evans have argued, a decision based on the superior cost–benefit performance of slaves but on the planters' decision to equip their properties with ade-

---

probably have been more dangerous for Africans. On the other hand, to the extent that seasoning mortality involved malaria, the risk to Europeans would have been higher. The issue continues to be debated. See David Galenson, *White Servitude in Colonial America: An Economic Analysis* (Cambridge and New York, 1981), pp. 152, 266–267.

32 Richard N. Bean and Robert P. Thomas, "The Adoption of Slave Labor in British America," in Henry A. Gemery and Jan S. Hogendorn, eds., *The Uncommon Market: Essays in the Economic History of the Atlantic Slave Trade* (New York, 1979), pp. 384–386.

33 The argument contained in this paragraph is persuasively made in Russell Menard, "From Servants to Slaves: The Transformation of the Chesapeake Labor System," *Southern Studies*, XVI (1971), pp. 355–390.

quate supplies of labor, even a less desired form of labor, rather than endure an insufficiency of agricultural workers.[34]

When the increase in slave labor did occur, was it attended in important part by a revised structuring of the tobacco farms? Eric Williams contended that plantations producing colonial staples (whether tobacco, cotton, or sugar) could only achieve economies of scale through high level technical organization and the use of disciplined slave gangs.[35] When applied to the Chesapeake, Williams's "technological determinism"[36] possesses little explanatory power; indeed, even for the seventeenth-century sugar colonies, it is not, as we shall see, an unassailable line of argument. Tobacco required delicate handling by cultivators. It benefited little from economy of scale and not at all from gang labor.[37] Although large plantations did arise in the Chesapeake, tobacco

---

34   Galenson's work confirms this argument. He offers the following decennial estimates of net immigration to the Chesapeake.

	WHITE	BLACK	TOTAL	20-YEAR TOTAL
1650–1660	17,523	1,332	18,855	
1660–1670	16,599	1,832	18,431	37,286
1670–1680	14,911	1,707	16,618	
1680–1690	9,131	7,259	16,390	33,008
1690–1700	−302	7,738	7,406	
1700–1710	18,470	10,747	29,217	36,623

It will be noted that there was a consistent pattern of immigration until the final two decades of the century. If we combined Galenson's decennial estimates to produce 20-year totals, we can see a consistency in the level of immigration for the whole 60 years. White immigration fell in the last half of the seventeenth century, but despite a growing demand for labor, the shortfall in white immigration was not compensated for by slave imports until the 1680's. In the 1690's, the deficiency of European immigrants was only partially made up by slaves. During the next decade, the very large white and black immigration largely redressed the shortfall of the nineties, bringing the 20-year total in line with earlier periods. If these estimates are generally correct, the takeoff in slave imports can be ascribed to a market shortage in white servant labor at a critical point in the expansion of tobacco exports. Galenson writes: "A sharp decline in the supply of servants to the region in the 1680s against an inelastic demand curve, in conjunction with a downward shift in the supply curve for slaves in the same decade, produced a dramatic increase of 57 percent in the price of servants relative to that of slaves between 1675 and 1690. This triggered a massive shift in the relative holdings of the two types of unfree labor. . . ." *White Servitude in Colonial America*, pp. 154, 217.
35   "Sugar, tobacco, and cotton," Williams wrote, "required the large plantation and hordes of cheap labor, and the small farm of the ex-indentured white servant could not possibly survive." *Capitalism and Slavery*, p. 23; see also, pp. 6, 7, 25, 27.
36   The term is used in Bean and Thomas, "Adoption of Slave Labor," p. 379.
37   Paul G. E. Clemens, *The Atlantic Economy and Colonial Maryland's Eastern Shore: From Tobacco to Grain* (Ithaca, N.Y., 1980), p. 84; and Gloria L. Main, *Tobacco Colony: Life in Early Maryland, 1650–1720* (Princeton, 1982), pp. 27–43.

continued to be grown on many small farms, and plantation production never acquired the centralized character of Caribbean sugar estates. Clearly, the growth of black slavery in Virginia cannot be accounted for in a single word, tobacco, as Williams asserted.

In Barbados, the shift from indentured to slave labor was earlier and swifter, but the details of the process are obscured by a paucity of social and economic data for the 1630–1650 period. We have no reliable measure of the island's population in the earliest decades of settlement, nor can we determine the ratio of whites to blacks.[38] That blacks were enslaved at an early date there can be little doubt;[39] moreover, we can presume with safety that by the late 1640's black slaves comprised a substantial portion of the working population and that the larger planters had become heavily dependent upon their labor.[40]

38 Population estimates vary from author to author. John Scott's contemporary claim (Sloane Manuscript, British Museum, 3662/54–62) that in 1645 the island contained nearly 6,000 slaves and over 18,000 whites, 11,200 of whom were landowners, has been adopted by most historians. See, for example, Vincent T. Harlow, *A History of Barbados 1625–1685* (Oxford, 1926), p. 45; Alfred D. Chandler, "The Expansion of Barbados," *Journal of the Barbados Museum and Historical Society*, XIII (1945), pp. 106–114; Carl and Roberta Bridenbaugh, *No Peace Beyond the Line: The English in the Caribbean 1624–1690* (New York, 1972), p. 33; and James A. Williamson, *The Caribbee Islands under the Proprietary Patents* (London, 1926), pp. 157–158. While adopting Scott's population figures, Williamson found his claim for 11,200 proprietors excessive since it implied that an average holding in the island would have been a mere 10 acres if "every inch of the island was occupied." Richard Sheridan repeats the figure 6,000 slaves, but considers the white population to have reached a maximum figure of 30,000 in 1645. See *Sugar and Slavery: An Economic History of the British West Indies, 1623–1775* (Baltimore, 1973), pp. 133, 143. Richard Ligon outrageously exaggerated the number of people in the island in the late 1640's, stating figures of 50,000 whites and double the number of blacks in his *A True and Exact History of the Island of Barbados* (London, 1657), p. 43. Everyone dismisses Ligon, and Richard Dunn dismisses Scott, describing him as a "notorious trickster" who probably fabricated his figures. Dunn thinks the island contained about 10,000 people in 1640 and that both the white and black population grew markedly, reaching 20,000 of each race by 1660. See Dunn's *Sugar and Slaves: The Rise of the Planter Class in the English West Indies, 1624–1713* (New York, 1972), p. 74.

39 In 1636, the Governor and Council declared "that Negroes and Indians that come here to be sold, should serve for Life, unless a contract was before made to the contrary." Quoted in Bridenbaugh and Bridenbaugh, *No Peace Beyond the Line*, p. 32. Richard Ligon divided the island population into masters, servants, and slaves—the latter with "their posterity, being subject to their Masters for ever." See *A True and Exact History*, p. 43. Modern historians of the island, Vincent Harlow and Richard Dunn, strongly affirm Ligon's view. The colonists, Dunn writes, "immediately categorized the Negroes and Indians who worked for them as heathen brutes and very quickly treated them as slaves." *Sugar and Slaves*, p. 227.

40 Whether we adopt Scott's figure of slightly under 6,000 slaves in 1645 or accept Dunn's view of a rapidly rising black population after 1640, we are bound to conclude

Most assuredly, the art of planting cane and manufacturing sugar was transferred to Barbados from Pernambuco through the good offices of the Dutch. The complex agricultural and manufacturing process that Ligon described as having existed at the end of the 1640's could not have been achieved in Barbados in a few years' time without the direct transfer of technology from an existing sugar culture.[41] If Ligon is correct in dating serious experimentation with cane around 1641–42, then 1645 might be considered a watershed year when, despite the continuing inferiority of their product, Barbados planters could be confident that cane offered them outstanding commercial prospects.

Williams identified the shift from tobacco and cotton to sugar with the installation of slave labor in the British Caribbean. "No sugar, no negroes," he wrote.[42] His emphasis fell upon the demand pull of the sugar plantation—in his words, the "establishment of the sugar industry created the demand for labor in the West Indian islands."[43]

Is this emphasis on demand appropriate? Is it true, as Williams repeatedly asserted, that African labor was cheaper than indentured labor, "eminently superior," and consequently preferred by the Barbados planters? Why did the Barbadian sugar

---

that the major planters, at least, had become heavily dependent on slave labor by the late forties. Beckles provides a table for the labor composition of 13 Barbadian estates, 1644–57: the five estates listed for 1644–48 had a total of 105 bondservants and 205 slaves. Hilary McD. Beckles, "The Economic Origins of Black Slavery in the British West Indies, 1640–1680: A Tentative Analysis of the Barbados Model," *The Journal of Caribbean History*, XVI (1982), p. 44. Apart from his exaggeration of total population figures for Barbados (see footnote 38) Richard Ligon was, as Dunn has observed, a "first-rate observer" though an "unreliable calculator." The estate with which he was most familiar, the Hilliard-Modyford property of 500 acres, had 96 black slaves, 3 Indian slaves, and 28 European servants in 1647. When Ligon prepared his elaborate model for a profitable Barbados property, he called for 100 blacks and "not above thirty" Christian servants. It is highly likely that Ligon's perception that blacks outnumbered whites by a margin of two to one on the island was owing to his constant involvement, over three years' time, with the highest echelon of planter society. Ligon, *A True and Exact History*, pp. 22, 115.

41 Ligon described a continuing process of edification—of tutelage "by strangers," of visitations in Brazil by Englishmen "covetous of the knowledge" of cane husbandry, of trial and error, until by 1647, there were many sugar works in the island, albeit "the Sugars they made, were but bare Muscovadoes, and few of them Merchantable commodities. . . ." *A True and Exact History*, pp. 85–86. Not until the end of the decade, when Barbadians learned to harvest cane at full maturity, was their product commercially sound. The system they had developed at that time persisted in the British Caribbean without significant modification for more than two centuries.

42 Williams, *Capitalism and Slavery*, p. 27.

43 Eric Williams, *The Negro in the Caribbean* (Washington, 1942), p. 11.

estate, the linear descendant of the Pernambuco plantation, assume a unitary character, rejecting the mode of cane farming commonly practiced in Brazil? Is there nothing to say here for Say's Law, for the notion that supply creates its own demand? Is it not possible that a readily available and abundant supply of black slave labor not only stimulated and accelerated the transition to cane culture in Barbados but dictated the character which that culture would assume? How else can we account for the unprecedented speed and unparalleled thoroughness of the Barbados sugar revolution?

It is universally affirmed that by 1640 the Barbados planters were seeking a new, more profitable staple crop. Prices for their tobacco, the poorest in the Atlantic trade, had fallen sharply in the mid-thirties, and cotton prices for 1640–41 were 30 percent below their 1630–35 average.[44] Two alternate possibilities existed—indigo and sugar—but both had to be manufactured and both required more labor than tobacco or cotton. Indigo was preferred. Its start-up costs were less burdensome than those of sugar, and in 1640–42 indigo was fetching its highest prices for the century.[45] Experiments with cane persisted, however, and by the late 1640's a fall in the price of indigo, improvements in the production of sugar, and a sharp rise in sugar prices sealed the destiny of the Barbadian economy.[46]

Before a sugar industry could be established in Barbados, certain vital prerequisites were necessary. First, prospective planters needed access to large amounts of capital for the consolidation of property, construction of works, purchase of utensils, and acquisition of animal stock and manpower. Second, planters who contemplated investments on this scale had to be assured that their future manpower requirements would be met by a continuing flow of abundant, reliable, and disciplined labor. Capital, labor, and land—the common ingredients of production—were not, however, sufficient. The colony required assurances of physical security. In this respect, Barbados was the most fortunate of

---

44 Robert Carlyle Batie, "Why Sugar? Economic Cycles and the Changing of Staples on the English and French Antilles, 1624–54," *The Journal of Caribbean History*, VIII (1976), pp. 12, 29, 30.

45 *Ibid.*, p. 15.

46 This price rise was caused by a fall in exports from Brazil occasioned by the rebellion of Portuguese planters against their Dutch overlords, beginning in 1645.

Britain's island colonies. Unlike others in the Lesser Antilles, Barbados had no Indian population capable of raiding newly established sugar works. Nor were the Barbados colonists, like their counterparts in St. Kitts, obliged to share their island with foreign nationals who might, at any time, endanger their security. Furthermore, Barbados, the most windward and the most populous of the "Caribbees," was least vulnerable to Spanish attack, though for protection against Spain, the island owed more to the Dutch than to westerly winds or the government in London. In fact, it was the Dutch who, by their indefatigable assaults upon Ibero-America, provided a security umbrella for the Barbados planters and delivered into the island the capital, labor, technology, and intelligence that promoted the sugar revolution.[47]

The search for a new staple in Barbados coincided with the onset of civil disturbances in England in 1639. During the ensuing Civil War, communication with the mother country was disrupted. The island declared its neutrality; it exercised virtual independence; and its trade passed largely to the Dutch. Although we have no reliable data on the flow of servants to Barbados during the initial years of the Civil War, we can assume that the trade in indentured laborers, like all other trade with England, was curtailed—or, at the very least, rendered irregular and unreliable. At the same time, Dutch merchants, eager to encourage a larger commerce with the island, were prepared to satisfy the planters' labor needs with African slaves.[48] Slaves arrived in in-

---

47 Goslinga contends that one aspect of the Dutch invasion of Brazil was to put Spanish intercolonial trade in the Caribbean at Dutch mercy. He adds, "coastal communication virtually ceased in 1629 and 1630, and Spanish defensive naval power in the area was reduced to zero." Cornelis Ch. Goslinga, The Dutch in the Caribbean and on the Wild Coast 1580–1680 (Gainesville, Fla., 1971), pp. 212–213. Kenneth Andrews, writing from the Spanish perspective, confirms this view: what permitted the maintenance of settlements by northern Europeans in the outer islands after 1624 was Dutch naval strength in the Caribbean. See The Spanish Caribbean: Trade and Plunder 1530–1630 (New Haven, 1978), p. 245. A. P. Newton observed that by virtue of Dutch marauding before 1630, "Spain's capacity for maritime defence in the waters of the West Indies had fallen to zero." The European Nations in the West Indies 1493–1688 (London, 1933), p. 154.

48 The Dutch were in constant need of raw materials to supply metropolitan processing industries. Dyeing, cloth making, and tobacco cutting were established Dutch industries, and Amsterdam was Europe's principal sugar-refining center. Amsterdam had 25 sugar refineries in 1620, 40 in 1650. Matthew Edel, "The Brazilian Sugar Cycle of the Seventeenth Century and the Rise of West Indian Competition," Caribbean Studies, IX (1969), p. 27. The ubiquitous presence of Dutch traders, legal and contraband, in ports of the Western Hemisphere during the 1630's and 1640's resulted in some measure from the

creasing numbers during the first half of the 1640's. Although they represented an earnest Dutch effort to prime the Barbadian pump,[49] most of them were put to work in cotton and tobacco fields, prompting the Bridenbaughs to assert that "the shift from indentured white servants to black slave labor in Barbados originated on the tobacco and plantations *before* sugar had become a regular staple. . . ."[50]

Too often, the supply of slave labor is viewed only as a response, not a stimulus, to sugar planting. Williams made this error. Bean and Thomas, Williams's critics, have repeated it. They argue that the Dutch West India Company, which "dominated the Atlantic slave trade in the 1640s," could not have sent a significant number of slaves to Barbados before 1648 or 1649.[51] In one sense, they are right. Having gained dominance over the African portals of the slave trade after 1637, the company concentrated its slave trading at Brazil for the next decade.[52] However, Bean and Thomas overlooked two other possibilities: slave captures from Iberian ships and interloping by private Dutch slave traders. The 80-year war between the Netherlands and Spain brought into the Caribbean swarms of Dutch privateers who, having disrupted Spanish commerce, conducted a vigorous contraband trade. Slaves were the most important product in that contraband.[53]

---

tactics employed by Spain in the war between the two countries, 1621–1648. The Spanish imposed strong economic pressure on the Dutch through embargoes. For the most part, the 800–900 Dutch vessels that normally traded with Spain were shut out, and had to find trade elsewhere. J. I. Israel, "A Conflict of Empires: Spain and the Netherlands 1618–1648," *Past and Present*, 76 (1977), pp. 41, 48, 73.

49 Harlow quotes from the Sloane MSS, 3662: "The Hollanders that are great encouragers of Plantacons, did at the first attempt of makeing sugar give great Credit to the most sober Inhabitants, and upon the unhappie Civill warr that brake out in England, they managed the whole Trade in or Westerne Collonies, and furnished the Island with Negroes, Coppers, Stills, and all other things Appertaining to the Ingenious for making sugar." See his *History of Barbados*, p. 42.

50 Bridenbaugh and Bridenbaugh, *No Peace Beyond the Line*, p. 33. The Bridenbaughs strongly emphasize the role of the Dutch in the early development of Barbados; see pp. 63–68.

51 Bean and Thomas, "Adoption of Slave Labor," pp. 381–382.

52 By 1636 the Dutch had conquered and pacified the sugar-producing districts of northeastern Brazil where, after years of turmoil, the demand for slaves was intense. In 1637, the company captured Elmina and subsequently took Luanda, Benguela, Axim, São Tomé, and other West African slave-trading ports.

53 Having little choice, Spanish colonists needing labor cooperated in the contraband trade. Goslinga, *Dutch in the Caribbean*, p. 355. In a letter to the King of Spain, Silva Solis

Using *asiento* figures as his main source, Philip Curtin determined that slave imports to Spanish America, 1626–50, should have averaged about 2,000 a year; to Brazil, 4,000 a year.[54] Between 1623 and 1636, however, 547 Iberian ships were captured by vessels of the Dutch West India Company, and we can assume that others were taken by noncompany Dutch marauders.[55] Many of those Iberian ships would have carried slaves; indeed, in the last months of 1636 alone, company ships captured 1,046 slaves at sea.[56] The first slaves to be landed at English settlements in Guiana, Virginia, and Barbados were prize seizures, and Mims has observed that among the earliest slaves deposited in French St. Christopher were Dutch captives taken from the Spanish.[57] In 1634, the Dutch seized Curaçao, a strategic island on the main Spanish access route through the Caribbean. The island quickly became a dispatching center for slaves and other contraband. There is no way to assess the number of captured slaves that might have been offered for sale at Barbados before 1645, but, by virtue of winds and currents, Barbados was the most likely and most convenient first port of call for Dutch captains who captured slave prizes anywhere along the whole South American coast north and west of Paraíba.

Dutch interlopers would have provided a second source of slaves for Barbadians. An intense debate developed in the Neth-

---

declared that the slave population of Mexico around 1640 was 80,000. Colin A. Palmer considers this figure too high. But it is the nature of Palmer's comment that is most interesting: if the official number of black slaves entering Mexico before 1640 was 110,525, contraband entries might have been sufficiently numerous to bring up the number to 150,000, making Solis's figure (80,000 in 1640) appear less outrageous. Palmer, *Slaves of the White God: Blacks in Mexico, 1570–1650* (Cambridge, Mass. 1976), pp. 28–29.

54 Philip D. Curtin, *The African Slave Trade: A Census* (Madison, Wisc., 1969), p. 119. Ernst van den Boogaart and Pieter C. Emmer provide a corrective to this, declaring the Brazilian figure too high for the 1630–50 period. See their "Dutch Participation in the Slave Trade, 1596–1650" in Gemery and Hogendorn, *The Uncommon Market*, p. 374.

55 C. R. Boxer, *The Dutch in Brazil 1624–1654* (Oxford, 1957), p. 66. Before the 1641 truce between the Dutch Portuguese, the latter's vessels were so heavily preyed upon by the Dutch that the Luso-Brazilian planters referred to themselves as "Dutch husbandmen." When the Pernambuco revolt erupted against the Dutch company in Brazil in 1645, the Dutch renewed their attacks in the Atlantic: 249 Portuguese ships trading with Brazil were lost between December 1647 and December 1648. Boxer, *Salvador de Sá and the Struggle for Brazil and Angola 1602–1686* (London, 1952), pp. 179–186.

56 Boogaart and Emmer, "Dutch Participation in the Slave Trade," p. 358. It should be noted that the slave trade to Brazil had fallen off after Dutch invasion; the demand for slaves was high; and the company took special efforts to seize Portuguese vessels carrying slaves.

57 Stewart L. Mims, *Colbert's West India Policy* (New Haven, 1912), p. 284.

erlands over whether the trade of Dutch Brazil would be open to all merchants or be reserved as a monopoly for the West India Company. Amsterdam merchants, notorious for trading wherever profits could be garnered, whether in enemy or friendly ports, strongly opposed the monopoly.[58] Compromise was achieved on most items of trade, but a monopoly was affirmed on the slave trade. That monopoly was immediately breached by interlopers fully capable of taking advantage of the distressed financial position of the company.[59] Although the WIC would have been helpless to deny interlopers from acquiring cargoes in Africa, it could severely limit, if not prevent, the illicit sale of slaves in Brazil.[60] At Barbados, however, Dutch interlopers would have confronted no impediment to the sale of slaves.

Did Barbados planters prefer the use of slave labor? Williams had no doubt of it. Hilary Beckles disagrees. In a paper that mirrors Menard's studies on the Chesapeake, Beckles declares that prior to 1660 black slaves were neither cheaper than bondservants nor preferred by the planters. Slave labor was double the price of bonded labor, and seasoning mortality was so high for Africans that the man/year price ratio of the two forms of labor favored indentures. Side by side, they performed the same tasks, producing about the same "daily marginal product." The slightly larger maintenance costs of Europeans was probably offset by their greater versatility, skill levels, and familiarity with English.[61]

58 Boxer declares that the Dutch would have traded with the Devil in Hell so long as their sails were not burned. *The Dutch in Brazil,* p. 237. Violet Barbour, among others, has traced the surreptitious flow of Amsterdam capital into a variety of enterprises which conflicted with other Dutch interests. The Danish and the Swedish West India Companies, for example, were organized by Hollanders in competition with the Dutch company. *Capitalism in Amsterdam in the 17th Century* (Ann Arbor, 1966). There is reason to believe that a Portuguese flotilla of 41 sail which set out to attack Dutch West India Company positions in 1638 would have been supplied, in part, by Dutch traders since many of the Portuguese transports were freighted in Danish ports where Dutch capital was pervasive.
59 Goslinga observes that interlopers "defied the West India Company monopoly and traded between Africa and America with impunity. . . ." For the whole history of the Company, "the illicit trade never abated." *The Dutch in the Caribbean,* p. 360.
60 Boogaart and Emmer are explicit in their argument that illicit imports of slaves to Dutch Brazil were insignificant. "Dutch Participation in the Slave Trade," p. 368.
61 Hilary McD. Beckles, "The Economic Origins of Black Slavery in the British West Indies, 1640–1680: A Tentative Analysis of the Barbados Model," *The Journal of Caribbean History,* XVI (1982), pp. 36–56. It is Beckles's view that the planters, having cheated bondservants of their freedom dues, were able to exploit them even more profitably as wage-earning agricultural proletarians when their indentures had expired.

How, then, do we reconcile this alleged preference for bondservants with the planters' increasing purchase of slave labor during the 1640's? Is it not a matter of economic security, of purchasing the vital ingredients of a productive system, even though they might be more costly or less favored, in order to avoid serious shortages in a time of rising need? The availability of labor and its certainty of supply was critically important to the Barbados colonists. In 1642, leading planters claimed a need for 2,000 indentured servants per year to maintain their tobacco and cotton cultures. They did not get them. No one knew when or in whose favor the English Civil War would end or what effect the war would have upon indentures. Furthermore, the climate of high adventure that pervaded the Indies in these years produced a constant exodus of freemen from the island. Everyone appreciated that existing crops would suffer and that serious experimentation with indigo or sugar would be impossible without reliable supplies of labor. Slaves were available through the Dutch, and Dutch vendors stimulated trade by permitting planters to delay payments for slaves until their next year's crop was taken.[62] In the early 1640's, the comparative advantage that Beckles claims for indentured servants would not have been fully apparent to the colonists. But even if it was and even if the planters favored white servants, the largest proprietors would have been inclined to buy slaves on easy credit terms rather than risk labor shortages at a critical juncture in the economic life of the settlement when the prospect of high profits from new crops was rising.

From the earliest years of the sugar revolution in Barbados, the sugar plantation assumed a unitary, or centralized, character. Having adopted Brazilian techniques of planting and manufacture, and even such Portuguese terms as *ingenio, muscovado,* and *bagasse,* why did the English colonists reject the Brazilian system of cane farming? Under that system, proprietors of plantations

---

62 The history of Dutch credits on slave sales is interesting in this period. Between 1636 and 1643, slave sales in Brazil were almost all undertaken on credit. In 1644 and 1645, when the Portuguese counterattack was getting underway, the percentage of slaves sold for cash was, respectively, 78 and 100. This does not reflect a strong cash position among the Brazilian planters, but growing Dutch apprehension. It has been argued that one reason for Portuguese insurgency in the forties was the desire to rid themselves of debts incurred in the purchase of slaves. While credit in Brazil was contracting, it was forthcoming in Barbados, and this should indicate something about the perceived long-term desirability of the two markets. Boogaart and Emmer, "Dutch Participation in the Slave Trade," p. 370.

rented the bulk of their land to small farmers who, with a few of their own slaves, planted, cultivated, and harvested the cane, transported it to the proprietor's mill, and shared its proceeds by prearranged agreement.[63] Surely, cane farming was possible in Barbados. Although there is considerable disagreement over the size and prosperity of the Barbados yeomanry in the 1640's,[64] there can be little doubt that small farmers were available to grow cane provided they could acquire ample labor. Also, time-expired servants were on hand to lease cane plots if economic conditions favored cane farming.

They did not. Despite the existence of many small farms, Barbados was not a colony of small proprietors. From the beginning of the settlement, land grants had been large, averaging about 100 acres but often ranging well above 300.[65] Large landowners commonly leased out property in the tobacco and cotton era, but the onset of sugar culture enabled them to consolidate holdings in order to achieve greater production efficiencies and economies of scale. Notwithstanding this, it is entirely conceivable that for a time at least Barbados planters would have relied on cane farming and indentured white labor had their cane culture evolved more gradually.

It was the swiftness of the Barbados sugar revolution that constituted its most striking characteristic. From the start, that revolution was a package arrangement, and the Dutch provided all parts of the package: technology, machinery, stock, slaves, credit, and guaranteed shipping at favorable rates. Dutch merchants concentrated their credit facilities on the larger, more creditworthy proprietors. Because the initial outlay for slaves was double that for servants, small and middling farmers had difficulty acquiring slaves in quantity. On the other hand, large planters

---

63 For descriptions of the Brazilian system, see C. R. Boxer, *Salvador de Sá and the Struggle for Brazil and Angola*, pp. 234–235, and *The Dutch in Brazil 1624–1654*, pp. 141–142.

64 For insight on this question, see Hilary McD. Beckles, "Land Distribution and Class Formation in Barbados 1630–1700: The Rise of a Wage Proletariat," *The Journal of the Barbados Museum and Historical Society*, XXXVI (1980), pp. 136–143.

65 F. C. Innis's survey of 771 land grants, 1628–38, produces an average unit size of 97.6 acres. See his "The Pre-Sugar Era of European Settlement in Barbados," *Journal of Caribbean History*, I (1970), pp. 9–11. Innis's work is confirmed in detail by P. F. Campbell's "Aspects of Barbados Land Tenure 1627–1663," *The Journal of the Barbados Museum and Historical Society*, XXXVII (1984), pp. 112–158.

who sought to expand their labor supplies could do so quickly with African slaves. Quite simply, prevailing landholding patterns coupled with the hothouse condition under which cane culture arrived in Barbados favored the creation of large unitary estates. In his superb analysis of that culture, Richard Ligon, drawing on experiences in the late 1640's, never contemplated anything but a unitary plantation where slaves would perform field work, and bondservants the artisans' tasks.

Although Eric Williams correctly recognized the importance of economy of scale and even unitary organization in sugar production, he carried his technological determinism too far. At its inception, there was no necessary connection between cane culture and slave labor in the British settlements, nor is it at all clear that African labor was cheaper, less vexatious, superior, or, in the last analysis, preferred in Barbados. It was available on easy terms at precisely the time when imports of indentured labor had become problematical and when, by virtue of a Portuguese rebellion against the Dutch in Brazil, supplies of sugar in the Atlantic were falling. Ironically, all Dutch actions, positive and negative, seemed to accelerate the sugar revolution in Barbados. Their attacks upon the Iberian colonies provided security for English settlements and generated a market in slaves; their commercial facilities satisfied colonial needs during the troubled decade of the English Civil War; and their political collapse in Brazil after 1645 sent sugar prices in Europe soaring, stimulating a rapid, even hectic, transformation of the Barbadian economy.

The Barbados sugar revolution was by no means inevitable. In its earliest stages, cane culture in the British Caribbean could have employed very different institutional strategies. Long-term growth trends would, at some point, have generated a heavy demand for slave labor, and the scale that the West Indian economy reached in the late seventeenth century could only have been achieved with slaves. But in his examination of the origins of Barbadian slavery, Williams overstressed demand and ignored supply. It is at least as appropriate to contend that ready supplies of African slave labor stimulated the sugar revolution as to argue that sugar production generated black slavery in Barbados. If, at the start, sugar and slaves were bound together in Barbados, the explanation is best found not in the superiority of slave labor nor in rigid technological determinism but in the pre-sugar pattern of land distribution, the remarkable commercial midwifery of the Dutch, and the peculiar concatenation of world events.

In his effort to separate race from slavery, Williams insisted that the decision for slavery, wherever it occurred, was an economically rational one. Virginia tobacco gave rise to black slavery. Barbados tobacco did not. Why? Because at the end of the seventeenth century there was a rise in demand for Virginia leaf. Barbadian tobacco was too coarse to generate important demand. By attributing the rise of black slavery to demand—European demand for colonial staples and a resulting colonial demand for cheap labor—Williams was able to explain the rise of slavery exclusively in rational economic terms. Race prejudice was unimportant.

But rationality and prejudice are not mutually exclusive. As we have seen, slavery in the British colonies did not wait upon demand. Black slavery was well established in the Chesapeake before the late-century spurt of exports; it was firmly installed in Barbados before there was a demand for the island's sugar. In both cases the supply of slaves came from beyond the British sphere of control, from the Atlantic dominions of the Iberian states and from the martial intrusion upon them by the Dutch. Although Williams focused exclusively on the English experience, the origins of slavery in the English colonies cannot be examined in isolation from the rest of the Atlantic world. English settlers in the New World may have had no experience with slavery, but they unhesitatingly enslaved Indians whom they encountered. Britons did not launch their American adventures ignorant of the low esteem in which blacks were held in Southern Europe, and it would be naive to assume that they were not influenced by the practice of slavery in various reaches of the Atlantic and the Mediterranean.[66]

---

66 Scholarly literature dealing with the racial attitudes of various early modern European societies has expanded dramatically in recent years, as has the literature on Iberian-American slavery. Studies on the Atlantic slave trade have begun to give new emphasis to Africa and to the supply side of the traffic. The comparative dimension offered in such work affords a broader context for analyzing the English colonial experience than was available to Williams. Literature appearing in the last decade alone includes: Anthony Baker, *The African Link: British Attitudes to the Negro in the Era of the Atlantic Slave Trade, 1550–1807* (Totowa, N.J., 1978); William B. Cohen, *The French Encounter with Africans: White Response to Blacks, 1530–1880* (Bloomington, Ind., 1980); Francis Jennings, *The*

Surely, Williams was right in arguing that American slavery "was not born of racism." Whether it was production-oriented, as in Virginia and Barbados, or laden with status value, as in Peru, black slavery was initiated and generally perpetuated for economic reasons. The other part of Williams's dictum, "that racism was the consequence of slavery," is far more problematical. In the most extreme sense, his point is undoubtedly valid. By intensifying degradation, slavery deepens prejudice. But to argue, as Williams has, that the origin of black slavery in the English colonies can be expressed in three words, "in the Caribbean, Sugar; on the mainland, Tobacco and Cotton," oversimplifies the problem monumentally. Williams's exclusive focus on the English colonies, his technological determinism, his untoward assumptions about the superiority of African slave labor, and his concentration upon the Old World's demand for New World staples caused him to neglect significant chronological details and to ignore important elements of supply.

Invasion of America: Indians, Colonialism, and the Cant of Conquest (Chapel Hill, 1975); Karen Ordahl Kupperman, *Settling with the Indians: The Meeting of English and Indian Cultures in America, 1580–1640* (Totowa, N.J., 1980); H. C. Porter, *The Inconstant Savage: England and the North American Indian, 1500–1660* (London, 1979); Bernard Sheehan, *Savagism and Civility: Indians and Englishmen in Colonial Virginia* (Cambridge and New York, 1980). Prominent works on early slavery in Spanish America include Frederick P. Bowser, *The African Slave in Colonial Peru, 1524–1650* (Stanford, 1974) and Colin A. Palmer, *Slaves of the White God: Blacks in Mexico, 1570–1650* (Cambridge, Mass., 1976). For the rising importance of supply factors in the slave trade, see Jan S. Hogendorn's review essay, "The Economics of the African Slave Trade," *The Journal of American History*, 70 (1984), pp. 854–861.

Part II. Caribbean Slavery and the Industrial Revolution

Barbara L. Solow

Capitalism and Slavery in the Exceedingly Long Run

> In the Mediterranean, Europe had developed on a large scale the sugar industry learned from India and the Middle East. Important centres of production were Sicily and Cyprus, and the large plantation and large factory had evolved. . . . European experience with colonial labor [had evolved] based firstly on the Moorish domination of Spain and secondly on the Portuguese conquest of West Africa. . . . When Columbus set out for the New World, his equipment included the European wanderlust, a powerful economic impulse, the requisite technical aids, a dominant crusading motive, all backed by the necessary political organization. Above all he took with him the knowledge that Africa was a capacious reservoir of labor which could become (as Gilberto Freyre of Brazil has described the Negro) "the white man's greatest and most plastic collaborator in the task of agrarian colonization."[1]

European expansion did not begin with Columbus, and the economic organization of the Atlantic economy is not of northern European origin. European expansion started at the end of the eleventh century when Christians from southern and western Europe conquered and exploited economically the lands of Muslim Palestine. The wave of expansion moved from east to west, terminating in the New World; in form and content it was one continuous movement. Atlantic colonization cannot be understood without considering the late medieval colonies of the Mediterranean, the Atlantic archipelagoes, and a large part of Africa, as well as the American continent and the countries of northern

---

1 Eric Williams, *From Columbus to Castro: the History of the Caribbean, 1492–1969* (London, 1970), 16–17. This quotation illustrates Williams' early understanding that Medieval Italy, Portugal, Holland, England, France, Brazil, Africa, and the Caribbean fitted into a historical pattern which linked slavery with capitalist development. The present article is an elaboration on his original vision.

Europe. The network of trade routes and of the international balance of payments joined Brazil with England, Madeira with Boston, Newfoundland with the Mediterranean, Holland with the West Indies, and Africa with northern Europe. The crucial importance of slavery to the development of the modern world will be missed by narrow nationalistic approaches.[2]

EARLY ITALIAN COLONIZATION IN THE MEDITERRANEAN   The Mediterranean phase of expansion was not confined to trade and commerce: the Italians, from the time of the First Crusade, engaged in colonial export-oriented sugar production. This production was not feudal: it was not based on a half-free caste of serfs owing labor dues, but involved plantation slavery from the beginning. To a large extent, it was via this first colonial sugar production that the medieval economy of the Mediterranean passed to the modern colonial economy of the Atlantic, and the history of sugar production is the history of slavery. Although Verlinden was concerned to show that it was the Italians who, "under a foreign flag, contributed powerfully to the realization and securing of the passage of civilization from the Mediterranean to the Atlantic world," it was the slaves who, through their labor, provided the principal economic vehicle of this passage. The slave–sugar complex was the bridge over which European civilization crossed from the Old World to the New, not the only bridge, but the first and for three centuries the most important and enduring: it organized the Atlantic economy and dominated it until the nineteenth century.[3]

From its origin in the South Pacific, sugar spread to Southeast Asia and India and was brought to the West by the Arabs in the Muslim era. In the late Sassanid period the southeastern region of Mesopotamia (Khuzistan) was the most important sugar-producing region, and sugar spread with Islam, appearing next in Egypt. From the Muslim era, sugar and slavery were associated.[4]

2 Charles Verlinden, *The Beginnings of Modern Colonization: Eleven Essays with an Introduction* (Ithaca, 1970), xix, xx.
3 *Ibid.*, 157.
4 Michael Lombard, *The Golden Age of Islam* (New York, 1975), 25; Daniel Pipes, *Slave Soldiers of Islam: Genesis of a Military System* (New Haven, 1981), 13. Paula Sanders, Harvard University, has kindly supplied me with important references to the medieval sugar–slave economy of Islam and Italy. See also, William D. Phillips, Jr., *Slavery from Roman Times to the Early Transatlantic Trade* (Minneapolis, 1984), 66–88.

It is not the volume of the sugar trade but its precedent as an economic organization that is significant. The Italians had sugar plantations among other forms of colonial exploitation; slaves worked these plantations among other occupations; and non-slave workers as well as slaves produced sugar in the Muslim areas. From these beginnings, however, there emerged a definite institution—the sugar plantation with slave labor producing for an export market—that would be transported westward in its developed state. By the fifteenth century, sugar plantations increasingly became not one form but *the* form of colonial exploitation in the Atlantic, and work on these plantations became not one occupation of slaves but *the* occupation, and slaves became not *one* form of labor for sugar production but *the* form. It is clear that slavery had an economic not merely a racial explanation. Plantation slaves were not all black at first, and black slaves were not plantation slaves at first—the black slaves of the Middle Ages were primarily in domestic service—but when colonization moved to the Atlantic, plantation slavery became black and blacks became plantation slaves. But there is a continuum from medieval slavery in Europe to Italian slavery in the Levant to colonial slavery in the Atlantic.

Europeans lost little time commercially exploiting the commodity they discovered during the First Crusade, and the Italian colonies in the Levant became the provider of sugar to all of Christian Europe. After the capture of Tyre from the Fatimids in 1123, Venice proceeded to engage in the sugar industry that it found in its new possessions. After the Fourth Crusade Venice acquired new territories, including Crete, where it expanded the existing sugar industry. After the last Christian fortresses fell and the Europeans withdrew to Cyprus, that island became Europe's principal sugar supplier. Both Venice and Genoa were extensively involved in the slave trade on Crete and Cyprus, and both utilized slaves in production.[5]

Although in Western Europe, by the tenth century, slavery had been succeeded by serfdom practically everywhere, along the shores of the Mediterranean it remained widespread. Until the fifteenth century the Mediterranean world used slaves in a variety of ways: as domestic servants, as soldiers, and in mining and

---

5 Verlinden, *Beginnings,* 18–19.

agricultural production. But the last would be the slave institution of the future: European colonization was associated with sugar; sugar was associated with slavery; and slavery was associated with blacks. The richest colonies were those that grew sugar with black slaves, and black slaves in greater numbers appeared in colonies which grew sugar. The slave-sugar complex which originated in the Italian colonies of the eastern Mediterranean shared with gold and silver the honors for first developing the New World and was the more important of the two. An even stronger statement can be made: the slave-sugar complex shared with spices and precious metals the honors for developing economic relations with the entire Third World and was the most important of the three.

Crete became the most important Venetian colony in the Levant, more valuable than the Holy Land colonies. From their occupation in the thirteenth century, the Venetians conducted an important slave market on Crete and cultivated the rural areas with the labor of Greek serfs and slaves. We know from a document of 1393 that Venice subsidized the purchase of slaves in order to develop unoccupied lands in the interior of the island. Furtado calls Brazil "the first large-scale colonial and agricultural enterprise in the Western Hemisphere," but Brazil was merely one stepping stone in a progression that began in the Italian colonies of the Mediterranean.[6]

Although Cyprus was acquainted with sugar from the Arab occupation of the seventh century, sugar's importance there dates from the collapse of the Christian kingdoms in the Holy Land. Along the south shore the royal family maintained plantations and used the sugar for debt repayment. The Hospitalers, the Bishop of Limassol, and the Catalan family of Ferrer all had sugar plantations on Cyprus, but most of our information comes from the holdings of the Cornaro family of Venice. Their methods were fully capitalistic. The plantations were worked by emigrants from the Holy Land, local serfs, and slaves of Arab and Syrian origin. Hydraulic mills were used to process the cane, and disputes

6 The documents on slavery in Crete are almost entirely unpublished. Verlinden published the principal work, "La Crete debouche et plaque tournate de la traite des esclaves aux XIVe et XVe siècles," *Studi di onore di A. Fanfani* (Milan, 1962), III, 593–669. My source on Cyprus is Verlinden, *Beginnings*, 19–20. Celso Furtado, *Economic Growth of Brazil: A Survey from Colonial to Modern Times* (Berkeley, 1963), 6.

over water rights were recorded. Capital equipment, in the form of huge copper boilers, was imported from Italy. The Cornaros even refined their own sugar and exported loaves and powdered sugar. It is clear that large investments and a complex economic organization were required for the entire undertaking.

Thus, while the agriculture of Western Europe was still characterized by manorial society—with serfs providing for their own consumption and meeting a traditionally set level of charges to lord, state, and church; generating most of their own inputs from their own holdings; and being hedged in by communal limitations on decision-making and by a tenurial system that was a web of customary rights and obligations—the members of the Cornaro family were involved in an international agri-business. Their aim was to maximize profits by combining inputs of labor and capital from different places, processing output, and selling the product through a distant marketing network. All of Europe was supplied with sugar from these Italian colonies, together with contributions from Sicily, Muslim Spain, and the Algarve. Slavery plays a role in the development of capitalist forms of economic organization from their first appearance.[7]

SLAVERY AND COLONIALISM   The slave–sugar complex became the premier institution of European expansion for reasons that are easy to understand. First, the effect of slavery as an economic institution was like abolishing child labor laws or factory acts which limited hours of work: an increased supply of labor was introduced into the economy. And to the extent that the supply of slave labor was more elastically supplied, it increased overall elasticity. Second, if slave labor were more productive than free labor—for example, if it were associated with economies of scale, as Fogel and Engerman maintain—then the introduction of slavery also resembled the invention of a new, improved factor of production, like a new kind of machine. Finally, in permitting slavery, society invented a new form of holding wealth: slave labor could be held as an asset in the portfolio of the saver. It brought this productive factor into the category of capital, since slave labor was purchased outright and delivered a stream of

7 Verlinden, *Beginnings*, 20.

services in future periods. Without slavery, labor could never be a capital asset because free labor could only be rented.[8]

The importance of the institution of slavery in unoccupied or underpopulated places like the Atlantic islands and the New World was great. (It had been foreshadowed in the case of the interior of Crete.) What ways were open to Europeans for the exploitation of newly conquered lands? If a flourishing economy existed, the conqueror could loot it, could engage in legitimate trade, or could introduce elements of coercion into the trade to his own advantage. Thus, the Spanish looted the gold of Peru when they ripped it off the walls; the Portuguese forced the trade of India into certain channels and levied exactions on it; and the Dutch forced deliveries in kind in their far eastern possessions. If there had been no economic activity in the colony, these avenues would not have been open. The Europeans could have sent settlers, but there would have been nothing to attract investment from Europe.

As Domar has shown, under some plausible assumptions, of the three elements of a simple agricultural structure—free land, free labor, and a landowning aristocracy—any two elements can exist but not all three simultaneously. Where land is free, its ownership receives no return. There is no way for Europeans at home to benefit by investing in land or capital in the simplest agricultural situation, and the empty colony will be characterized by family farms whose modest capital needs will be supplied by their own savings. The development of such an economy depends on population growth and domestic capital accumulation. Growth may be vast in the long run but it will be slow to develop.[9]

But if society invents or adopts a productive asset (like slaves) in which capital can be immediately invested, the colony can be built up without waiting for population voluntarily to immigrate or capital to be generated. The factors of production can be assembled at once, and the return to the European investor can be transferred by the export of colonial produce. The existence of the slave institution could have increased the incentive to save

8 Robert W. Fogel and Stanley Engerman, *Time on the Cross* (Boston, 1974), I, 192–194. Furtado, *Economic Growth of Brazil*, 148.
9 Evsey D. Domar, "The Causes of Slavery or Serfdom: A Hypothesis," *Journal of Economic History*, XXX (1970), 18–32.

in Europe; it is even likelier that it would have switched existing savings to more productive uses. If the alternative uses for savings had been wars, cathedrals, and luxury consumption, the adoption of slavery could have been important. If the demand for investment had hitherto been a restraint on growth, the invention of slavery as a productive asset could have played a role. Potentially then, slavery, by introducing an elastic supply of an especially productive sort to the economy, by possibly increasing savings rates, and by enabling savings to be invested more productively, resulted in greater European income and more trade, with all the benefits that division of labor and gains from trade provided. To the extent that colonial slave production was in agriculture, Europe's comparative advantage shifted to manufactures. Had the slaves been engaged in the production of transistors, European agriculture would have been encouraged.[10]

It is neither necessary nor sufficient that this scenario lead to an industrial revolution. Whether it did remains to be seen from the historical record. The historical story is that the Italians transferred the sugar-slave complex, which they had developed as a means of colonial exploitation, to Madeira, the Canaries, and the West African islands. The consequent flows of capital, labor, sugar, and manufactures turned these colonies one by one into centers of international trade, uniting them with Europe and Africa in a complex web of transactions. Slavery opened investment opportunities for Europe and allowed northern Europe to trade its manufactures for sugar. I argue that the spread of the slave-sugar complex played a major role in the discovery and economic exploitation of America, as first the Dutch and then the English and French transferred these institutions to Brazil and the Caribbean. This microcosm of capital and trade flows associated with plantation slavery became quantitatively important for British economic development in the eighteenth century. But the *mechanism* which accomplished this development existed in miniature all along the route from Palestine to Crete to Madeira to the Canaries to São Tomé to Brazil and to the Caribbean.

---

10 Aside from the example of slavery, Europeans did not engage in the organization of much productive activity in the rest of the world until the nineteenth century. European entrepreneurship and European direct capital investment assume large proportions only in the last quarter of the century.

TRANSFER OF THE SUGAR-SLAVE COMPLEX TO THE ATLANTIC   Already known to the Genoese in the fourteenth century, Madeira was rediscovered in 1425 by two Portuguese in the service of Prince Henry the Navigator. The islands were entirely uninhabited. The Portuguese exploited their discovery by introducing the slave-sugar complex.

When the Turkish conquest reduced Europe's sugar supply from the eastern Mediterranean, parts of Spain, Portugal, and Italy became alternative sources. Of these, Sicily was the most important. The Sicilian sugar industry had been in trouble at various times, and when it finally declined the Genoese introduced sugar cane production to Madeira. Before the middle of the century (1443), the importation of African slaves began. It was black slavery that was chiefly used in Madeiran sugar production. By 1456 sugar was being exported to England and later to Flanders.

> Madeiran cultivation was so successful, and the production so plentiful, that the price of sugar on European markets probably fell by about 50 per cent between the years 1470 and 1500. . . . Madeira, by the time Columbus sailed to the Americas, had become well integrated into the economies of Europe and Africa. The island was the prototype of that momentous and tragic social and economic system of sugar and slavery that was to be repeated, on a far larger scale, in the West Indies and Brazil. By 1500, when Madeira had reached only its seventy-fifth year of settlement, the island had become the world's largest producer of sugar and, with its complex European and African connections, was also an important center for commercial shipping and navigation. . . . The development of the virgin territory of Madeira was, one may say, quite rapid; within two generations the colonists had seized upon their indispensable cash crop and promoted it with astounding success.[11]

Duncan should have added that the colonists had also seized upon their indispensable labor supply.

Compare the quotation above with Furtado's description of sugar production in Brazil. And we meet it again in Barbados: "Few enterprises in the history of agriculture in modern times approach this in ingenuity, completeness, and ultimate conse-

11   T. Bentley Duncan, *Atlantic Islands: Madeira, the Azores, and the Cape Verdes in Seventeenth-Century Commerce and Navigation* (Chicago, 1972), 10–11; Verlinden, *Beginnings*, 98–112.

quences." The historians of Madeira, of Brazil, and of Barbados, independently of one another, are describing in similar words the same phenomenon. Historians of slavery would recognize the identity of the three cases: in each case slavery is critical. So distinguished an authority on the Atlantic as Chaunu, however, missed the role of slavery. Chaunu emphasizes that the first long phase of European growth "was rooted in the Atlantic adventure and secondly in the Oriental one"; that "it was the dynamism of sugar interests that led to the exploitation of the Atlantic islands"; and that "sugar was the raison d'être of the original settler populations in the Canaries and Madeira." But he misses the significance of slavery by explaining that sugar came to the islands because "sugar requires a rich soil and a readily available labor force. The islands had these." Madeira had no labor force at all, and the Canaries had to import one. What had to be readily available was slave labor for import.[12]

The first deed for sugar production on Madeira was a contract from Prince Henry: "the contract had no trace of feudal or demesnial form. . . . It started a sort of partnership between the Infante and his squire for the production of sugar." Thus, to an uninhabited island, when it was profitable to do so because of demand and cost conditions in the world market, sugar was introduced, slave labor and capital for plant and equipment were imported, the product was processed and exported to the European market, and the island was integrated into an international economy involving several continents in a thoroughly capitalistic network. A brief period of dominance in sugar ended when new cost and demand conditions emerged, and the pattern was repeated elsewhere. Newly discovered islands without the potential for sugar, like the Azores, were characterized by lagging, hesitant, and intermittent growth and were less important members of the world economy.[13]

Madeiran production began to decline after 1570 as Brazilian sugar undercut it in price. Duncan puts production at 45,000 arrobas (an arroba was about 25 pounds) in 1600, compared with the maximum of 150,000. By the beginning of the seventeenth century wine had replaced sugar as Madeira's chief export. But

---

12   Carl and Roberta Bridenbaugh, *No Peace Beyond the Line: The English in the Caribbean, 1624–1690* (New York, 1972). Pierre Chaunu (trans. Katharine Bertram), *European Expansion in the Later Middle Ages* (Amsterdam, 1979), 63, 98, 107.
13   Verlinden, *Beginnings* 216, 217.

the sugar–slave plantations were not a stepping-stone to the new Atlantic economy in the restricted sense that their importance ended when the next step was taken. On the contrary, when sugar moved on, Madeira remained an important link in the development of Atlantic commerce.[14]

As sugar moved to the Western Hemisphere, first Brazil, then the Caribbean and North America became the most important customers for the wines of Madeira. The wine trade of Madeira was in English hands. English merchants acquired wine by selling English textiles and manufactures, salt fish, and Azorean wheat. The Devonshire towns of Topsham and Barnstaple were large suppliers to Madeira, as was Colchester. The wine ships went either directly to the West Indies or stopped first at Cape Verdes for salt. With the West Indian cargoes of sugar, rum, and molasses, they went directly to England or to New England where they traded for codfish, lumber, and pipe staves. The extent of the market for Madeiran wines depended then on the slave-produced commodities of the Americas, and, although insignificant in quantity, so did the textile trade of some Devon and Suffolk towns. The network of eighteenth-century trade was already in existence, in miniature.

The colonization of the Canary Islands followed that of Madeira, although they had been discovered about 1336 by Lazarotto Malocello, a Genoese in the service of Portugal. The islands were conquered by Castile in the mid-fifteenth century. They were originally occupied by the Guanches, whose simple culture was not unlike that of the Arawak of the West Indies. At an early stage of European occupation the Guanches were enslaved, either for domestic use or export; they also fell prey to plague and obscure sicknesses, much like the indigenous peoples of the New World. They were no bar to Spanish conquest. The earliest European settlers were Portuguese, possibly from Madeira, who farmed small holdings of wheat. When European demand for sugar increased in the fifteenth century, its production spread to those parts of the Canaries where it could be grown. The Canaries became sugar producers because that was the way the Spanish could exploit them economically.[15]

---

14 Duncan, *Atlantic Islands*, 31.
15 Felipe Fernández-Armesto, *The Canary Islands after the Conquest: The Making of a Colonial Society in the Early Sixteenth Century* (Oxford, 1982), 32, 203.

From the beginning, sugar production was carried on by foreign capital. Genoese, Portuguese, and the German banking family of Welzer were sources of the considerable requirements. Portuguese from Madeira probably contributed technical skill in sugar-making. The industry grew rapidly from the establishment of the first mill (1484), until, in the early sixteenth century, production was estimated at 70,000 arrobas, equal to Madeira's at the time but below its peak. Sugar never completely dominated the Canaries; it would only grow in certain areas. Foreigners with large holdings grew sugar on irrigable land, whereas small settlers, usually Portuguese, raised wheat and wine on rain-fed acreage. Conflict between them was sharp, but efforts to limit foreigners' holdings were nullified by Crown exemption. For example, the Welzers were granted such an exemption, not surprisingly since they were in partnership with the royal secretary.[16]

The role of slavery in Canarian sugar production is not clear. Guanches were not used in sugar, although some of those exported to Madeira may have been. In the Canaries the Guanches were domestic slaves. It is known that Christian pirates from the Canaries kidnapped Berbers and enslaved them on sugar plantations and that black slaves were taken from the nearby African mainland and from Portuguese slave markets. Ordinances existed prohibiting the use of imported slaves in the home, so they must have been brought in for sugar. Fernández-Armesto believes that they were used in refining, with field labor managed by white sharecroppers with white tenants. Verlinden cites a will of 1527 in which a Spanish plantation owner mentions twenty-three male slaves (of whom twenty were black), two female slaves, and skilled free workers. It seems a fair presumption that black slaves were used in the fields. With all respect to Fernández-Armesto, if black slaves did not work in the fields and were not allowed to be domestics, and we know that black slaves were being imported, where did they all go?[17]

With only partial use of slaves then, the Spanish monarch chose to exploit the Canaries by joining foreign capital to immigrant labor. The combination produced sugar for the European market. Thenceforth the Canaries took their place in the devel-

---

16 Queen Juana to Anton Welzer and Company, Valladolid, Jan. 1513, reproduced in *ibid.*, 219. The conflict between the small settlers and the plantation owners has a familiar ring to Americans.

17 Verlinden, *Beginnings*, 113–131, 153.

oping Atlantic economy: capital from Italy, labor from Portugal and Africa, sugar to northern Europe, and textiles from London, Bristol, and the Low Countries. By analyzing forty documents relating to the activities of one merchant, Verlinden shows how this bazaar "functioned as a minute nerve-center on the roads of world trade, uniting by land and sea, England and Flanders with Spain and Italy, and, in the Atlantic, Spain with its possessions in the Antilles." By using the known notarial records, Verlinden shows how sugar incorporated a whole web of international transactions. There was an Atlantic economy in existence before the New World began its economic life, and, when Brazil and the West Indies appeared on the scene, they took starring roles in a play already long in progress.[18]

On his first voyage Columbus stopped at the Canary Islands for nearly a month for repairs to the *Pinta*'s rudder and a sail change for the *Nina*. In his first notes from America, on October 12, 1492, he compared the Amerindians with the Guanches. He had set out in the hope of founding monopolistic trading posts in the East but this goal was soon abandoned. In his journal he outlined almost at once the two ways in which Spain could exploit his discovery: by the institution of coerced labor in agriculture or by the extraction of precious metals. On December 16, 1492, he wrote:

> I must add that this island (Hispaniola), as well as the others, belongs to Your Highnesses as securely as the kingdom of Castile. It only needs people to come and settle here, and to give orders to the inhabitants who will do whatever is asked of them. . . . The Indians have no weapons and are quite naked. They know nothing about the art of war and are so cowardly that a thousand of them would not stay to face three of our men. . . . they need only to be given orders to be made to work, to sow, or to do anything useful.

Ten days later exploitation by coerced labor had been forgotten. On December 26, in a frenzy to acquire the baubles Columbus' men had brought, the Indians offered in Columbus' words "incredible quantities of gold for almost anything."[19]

18 *Ibid.*, 143.
19 Chaunu, *European Expansion*, 164, 190, n.129.

Chaunu comments: "the principles of despoiling a traditional society were established." The Spanish, in fact, did base their policy on the extraction of precious metals. But Chaunu draws attention to the astonishing insight of Columbus' first views of October 12: "They bear the mark of genius. After such a trial and amid such anxiety and uncertainty, he could show this lucidity and this unhurried attention." Chaunu attributes Columbus' initial idea to his familiarity with the Portuguese slave trade. (Between 1482 and 1484 Columbus had participated in at least one voyage to the site of the fort at Elmina on the Gold Coast.) Certainly Madeira was where he saw slaves "working and sowing."[20]

The two methods that Columbus described forecast the main direction of Western Hemispheric history for the next 300 years. The Spanish aim was the extraction of precious metals, and the history of Spanish Latin America, San Domingo (the Dominican Republic), Puerto Rico, Cuba, and Mexico for three centuries reflect this choice. The Portuguese took the other road and introduced plantation slavery; the history of Brazil, the Caribbean islands of France and Britain, the Chesapeake, South Carolina, and Georgia were dominated by that strategy.

PORTUGAL AND SPAIN IN THE WESTERN HEMISPHERE   The great achievements of the Portuguese explorers and the brilliant strategy of Affonso de Albuquerque in gaining complete mastery over the Asian sea routes in the sixteenth century should not obscure Portugal's failure to make much of its vast Asian conquests. It was unopposed by other Europeans for the whole century, and at its end it had nothing to show for its pains but Goa, Macao, and Timor. Its eastern trade declined from the beginning of the seventeenth century, and the economic links of its remaining colonies with Europe were of the frailest.

Portugal's policy was to monopolize trade in certain commodities and to force trade into specific ports where it could exact tolls. But the Portuguese also engaged in legitimate trade, acquiring Asian spices with their earnings as merchants and shippers in the traditional trade of Asia. The spices were shipped to Lisbon where the Dutch transshipped them to the rest of Europe. Only

20 *Ibid.*, 162.

Eurocentric vision prevents us from seeing that quantitatively and qualitatively the important Asian trade was between Asians, not between Europe and Asia. Portugal sent few men, few goods, and little capital, and organized little or no productive activity in Asia. Its simple aim was to divert to its own sea routes a small portion of the great Asian trading system that lay at hand. Indeed, three and a half centuries would pass before Europe became the most important trading partner of Asian countries, before Europeans exported capital and organized production in Asia, and before Asia was turned into a food- and raw-materials-producing exporter and an importer of European manufactures. These revolutionary changes date from the second half of the nineteenth century, not from the sixteenth. In that century the transatlantic trade between Spain and Spanish America employed far more shipping and moved far more goods than did the trade from Portugal to India. If we add Portugal's trade with Africa and Brazil, the predominance of the Atlantic becomes even clearer.[21]

Chaunu describes 1441 as something of an *annus mirabilis* in Portuguese exploration: the caravel was built and the first African slave hunt by Europeans took place. In 1444 Prince Henry personally watched his share of a shipment from Guinea being unloaded. The trade between the Senegal and Sierra Leone was managed from the Cape Verde islands. Some of these barren, arid islands (there are ten of significant size) had been discovered between 1456 and 1460. The islands could support little except goats and a small amount of agriculture; three of them had salt deposits. At first they were the site of a complex trade, involving not only slaves but also wax, ivory, hides, and gum from the mainland; manufactures, metal goods, spirits, baubles, and textiles from Europe; Indian cottons and Molucca spices from Asia via Lisbon; and silver from Latin America. This lively trading economy soon waned and by the seventeenth century "slave-holding and slave-trading were the archipelago's raison d'être, [and] the very basis of its existence as a social and economic complex." The islands were an especially horrible entrepôt: slaves were always the first victims of chronic droughts.[22]

---

21 John H. Parry, "Transport and Trade Routes," *Cambridge Economic History of Europe* (Cambridge, 1967), IV, 199.
22 Chaunu, *European Expansion*, 120; Duncan, *Atlantic Islands*, 230.

A decade divides the discovery of the Cape Verdes from the mapping out of the great curve of the Gulf of Guinea. In 1471/72 the Grain Coast, the Ivory Coast, and the Gold Coast were discovered. The following year the Slave Coast was reached and then the Niger Delta. On December 21, 1471 São Tomé was discovered, and on New Year's Day Annobon and Príncipe. Fernando Po was probably discovered on the next expedition. The Southern Hemisphere had been reached.

Scarcely more than a generation later, the Malagueta pepper of the Grain Coast proved inferior, the ivory of the Ivory Coast proved exhaustible, and the climate of the Niger Delta proved too unhealthy for Portuguese occupation. The settlers withdrew to São Tomé and Fernando Po. Unable to exploit the islands by the methods that they had used in Asia, they repeated the old pattern. They brought kidnapped Jews from home and black slaves from Africa and set up sugar plantations. São Tomé was producing sugar for export by 1522 and became a major supplier to Europe. "São Tomé became the true economic and political center of Portuguese power north of Angola," and Angola became a tributary, supplying slaves first to São Tomé then to Brazil. Without them Angola was economically insignificant.[23]

Not only did the Asian trade of the Portuguese dwindle, but so too did the African trade of any commodity except slaves. The most enduring legacy of Portuguese exploration was to open up the coast of Africa for slave supplies.

São Tomé's sugar era was short-lived. Estimates of production suggest a rise until perhaps the last quarter of the century and a decline thereafter. There were slave rebellions in 1580, 1595, and 1617 and more or less continuous guerilla resistance. But it was the entry of Brazil into the sugar market in the last quarter of the century that changed São Tomé from a sugar producer to a slave entrepôt. The great profitability of that business attracted the Dutch, and the worldwide Luso-Dutch wars of the seventeenth century—if we can call Asia, Africa, and Latin America worldwide—in fact began with a Dutch attack on São Tomé and Príncipe in 1598/99.

Brazil was not planned as a sugar plantation; it became one by the logic of the situation. Portugal hoped for precious metals.

23 Antonio H. de Oliveira Marques, *History of Portugal* (New York, 1972), 274.

Until these turned up it needed an economic foothold to make Brazil a paying proposition and to keep rivals away. Of the ten captaincies created in the original settlement, only three took hold: two where sugar thrived and one where slave-hunting was the settlers' occupation. The crown soon undertook to encourage sugar production as the most likely road to riches until gold was found. Development was slow at first, but by the middle of the sixteenth century the industry was well established; in the last quarter of the century production increased tenfold. From 1575 to 1650 Brazil supplied most of Europe's sugar and imported considerable quantities of manufactured goods and slaves, not only for itself but also (illicitly) for the Spanish colonies in the Caribbean and on the mainland. The main source of these goods— textiles and hardware—was not Portugal but northern Europe.

The planter who claimed that the sugar of Brazil was more profitable than all the pepper, spices, and luxury goods of Asia was right. Between 1575 and 1650 Pernambuco and Bahia produced several million arrobas of sugar, and Brazil's production exceeded that of the Atlantic islands by a factor of twenty. "From mere plundering and mining ventures . . . the Western Hemisphere started to become an integral part of the European reproductive economy, the technology and capital of which were therefore to be guided and invested in such a manner as to create a permanent flow of goods to Europe."[24]

Furtado makes a crude calculation that Brazil had 120 sugar mills at the end of the century at an average value of £15,000 (gold), amounting to investment in plant and equipment of £1.8 million. Valuing 20,000 slaves at £25 and assuming that 75 percent were engaged in sugar adds £375,000, for a total investment of £2.175 million. Income can be no more than "a vague conjecture." Furtado estimates sugar exports in a good year at £2.2 million, of which 60 percent is ascribed to value added in Brazil, and of this 75 percent is ascribed to the sugar sector. The resulting income estimate of £2 million to be divided among the 300,000 whites of Brazil "was evidently far higher than that prevailing in Europe at the time, and at no other period of its history—even at the height of the gold cycle—did Brazil regain this level of income."[25]

24 Furtado, *Economic Growth of Brazil*, 5.
25 *Ibid.*, 47. If Furtado were writing today he might revise the statement, but that would not detract from its forcefulness.

The formidable difficulties of erecting an agricultural export industry of this size in the virgin territory of the Western Hemisphere in the sixteenth century were overcome because the required institutions had already been developed, and Brazil took over from São Tomé the pattern that had been bequeathed from the Italian Mediterranean colonization. But the Dutch now played the role of the Italians. From mid-century the Portuguese sugar industry was amalgamated with Dutch and Flemish interests. Dutch capital financed the acquisition of slaves from Africa and the setting up of plantations; the Dutch had perhaps a half to two thirds of the carrying trade between Europe and Brazil; Antwerp and Amsterdam (after the sack of Antwerp) refined the sugar; and the Dutch marketed it.[26]

If the sixteenth were Portugal's imperial century in Asia and Africa, and Portugal's and Spain's in Latin America, the seventeenth century was Holland's. Its war of independence against Spain was waged equally against Portugal during the union of the crowns. According to Boxer's succinct scorecard, Holland played Portugal in Africa and tied, Holland played Portugal in Asia and won, Holland played Portugal in Brazil and lost. In Africa the Dutch originally succeeded in taking not only the slave forts at Elmina, Shama, and Axim, but also Luanda, Benguela, São Tomé, and Annobon. The latter group they could not retain, thus the tie score, but they had gained enough of a foothold to become a dominant force in the slave trade. In Asia, the Dutch reached the East Indies at the end of the sixteenth century. The Portuguese strategic position, based on facing a mainland enemy, was now outflanked. The Dutch could attack the Portuguese strongholds and attack they did. Malacca, Ceylon, Cochin, and the Malabar coast fell one by one, and the Asian trade was reoriented from the Red Sea, the Persian Gulf, and East Africa to a direct route from Batavia (Jakarta) round the Cape of Good Hope.

Meanwhile, in Brazil, Dutch occupation had begun in 1630. Portugal, with its limited resources, made the choice to give up Asia in favor of Brazil and its complementary ports in Africa. The Dutch were expelled from Brazil, retaining only Surinam, Essequibo (Guyana), and Demerara (Guyana). The Dutch attack on Spanish shipping in the Western Hemisphere also succeeded. As a result of its depredations "official shipping between Seville

26 C. R. Boxer, *The Dutch in Brazil* (Oxford, 1957), 20.

and the Indies shrank by 1640 to less than 10,000 tons annually" and continued to shrink for the rest of the century. Spain retained its mainland colonies, but its seapower monopoly had been broken, and it could not prevent French and British settlers from occupying the smaller Caribbean islands.[27]

In the short term, Holland secured a dominant role in the slave trade of Africa and the spice trade of Asia, and, although it lost the sugar trade of Brazil, Brazil lost much of it too when production was introduced into the Caribbean islands. But Dutch commercial and shipping resources made the Caribbean for the first half of the seventeenth century "a Dutch lake."

Sugar production never disappeared from Brazil; nor did Brazil disappear from the Atlantic economy. When sugar revenues declined severely at the end of the seventeenth century, Portugal tried to compensate by encouraging manufacturing in Brazil. It adopted a protectionist policy and almost succeeded in ending textile imports altogether. The powerful Portuguese wine interests found that they could sell less to England if England earned less foreign exchange in Portuguese markets. Together the English and these wine interests manuevered the Methuen Treaty of 1703: English textiles would no longer be embargoed and Portuguese wines would receive preferential treatment in England. Furtado observes that, in view of the conditions in 1703, the treaty probably had no great effect. The low value of the wine exports could hardly be expected to have balanced textile imports; perhaps the treaty would not have survived. But, by the eighteenth century, gold was finally discovered in Brazil, earning perhaps £2.5 million for Portugal at the peak of production in 1760. The Methuen Treaty provided the mechanism for British manufactures to satisfy the large Brazilian demand for goods. The gold went to Britain and Portugal could only skim off some taxes and brokerage.[28]

---

27 De Oliveira Marques, *History of Portugal,* 338; Edwin E. Rich, "Colonial Settlement and its Labour Problems," *Cambridge Economic History,* IV, 204.

28 Furtado, *Economic Growth of Brazil,* 92:

> England found in the Portuguese-Brazilian economy a fast expanding and nearly unilateral market. Her exports were paid for in gold, which gave the English economy exceptional flexibility in its operations on the European market. She thus found herself for the first time in a position to balance indirectly her trade in construction materials and other raw materials from northern Europe with manufactured products. The English economy thus acquired greater flexibility and a tendency to concentrate on investments in the manufacturing sector as the most indicated for rapid technological evolution. Further, by receiving most of the gold then being

As the Marquis de Pombal, the great Portuguese statesman, is supposed to have said, gold meant nothing more than fictitious riches for Portugal: "even Negroes working in the mines had to get their loincloths from the British." What Portugal did get from the transaction was a British guarantee of its national sovereignty and of its possession of Brazil. Without backing it would have been at the mercy of France and Spain.

Brazil, founded on slaves and functioning with slaves until the late nineteenth century, was an important participant in the Atlantic economy in the sugar and gold eras from the late sixteenth century. The combination of empty land, European capital, and African labor led to production on a much larger scale than its earlier incarnations had ever achieved.

Spain's Latin American colonies, however, never played a major role in international trade after the mining era. The Spanish limited their colonial aims to generating a surplus in gold and silver and remitting it annually to the home country. Settlement was made only along an axis connecting the mining properties and the necessary supply and transport routes. Aside from precious metals, no economic links between the mother country and the colonies were encouraged, nor was any intercolonial trade. In pursuit of this policy Spain tried to monopolize and regulate all the trade to the colonies. Consequently, the supply of shipping, capital, slaves, and settlers was severely limited. When the mining industry declined, the vast Spanish empire sank into stagnation and decay. Not until the Spanish colonies were opened to foreign capital at the end of the eighteenth century did the sugar-slave complex take hold in Cuba, replicating on a grand scale the cases I have described.

CARIBBEAN SLAVERY AND BRITISH ECONOMIC GROWTH   The Atlantic economy in the eighteenth century found the Spanish colonies moribund, the Portuguese colony pouring out gold, and the French and British established in the Caribbean and on the seaboard of North America.

---

produced in the world, English banking houses reinforced their position even more and Europe's financial center transferred from Amsterdam to London. According to English sources, imports of Brazilian bullion in London were at one time as high as £50,000 a week, permitting a substantial accumulation of reserves without which Britain could hardly have carried on the Napoleonic Wars.

The earliest Caribbean colonists struggled to survive by growing tobacco, indigo, cocoa, cotton, ginger, and the like on small plots with indentured labor and some slaves. It was a losing battle. Sugar was introduced to Barbados about 1640, and within a decade the large numbers of small holders and white servants were replaced by large plantations and black slaves. Brazilian sugar could no longer compete, and its markets were henceforth limited to southern Europe. The transformation of Barbados to an economy based on slaves and sugar was followed by that of the Leeward Islands, Guadeloupe, and Martinique, and much later and on a larger scale by Jamaica and Saint Domingue (Haiti). Total sugar production in the Western Hemisphere can be estimated roughly at 54,000 tons in 1700; it doubled by 1740; tripled by 1776; and nearly quadrupled by the end of the American Revolution.

"By 1750 the poorest English farm laborer's wife took sugar in her tea." Rum from West Indian molasses catered to the notorious drinking habits of eighteenth-century Britain and supplied the navy. By 1660 the value of sugar imports exceeded that of all other colonial produce combined; by 1774 sugar accounted for 20 percent of the total import bill, far surpassing any other commodity. The British took a third of Europe's consumption in the first half of the century, and the rapid increase after that has been described as "astonishing"; per capita consumption was eight times that of the French. Slave labor produced this sugar. Of the six million slaves taken from Africa in the eighteenth century, the Caribbean imported more than half and Brazil another third.[29]

Once the sugar-slave plantation arrived in the British colonies, the external trade of Britain turned in that direction. At the beginning of the seventeenth century the woolen industry dominated English trade and manufacturing, accounting for four fifths of English foreign trade, mainly with Europe. Trade with the Levant, India, and Indonesia were sources of imports rather than destinations for exports; the East was a notorious sink for bullion. With the appearance of slave-grown tobacco and sugar, British commerce turned to the West, and Britain became the entrepôt

29 Ralph Davis, *Rise of the Atlantic Economies* (Ithaca, 1973), 351. For a full discussion of the rise of sugar consumption in England, see Sidney W. Mintz, *Sweetness and Power: The Place of Sugar in Modern History* (New York, 1985), 74–151. Philip D. Curtin, *The Atlantic Slave Trade: A Census* (Madison, 1969), 216, Table 65.

for Europe's supply of these goods. By the end of the seventeenth century the re-export of colonial and Asian goods amounted to over a quarter of British exports. But American trade was just beginning and Asia's share was declining. Demand for spices was satiated and inelastic, and European governments began to ban imports of Asian textiles. The share of Oriental trade would not revive until the rise in the popularity of tea well into the next century.

The total production of sugar and much of the production of tobacco, their cheapness, and their elasticity of supply were dependent upon the continuing flow of the productive labor of slaves to the colonies. The eighteenth century saw the full fruition of this trade reorientation. Total trade increased greatly, and the Atlantic was crisscrossed by British ships carrying manufactured goods to Africa, the West Indies, Brazil, Portugal, and British North America. The Atlantic islands were exporting wine, Africa slaves, Brazil gold, and the West Indies sugar and molasses. Some of the British North American colonies were sending rice and tobacco to Britain; others were sending fish, lumber, horses, and flour to the West Indies and were buying British manufactures with the proceeds. Every one of these flows depended on the product of slave labor.

In particular this dependence on slave labor is true of the North American nonslave colonies. Their land was suited to agricultural commodities which could not easily bear the cost of transport to Britain. They could import British manufactures only by shipping their surplus food and raw materials to the slave colonies of the West Indies and earning there the foreign exchange that enabled them to meet their balance of payments deficits in Britain. Thus, the international trade of the northern colonies depended on slave production as much as did the trade of Virginia and South Carolina. The population of British North America increased tenfold between 1700 and 1774 and was responsible for most of the expansion of British overseas trade during the middle decades of the century.[30]

Wherever the slave-sugar complex went, a network of international trade flows followed: flows of labor, capital, manufactures, sugar, raw materials, shipping, banking, and insurance. The

30 Davis, *Rise of the Atlantic Economies*, 303.

Atlantic network centered on the Caribbean was similar in form to that centered on the eastern Mediterranean in the late Middle Ages and those centered on the Atlantic islands, the African islands, and Brazil in the early modern period. But this eighteenth-century trading network had a vastly greater significance: it was important to the economic growth of Great Britain at the beginning of the Industrial Revolution. Slavery did not cause the Industrial Revolution, but played an active role in its pattern and timing.

The slave institution increased economic activity in the Atlantic economy: it did not merely direct economic activity from alternative, equally productive channels. Slavery introduced a more elastic supply of labor into the colonial system, counteracting the diminishing productivity of investment, and permitting a period of constant returns to colonial investment, thus raising the rate of return on investment in the whole colonial system over what it would otherwise have been. To the extent that this new slave labor was more productive than free white labor, the return to investment was multiplied even further. In sum, slavery in the colonies raised the rate of return on investment in the empire—made investment more productive—and thereby increased national output. Capital investment in the colonies, amounting to £37 million in 1773, was large enough to make this a significant force.[31]

At higher levels of national output, the British colonial empire enjoyed an extension of the market and a concomitant division of labor, which encouraged British manufacturing activity in particular. The gains accrued to Britain irrespective of the original level of employment in the home country. But if there was underemployment associated with a Keynesian demand shortfall—as I have suggested—the slave colonies made an additional contribution to economic activity through raising total demand.

How do these mechanisms fit with the concrete historical circumstances of British growth in the eighteenth century? It is now generally agreed that national output grew more slowly than previous estimates suggest, and that the acceleration of investment and of industrial growth was more gradual than earlier scholars

---

31 Solow, "Caribbean Slavery and British Growth: The Eric Williams Hypothesis," *Journal of Development Economics*, XVII (1985), 99–115.

believed. Amidst these revisions, however, the one relationship that is confirmed more than ever is the importance of exports to industrial growth. There is a solid connection between slave production in the Americas and British production of industrial goods. "In the last two decades of the eighteenth century (the early rather than the decisive phase of the industrial revolution), almost sixty percent of additional industrial output was exported." Industrial exports led industrial growth, and industrial growth meant structural change and overall growth. American slavery contributed substantially to these exports.[32]

To argue that slavery was important for British economic growth is not to claim that slavery caused the Industrial Revolution. British incomes grew over the eighteenth century when population growth was accompanied by increased agricultural productivity, leaving both a demand for nonagricultural commodities, not only by the rich but also by people of middle income levels, and a supply of labor to produce these goods. This entire process paved the way for the technical change which began late in the century and assumed greater quantitative importance in the first quarter of the nineteenth century. One of the new demands was for sugar; and the demand for sugar, originating in the home economy, was a necessary condition for the Atlantic trading system. But so too was the elastic supply of productive labor to produce that sugar.

The late eighteenth century was an era of radical change for the British economy, and its importance should not be obscured by comparison with future decades. It is hardly surprising that changes in the growth of aggregate output or output per capita show up only with a lag. Industrial growth was marked in the late eighteenth century even though it was smaller than Deane and Cole thought and smaller than it later became. According to Crafts' revised figures, the annual growth rate of industry more than doubled from the period 1700 to 1760 (when it was .71) to the period 1760 to 1780 (1.51), and grew half as much again between 1780 and 1801 (2.11). Aside from government and defense, only one other sector of the eighteenth-century economy grew at a rate exceeding 1 percent over the entire century. All

32 Nicholas F. R. Crafts, "British Economic Growth," *Economic History Review*, XXXVI (1983), 177–199.

sectoral growth rates exceeded 1 percent after 1801 and industry continued to lead.[33]

Investment grew markedly at the end of the eighteenth century whether one accepts Feinstein's estimates or Crafts'. For Feinstein, gross domestic investment as a percent of gross domestic product rose from 8 percent between 1761 and 1770 to 13 percent between 1791 and 1800, or by five percentage points in one generation. For Crafts, the corresponding rise was from 5.7 percent in 1760 to 7.9 percent in 1801, a faster rate of increase than in the period before 1760.[34]

In the late eighteenth century, investment and industrial growth were accelerating and national output began to grow faster. Crafts' Table 5 shows output growth rates of .69 for 1700 to 1760 and .70 for 1760 to 1780, but 1.32 for 1780 to 1801. I have argued that some portion of the investment increase is attributable to the slave-based American economy, and that much of the incremental industrial output of the period depends on the export demand associated with that economy.

Crouzet estimates the growth rate of exports between 1781 and 1800 as more than 5 percent and attributes the export spurt of the 1790s to increased demand from American markets. Export growth accounts for nearly 60 percent of additional industrial growth in this period, and industrial growth contributes to the growth of output. Without the demand for exports generated by the slave-grown crops of the Atlantic economy, Britain would have begun the nineteenth century with a much slower-growing industrial base and a slower-growing economy.[35]

Decadal turning points in the late eighteenth century were fragile because of the effect of the American Revolution. But over the century it remained true that the growth of output, of the investment rate, and of industrial production accelerated. The share of exports in national output doubled over the century and was a source of dynamic changes: export growth led industrial growth which led to accelerated growth in national output. There

33 *Ibid.*, Table 5. Phyllis Deane and William A. Cole, *British Economic Growth 1688–1959: Trends and Structure* (Cambridge, 1967; 2nd ed.).
34 Charles H. Feinstein, "Capital Accumulation and the Industrial Revolution," in Roderick Floud and Donald McCloskey (eds.), *The Economic History of Britain since 1700* (New York, 1981), I, Table 7-3, 133.
35 François Crouzet, "Towards an Export Economy: British Exports during the Industrial Revolution," *Explorations in Economic History*, XVII (1980), 48–93.

is no reason to dispute Deane and Cole's conclusion that "the existence of exploitable international markets at the end of the eighteenth and beginning of the nineteenth centuries was probably crucial in initiating the process of industrialization and the growth of real incomes which was associated with it." They claim that "it was the American market (including the valuable West Indies) which provided the greatest scope for growth."[36]

The importance of Caribbean slavery to British growth depended on particular circumstances and was confined to a particular historical period. The old colonial system benefited Britain when investment was lagging, technical change was slow, growth in domestic demand for manufactures was less than that in external demand, and when the North American colonies depended on Britain for manufactures and on the West Indies for the foreign exchange with which to buy them. None of these conditions obtained after the Napoleonic Wars (or by the 1820s at the latest).

By 1820, Britain had moved decisively toward industrialization. Investment and technical change picked up; exports mattered less; within the diminished export sector, North America and the West Indies mattered less; and market-widening gave way to market-deepening as a driving force for exports.

British export growth rates declined after 1802 and remained slow until the middle of the nineteenth century. "It is clear that it was only after 1850 that Britain really became an 'export economy'." Saul confines the term export economy to the period 1870 to 1914. Exports as a percentage of national income (which had doubled over the eighteenth century to a peak of 18 percent in 1801) fell and stagnated thereafter. The leading role of exports in British economic growth did not survive the eighteenth century, whichever measure one chooses. The home market was expanding faster than demand from abroad, and domestic consumption and investment replaced exports as an engine of growth.[37]

Within the diminished export sector, trade moved away from the United States and West Indies. The American market, which had translated more than half of the British West Indian sugar earnings into British exports, lost importance during the wars

---

36 Deane and Cole, *British Economic Growth*, 312, 34.
37 Crouzet, "Towards an Export Economy," 81; S. Berrick Saul, "The Export Economy, 1870–1914," *Yorkshire Bulletin of Economic and Social Research*, XVII (1965), 5–18.

and never mattered so much again. This timing is necessarily clouded because Britain had control of Europe's access to overseas trade during the wars, so what was developing was not immediately apparent. The American market ceased to depend on imports from Britain, which, as a colony, she had been constrained to take. The United States began to control her own commercial policy, produce her own textiles and manufactures, and meet her foreign exchange needs from the export earnings of the Cotton South.

The share of the United States in British export growth to the end of the War of 1812 was large, but this was a false dawn. "The Americas, though playing a vital role from the 1780's to the end of the French wars, were thereafter far less important." The mean growth rate of British exports to the United States between 1814 and 1846 was −0.6 in current values, indicating an absolute decrease. Cain and Hopkins go so far as to say that "the rise of an export economy based on cotton manufacturing after 1780 was accomplished only by dismembering the old colonial system." One can quibble about the date, and Americans can question the word "dismembering," but the statement is otherwise correct.[38]

In the era of cotton dominance it was India, Australia, and Latin America which were increasingly Britain's customers. Cain and Hopkins calculate that four fifths of the increase in exports from 1816–1820 to 1838–1842 came from outside the old colonial system. Even in the export field it was the cheapening of British goods that led to export growth, as lower prices expanded foreign demand. Export volumes increased while values stayed fairly steady: market-deepening not market-widening dominated at home and abroad in the first half of the nineteenth century, but the main sources of growth were at home.

British resources directed toward the acquisition of slaves in the eighteenth century were very productive: they hastened the development of the New World; the rate of return on investment in the empire was enhanced; and the earnings associated with slave-produced crops enabled Britain's manufacturing sector to expand very much faster than domestic demand permitted. In the

---

38 Crouzet, "Towards an Export Economy," 77, 73; P. J. Cain and Anthony G. Hopkins, "The Political Economy of British Expansion Overseas, 1750–1914," *Economic History Review*, XXXIII (1980), 489.

first half of the nineteenth century, with higher investment and faster technical change, market widening through exports mattered much less to British growth, and slavery no longer had a starring role. Emancipation meant buying more sugar from Cuba and Brazil rather than from Trinidad and Demerara. The end of slavery would have been costly to Great Britain had it come in the middle of the eighteenth century. When it came toward the middle of the nineteenth, it was a bargain. Until the nineteenth century, wherever sugar and slavery went, a web of international trading flows in capital, merchandise, labor supply, and shipping was woven. Where slavery did not go, less trade flowed between Europe and the rest of the world. Fanciful tales that European growth was due to exploitation of "the periphery" by "the metropolis" do not withstand scholarly examination. The exploitation that really mattered for 300 years was the exploitation of African slaves.

Joseph E. Inikori

Slavery and the Development of Industrial

Capitalism in England   Studies of the relationship of the
Atlantic slave economy to the development of eighteenth-century
English industrial capitalism have traditionally focused on narrow
issues of capital and finance. To understand the broader relationships, however, the emphasis must be shifted from profits and
the availability of investible funds to long-term fundamental
changes in England: the development of the division of labor and
the growth of the home market; institutional transformation af-
fecting economic and social structures, national values, and the
direction of state policy; and the emergence of development centers. The Atlantic region must be seen as a single interdependent
economic region within which the major forces operating on the
individual economies were significantly dependent upon the operation of the whole system. Thus it is inadequate to isolate the
analysis of the relationship between England and the British West
Indies from the whole Atlantic region: it must be considered in
the context of the entire region, south and north, east and west.

Economists grappling with the problems of present-day
Third World economies have long realized the inadequacy of
neoclassical economic analysis for their purposes. That analysis is
designed specifically for short-term minute changes at the margin,
and it presupposes economies where certain fundamental institutional and structural arrangements are already in place. Students
of the Third World, facing economies undergoing long-term institutional and structural change, have found the existing tools of
neoclassical economics inadequate; hence the emergence of the
subdiscipline called development economics.[1]

---

1 See A. N. Agarwala and S. P. Singh (eds.), *The Economics of Underdevelopment* (London,
1958); Gerald M. Meier, *Leading Issues in Economic Development: Studies in International
Poverty* (Oxford, 1970; 2nd ed.).

Since all developed economies were once less developed, it is surprising that students of the Industrial Revolution in England have not shown sufficient awareness of the similarity of their issues to those of the presently developing nations. Instead of addressing long-term processes of institutional and structural change, they have persisted in applying the unmodified tools of neoclassical economics to the study of the Industrial Revolution.[2]

The analytic framework of the present article is designed to capture these long-term processes by combining some neoclassical tools with the base-superstructure model of Marxian analysis.[3] We take as our point of departure a hypothetical agricultural economy based predominantly on subsistence production. The essential characteristics of the economy are as follows:

2 One important exception is Douglass C. North, who has employed considerably modified tools of neoclassical economics in his study of long-term institutional and structural changes leading to the industrial revolutions in the West. See, for example, North and Robert Paul Thomas, "An Economic Theory of the Growth of the Western World," *Economic History Review*, XXII, (1970), 1–17; North, *Structure and Change in Economic History* (New York, 1981).

3 The base-superstructure model of Marxian analysis views society as an organic structure made up of a material base and superstructure. The material base comprises the essential elements of production, including the natural environment and man himself. The superstructure is made up of two spheres: the sphere of the state, with its laws; and the cultural sphere, with its science, philosophy, technology, religion, morality, and customs. The process of social transformation is led by the material base, the changes in which influence the nature of the state and its laws, and the character of the cultural sphere in terms of the nature of science, technology, and ideology. Each round of modifications in the superstructure arising from influences emanating from the material base provides the necessary superstructural conditions for the efficient functioning of the material base in its current form.

The model is being applied here in a modified form. On occasion nationalism, provoked by external forces, may bring about important changes in the superstructure and the material base, changes that cannot be explained in terms of the base-superstructure model. Again, cultural intrusion from outside may provoke important changes in the superstructure unrelated to any change in the material base, but may have important influences on the base subsequently. These modifications are necessary, but they do not weaken the explanatory power of the model. For some discussion of the model, see Melvin Rader, *Marx's Interpretation of History* (New York, 1979). A high level development of the division of labor resulting in an industrial revolution has happened in history in two ways. One is through the market and the other is through state coercion. Other forms have been a mixture of the two. I hold that industrial revolution through state coercion became possible only after the first type of development had provided an example of industrial revolution that could be forcefully transplanted through state coercion. It is therefore to be expected that the first industrial revolution in history had to be the product of the market.

1. Cultivable land is surplus, so that there is no commercial value for agricultural land. Hence, there is no land market.

2. There is no wage labor and no wage labor market. Either the availability of land for all makes everyone self-employed, producing mainly to meet the needs for immediate consumption by family labor, or else labor is provided by serfs who are tied to their lords.

3. Trade and the opportunity to trade are severely limited because of the low level of development of the division of labor internally, and the nonexistence of external commodity trade. In consequence, the area within the national boundary is made up of several regional economies that are scarcely linked.

4. Opportunity for capital investment and capital accumulation is limited because of a limited commodity market and the nonexistence of a wage labor market.

5. Opportunity for surplus extraction from the direct producers is limited because of the nonexistence of wage labor as a dominant element, and because of a limited commodity market. In general, surplus is extracted through the direct appropriation of surplus labor power in the form of labor dues or slavery, or by tax payment in kind.

6. Surplus extraction is for the subsistence of the expropriators and their agents, and not for investment and accumulation.

7. Manufacturing is scarcely separable from agriculture and is based on handicraft techniques and family labor.

8. There is a limited opportunity for technological innovation on a regular basis.

9. The state may perform some important economic functions in the form of public works, such as irrigation, depending on the physical characteristics and the general climatic conditions of the area. In general, however, the state performs limited economic roles. Its main function is the provisioning of its officials, the administration of justice, and the protection of the people.

10. The character of the state, the form of political organization, the nature of science, technology, philosophy,

religious practice, and other elements of culture reflect the characteristics of the economy and the geographical environment.

This economy is undeveloped, not in that it has remained static since the time of Adam and Eve, but in the conceptual sense that capitalist relations of production, institutions, and technology have not developed in any significant way. Conversely, the economy is not underdeveloped, because its path to development is still clearly open, with no obstructions or blockings due to distortions of its institutions and class structures as a result of a historical process.

What kind of factors will operate over time to transform this economy institutionally, structurally, and technologically? How will these factors operate, and what is the nature of their interaction in the process? The dominant factors are population and external commodity trade. The subordinate factors are government policies and science, invention, and technological innovation.

Population growth, by raising the ratio of cultivators to land, and by forcing the movement of people into previously unsettled or lightly settled territories, stimulates the development of the division of labor, the growth of trade, class differentiation, and general institutional change in the direction of capitalist relations of production. However, left to itself, population growth would reach a point where efforts by society to maintain an equilibrium between population and resources limit further growth and render incomplete the process of capitalist transformation. The existence of an external commodity trade of significant magnitude is required.[4]

4 For the role of population in the capitalist transformation of undeveloped economies, see Ester Boserup, *The Conditions of Agricultural Growth: The Economics of Agrarian Change under Population Pressure* (London, 1965); David B. Grigg, *Population Growth and Agrarian Change: An Historical Perspective* (Cambridge, 1980); idem, *The Dynamics of Agricultural Change: The Historical Experience* (London, 1982); North and Thomas, "The Growth of the Western World." See also the debate on the subject provoked by Robert Brenner, "Agrarian Class Structure and Economic Development in Pre-Industrial Europe," *Past & Present*, 70 (1976), 31–75: J. P. Cooper, "In Search of Agrarian Capitalism," *ibid.*, 80 (1978), 20–65; Michael M. Postan and John Hatcher, "Population and Class Relations in Feudal Society," *ibid.*, 78 (1978), 24–37; Brenner, "The Agrarian Roots of European Capitalism," *ibid.*, 97 (1982), 16–113. There are four other contributions to this debate in the same journal.

In several instances, significant external commodity trade develops earlier than domestic trade, because of the initial problems of internal communication. The super-imposition of an important export-import sector on the hypothetical economy described above provokes a host of developments, depending on the character of the commodities and the magnitude of the trade. If the commodities are agricultural and require extensive land for their production, then, as exports increase, land that was previously abundant will become scarce. Private property rights will develop and a landless class will emerge, accompanied by changes in the social relations of production. These changes are also communicated to regions not directly involved in export production. In consequence, there is an expansion of internal trade and of the growth of opportunities for capital investment and capital accumulation.

The increasing development of the division of labor and the growth of income per capita provide the necessary conditions for the expansion of an industrial sector. As the expansion of the industrial sector provides more employment opportunities, population grows and further increases the size of the domestic market. The pace of transformation will be accelerated if there is an expanding export market for the products of the industrial sector. The institutional and structural changes provoked by these developments provide the legal framework, the necessary direction of state policies, and the sociological milieu for the development of science and technology and their regular application to production.[5]

---

[5] An important analytical problem is to determine the extent to which science, invention, and technological innovation have autonomous lives of their own in the kind of process in question, and the extent to which, in the context of the base-superstructure model, their development is dependent on social and political change related to economic processes. Individuals are differently gifted, but the use to which individuals put their natural gifts, and whether or not individuals' talents are fully developed and fully utilized, depends on the nature of the economy, the class character of the state, and the dominant ideology or ideologies in a given society. All societies with several million people are equally endowed with people of all talents, proportionately. The manifested differences in performance in different fields between one society and another result from differences in economic structure, social and political organization, and the prevailing ideologies. For example, in a society where priesthood is of the highest esteem, the best scientific minds may all be attracted to the philosophy of religion rather than to physics, chemistry, mathematics, and engineering. This is why it is not realistic to isolate the development of science and technology from the whole social process. See A. E. Musson (ed.), *Science,*

For the export-import led process of transformation to be completed successfully, certain conditions must be met.

1. There must be a national government (as opposed to a colonial government) that regularly focuses state policy on the elimination of bottlenecks or barriers to the successful completion of the process.
2. The size of the export-import sector must be large in relation to the domestic economy.
3. A substantial proportion of the incomes directly generated by the external sector must be retained and spent within the economy.
4. Incomes must be evenly distributed.
5. Over time, more income must be spent on the consumption of domestically produced rather than imported goods.
6. The process has to continue for a long period of time without serious and prolonged interruption.

In the areas that matter, the English economy by the twelfth century can be said to have possessed characteristics similar to those of our hypothetical economy. From this time to the Industrial Revolution the English economy was continuously involved in external commodity trade of a considerable magnitude. From the twelfth to the fourteenth century, the external wool trade dominated the process of economic transformation, to be followed later by a large-scale export trade in woolen textiles. From the seventeenth century to the Industrial Revolution, England was one of the major trading nations in the Atlantic region.

From the thirteenth and fourteenth centuries, annual exports of raw wool from England were of considerable magnitude relative to the domestic economy. This trade, aided by wartime government policies, gave rise to the woolen textile industry in England in the fourteenth century as an import-substitution industry. By the sixteenth century England had been transformed from an exporter of raw wool to an exporter mainly of woolen

---

Technology and Economic Growth in the Eighteenth Century (London, 1972), for a discussion of some of the issues, especially the editor's introduction, 1–68, which argues a different view.

cloth, and the export market was absorbing about two thirds of the total output of the woolen textile industry.[6]

From the twelfth century to the Black Death, population growth accompanied the rise of the wool trade. This simultaneous

6   English Wool Exports, 1279–1482

Period	Annual Average (lbs)	Estimated Number of Sheep
1279–1290	9,737,000	5,124,737
1290–1294	10,920,000	5,747,368
1297–1304	10,108,644	5,320,339
1304–1311	14,408,576	7,583,461
1311–1313	13,742,456	7,232,872
1313–1323	9,837,828	5,177,804
1323–1329	8,644,636	4,549,808
1329–1336	11,263,980	5,928,411
1355–1358	12,123,384	6,380,728
1365–1368	10,506,496	5,529,735
1399–1402	5,505,500	2,897,632
1425–1428	5,786,508	3,045,531
1445–1448	3,921,008	2,063,688
1465–1468	3,320,044	1,747,392
1479–1482	3,532,984	1,859,465

SOURCE: Constructed from data in T. H. Lloyd, *The English Wool Trade in the Middle Ages* (Cambridge, 1977), 79–80, 123, 311. The quantities presented by Lloyd are shown in sacks. These quantities have been reduced to lbs and the number of sheep estimated, following the method suggested by Bowden: 364 lbs to a sack of wool and 1.9 lbs to a sheep's fleece. See Peter J. Bowden, *The Wool Trade in Tudor and Stuart England* (London, 1962), 37. Allowing for the conflicts in the estimates of England's population during this period, the indication is that export production of raw wool was approximately 4 lbs per capita p.a. in the thirteenth century and about 3 lbs in the first half of the fourteenth. The number of sheep in the export production of raw wool considerably exceeded the human population during the period. See Edward Miller and Hatcher, *Medieval England: Rural Society and Economic Change, 1086–1348* (London, 1978), 29, for discussion of the human population of England during the period in question.

For details of the development of the English woolen textile industry during this period, and the government policies that aided it, see E. M. Carus-Wilson, "Trends in the Export of English Woollens in the Fourteenth Century," *Economic History Review*, III (1950), 162–179. Although the evidence shows that cloth production in England long antedated the growth of raw wool exports, this earlier industry had been severely constricted before the fourteenth century by the superior competitiveness of the formidable woolen textile industry of Flanders. Lloyd, *The English Wool Trade*, 314. As Carus-Wilson points out, the most striking feature of the industry in its first phase of expansion in the 1330s and 1340s was the capture of the home market from Flemish suppliers by English manufacturers. Carus-Wilson, "Export of English Woollens," 164. Bowden estimated the total annual average production of raw wool in England in the years 1540–1547 at 50,723 sacks. Of this quantity, 5,025 sacks of raw wool were exported, 28,790 sacks were employed in the production of 124,750 cloths that were exported, and 14,395 sacks were employed in the production of cloths for the home market. Bowden, *The Wool Trade*, 37–38.

development, by decreasing the supply of arable land at the same time that population growth increased the demand for it, drove England to arrange a land system that would permit a more efficient use of the scarce resource. It thus emerged from the late Middle Ages with an agrarian structure more conducive to capitalist development than that of the major continental countries, especially France, and it was better placed to respond more vigorously when the great period of Atlantic trade opened in the sixteenth century.

From the second half of the sixteenth century, as the woolen industry ran into exporting difficulties that continued into the seventeenth, population growth provided enough stimulus to sustain the ongoing process of capitalist transformation. But, by the middle decades of the seventeenth century, population densities throughout England reached a point where, under the prevailing agrarian structure, further population growth depended strictly on the growth of employment opportunities outside agriculture. As the crisis of the seventeenth century continued all over Western Europe, there was every possibility that the process of capitalist transformation in England would be reversed, as happened in some other major economies of Western Europe, particularly in Italy. However, the growth of English overseas trade in the seventeenth and eighteenth centuries prevented that possibility and provided the conditions for the completion of the capitalist transformation process.[7]

As Davis has shown, the expansion of English overseas trade in the seventeenth century was due mainly to the rapid growth of re-exports. The growth of external trade during the period stimulated much greater mercantile than industrial investment. However, there were two other important developments during the period: the opening up of expanding markets for English woolens in southern Europe and the growth of manufactured exports other than woolen textiles. By the eighteenth century these two developments combined to make export demand the leading factor in the development of industrial capitalism in England. The annual average value of woolens exported from England was £3,045,000 between 1699 and 1701, £3,930,000 between

7 *Ibid.*, 6, 43–44; David Levine, *Family Formation in an Age of Nascent Capitalism* (New York, 1977); Eric J. Hobsbawm, "The General Crisis of the European Economy in the 17th Century," *Past & Present*, 5 (1954), 33–53; 6 (1954), 44–65.

1752 and 1754, and £4,186,000 between 1772 and 1774. During the same periods, the export of non-woolen manufactures amounted to £828,000, £2,420,000, and £4,301,000, respectively.[8]

For the whole eighteenth century, the data assembled by Deane and Cole show that export demand for English manufactures grew much faster than home demand. This growth in exports is further confirmed by the more rapid expansion of the woolen industry in the West Riding of Yorkshire, the main area of woolen export, than elsewhere in England during the eighteenth century. Yorkshire's share of the total output of the English woolen industry rose from about a third in 1772 to about 60 percent by the end of the century. The bulk of the woolen output in Yorkshire and Lancashire in the eighteenth century was exported, being about 73 percent in 1772.[9]

The leading role of the external sector in the eighteenth-century transformation process cannot be fully appreciated if we restrict our view to the value of commodity exports alone. The external sector stimulated the growth of income and employment in various ways that were crucial to the structural transformation of the English economy and society in the eighteenth century.

Table 1 shows how commodity production for exports also directly stimulated the growth of incomes and employment through trade and transport. Because of the relatively large volume of English overseas trade in the eighteenth century, and the long distances involved, the external sector of trade and transport regularly generated more income than the domestic sector.[10]

8 Ralph Davis, "English Foreign Trade, 1660–1700," in Walter E. Minchinton (ed.), *The Growth of English Overseas Trade in the Seventeenth and Eighteenth Centuries* (London, 1969), Table 4, 92. This table shows that, while English domestic exports rose from an annual average of £3,239,000 in 1663–1669 to £4,433,000 in 1699–1701 (an increase of 36.9%), re-exports grew from £900,000 to £1,986,000 during the same periods (an increase of 120.7%). *Ibid.*, 108.

9 Phyllis Deane and William A. Cole, *British Economic Growth, 1688–1959: Trends and Structure* (Cambridge, 1967; 2nd ed.), Table 19, 78. Industries producing largely for exports increased by a factor of 5.44 between 1700 and 1800; industries producing mainly for the home market grew by a factor of 1.52 during the same period. Deane, "The Output of the British Woolen Industry in the Eighteenth Century," *Journal of Economic History*, XVII (1957), 220, Table 2, 215.

10 This view is also supported by the calculations in one of the best contemporary estimates of British national income during the period of the Industrial Revolution. In his estimates of the national income of Great Britain and Ireland for 1811, Patrick Colquhoun estimated the total income accruing from trade and transport as £79,873,748. See his *Treatise on the Wealth, Power, and Resources of the British Empire* (London, 1815), Table 3,

Table 1   Total Output of English Manufactures, Mining, Building, Trade, and Transport (in value, analyzed to show the relative magnitudes of the home market and foreign trade over time)

	(1) Manufacture Mining Building (£m.)	(2) Of which Exports (£m.)	(3) (%)	(4) Of which Home Consumption (£m.)	(5) Trade and Transport (£m.)	(6) Of which Foreign Trade (£m.)	(7) Of which Home Trade (£m.)
1700	18.5	3.8	20.6	14.7	5.6	3.4	2.2
1770	36.9	11.2	30.3	25.7	17.0	9.3	7.7
1801	54.7	21.0(28.5)	38.4	33.7	40.5	22.9	17.6
1811	62.5	28.2(38.2)	45.1	34.3	50.1	26.0	24.1

NOTES & SOURCES *Columns (1), (2), (3), and (4):* Figures for 1700 and 1770 are all taken from Cole, "Factors in Demand 1700–1780," in Roderick Floud and Donald McCloskey (eds.), *The Economic History of Britain since 1700* (Cambridge, 1981), I, Table 3.1; for 1801 and 1811, the figures in Column (1) are from Deane and Cole, *British Economic Growth*, Table 36; those in Column (2) are computed from Davis, *The Industrial Revolution and British Overseas Trade* (Leicester, 1979), Table 38, the figures in brackets being, respectively, the mean for 1794, 1795, 1796, 1804, 1805, and 1806 (for 1801), and 1804, 1805, 1806, 1814, 1815, and 1816 (for 1811). The other figures, £21.0m. (1801) and £28.2m. (1811), have been computed on the ground that 26.2% of the value of British manufactures exported was made up of imported and domestic raw materials other than mining products, following Deane's data for the Yorkshire and Lancashire woolen industry in 1772. See Deane, "British Woolen Industry," 215. *Column (5):* All the figures in the column are from Deane and Cole, *British Economic Growth*, Tables 35 and 36. *Column (6):* The figures in the column are computed from *ibid.*, Table 85, by calculating insurance and freight on imports and multiplying the result by 2 in order to include insurance and freight on exports. The figure for 1811 was produced by calculating the annual average of the first cost (official value) of imports for 1809–1811, using the import figures in Brian Redman Mitchell, *Abstract of British Historial Statistics* (Cambridge, 1962), 282. This number was multiplied by the ratio of insurance and freight to the first cost of imports for the years 1798–1800, as calculated from the data in Deane and Cole, *British Economic Growth*, Table 85. All the figures in column (6) are annual averages for 1697–1700, 1766–1770, 1798–1800 (for 1801), and 1809–1811, respectively. They do not include merchants' profits and freights and insurance on slaves transported by British merchants from Africa to the New World. These omitted elements should more than offset freight and insurance on British imports and exports earned by foreigners but included in column (6).

For all the columns in the Table, the figures for 1700 and 1770 are for England and Wales; those for 1801 and 1811 are for Great Britain.

Table 1 shows clearly the leading role of the external sector in the structural transformation process. Taking industry, trade, and transport together, the contribution of foreign trade to the combined incomes of the sector rose from £7.2 million in 1700, or 29.9 percent of the total, to £54.2 million in 1811, or 48.1 percent. These figures mean that the growth of the non-agricultural sector (the modern sector) in the eighteenth century was due primarily to the growth of the external sector, as had been the case in the earlier centuries. In fact, in the light of the resolution of the conundrum of English population growth in the eighteenth century, even the expansion of the domestic market is to be explained largely in terms of the growth of the external sector.

Until recently, the unresolved debate about the causes of population growth in England in the eighteenth century made it impossible to say with certainty whether population growth was an autonomous factor in the transformation process of the period. The growth of England's population from 4.9 million in 1680 to 11.5 million in 1820 was a major factor in the expansion of the domestic market which played an important role in the transformation process. If this population increase were caused by improved medical care, as some had argued, then it would be an autonomous factor in the process. However, it is now clear that population growth was a dependent factor in the process of structural change in England in the eighteenth century. As Wrigley reports, recently concluded research has established beyond doubt that "The great acceleration in population growth [in England] during the 'long' eighteenth century was principally due to earlier and more universal marriage."[11]

The relationship between the timing and incidence of marriage in seventeenth- and eighteenth-century England and the existence of employment opportunities outside agriculture has been discussed by Wrigley. He concludes that "it is not difficult to show that nuptiality trends bear a striking resemblance to trends in the one relevant economic index which covers the whole early modern period," but he questions whether that one index—

---

95. Of this amount, he calculated the total earned directly in the external sector as £46,373,748, or 58.1%. The comparable figure for our Table 1, which relates to Great Britain alone, is 51.9%.

11 E. Anthony Wrigley, "The Growth of Population in Eighteenth-Century England: A Conundrum Resolved," *Past & Present*, 98 (1983), 121–150.

the Phelps-Brown and Hopkins series—is satisfactory in resolving the question.[12]

Levine's study of four villages between 1600 and 1850 provides strong support for the relationship between demographic trends and industrial economic development. Levine studied two agricultural villages and two industrial villages, one in which activity was increasing and one in which it was decreasing. The village which lost its markets (Colyton) showed a dramatic drop in its rate of reproduction over the seventeenth century, whereas the village facing industrial expansion (Shepshed) showed rapid population growth based on earlier and more universal marriage.

> The great increase in the number of marriages celebrated in the later 1750s and 1760s coincided with a boom in exports and a period of great technical innovation. The American colonists' embargo on British goods deprived the stocking industry of its largest overseas market, and during the years of the American Revolution the bottom fell out of the export market. In these years there was also a fall in the number of marriages celebrated in Shepshed. The end of the hostilities in America and the 1786 treaty with France, which gave British manufacturers the opportunity to sell their goods in this large and lucrative market, ushered in a period of prosperity that lasted until 1815. Moreover, the effects of this heady economic climate were reinforced by the entry of the generation born between 1755 and 1770 into the marriage market. Again, in the 1780s there was a great increase in the number of marriages celebrated in Shepshed.[13]

Wrigley's and Levine's evidence together with the data of Table 1 lead to the conclusion that the growth of the external

12 The result of the investigation shows that, although reduced mortality made some contribution, it was increased fertility that accounted for the lion's share of the acceleration in population growth and increased fertility was due, in turn, to earlier and more universal marriage. *Ibid.*, 126, 131.

13 Levine, *Family Formation*, 60, 108. For the agricultural villages, Levine found that population growth was restricted through the mechanism of delayed marriage and reduced fertility within marriage, the former being the more important. However, Levine's emphasis on proletarianization is unnecessary. It is enough to say that industrial expansion by creating growing employment opportunities encouraged early and regular marriage and so stimulated population growth, which is what his evidence points to. For a criticism of this point, see Inikori (ed.), *Forced Migration: The Impact of the Export Slave Trade on African Societies* (New York, 1982), editor's introduction, 18–19; also Wrigley, "The Growth of Population," 144.

sector in the seventeenth and eighteenth centuries was a major factor explaining the growth of population in England in the eighteenth century. This growth of population and its concentration in important trading and manufacturing centers reinforced the stimulating impact of foreign trade in providing the final push that propelled the economy into industrial capitalism. The evidence suggests that portions of the same industries located in the different regions of England were differently affected by external trade. Because of the leading role of the external sector, the industries concentrated in the long run in those regions that produced more for export. This tendency seems to be reflected also in the long-term regional redistribution of wealth in England from 1086 to 1843. If we recall the regional nature of the Industrial Revolution in its initial stages, it can be shown that the role of the external sector in the capitalist transformation process was in fact greater than the national figures show.[14]

To summarize, several centuries of vigorous foreign trade resulted in an English economy with modern institutional features, a capitalistic agrarian sector, and a population density unique in Western Europe, which in turn contributed to the development of the domestic market. It would be difficult to find another European country where the powerful impact of external trade was felt so early and continued so long. Had the external sector weakened in the seventeenth and eighteenth centuries, as threatened to be the case, England would have lost her chance to launch the first industrial revolution. It was the economic, social, and political changes brought about by this long-term transformation process, led by the external sector, that explain the inventions and technological innovations of the industrial revolution period.

The vigor of the external sector in the seventeenth and eighteenth centuries depended entirely on the growth during that period of an Atlantic system based on the slave trade and African slavery

---

14   See E. J. Buckatzsch, "The Geographical Distribution of Wealth in England, 1086–1843: an Experimental Study of Certain Tax Assessments," *Economic History Review*, III (1950), 180–202. Of the 39 counties ranked according to the amount of wealth assessed over time periods for tax purposes, Yorkshire moved from the 34th position in 1660 to the 18th in 1803. During the same period, Lancashire moved from the 35th position to the 3rd, and Warwickshire from the 20th to the 5th (Table 1, 186–187).

in the New World. Hence, the export slave trade from Africa and New World slavery were crucial to the capitalist transformation of England in the seventeenth and eighteenth centuries. Without the opportunities offered by the expansion of the slave-based Atlantic system, the English economy and some other major Western European economies would have suffered the fate of the Mediterranean countries after the crises of the seventeenth century.

The issue has been well posed by Hobsbawm: "Why did the expansion of the later fifteenth and sixteenth centuries not lead straight into the epoch of the eighteenth and nineteenth century Industrial Revolution? What . . . were the obstacles in the way of capitalist expansion?" His answer is that neither technical nor organizational capabilities were lacking, nor was there a shortage of capital: the origin of the crises can be summarized in one phrase, inadequate economic opportunity.[15]

That economic opportunities in seventeenth-century Europe were limited can be explained in terms of the low level which the development of the division of labor had reached in each European economy at the time. The situation was made much worse by the atmosphere of economic nationalism, bordering on economic warfare, which prevailed in Western Europe in the seventeenth century. It is clear that, in the seventeenth century, not a single country in Western Europe possessed a domestic market sufficiently large and self-propelling to provide the steam that could burst the remnants of traditional social structures and launch the economy into industrial capitalism. Yet virtually all of them embarked on policies of industrial self-sufficiency. As the national industries grew behind high tariff walls, intra-European trade declined, especially trade in manufactures. Several countries, including England, were hard hit. Yorkshire exports were adversely affected by competition from German industries in the early seventeenth century. The same thing was true of France which, for many years, was the largest market for England's woolen products, called kersies, but from the 1660s that market contracted violently due to rising tariffs. In the same way, English imports of continental manufactures declined drastically.[16]

15 Hobsbawm, "Crisis of the European Economy," 39.
16 Bowden, *The Wool Trade*, 45; Davis, "English Foreign Trade," 102. According to

The consequence of the general crisis for several West European economies was far-reaching. A number went through a process of deindustrialization, the most notable of which was Italy, which Hobsbawm describes as transforming "itself from the most urbanized and industrialized country of Europe into a typical backward peasant area." The situation in Italy illustrates vividly the point that inadequate economic opportunity was central to the crisis. "Sixteenth century Italians," says Hobsbawm, "probably controlled the greatest agglomerations of capital, but misinvested them flagrantly. They immobilized them in buildings and squandered them in foreign lending." But the Italians were behaving rationally. In the European economies of the seventeenth century the alternative to investing resources in the production of manufactures for export was not a simple switch to investing resources into production for the domestic market. If export demand were lacking, investment alternatives were limited and the opportunity for growth was squandered.[17]

The expansion of the Atlantic system from the second half of the seventeenth century made it possible for France, Holland, and, more so, England to escape the fate of Italy. First, the effect of the Atlantic system on each individual country depended upon the possession, size, and type of colonies, together with the economic and social structures prevailing in the mother country. Second, although the mercantilist policies succeeded in channelling the flow of goods, they did not prevent the development of an Atlantic-wide division of labor. For this reason, although the restrictive policies largely determined which European nation received which benefit, it is still possible to observe the Atlantic area operating in the seventeenth and eighteenth centuries as a truly single economic unit: a common market of sorts. This is an important point.

The division of labor between the New World and western Africa was brought about by the operation of the Atlantic area as a de facto common market. The variables in the simultaneous equation are as follows: (1) vast natural resources and thin pop-

---

Davis, English imports of manufactures from Germany, Holland, Flanders, and France declined from a total of £1,015,000 to £471,000 per annum in the first three quarters of the eighteenth century.

17 Hobsbawm, "Crisis of the European Economy," 35, 42–43.

ulation in the New World, following the early sixteenth-century demographic catastrophe among the indigenes; (2) the extremely high cost of white labor under conditions of freely available land in mainland North America; (3) relatively large populations, political fragmentation, and low development of the division of labor in West Africa. The simultaneous combination of these elements in a de facto common market produced slave prices high enough to offer to a class of people in West Africa private gains greater than they could have obtained in ways other than the "production" of captives for export. Once that "production" process was established, it became self-perpetuating and prevented the emergence of other forms of more profitable employment of resources, such as the production of commodities for export or the production of commodities for the domestic market. These alternatives would have been socially more beneficial.

Within Europe, in spite of the prevailing atmosphere of economic warfare, the Atlantic system still imposed some important elements of division of labor. The bulk of New World commodities had no close substitutes in Europe. Hence, from gold to tobacco to sugar, they were in demand everywhere. The control of the distribution of these commodities by the European colonial powers enabled them to engage in a lucrative re-export trade in New World products with the rest of Europe. Again, while the home markets for manufactures in Europe were strongly protected, the European colonial powers were prepared to tolerate the export of certain manufactures of foreign origin to their colonies if such goods could not be easily procured at home and if they were sent via the colony-owning country by its nationals and in its own ships. The latter policy was particularly important for the countries with mineral producing colonies.

In the face of easy revenues from colonial minerals, the dominant classes in these countries had no economic and political pressures to develop their productive forces. They imported large quantities of foreign manufactures for both domestic consumption and for re-export to their colonies. Spain and Portugal were the most liberal of the major countries of Western Europe in the seventeenth and eighteenth centuries in matters of manufactured imports. In the early eighteenth century, Zabala, a Spanish economist, stated that the total value of foreign goods exported yearly from Seville to the Indies was between £3,125,000 and £4,166,666.

The same situation was true of Portugal, especially during the boom years of the Brazilian gold trade, from 1700 to 1760.[18]

In the New World, the development of interregional division of labor was on an even greater scale. The British West Indian colonies carried on a large amount of trade with the Spanish colonies, and English manufactured goods were also exported to Spanish America through Britain's West Indian colonies. By the end of the seventeenth century, the trade between the British West Indies and Spanish America was worth about £1.5 million, and was introducing into Jamaica and Barbados quantities of bullion worth about £150,000 (sterling), annually.[19]

By far the most important interregional division of labor in the New World in the eighteenth century was between the temperate territories of mainland North America and the tropical territories. The British North American colonies traded with all the tropical territories of the New World without regard to British mercantilist laws. Williams puts it well: "It was prophetic that the appearance of North America in the Caribbean was marked, almost from the beginning, by a disregard of national boundaries." The foodstuffs of North America became indispensable for the plantation economies of the Caribbean, British and foreign. So too did lumber, horses, fish, and a host of other goods. The North American traders and shipowners also exported a considerable amount of services to these tropical territories.[20]

Thus, mercantilist restrictions notwithstanding, the Atlantic area operated in the seventeenth and eighteenth centuries like a common market, with an important Atlantic-wide division of labor. The forces which operated in this de facto common market were the outcome of a simultaneous combination of several elements and, in consequence, were largely independent of the forces operating within any single member economy at any point in time.

---

18 Jean O. McLachlan, *Trade and Peace with Old Spain, 1667–1750: A Study of the Influence of Commerce on Anglo-Spanish Diplomacy in the First Half of the Eighteenth Century* (Cambridge, 1940), 12. The amounts are stated in Spanish dollars as 15,000,000 and 20,000,000. These amounts have been converted to pounds sterling at the rate of a Spanish dollar to 4s 2d as stated by McLachlan. *Ibid.*, 11. H. E. S. Fisher, "Anglo-Portuguese Trade, 1700–1770," in Minchinton, *English Overseas Trade*, 144–164.
19 Eric Williams, *From Columbus to Castro: The History of the Caribbean, 1492–1969* (London, 1970), 169.
20 *Ibid.*, 219.

England's participation in the expanding Atlantic system enabled it to escape the fate of others in the crisis of the seventeenth century. The impact of the Atlantic system on the English economy came through three important channels: the trade of African slaves to the New World, which England came to dominate in the eighteenth century; the trade of the British colonies, which linked them to one another, to the rest of the New World, and to the mother country; and the trade of Spain and Portugal through which the English economy was firmly linked to the Latin American territories in the New World. The British colonies played three crucial roles. They provided commodities for England's re-export trade. They spent the purchasing power built up, inter alia, through their linkages with the other New World territories on English manufactures. And they provided outlets through which English manufactures reached the rest of the New World.

Once England had succeeded in preventing Holland from trading with the British New World colonies, the distribution in Europe of colonial products became a major source for the expansion of England's external trade. The contribution of re-exports came entirely from the products of these colonies. In the area of manufactured exports, the evidence clearly shows that the Atlantic system was entirely responsible for expansion in the seventeenth and eighteenth centuries (see Table 2).

English manufactures exported to Europe (excluding southern Europe) declined from £1,927,000 between 1699 and 1701 to £1,613,000 in 1774 (computed as three-year moving averages). This is a decrease of 16.3 percent and is accounted for by decreased

Table 2 Regional Distribution of Exports of English Manufactures, 1699–1774, Three-Year Annual Averages (£000)

| YEARS | REST OF EUROPE | | SOUTHERN EUROPE | | AMERICA AND AFRICA | |
	WOOLEN GOODS	OTHER GOODS	WOOLEN GOODS	OTHER GOODS	WOOLEN GOODS	OTHER GOODS
1699–1701	1,544	383	1,201	73	185	290
1722–24	986	141	1,606	226	303	376
1752–54	1,325	257	1,954	390	374	1,197
1772–74	963	650	1,667	337	1,148	2,533

SOURCE: Computed from Davis, "English Foreign Trade," 108, 120.

woolen exports. At the same time, woolen exports to southern Europe increased from £1,201,000 to £1,667,000 and to Africa and America increased from a mere £185,000 to £1,148,000 over the same period. Total manufactured English exports to these two sub-regions of the Atlantic rose from £1,749,000 to £5,685,000 over this period. There was a phenomenal expansion of a wide range of new manufactured exports to America and Africa, with exports rising from £290,000 between 1699 and 1701 to £2,533,000 between 1772 and 1774. Rising exports to southern Europe in this period were dependent either directly or indirectly on the New World. Apart from the evidence summarized above, Fisher's data show that English export of manufactures to Portugal in the seventeenth and eighteenth centuries had a strong positive correlation with trends in the Brazilian economy.[21]

In the words of Deane, "the Industrial Revolution was preceded by three quarters of a century or more of marked . . . expansion in the English woolen industry," which, she thought, "contributed significantly to the creation of a favourable environment for the more revolutionary developments in industrialization which began at the end of the century."[22] The evidence that I have adduced in this article shows that this expansion of the woolen industry was owed entirely to the expansion of the Atlantic system during the period. But for this latter expansion, the English woolen industry, which had been export dependent for many centuries, would have declined absolutely, thereby provoking a nation-wide process of deindustrialization (as occurred in Colyton). In particular, the industrial development of Yorkshire in the eighteenth century can be seen to have depended entirely on the expansion of the Atlantic system. The evidence also shows that the broadening of the industrial base of the English economy beyond woolens was directly and indirectly a function of the expanding Atlantic system. Finally, the overall expansion of the modern sector, that was discussed earlier, can now be seen to have depended almost entirely on the expansion of the Atlantic system.

The expansion of the Atlantic system in the seventeenth and eighteenth centuries depended on the slave trade and New World

21 Fisher, "Anglo-Portuguese Trade."
22 Deane, "British Woolen Industry," 223.

slavery. It is common knowledge that production in the New World in the late seventeenth and eighteenth centuries depended on slave labor. In general, the New World territories moved from a period of predominantly subsistence production to a period of predominantly export production of cash crops. This transition was accompanied by the entrenchment of slave labor as the dominant mode of production, which is reflected in the transformation of the racial composition of their populations.

Recent research shows that slaves of African origin were crucial to the working of the gold and silver mines of Mexico, Peru, and Brazil. In Brazil, the early development of large-scale export production of sugar in the sixteenth century depended entirely on slaves of African origin. The same is true of the later development of gold production. By 1798, there were 1,988,000 people of African origin in Brazil, comprising 61.2 percent of the total population. The number was this high despite the eighteenth-century gold rush that brought many Europeans into Brazil as mine owners and traders.[23]

In the Caribbean, the transition from subsistence agriculture to large-scale export production of cash crops was effected in the seventeenth century through slavery. The population of Barbados in 1660 comprised 22,000 whites and 20,000 blacks; by 1713, blacks formed 73.8 percent of the island's population of 61,000. In Jamaica, there were 3,000 whites and 500 blacks in 1660; by 1713, there were 7,000 whites and 55,000 blacks. In the Leeward Islands, the racial composition of the population changed from 8,000 whites and 2,000 blacks in 1660 to 9,000 whites and 30,000 blacks in 1713. In the French West Indies, where large-scale production of cash crops for export occurred later, the course of events was the same. The composition of Martinique's population changed from 2,450 whites and 5,085 African slaves in 1678 to 12,450 whites and 70,966 African slaves in 1770; in St. Domingue,

23 A census taken in Spanish America by the clergy in 1796 was reported to have shown that people of African origin numbered 679,842 in Mexico and 539,628 in Peru. Inikori, "Measuring the Atlantic Slave Trade: an Assessment of Curtin and Anstey," *Journal of African History*, XVII (1976), 204. See also Enriqueta Vila Vilar, "The Large-Scale Introduction of Africans into Veracruz and Cartagena," in Vera Rubin and Arthur Tuden (eds.), *Comparative Perspectives on Slavery in New World Plantation Societies* (New York, 1977), 267–280; Colin A. Palmer, *Slaves of the White God: Blacks in Mexico, 1570–1650* (Cambridge, Mass., 1976). Thomas W. Merrick and Douglas H. Graham, *Population and Economic Development in Brazil, 1800 to the Present* (Baltimore, 1979), Table III-2, 29.

the composition changed from 4,336 whites and 2,312 African slaves in 1681 to 32,650 whites and 249,098 African slaves in 1779.[24]

In North America, there were two regimes of commercial agriculture. In the middle colonies there was production of commercial foodstuffs for the export markets in the plantation economies of the Caribbean. Such production occurred on medium-sized family farms, where family labor was dominant. But in the southern colonies, where large-scale export production of cash crops was organized in plantations, the slave mode of production was dominant. In consequence, the slave populations of what became the southern United States rose as export production in plantations expanded; the white population of the rest of the United States that depended on trade, shipping, commercial food-stuff production, and subsistence farming multiplied as economic opportunities increased.

The white population of the New World grew rapidly in the nineteenth century, as capitalist development took root in the United States and pockets of capitalism developed in mainland Latin America. Even so, a summary of New World populations in 1820 still shows the dominance of the slave mode of production. As Table 3 shows, it was only in the United States and in Spanish America that African slaves and people of African origin did not constitute the bulk of the population by 1820. Even in the United States, a large proportion of the population in the export producing South was African in origin. It is thus clear that the expansion of the Atlantic system from the second half of the seventeenth century to the end of the eighteenth depended on African slave labor in the New World. Without African slaves the Atlantic system would have operated on a considerably reduced scale.

We have argued that the development of industrial capitalism in England in the eighteenth century was made possible by the expansion of the Atlantic system in the seventeenth and eighteenth centuries. This expansion, in turn, was produced by the Atlantic

24 Richard S. Dunn, *Sugar and Slaves: The Rise of the Planter Class in the English West Indies, 1624–1713* (New York, 1972), Table 26, 312; Richard Sheridan, *The Development of the Plantations to 1750. An Era of West Indian Prosperity 1750–1775* (Aylesbury, 1970), 35, 49.

Table 3 Ethnic Composition of New World Population
c. 1820

	POPULATION	
TERRITORY	BLACK AND FREE COLORED	WHITE
United States	1,771,656	7,866,797
British West Indies	839,000	57,000
French, Danish, and Dutch West Indies	814,600	73,600
Brazil	2,660,000	920,000
Spanish America, excluding Peru	5,150,000	3,429,000

SOURCE: David Eltis, "Free and Coerced Transatlantic Migrations: Some Comparisons," *American Historical Review*, LXXXVIII (1983), Table 3.
NOTE: For Spanish America, Indians, mestizos, and mulattos form the bulk of the non-white population. For the other territories, the non-white population was almost entirely African slaves and people of African origin.

slave trade from Africa and the employment of African slave labor in the New World. Hence, the slave trade and African slavery in the New World were central to the development of industrial capitalism in England in the eighteenth century. In order to provide a proper historical perspective for the analysis leading to this position, we have examined the long-term process of institutional and structural transformation in England from the Middle Ages. The evidence we have produced makes it clear that the process was dependent on the external sector over the long run. By the time the great period of the Atlantic system opened up in the sixteenth century, the economic and social structure that had developed in response to stimuli from the external sector placed the English economy in a position to derive maximum benefits from the expansion of world trade and achieve full capitalist transformation.

There was a clear possibility of a reversal in the seventeenth century, as the countries of Western Europe tried to develop industrial capitalism simultaneously in a situation of limited economic opportunities. Our evidence shows that the expansion of the Atlantic system in the seventeenth and eighteenth centuries provided opportunities that enabled some of the Western European countries to survive the crisis with limited damage and to continue their transformation process. Those countries, like Italy, who could not participate effectively in the Atlantic system for various reasons, were unable to escape the reverse process. Deriving maximum benefits from the expansion of the Atlantic system, partly because of the nature and size of its colonies, partly because of its economic and social structures, and partly because of specific developments in the other Western European countries during the period, England was able to launch the first industrial revolution.

We have produced evidence to show that the seventeenth- and eighteenth-century expansion of the Atlantic system, which provided England with all of these opportunities, was a function of the Atlantic slave trade and African slavery in the New World. Our analysis is not based on private profitability of the slave trade and slavery. We have argued elsewhere that the slave trade was privately profitable to the British traders. But, the analysis developed here does not depend simply on that premise. The slave-based Atlantic system provided England with opportunities for the division of labor and for the transformation of economic and social structures: these are more important considerations.[25]

Eighteenth-century European governments were very aware of this fact. It explains why the French government was prepared to offer a subsidy to French traders to enable them to make African slave labor available in French America. The private profits of the slave trade and slavery did make important contributions to the financing of the capitalist transformation process. More important, however, the private profits from the slave trade and slavery were large enough for the British entrepreneurs to expand the system without depending on government subsidies that would have increased the tax burden for British citizens, with all the negative economic implications that such a levy would have entailed. In this way, the expansion of the Atlantic system provided adequate opportunities for the launching of industrial capitalism in England from the late eighteenth century, thanks to the Atlantic slave trade and African slavery in the New World.

25 Inikori, "Market Structure and the Profits of the British African Trade in the Late Eighteenth Century," *Journal of Economic History*, XLI (1981), 745–776.

David Richardson

The Slave Trade, Sugar, and British Economic Growth, 1748–1776

> That from the encreasing luxury of our Country [i.e. Britain], the
> advance of the sugar keeps pace with the advance upon the Slaves.[1]

British overseas trade grew substantially during the eighteenth
century. Data derived from customs records indicate that the
official value of British exports (excluding re-exports) rose almost
sixfold over the century while imports increased over fivefold.
The growth of trade was by no means steady and was frequently
disrupted by war, but it accelerated distinctly over the course of
the century; the annual level of trade rose by 0.8 percent before
1740, by 1.7 percent between 1740 and 1770, and by 2.6 percent
thereafter. Overall, overseas trade grew faster than either British
population or total output. Per capita imports and exports thus
increased significantly during the century, and a rising share of
British output, especially industrial output, was exported. It has
been estimated that exports' share of output doubled over the
century, rising from 7 or 8 percent at the beginning to 16 or 17
percent at the end. Exports' share of industrial production is
calculated to have grown from one fifth to one third during the
same period.[2]

Although there appears to be widespread agreement about
the general contours of British overseas trade and its share of
British output, there is little consensus about either the causes of
the growth of trade or its relationship to British industrialization.
Some historians have regarded the expansion of demand for Brit-

1 Thomas Melvil to the Company of Merchants Trading to Africa, 17 Mar. 1755, Cape
Coast Castle, Public Record Office (PRO), C.O. 388/46, Ee 59.
2 Phyllis Deane and William A. Cole, *British Economic Growth, 1688–1959* (Cambridge,
1967), 46; Roderick Floud and Donald McCloskey (eds.), *The Economic History of Britain
since 1700,* (Cambridge, 1981), I, 38–39, 89.

ish goods overseas as stemming from essentially autonomous developments abroad, whereas others, notably Deane and Cole, have argued that the growth of British exports, particularly after 1745, was primarily a consequence of the British demand for imports, the resulting expansion of purchasing power abroad filtering back to British exporters by means of a network of colonial trading connections. Similarly, the extent and timing of the expansion of British exports, notably after 1783, has led some scholars to attribute to overseas trade a major role in causing British industrialization, whereas McCloskey and Thomas have recently concluded that "the horsepower of trade as an engine of growth seems [to have been] low" in the century or so before 1860. Historians resident in Western industrialized nations are generally divided in their explanations of the growth of eighteenth-century British exports and in their assessment of exports' impact on the Industrial Revolution.[3]

Caribbean-based historians, by contrast, have generally been much more united in attributing to British overseas trade—particularly the slave trade and related trades in plantation staples—a positive and substantial role in fostering British industrialization. Williams, the major exponent of this view, claimed that profits from the triangular or slave trade "fertilized the entire productive system of the country." Despite recent demonstrations that the slave trade was probably less profitable than Williams alleged and could not carry the weight of responsibility for financing British industrialization that he assumed, his views continue to influence the debate over the origins of British industrial growth during the eighteenth century. In part at least, this influence arises from the fact that Williams presented his argument in broad and sweeping terms, and failed, for instance, to indicate clearly whether he was referring to profits from the slave trade alone or from the combined triangular and bilateral colonial trades. Furthermore, he frequently neglected to locate precisely in time and place the connections that he believed existed between the slave trade, associated plantation trades, and British industrial development.[4]

3 Timothy J. Hatton, John S. Lyons, and Stephen E. Satchell, "Eighteenth Century British Trade: Homespun or Empire Made," *Explorations in Economic History*, XX (1983), 164; Deane and Cole, *Economic Growth*, 83; Cole, "Factors in Demand, 1700–80," in Floud and McCloskey, *Economic History*, I, 42–44; McCloskey and Robert P. Thomas, "Overseas Trade and Empire, 1700–1860," in *ibid.*, 102.
4 Eric Williams, *Capitalism and Slavery* (London, 1964; orig. pub. 1944), 105. See, e.g.,

This article investigates these possible connections during the period 1748 to 1776. The investigation ranges outside the question of the relationship of profits from the slave trade and British industrial investment to which several scholars have addressed themselves and seeks instead to explore the impact of Caribbean slave economies and their related trades upon the growth of markets for British industrial output. An examination of market connections among the slave trade, plantation agriculture, and British industry during the third quarter of the eighteenth century is particularly revealing, for available evidence now indicates that there occurred at this time both a substantial rise in the level of British slave trading activity and colonial sugar production on the one hand, and a marked acceleration in the rate of growth of British industrial production on the other. I argue that these developments were not unrelated but that their relationship was more complex than Williams indicated. In particular, the slave trade and slavery should be viewed not as some peculiar promoter of industrial expansion and change in Britain, but rather as integral though subordinate components of a growing north Atlantic economy, the expansion of which was largely dictated by forces from within British society, notably rising consumer demand for colonial staples such as sugar. Rising British sugar imports in turn created enhanced export opportunities for British manufacturers in colonial and African markets and thereby made a significant contribution, as Deane and Cole have argued, to the acceleration in the rate of growth of British industrial output in the middle of the eighteenth century.

During the last fifteen years historians have made major advances in their efforts to ascertain the general volume and temporal distribution of the eighteenth-century British slave trade. Published estimates have suggested that British traders may have carried between 2.5 and 3.7 million slaves from Africa between

---

Roger Anstey, *The Atlantic Slave Trade and British Abolition* (London, 1975), 38–57; Thomas and Richard N. Bean, "The Fishers of Men: The Profits of the Slave Trade," *Journal of Economic History*, XXXIV (1974), 885–914. The debate over profitability still continues however. See Joseph E. Inikori, "Market Structure and the Profits of the British African Trade in the Late Eighteenth Century," *ibid.*, XLI (1981), 745–776, and the comment by Bruce L. Anderson and Richardson, with a rejoinder by Inikori in *ibid.*, XLIII (1983), 713–729. Compare Williams' comment in *Capitalism and Slavery*, 5, with his comments on 52 and 105. See also, *ibid.*, 51–84.

1701 and 1807, with the most recent survey carried out by Lovejoy suggesting a figure of just over 2.8 million. Although there remains much scope for disagreement about the overall size of the British trade after 1701, all estimates indicate that it grew substantially over the course of the century, reaching its peak after 1783. The most widely accepted figures indicate that annual shipments of slaves by the British probably tripled over the eighteenth century, rising from 12,000 to 14,000 before 1720 to around 42,000 during the 1790s.[5]

Currently published estimates of the British trade are invariably constructed on decadal bases and have only limited usefulness for exploring in detail the relationship between the slave trade and economic change in Britain, Africa, and the Americas. For such purposes estimates of the annual levels of the trade are needed. Using new sources of shipping data, I have been able to produce such estimates for the period 1698 to 1807. As yet unpublished, these estimates largely confirm the overall rate of expansion of the trade suggested by most other historians. But they also indicate that expansion was far from smooth. It was largely confined in fact to two main periods: the 1720s and early 1730s and the third quarter of the century. The increase in British slaving during the latter period was especially marked, as annual British shipments of slaves from the African coast in peacetime rose from an estimated 25,800 between 1749 and 1755 to 43,500 between 1763 and 1775. During these last years, British vessels carried more slaves from Africa than in any previous or subsequent period of thirteen consecutive years. The British slave trade may therefore have reached its peak before, not after the American Revolution as most recent scholars have suggested.[6]

Irrespective of whether the British slave trade peaked before 1776 or not, its substantial expansion over the third quarter of the century requires explanation. A detailed investigation of the matter is impossible here, but the evidence suggests that the

5 See Paul E. Lovejoy, "The Volume of the Atlantic Slave Trade: A Synthesis," *Journal of African History*, XXIII (1982), 474–501, for a summary of recent estimates. The annual figures here are based on estimates contained in Philip D. Curtin, *The Atlantic Slave Trade: A Census* (Madison, 1969), 150; Anstey, "The British Slave Trade 1751–1807: A Comment," *Journal of African History*, XVII (1976), 606–607; Seymour Drescher, *Econocide: British Slavery in the Era of Abolition* (Pittsburgh, 1977), 205–213; Lovejoy, "Synthesis."
6 Copies of my tables are available on request. The next highest thirteen-year total in the number of slaves carried was 1783 to 1795.

expansion of the trade owed little to improvements in commercial conditions in West Africa. In comparison with earlier years, the costs of procuring slaves on the coast probably rose significantly after 1750 as dealers in West Africa were unable to accommodate an acceleration in the growth of international demand for slaves within existing cost and price schedules. Data compiled by Bean reveal that the average current price for adult male slaves at the coast increased by some 25 percent between 1748 and 1775 or from £13.9 in 1748 to 1757 to £17.5 in 1768 to 1775. Furthermore, procuring slaves even at these rising prices required British traders to accept mounting shipping costs. My own estimates, based on Bristol and Liverpool shipping data, indicate that the average time spent by British vessels slaving on the coast lengthened considerably during the third quarter of the century and that daily loading rates of slaves at times fell to historically low levels, thereby raising average shipping costs per slave purchased.[7]

Faced with rising expenses in West Africa, British merchants continued in the slave trade because they either anticipated equivalent cost savings on other sections of the slaving voyage or expected proportionately higher prices for slaves in the New World. How much scope there was for achieving economies on mid-eighteenth-century slaving voyages is difficult to assess, but the introduction of new payments mechanisms for slaves in the Caribbean and elsewhere around mid-century and the use of copper sheathing from the 1770s onward to protect the hulls of slave ships from attack by toredo worms—a practice pioneered by the Royal Navy—were both cost-saving innovations. Innovations of this sort, however, took time to introduce and brought uncertain and essentially long-term benefits.[8]

Failing immediate short-term cost-cutting opportunities, merchants had to rely on higher prices for slaves in the New World in order to offset the upward pressure on costs in West Africa after 1748. They were not disappointed. Published data

7 See Ben T. Wattenberg (ed.), *The Statistical History of the United States from Colonial Times to the Present* (New York, 1976), 1174. These estimates are presented in Richardson, "The Efficiency of English Slave Trading in West Africa during the Eighteenth Century: Estimates and Implications," unpub. ms. (1981).

8 Gareth Rees, "Copper Sheathing: An Example of Technological Diffusion in the English Merchant Fleet," *Journal of Transport History*, II (1972), 85–94; Henry A. Gemery and Jan S. Hogendorn, "Technological Change, Slavery and the Slave Trade," in Clive Dewey and Anthony G. Hopkins (eds.), *The Imperial Impact* (London, 1978), 257–258.

indicate that during the first half of the eighteenth century the average current price for adult male slaves in British America varied between £23 and £27, but then rose to £31.9 between 1748 and 1757, to £35.0 between 1758 and 1767, and to £40.7 between 1768 and 1775. A rise of some 27.6 percent between 1748 and 1775, this matched the rise in slave prices in West Africa over the same period and created a rate of mark-up on prices between the coast and the New World after 1748 that was even higher than that prevailing during the previous period of expansion in the trade in the 1720s and early 1730s. Expansion and success in the British slave trade between 1748 and 1776 thus appears to have rested primarily on the buoyancy of markets for slaves in the Caribbean and other parts of British America.[9]

Various factors influenced the demand for slaves in British America; these included the inability of slaves to maintain their numbers through natural reproduction, particularly in the Caribbean, and the regular extension of credit by British merchants to New World planters to assist them in purchasing slaves. However, the main determinant of demand for slaves was the level of income that planters derived from the production and sale of basic staples such as sugar, tobacco, rice, and indigo. Although the number of slaves sold by the British to planters in North American mainland colonies such as Virginia and South Carolina was sometimes considerable, the central markets for British slavers before and after 1776 were in the sugar islands of the Caribbean. Sugar exports constituted the largest single component of British Caribbean planter incomes, and it was revenue from this crop that essentially shaped demand conditions for British slavers between 1748 and 1776.[10]

Detailed evidence about Caribbean planters' incomes is, unfortunately, relatively sparse, but information about the volume and prices of sugar shipped annually to Britain from the islands during the eighteenth century is readily available. From this information it is possible to calculate the gross annual revenues received by planters from sugar exports to Britain. Some sugar

9 Wattenberg (ed.), *Statistical History*, 1174. Mark-ups were 129% and 132% in 1748–1757 and 1768–1775 compared to 94% in 1728–1732 and 101% in 1723–1727. *Ibid.*, 1174.
10 On the role of credit, see Jacob M. Price, *Capital and Credit in British Overseas Trade: the View from the Chesapeake 1700–1776* (Cambridge, Mass., 1980). Curtin, *Census*, 140.

was shipped from the islands to markets other than Britain, notably the British North American colonies, but most of the sugar produced in the islands was shipped initially to the mother country; up to 20 percent was re-exported to Ireland and the European Continent. Gross receipts from sugar shipments to Britain offer a clear indication of the total revenues accruing to planters from their sugar exports. Gross receipts provide an imperfect measure of net incomes from sugar sales, but it is reasonable to assume that variations in such receipts over time probably reflect both the short-term fluctuations in planters' fortunes and long-term trends in their net incomes.[11]

Detailed estimates of gross annual receipts accruing to Jamaican planters from sugar shipments to Britain from 1748 to 1775, together with figures on retained annual slave imports into the island, are set out in Table 1. Estimates of the gross revenues received from shipments to Britain by all British Caribbean planters for various periods between 1713 and 1775 are provided in Table 2.

It appears from Table 1 that there existed a direct but lagged relationship between changes in Jamaican planters' gross receipts from sugar shipments to Britain between 1748 and 1775 and the number of imported slaves retained in the island. Excluding war years when trading conditions were uncertain, annual variations in Jamaican revenues from sugar were generally reflected one year later by similar variations in retained slave imports during seventeen of the twenty peacetime years between 1748 and 1775.

11 See John R. Ward, "The Profitability of Sugar Planting in the British West Indies, 1650–1834," *Economic History Review*, XXXI (1978), 197–213, on planter profits. Richard B. Sheridan, *Sugar and Slavery: An Economic History of the British West Indies 1623–1775* (Baltimore, 1974), 22, 32–34, 493–497. The sugar trade statistics provided by Sheridan refer to England and Wales only before 1755 but include Scotland thereafter. Throughout this article I refer to Britain in describing trade figures even when, as in my present discussion of sugar imports or my later discussion of British exports generally, the data relate to England and Wales. As far as sugar imports or British-produced exports are concerned, trade statistics for England and Wales are close approximations to British trade in this period. Available statistics on Scottish trade after 1755 reveal that less than 4% of British sugar imports entered through Scottish ports before 1776 and that less than 5% of total British-produced exports were dispatched from Scotland. Henry Hamilton, *An Economic History of Scotland in the Eighteenth Century* (Oxford, 1963), 414, 419. The omission of Scottish figures from the trade statistics used in this article does not affect the trends suggested by such statistics.

Table 1 Gross Revenues from Sugar Exports to Britain and Retained Slave Imports in Jamaica, 1748–1775

YEAR	SUGAR REVENUES £000	RETAINED SLAVE IMPORTS
1748	688	8004
1749	603	4730
1750	561	2866
1751	569	4127
1752	586	5079
1753	718	6759
1754	702	7959
1755	836	12125
1756	777	9264
1757	754	6992
1758	922	2994
1759,	1015	4531
1760	1622	5205
1761	1556	5838
1762	1020	6047
1763	994	8497
1764	1104	7574
1765	1001	6945
1766	1070	9536
1767	1234	2873
1768	1278	5465
1769	1210	3155
1770	1350	5988
1771	1294	3512
1772	1264	4355
1773	1501	8876
1774	1856	15937
1775	1618	7663

NOTE: Sugar revenues relate to the gross proceeds from sales in England for the year *prior* to that stated.

SOURCES: Sugar prices: Sheridan, *Sugar and Slavery*, 496–497. Sugar imports from Jamaica: Noel Deerr, *History of Sugar* (London, 1949), I, 193–202. Slave imports: PRO, C.O. 137/ 38, Hh, 3, 4.

Since the time interval between the dispatch of slaving voyages from British ports and their arrival in the New World was nine to twelve months by the mid-eighteenth century, this twelve-month lag between Jamaican planters' receipts from sugar and their purchase of slaves suggests a high degree of supply responsiveness among British slavers to shifts in Jamaican demand for slaves during the third quarter of the eighteenth century.[12]

An inspection of Table 2 shows that gross annual receipts by Caribbean planters from their total shipments of sugar to Britain rose by some 237 percent between 1713 and 1775, from £959,000 per annum between 1713 and 1716 to £3,235,000 between 1771 to 1775. However, the growth in receipts was by no means steady and was affected by different factors over time. Revenues actually fell after 1716 largely as a result of falling sugar prices, but then rose steadily during the 1720s as shipments of sugar increased markedly and prices stabilized. Declining re-export markets and a collapse in London sugar prices brought about another fall in planter revenues during the early 1730s; they remained below the levels of 1726 to 1730 through the rest of the decade. Sugar prices began to recover in the late 1730s and the 1740s, however, and, despite a doubling in the quantities of sugar shipped to Britain

Table 2   Average Annual Gross Revenues from Sugar Shipments to Britain from the Caribbean, 1713–1775

	AVERAGE GROSS PROCEEDS (£000 PER ANNUM)	SUGAR PRICE INDEX (1713–16 BASE)	CONSUMER PRICE INDEX (1713–16 BASE)
1713–16	959.1	100	100
1721–25	805.6	72	94
1726–30	1049.3	74	98
1731–35	824.8	60	88
1736–40	965.1	75	91
1741–45	1209.5	95	93
1746–50	1479.9	103	93
1751–55	1675.1	105	90
1756–60	2652.1	120	101
1761–65	2617.2	108	98
1766–70	2952.1	110	104
1771–75	3234.8	108	114

SOURCES: Sugar imports: Elizabeth B. Schumpeter, *English Overseas Trade Statistics 1697–1808* (Oxford, 1960), 52–56. Sugar prices: Sheridan, *Sugar and Slavery,* 496–497. Consumer prices: Brian R. Mitchell and Deane, *Abstract of British Historical Statistics* (Cambridge, 1962), 468–469.

12   Richardson, "Efficiency of English Slave Trading." A similar responsiveness of slave supply to changes in planter revenues was apparent in South Carolina after 1748. *Idem,* "The Volume and Pattern of the English Slave Trade to South Carolina before 1776," unpub. ms. (1983).

during the third quarter of the century, these higher sugar prices were sustained through to the American Revolution. During this quarter century, prices of muscovado sugar on the London market only occasionally fell below 33 shillings per cwt., and were usually 40 percent or more higher than they had been in the two decades before 1740. Based in part on a revival in re-exports of sugar after 1748, notably to Ireland, this sustained recovery in sugar prices was due primarily to the buoyancy of the domestic sugar market in Britain. Despite substantially increased imports, the price of muscovado sugar appears to have risen relative to the prices of other consumer goods in Britain during the third quarter of the century. At the same time, the share of British imports coming from the Caribbean rose significantly from 20.9 percent by value between 1748 and 1752 to 28.7 percent between 1773 and 1777. Growing British sugar consumption thus provided the foundation for the silver age of sugar between 1763 and 1775 and the associated rapid expansion in British slaving activity.[13]

Statistics on population and retained sugar imports indicate that sugar consumption per head in Britain rose from 6.5 lbs around 1710 to 23.2 lbs in the early 1770s. By this latter date, per capita sugar consumption in Britain was several times higher than in continental Europe. Explanations for the growth of British sugar consumption and its divergence from continental levels have largely focused upon changes in taste and diet, particularly the growth of tea and coffee drinking in Britain during the eighteenth century. Apparently confined in the seventeenth century to the wealthier strata of British society, tea drinking in particular became widespread in the eighteenth century. Thus contemporary writers often mentioned the growing habit of taking tea with sugar among even the poorest sections of British society.[14]

That increased tea drinking was probably a major factor in extending the market for sugar in eighteenth-century Britain is not to be denied, but available statistics indicate that the increase in sugar consumption in Britain was not steady and may have

13 Sheridan, *Sugar and Slavery*, 32; Drescher, *Econocide*, 22. For the use of the phrase "silver age of sugar" to describe the period 1763 to 1775, see Richard Pares, "Merchants and Planters," *Economic History Review*, Suppl. 4 (1960), 40.
14 Sugar consumption figures are based on Sheridan, *Sugar and Slavery*, 493–495; Floud and McCloskey, *Economic History*, I, 21. Sheridan, *Sugar and Slavery*, 18–35.

also been influenced by other factors. Close examination of import figures and population estimates shows that per capita sugar consumption increased markedly during the second and third decades of the century and again between 1750 and 1775 but remained relatively static during the intervening period. This leveling out of sugar consumption per head between 1730 and 1750 may have been more apparent than real, reflecting weaknesses in customs records; the period from 1730 to 1750 is thought to have been one in which smuggling, for instance, was particularly rife. However, smuggling was associated more with spirits, tea, and tobacco than muscovado sugar, and it is unlikely that the variations in the rate of growth of British per capita sugar consumption in the half century before 1775 can be attributed to deficiencies in trade statistics.[15]

Available price data suggest that the growth of sugar consumption in Britain during the two decades before 1730 stemmed essentially from improved efficiency in supplying the product. With 1713 to 1716 as a base, the wholesale price of muscovado on the London market fell by over 30 percent between 1713 and 1730 while the fall in price of consumer goods generally was less than 10 percent. From the mid-1730s onward, however, sugar prices rose relative to other prices. Despite substantial increases in sugar imports after 1750, wholesale prices on the London sugar market were some 5 to 20 percent higher than the 1713 to 1716 base throughout most of the third quarter of the century, whereas prices of consumer goods in general, but particularly consumer goods other than cereals, remained below or near to the 1713 to 1716 base until about 1770. In contrast to the period before 1730, the growth of sugar consumption between 1748 and 1776 was essentially the result of rises in incomes or changes in consumer preferences rather than improvements on the supply side.[16]

15 The exact figures of consumption per head are: 1731, 15.7 lbs; 1741, 13.9 lbs; 1751, 15.0 lbs; 1761, 18.0 lbs. Consumption in each year is the average of 5 years centering on the year specified. Cole, "Trends in Eighteenth-Century Smuggling," *Economic History Review*, X (1958), 395–410. On tobacco, see Robert C. Nash, "The English and Scottish Tobacco Trade in the Seventeenth and Eighteenth Centuries: Legal and Illegal Trade," *ibid.*, XXXV (1982), 354–372.

16 Sugar prices based on Sheridan, *Sugar and Slavery*, 496–497; consumer goods on the Schumpeter-Gilboy index as reprinted in Mitchell and Deane, *Abstract of British Historical Statistics*, 468–469. By 1770, the exclusion of cereals from the consumer goods price index lowered the consumer goods index by around 10%.

This last suggestion raises some interesting problems, for most recent studies of eighteenth-century British output and income have indicated that, largely because of changes in the relative growth rates of population and agricultural output and productivity, per capita real incomes in Britain probably rose faster in the half century before 1760 than during the ensuing two decades. In particular, it has been suggested that per capita real incomes may have grown relatively quickly between 1730 and 1750—the era of the so-called "Agricultural Depression"—when unusually low grain prices are alleged to have stimulated consumption of non-agricultural goods, notably manufactures. Recent work has cast doubt on the extent of the depression in British agriculture at this time, however, and its assumed impact on consumer demand and British economic growth may thus have been exaggerated.[17]

Nevertheless, available evidence still points toward a distinct slowing down in the rise of real per capita income nationally around 1760 as the growth rate of agricultural output slackened, grain prices rose both absolutely and relatively, and Britain became periodically a marginal net importer of grain instead of a regular grain exporter. Furthermore, an analysis of data on British wage rates and prices between 1750 and 1792 has led Flinn to conclude that "it would be a brave historian who would assert that real wages were advancing in this period." In view of such evidence, the fact that per capita sugar consumption in Britain appears to have increased by around 50 percent between 1750 and 1775 is especially intriguing.[18]

17 Nicholas F. R. Crafts, "British Economic Growth, 1700–1831: A Review of the Evidence," *Economic History Review*, XXXVI (1983), 177–199; Arthur H. John, "Agricultural Productivity and Economic Growth in England, 1700–1760," *Journal of Economic History*, XXV (1965), 19–35; John V. Beckett, "Regional Variation and the Agricultural Depression, 1730–1750," *Economic History Review*, XXXV (1982), 35–52.

18 On trends in grain exports see John, "English Agricultural Improvement and Grain Exports, 1660–1765," in Donald C. Coleman and John (eds.), *Trade, Government and Economy in Pre-Industrial England* (London, 1972), 45–67; Walter E. Minchinton (ed.), *The Growth of English Overseas Trade in the Seventeenth and Eighteenth Centuries* (London, 1969), 63. See also R. V. Jackson, "Growth and Deceleration in English Agriculture, 1660–1790," *Economic History Review*, XXXVIII (1985), 333–351. Michael W. Flinn, "Trends in Real Wages, 1750–1850," *ibid.*, XXVII (1974), 408. See also Peter H. Lindert and Jeffrey G. Williamson, "English Workers' Living Standards During the Industrial Revolution: A New Look," *ibid.*, XXXVI (1983), 1–25, which includes wage data on the period 1755 to 1781. Their data indicate some squeezing of real adult male earnings between these benchmark dates.

Pending further detailed research, any explanation of rising British sugar consumption after 1750 must be regarded as speculative, but two reasons suggest themselves. The first relates to regional variations in income growth and the second to changes in the supply and relative price of beverages, notably beer and tea, after 1750.

Frequent references by early eighteenth-century writers to the growth of new consumption habits among working families and the poor have led historians to exaggerate the extent to which a national market for sugar developed in Britain before the mid-eighteenth century. Despite some transport improvements in the century or so after 1660, Britain continued to exhibit considerable regional diversity in terms of social structure, labor markets, and levels of prosperity and wealth before 1750. As a result the rate at which consumption patterns changed almost certainly varied significantly from one area of the country to another. Comments by eighteenth-century writers about changing habits of consumption should therefore be approached cautiously, for, as Gilboy reminded us, "most of the writers were Londoners, writing either consciously or sub-consciously about London or other growing towns."[19]

Although data on local or regional levels of sugar consumption are presently unavailable, sugar consumption per head probably was higher in London and its surrounding area than in other regions during the first half of the eighteenth century. London was, after all, the center of the British tea and sugar trades and also had a large servant population who were "the chief intermediaries between their masters and the lower classes in spreading standards of conspicuous consumption." Furthermore, available data indicate that, throughout the eighteenth century, money wages of laborers and craftsmen were higher in London than elsewhere, and moreover that the differential was greatest during the first half of the century. Such evidence suggests that general trends in Britain's sugar consumption up to 1750 were determined largely by economic and social conditions in the nation's capital.[20]

However, there are signs that, by the middle of the century, sugar consumption was growing among even the poorest mem-

19 See Sheridan, *Sugar and Slavery*, 18–35; Elizabeth W. Gilboy, *Wages in Eighteenth-Century England* (Cambridge, Mass., 1934), 240.
20 *Ibid.*, 235, 219–227.

bers of society in areas some distance from London. Contemporary writers referred also to the wider use of meat, tea, and sugar in northern working-class diets. Such dietary changes were made possible by relative improvements in real wages after 1750 in industrializing counties such as Lancashire. Recent studies have revealed that, although real wages nationally may not have improved significantly between 1750 and 1790, wages in Lancashire and perhaps other industrializing areas rose markedly, reflecting a growing demand for labor as industrial and urban expansion gathered pace. Thus, between 1750 and 1792, money wages of Lancashire laborers and building craftsmen rose by some 64 percent and 40 percent respectively, whereas Kentish laborers' wages rose by just under 20 percent and London laborers' wages by under 4 percent. Even allowing for price increases, Lancashire workers seem to have made notable gains in real terms after 1750 and, by narrowing the gap in wage levels that existed between themselves and their counterparts in the southeast before 1750, were able to share more fully in the consumption of products that the latter had enjoyed for almost half a century. Increases in per capita sugar consumption after 1750 may thus reflect the emergence of a national market in sugar brought about by dietary changes in industrializing regions experiencing rising prosperity during the third quarter of the eighteenth century.[21]

Rising sugar consumption after 1750 may also have stemmed from shifts in the relative elasticities of supply of tea and more traditional British beverages such as beer and ale. Official statistics on eighteenth-century British tea imports are notoriously unreliable because tea was invariably subject to such high import duties that it was regularly smuggled into Britain on a large scale. Research has suggested, however, that lower duties introduced in 1745 probably reduced levels of tea smuggling during the ensuing

21 Jonathan D. Chambers, "The Vale of Trent, 1670–1800," *Economic History Review,* Suppl. 3 (1957), 24; Thomas Percival, "Observations on the State of the Population of Manchester, and other Adjacent Parts, 1773–74," in Bernard Benjamin (ed.), *Population and Disease in Early Industrial England* (Farnborough, Hants., 1973), 43–45; Soame Jenyns, *Thoughts on the Causes and Consequences of the Present High Price of Provisions* (London, 1767), 10–12; G. Nick von Tunzelmann, "Trends in Real Wages, 1750–1850, Revisited," *Economic History Review,* XXXII (1979), 39; Gilboy, *Wages,* 220–221. A sharp deterioration in real wage rates for building craftsmen in London took place in the 1750s and 1760s. See L. D. Schwarz, "The Standard of Living in the Long Run: London, 1700–1860," *Economic History Review,* XXXVIII (1985), 24–41.

quarter century or so. Trends in legal imports may thus reasonably closely reflect patterns of British tea consumption in the twenty years after 1748.[22]

Total legal imports and consumption per head both increased substantially during this period. Recorded tea imports per annum rose by some 123 percent between 1748 and 1767, or from just over 3 million to almost 7 million pounds. As a result per capita tea consumption doubled. During the same period, market prices for tea, including duty, fell by nearly 10 percent while real prices fell by over 15 percent. Even allowing for the possibility of diminishing levels of smuggling between 1748 and 1767, tea supplies in Britain were highly elastic during the third quarter of the eighteenth century.[23]

Any attempt to assess the elasticity of beer and ale supplies over the same period is complicated by two factors. First, retail prices for traditional alcoholic beverages such as beer, ale, and porter were subject to official control during the eighteenth century and often remained fixed for lengthy periods. Information on the price of beer in differing localities is unavailable, but if we extrapolate from information on the price of porter, the staple beer drunk in the London metropolitan area from the 1720s on, retail prices of strong beer and ale may have risen by around 15 percent between 1748 and 1776, or from 3d to 3½d per quart pot, largely as a consequence of an increase in the duty on beer in 1761.[24]

Second, although detailed figures on the annual English output of beer throughout the eighteenth century are readily available, they derive essentially from the excise duties levied on beer sales and as a result almost certainly underestimate actual beer production. The most thorough investigation of the eighteenth-century brewing industry has concluded, nevertheless, that despite the onerous levels of duty on beer, which amounted at times to over 50 percent of all other costs, the excise returns "are more

22   Cole, "Eighteenth-Century Smuggling."
23   Tea imports from Schumpeter, *English Overseas Trade Statistics,* 60–61; population estimates from Floud and McCloskey, *Economic History,* I, 21. Cole, "Eighteenth-Century Smuggling," Table 1.
24   Peter Mathias, *The Brewing Industry in England* (Cambridge, 1959), 109–113, 546. Thomas S. Ashton, *Economic Fluctuations in England 1700–1800* (Oxford, 1959), 65, notes a high level of price elasticity of demand for beer.

reliable as a guide to actual production over a series of years than most other eighteenth-century statistics."[25]

From these returns it appears that, after experiencing either modest growth or, at worst, stability up to the 1740s, per capita beer production in England declined moderately, if somewhat irregularly, during the ensuing thirty years before the American Revolution. Attributable in part to the rising price competitiveness of tea, this decline may also have been caused by the impact of harvest failures and generally rising barley and malt prices on brewers' costs and profits after 1750. Faced with increasing raw material costs and deterred by custom and official restriction from raising retail prices to cover them, many brewers, particularly the smaller victualling brewers, experienced an erosion of profit margins during the third quarter of the century. As a result they were obliged either to adulterate their product· by watering it down and using additives to simulate alcoholic strength, which ultimately damaged the reputation of their product, or to cease production altogether, thereby increasing opportunities for alternative beverages. By constraining the growth of beer production, the failure of grain supplies to match increases in British population after 1750 may thus directly have assisted tea and its associate, sugar, in improving their share of the expanding British market for food and drink.[26]

Variations in regional wage movements and shifts in the relative prices of beverages in Britain may have enhanced economic opportunities for Caribbean planters between 1748 and 1776. The 50 percent rise in per capita sugar consumption in Britain in this period is, however, greater than might be predicted by known income or price elasticities of demand for agricultural products at this time; other factors must have contributed to the

25 Mathias, *Brewing*, 345.

26 *Ibid.*, 542–543 for beer output statistics. According to Crafts' calculations, beer output fell in the 1760s, whereas output of most major industries experienced accelerated growth compared to 1700–1760. See Crafts, "British Economic Growth," 181. The problems confronting the brewing industry after 1750 may have affected the relative numbers of common and victualling brewers. See Mathias, *Brewing*, 542–543. For trends in Scottish and Yorkshire brewing at this time, see Ian Donnachie, *A History of the Brewing Industry in Scotland* (Edinburgh, 1979), 16–37; Eric Sigsworth, *The Brewing Trade during the Industrial Revolution: the Case of Yorkshire* (York, 1967). The potential of tea as a substitute for alcoholic beverages was noted by Gilbert Blane, writing in the early nineteenth century; see Mary D. George, *London Life in the Eighteenth Century* (London, 1925), 339.

sharp increase in sugar consumption. It is possible, for instance, that greater resort to non-alcoholic beverages reflected public reaction to the excesses associated with the gin age. One should not overlook, either, the contemporary comments about the spread of tea drinking among the laboring population or the more recent evidence produced by historians that the number of families with "middling" incomes of £50 to £400 per annum grew from 15 to 25 percent of the English population between 1750 and 1780.[27]

Why this increase in the number of middle-income families took place at this time, when agricultural prices generally were rising, is still uncertain, but the increase provided a major impetus to the growth of the home market for British industrial products during the third quarter of the eighteenth century. Such families, headed by merchants, wealthy tradesmen, clergymen, members of the legal and other professions, and government servants, were substantial consumers of imported beverages and sugar, being classified, for instance, by Joseph Massie in 1760 among those who "drink Tea or Coffee in the Morning" or even "Tea, Coffee, or Chocolate, Morning and Afternoon." As consumers not only of home-produced manufactures but also of slave-grown products such as sugar, such families, in conjunction with Caribbean planters and slave merchants, played a prominent part in promoting the economic growth and expansion of the north Atlantic world after 1748.[28]

Recent studies of eighteenth-century British output have indicated that, despite an overall deceleration in the growth rate of total

27 Income and price elasticities are discussed in Jackson, "Growth and Deceleration," 333–351; Crafts, "Income Elasticities of Demand and the Release of Labour by Agriculture during the British Industrial Revolution," *Journal of European Economic History*, IX (1980), 153–168. On the spread of tea drinking, see Mathias, *The Transformation of England* (London, 1979), 162; Floud and McCloskey, *Economic History*, I, 58; Jonas Hanway, *A Journal of an Eight Days Journey. . . . with an Essay on Tea* (London, 1755), II, 274–275. Hanway believed that 25,000 hogheads of sugar or some 29 to 35% of British sugar imports a year "are supposed to be expended with tea" (II, 151). Neil McKendrick, John Brewer, and John H. Plumb, *The Birth of a Consumer Society* (London, 1982), 24.
28 David E. C. Eversley, "The Home Market and Economic Growth in England, 1750–80," in Eric L. Jones and Gordon E. Mingay (eds.), *Land, Labour and Population in the Industrial Revolution* (London, 1967), 206–259. Lindert and Williamson, "Revising England's Social Tables 1688–1812," *Explorations in Economic History*, XIX (1982), 349–399; Mathias, "The Social Structure in the Eighteenth Century: A Calculation by Joseph Massie," *Economic History Review*, X (1957–58), 30–45.

output between 1760 and 1780, industrial output increased faster during this period than during the previous sixty years. As a result, growth rates of agriculture and industry, which had largely moved in harmony before 1760, diverged sharply during the following two decades. It is estimated that industrial output rose annually by 0.7 percent before 1760, by 1.5 percent between 1760 and 1780, and by 2.1 percent between 1780 and 1801. Annual growth rates for agriculture were 0.6 percent, 0.1 percent and 0.8 percent respectively.[29]

The flimsiness and unreliability of eighteenth-century statistics and the arbitrary nature of the periods chosen for investigation make one hesitant about accepting these estimates too uncritically, but there is little doubt that the growth rate of British industrial output rose discernibly and diverged perceptibly from that of agriculture during the third quarter of the century. To what extent was this acceleration in industrial growth based on exports and, more specifically, on the purchasing power generated in the Caribbean by rising British sugar imports after 1748?

The debate among historians about the relationship of exports to Britain's industrial expansion during the eighteenth century has to date largely centered on the period after 1783. Despite suggestions by Williams, for instance, that the expansion of eighteenth-century British manufacturing was encouraged substantially by the markets created by the slave trade and Caribbean sugar production, recent work has suggested that British industrial growth before 1780 was largely based on the home market. The importance of the home market has been particularly stressed by Eversley, who pointed not only to the importance of the growth of income of certain middle-income social groups in Britain between 1750 and 1780, but also to the modest rate of growth of British-produced exports and the low ratio of exports to total output in Britain before 1783.[30]

That the home market remained buoyant and British exports in general grew relatively modestly before 1783 is undeniable. The expansion of sugar imports between 1748 and 1776 is itself testimony to rising incomes and changing consumer tastes in Britain at this time. Furthermore, customs statistics indicate that,

29 Crafts, "British Economic Growth," 187.
30 For Williams' views, see his *Capitalism and Slavery*, 65–84. Eversley, "Home Market," 206–259.

in official values, average annual home-produced exports from Britain rose from £7.22 million between 1745 and 1749 to £10.05 million between 1770 and 1774 or by 39.3 percent. This modest increase in exports was no greater than that achieved during the thirty years prior to 1745, particularly when one takes demographic changes into account. Thus, again in official values, exports per capita rose from £0.86 between 1715 and 1719 to £1.11 between 1745 and 1749 and to £1.26 between 1770 and 1774. Overall, the ratio of exports to output in Britain failed to rise sharply after 1750 or to exceed more than 13 percent of total output before 1783.[31]

The recent discovery that trends in industrial and agricultural output diverged sharply around 1760, however, raises some doubts about an explanation of market expansion for Britain's industrial output based almost wholly on home demand. Furthermore, an analysis of export demand which is based primarily on aggregate trade and output figures and neglects to examine the changing composition of British exports after 1748 and their relationship to the shifting regional balance of Britain's manufacturing base is misleading and too pessimistic about the contribution of exports to Britain's industrial performance between 1750 and 1780. Investigation of the connections between exports and growth and structural change in British industry after 1750 requires one to distinguish exports of industrial goods from other goods and, within the group of industrially based exports, to distinguish more traditional exports such as woolens and worsteds, which were already experiencing relative decline by 1750, from new and emerging exports such as cotton and linen textiles.

A division of home-produced exports from Britain between 1745 and 1774 is given in Table 3. Two important characteristics of exports in this period are highlighted by this table. First, exports of non-industrial goods, primarily grain and fish, which together regularly contributed 15 percent of British home-produced exports before 1750, declined both relatively and even absolutely over the third quarter of the century, thereby lowering the overall rate of growth of total domestically produced exports. Whereas total home-produced exports rose by only 39.3 percent

---

31 Schumpeter, *Trade Statistics*, 15. The ratio of exports to industrial output, however, increased in this period. See Floud and McCloskey, *Economic History*, I, 40.

Table 3 Average Annual Domestically Produced British Exports, 1745–1774, Distinguishing Corn, Fish, and Woolens from All Other Exports

	ALL EXPORTS £000	CORN & FISH £000	WOOLENS £000	OTHER EXPORTS[a] £000
1745–49	7,217	1,132	4,477	1,608
1750–54	8,705	1,370	5,023	2,312
1755–59	8,793	570	5,591	2,632
1760–64	10,448	1,056	5,623	3,769
1765–69	9,639	173	5,267	4,199
1770–74	10,030	93	5,395	4,542

a   Other exports consisted overwhelmingly of industrial goods.

SOURCE: Schumpeter, *Overseas Trade Statistics*, 19–22, 25, 37–39; John, "English Agricultural Improvement," 64; Minchinton, *English Overseas Trade*, 63.

between 1745–1749 and 1770–1774, exports of industrial products rose by 63.2 percent, or from £6.09 million annually to £9.94 million.

Second, among exports of industrial goods, woolen and worsted exports grew very slowly between 1750 and 1775, despite the fact that the rising West Riding branch of the industry increased its exports substantially during the third quarter of the century. Official statistics indicate that annual exports of woolens and worsteds rose by less than 21 percent or some £918,000 between 1745–1749 and 1770–1774, with Yorkshire contributing the lion's share of this increase. By comparison, exports of other industrial goods during the same period rose in official values by 182.5 percent or by £2.93 million annually. Notably fast rates of growth were attained by coal, wrought iron, copper and brass, and linen and cotton textiles, all of which achieved increased exports of up to 290 percent by value during the quarter century after 1749, thereby raising their share of domestically produced British exports from 8.5 percent in 1745–1749 to 20.2 percent in 1770–1774.[32]

Symbolic of the changing regional balance of Britain's industrial base in the mid-eighteenth century, each of these growing sectors of British industry, with the exception of coal, exported an increasing share of its output up to 1776 and beyond. Series

32   Richard G. Wilson, *Gentlemen Merchants* (Manchester, 1971), 41–42; Schumpeter, *Trade Statistics*, 21–22, 25.

of production statistics for eighteenth-century British industries are rare and in most cases of doubtful reliability. Estimating the output of particular British industries at any stage during the eighteenth century is thus extremely difficult. Nevertheless, available information indicates that most of the growing export industries had developed significant export markets by 1750 and that their ratio of exports to output rose further between 1750 and 1775. Wilson's study of Leeds' clothiers, for instance, shows that the West Riding's expanding share of British woolen and worsted output during the eighteenth century arose essentially from its successful penetration of export markets, particularly during the 1720s and 1730s and again after 1760. Available data suggest that about 40 percent of the area's output of woolens went abroad around 1700 but, by 1771/72, when a detailed and apparently reliable census of the Yorkshire industry was made, 72.3 percent of the region's estimated output of woolens, valued at £3.5 million, was exported; over 90 percent of the area's staple product, broad cloth, was sold abroad.[33]

Output estimates for other prominent export industries after 1750 are even more sketchy than those for West Riding woolens, but they too suggest an increasing dependence on exports in general after 1750. For example, estimates of British pig-iron output together with imports of bar iron indicate that supplies of raw materials to wrought iron manufacturers may have risen by 70 percent during the third quarter of the century, whereas wrought iron exports increased by 141 percent during the same period. Similar calculations reveal that exports of linen and cotton textiles rose at least twice as fast as the raw materials available to manufacturers in the same period. Only in the case of copper and brass did export markets fail to absorb a rising proportion of the industry's output between 1750 and 1775, but available figures suggest that exports still took as much as 40 percent of British copper and brass production on the eve of the American Revolution.[34]

33 Wilson, *Gentlemen Merchants*, 41–42, 51–52.
34 For pig iron output, see Philip Riden, "The Output of the British Iron Industry before 1870," *Economic History Review*, XXX (1977), 442–459. Bar iron imports and wrought iron exports from Schumpeter, *Trade Statistics*. Much bar iron was re-exported; therefore these calculations may understate the importance of export growth after 1750. Estimates of linen and cotton exports are based on data from Schumpeter, *Trade Statistics*. Calcula-

For each of these industries—wrought iron, copper and brass, cotton and linen textiles, and even Yorkshire woolens—export success during the third quarter of the century lay essentially in African and American markets. Detailed information on the proportion of Yorkshire woolens exported to different markets overseas is unavailable, but the most recent work on the industry indicates that its expansion depended heavily on North American markets from about 1760 onward. Fuller information about export markets for the other industries mentioned above shows that dependence on America and Africa as export markets was also pronounced in most instances by 1750; in the case of wrought copper, for instance, over 80 percent of its admittedly small exports in 1750 went to Africa and America. Almost invariably, however, sales to these markets rose both absolutely and proportionally, in some cases markedly, between 1750 and the early 1770s. Excluding Yorkshire woolens, each of the industries dispatched at least 70 percent of its exports to America and Africa by the 1770s, a notable achievement given the considerably enhanced level of exports produced by each of them between 1750 and 1775.[35]

The combined effect of this increased dependence of most leading growth sectors of British exports upon African and American markets was closely reflected in the overall distribution of English exports after 1750. Several historians, most notably Davis, have noted that links with non-European economies exerted a growing influence on the pattern of British overseas trade during the eighteenth century. Africa and America's share of British exports rose from less than 10 percent of total exports at the beginning of the century to almost 40 percent at the end. Closer examination of the trade figures reveals, however, that the shift in this distribution of British exports toward Africa and America largely occurred between 1748 and 1776. Up to 1747 exports to Africa and America fluctuated between 12 and 15

---

tions by Durie suggest that the share of Scottish produced linen that was exported rose from 18% between 1748 and 1752 to around 30% between 1768 and 1777. Alistair J. Durie, "The Markets for Scottish Linen, 1730–1775," *Scottish Historical Review*, LII (1973), 38. A rising proportion of these exports was directed through English ports. On copper and brass, see John R. Harris, *The Copper King* (Liverpool, 1964), 12.

35 Wilson, *Gentlemen Merchants*, 50; Schumpeter, *Trade Statistics*, 63–69; Alfred P. Wadsworth and Julia de L. Mann, *The Cotton Trade and Industrial Lancashire 1600–1780* (Manchester, 1931), 145–169; Durie, "Scottish Linen," 41–42.

percent of total exports, including re-exports, but then rose dramatically over the third quarter of the century, reaching 35 percent of the early 1770s.[36]

Underpinned by the changing regional distribution of traditional British industries such as woolens and worsteds and by the displacement of exports of primary goods such as grain and fish by goods from relatively recently established manufacturing industries located in the northwest and midlands of England as well as west-central Scotland, this decisive shift in the general direction of exports was essentially responsible for sustaining the overall growth of British exports between 1748 and 1775. Almost two thirds of the increase in recorded British exports during the third quarter of the century can be accounted for by rising sales in Africa and America, the remaining third being attributable largely to increased sales, notably of re-exported colonial produce, to Ireland. Such changes suggest that, although at the national level home demand may have played a preponderant role in sustaining growth after 1750, exports to Africa and America were at least a capable handmaiden in promoting further expansion in Britain's emerging industrial regions before 1775.

Various factors contributed to the growth of exports from Britain to Africa and the New World between 1748 and 1775. These included the continuing expansion of tobacco and rice exports from the southern mainland colonies and the development of supplementary, subsidized staples such as indigo; the expansion of North American food exports to southern Europe as British grain exports dwindled and cereal prices nudged upward in European markets; and the impact of the Seven Years' War on British government expenditure in the Americas.[37]

The most important single factor, however, was rising Caribbean purchasing power stemming from mounting sugar sales to Britain. As receipts from these sales rose, West Indian purchases of labor, provisions, packing and building materials, and con-

36 Ralph Davis, "English Foreign Trade, 1770–1774," *Economic History Review*, XV (1962), 285–303; Mitchell and Deane, *Abstract*, 309–310. Schumpeter, *Trade Statistics*, 17, Table V, also contains a breakdown of destinations of exports but seems defective for the period 1771–1775. Drescher, *Econocide*, 23, presents data on the shifts in the destinations of exports from England from 1713 onward but fails to comment on the marked change in the destination of exports between 1750 and 1775.
37 For the impact of the Seven Years' War on exports from England to America, see Davis, "Foreign Trade," 296.

sumer goods generally increased substantially after 1748, reinforcing and stimulating in the process trading connections between various sectors of the nascent Atlantic economy. Data on changes in West Indian incomes and expenditure at this time are unfortunately lacking, but Table 2 shows that gross receipts from British West Indian sugar exports to Britain rose from just under £1.5 million annually between 1746 and 1750 to nearly £3.25 annually between 1771 and 1775 or by about 117 percent.

Rising West Indian proceeds from sugar sales had a direct impact on exports from Britain to the Caribbean and, as planters expanded their purchases of slaves from British slave traders, on exports from Britain to Africa also. Customs records reveal that the official value of average annual exports from Britain to the West Indies rose from £732,000 between 1746 and 1750 to £1,353,000 between 1771 and 1775, and that exports to Africa rose over the same period from £180,000 to £775,000 per annum. Annual exports from Britain to the Caribbean and Africa thus rose by just over £1.2 million over the third quarter of the century, a figure equivalent to 27.5 percent of the total increase in annual recorded British exports during the same period. It may be argued that these export data understate the full impact of Caribbean purchases of slaves on exports to Africa. They exclude British goods ultimately bound for Africa which were carried by the small number of British slave ships which first visited continental, notably Dutch, ports in order to complete their cargoes of African trade goods before proceeding to the coast for slaves. Such ships naturally cleared customs from Britain for continental destinations rather than for African ports. At the same time, however, about 5 percent of British vessels clearing for Africa were non-slavers and around 10 percent of British slavers sold their slaves purchased in Africa in non-Caribbean, mainly North American, markets. Overall, available export data provide as accurate a picture of the increases in British exports to the West Indies and Africa after 1748 as eighteenth-century trade statistics permit.[38]

In addition to their direct impact on British exports, rising Caribbean expenditures from 1748 on had more indirect effects on British trade. Two effects in particular are worth stressing.

---

38 Schumpeter, *Trade Statistics*, 17. Details of the proportion of slaves sold in non-Caribbean markets are to be found in my unpublished ms., "The Volume and Pattern of the English Slave Trade to South Carolina before 1776" (1983), 3.

First, exports from Britain to Africa especially consisted not only of home-produced goods but also of foreign, notably East India, goods. Trade between Britain and the East Indies grew substantially over the third quarter of the eighteenth century, with imports from the East Indies rising from some £960,000 per annum between 1746 and 1750 to £1,750,000 between 1771 and 1775 and annual exports to the area rising from £520,000 to £910,000 during the same period. The expansion of British trade with Africa after 1748 provided an important stimulus to trade with the East, for available data suggest that some 25 percent of exports from Britain to Africa comprised East Indian produce at this time. The growth of Britain's trade with Africa therefore may have boosted East Indian purchasing power by as much as £150,000 per annum between 1748 and 1776. Assuming this increased income was spent wholly on purchasing imports from Britain, such a sum was equivalent to almost one third of the growth of exports from Britain to the East Indies and represented 3.4 percent of the growth of total annual exports from Britain between 1748 and 1776.[39]

Second, Caribbean planters purchased increased quantities of foodstuffs, packaging, and building materials, largely from Ireland and the mainland colonies, and in the words of one contemporary, George Walker, agent for Barbados, "in proportion to their dependence on North America and upon Ireland, they enable North America and Ireland to trade with Great Britain."[40]

Calculating the effect of Irish and North American sales to the West Indies on their own purchases of British goods is more problematical than Walker assumed, however, for detailed information about the level of Irish and North American trade with the Caribbean over any length of time is presently lacking. In the case of Ireland, published trade statistics show that Irish exports generally experienced a significant and largely sustained rise from about £1.25 million in 1740 to almost £3.2 million in 1770. Imports also rose strongly during the same period from £850,000 to

39 Schumpeter, *Trade Statistics*, 17–18; Richardson, "West African Consumption Patterns and their Influence on the Eighteenth-Century English Slave Trade," in Gemery and Hogendorn (eds.), *The Uncommon Market: Essays in the Economic History of the Atlantic Slave Trade* (New York, 1979), 306–307. East India goods comprised up to 85% of foreign goods re-exported from England to Africa.
40 Cited in Sheridan, *Sugar and Slavery*, 475.

over £2.5 million. Founded primarily on expanding sales of linen
to Britain, some of which was then re-exported to the American
mainland colonies, Irish exports were given a further boost from
the 1740s onward by growing sales of provisions, particularly salt
beef, pork, and butter. According to one authority, the markets
for beef arose mainly from the slave populations of West Indian
plantations and the victualling of ships engaged in colonial voyages.[41]

Although recent research has indicated that consumption of
beef and other Irish provisions by the slave population of the New
World probably was very small, sales of Irish provisions in the
British Caribbean rose markedly during the third quarter of the
century, reflecting buoyant demand among the white population
of the islands. Figures produced by Nash show that exports of
provisions from Ireland to the Americas rose from an annual
average of £129,000 Irish between 1748 and 1752 to £213,000 Irish
between 1773 and 1777, the bulk of these sales taking place in the
Caribbean.[42]

Such sales allowed Ireland to create a favorable trade surplus
with the Caribbean averaging about £161,000 (Irish) per annum
between 1773 and 1777. However, this surplus was more apparent
than real, for most of Ireland's export trade to the Caribbean was
carried on in British-owned vessels to which Irish shippers were
obliged to pay freight and other charges. In any case, exports to
the Caribbean constituted less than 10 percent of Ireland's total
exports in the early 1770s and the superficial surplus on its dealings
with the region between 1773 and 1777 was no more than 12
percent of its recorded exports to Britain in 1771.[43]

By comparison with linens, which constituted some 70 percent of Irish exports to Britain in the period from 1740 to 1770,
Irish earnings from sales of provisions to the British West Indies
could at best have contributed only marginally to advancing sales
of British products in Ireland before 1776. Indeed, in view of the

41 Louis M. Cullen, *An Economic History of Ireland since 1660* (London, 1972), 55.

42 Nash, "Irish Atlantic Trade in the Seventeenth and Eighteenth Centuries," *William and Mary Quarterly*, XLII (1985), 330–341. The £ (sterling) exchanged for between £1.07 and £1.12 (Irish) during the eighteenth century.

43 *Ibid.,* 339. Another calculation which suggests a trade surplus of £142,000 per annum in 1772–1774 can be found in Sheridan, *Sugar and Slavery,* 470. See Cullen, *Anglo-Irish Trade 1660–1800* (Manchester 1968), 45, for Irish exports to England.

fact that re-exported colonial goods constituted over half of Britain's exports to Ireland after 1750, it is probable that Irish linen exports to Britain did more to sustain markets in Ireland for Caribbean goods than sales of Irish provisions to the Caribbean bolstered Britain's exports of home-produced goods to Ireland.

British exporters perhaps derived greater benefits from North American sales of produce to the Caribbean. Hard statistical information about the scale of American mainland dealings with the British sugar islands is largely confined to the years 1768 to 1772. Shepherd and Walton have calculated that the current value of North American exports to the British West Indies averaged £710,000 annually between 1768 and 1772; imports from the islands averaged £684,000 annually during the same period, yielding an average annual surplus on trade of £26,000 in favor of the mainland. This small surplus on commodity trade was supplemented by sales in the islands of slaves purchased by mainland colonists in West Africa and, even more significantly, by mainland earnings from shipping, insurance, and commissions associated with their Caribbean transactions. Mainland exports to Africa which provide one indication of the value of their Caribbean sales of slaves averaged £21,000 a year from 1768 to 1772; earnings from shipping and invisibles associated with Caribbean trade, such as insurance and commissions, have been estimated to have averaged no less than £323,000 and £137,000, respectively, during the same five years.[44]

If these other earnings are added to the small trade surplus, it appears that North Americans achieved an overall balance of payments surplus of some £507,000 annually on their business with the Caribbean between 1768 and 1772. The bulk of this surplus accrued to colonies north of the Delaware, which also accumulated the largest trade deficits with Britain. The official value of annual exports from the thirteen colonies to Britain averaged £1.69 million between 1768 and 1772; their annual imports from Britain averaged £2.83 million. Surpluses on Caribbean trade were thus vital to the mainland colonies, allowing

44 James F. Shepherd and Gary M. Walton, *Shipping, Maritime Trade and the Economic Development of Colonial North America* (Cambridge, 1972), 128, 134, 223–226, 227, 229–230.

them to pay for almost 18 percent of their recorded imports from Britain around 1770.[45]

In the absence of detailed trade and shipping data for earlier periods, it is difficult to assess the contribution of surpluses on Caribbean transactions to mainland purchases of imports from Britain in 1750. However, the level of Caribbean sugar revenues and slave purchases during the 1750s and 1760s, together with the evidence of sharply rising foodstuff exports to the islands from several of the major mainland colonies after 1748, point to a rapid growth in mainland trade and shipping activity with the Caribbean during the third quarter of the century, and therefore to much lower levels of exports from North America to the islands around 1750. Estimates by Shepherd and Walton, based on admittedly flimsy information, suggest that mainland exports to the sugar islands were probably no greater than £200,000 a year in the 1750s, or less than one third of the level reached around 1770. If we apply this tentative figure to the period 1748 to 1752 and also assume that the ratio of mainland commodity exports to their realized surplus on total dealings with the Caribbean was the same in this period as twenty years later, then Caribbean transactions would have yielded a sum of £143,000 annually to North America between 1748 and 1752, a figure equivalent to 11 percent of its average annual imports from Britain in those same years. Comparison of this estimated surplus with that between 1768 and 1772 suggests that, during the intervening twenty years, North American mainland surpluses on exchanges with the West Indies grew by £364,000 per annum. During the same period the official value of average annual mainland imports from Britain rose by £1.53 million to £2.83 million. Surpluses derived from Caribbean trade appear to have paid for almost a quarter of the increased imports that North Americans bought from Britain between 1750 and 1770.[46]

These crude calculations, based essentially on British trade with Africa, the West Indies, and the East Indies, and on North

45 Price, "New Times Series for Scotland's and Britain's Trade with the Thirteen Colonies and States, 1740 to 1791," *William and Mary Quarterly*, XXXII (1975), 322–325.
46 On grain exports see, for instance, David Klingaman, "The Significance of Grain in the Development of the Tobacco Colonies," *Journal of Economic History*, XXIX (1969), 268–278; Geoffrey Gilbert, "The Role of Breadstuffs in American Trade, 1770–1790," *Explorations in Economic History*, XIV (1977), 378–388. Shepherd and Walton, *Shipping*, 174; Price, "Time Series," 322–325.

American trade with the islands, suggest that the growth of Caribbean purchasing power may, directly and indirectly, have increased total exports from Britain by almost £1.75 million per annum between the late 1740s and the early 1770s. As total annual exports from Britain rose by some £5.0 million over the same period, West Indian demand may have accounted for some 35 percent of the growth in total British exports during these years.

In common with British exports generally, however, exports to the West Indies, Africa, and North America in particular comprised both domestically produced and re-exported goods. Trade statistics indicate that the share of re-exports in total exports from Britain rose from 32 to 36 percent over the third quarter of the century. They also suggest that, although re-exports constituted only a small proportion of Britain's exports to the East Indies, averaging less than 10 percent, their share of Britain's exports to Africa was close to the national figure. Compared to the African trade, re-exports comprised a lower proportion of Britain's exports to the Caribbean and North America, but still provided some 20 percent of exports to these areas in the third quarter of the century. Deducting appropriate proportions from British exports to Africa, the West Indies, and North America to account for re-exports leaves a figure of £1.33 million as the estimated increase in domestically produced exports from Britain arising from Caribbean-generated demands in the quarter century before the American Revolution. As total home-produced exports from Britain increased by no more than £2.8 million annually during the same period, West Indian demands, directly and indirectly, may have been responsible for almost half of the growth of Britain's domestically produced exports between 1748 and 1776.[47]

Impressive though such a figure is, its real significance lies in its relationship to British industrial expansion in the third quarter of the eighteenth century. Available trade statistics suggest that some 95 percent of home-produced exports from Britain to Africa, the East Indies, and the New World consisted of manufactured goods after 1748. Caribbean-related demands, therefore, stimulated the growth of British industrial output by some £1.26 million during the third quarter of the eighteenth century. De-

---

47 Schumpeter, *Trade Statistics*, 15–16; Davis, "Foreign Trade," 300–303; Shepherd and Walton, *Shipping*, 235; Richardson, "West African Consumption," 306–307.

tailed figures on British industrial production from 1750 to 1775 are unavailable, but according to Cole's estimates, England's annual industrial output rose by some £10.8 million from the late 1740s to the early 1770s, or from £25.9 million to £36.7 million. Using these figures, it appears that Caribbean-based demands may have accounted for 12 percent of the growth of English industrial output in the quarter century before 1776. Furthermore, the indications are that a similar proportion of the increased output between 1750 and 1775 of Scotland's leading industry, linen, was sold in Caribbean markets. Although West Indian and related trades provided a more modest stimulus to the growth of British industrial production than Williams imagined, they nevertheless played a more prominent part in fostering industrial changes and export growth in Britain during the third quarter of the eighteenth century than most historians have assumed.[48]

This article, by examining the relationships between the slave trade, Caribbean sugar, and British economic growth from 1748 to 1776, shows that these relationships were more complex than Williams suggested. Concentrating essentially on eighteenth-century British capital accumulation, Williams perceived of profits from the slave trade and the slave-based plantation regime of the West Indies as providing a powerful exogenous input into British industrial growth. For him British economic growth, to borrow a phrase from a more recent distinguished historian in this field, was "chiefly from without inwards."[49]

It is the contention of this article that an approach which first draws a sharp distinction between external and internal promoters of change and then seeks to give primacy to one, in Williams' case an external one, is particularly artificial in Britain's case. It fails to appreciate the essential interweaving and mutual reinforcement of internal and external forces of change that occurred in eighteenth-century Britain. In the process of linking internal and

---

48 Davis, "Foreign Trade," 300–303. Data on industrial output are provided by Cole in Floud and McCloskey, *Economic History,* I, 40. Cole's figures relate to England and Wales, not just England. In estimating output for the late 1740s I have averaged Cole's figures for 1745 and 1750 and for the early 1770s have averaged his figures for 1770 and 1775. On Scottish linens, see Durie, "Scottish Linen," 30, 38. I assumed that one quarter of Scottish linen exports were sold in the West Indies in this period. *Ibid.,* 41–42.
49 Sheridan, *Sugar and Slavery,* 475.

external stimuli to structural change and industrial expansion, increases in British sugar consumption in the third quarter of the eighteenth century may have played an important role. In their efforts to satisfy these demands, which arose ultimately from changes in British agriculture, incomes, and consumer tastes, Caribbean planters and their slaves created additional opportunities after 1748 for manufacturers and their employees in Britain's emerging industrial regions. In forging more closely than previously a pattern of interdependence between industrial Lancashire, Yorkshire, the English Midlands, and west-central Scotland on the one hand, and American slavery on the other, British sugar imports after 1748 had a substantial long-term influence in shaping social and economic conditions on both sides of the Atlantic over the next century or so.[50]

50 Williams, to be fair, recognized that internal factors may have been important in determining British industrialization, but he failed to discuss them. See Williams, *Capitalism and Slavery*, 105–106.

Part III. The Decline of the British West Indies

Selwyn H. H. Carrington

The American Revolution and the British West

Indies' Economy The plantation system in the British West Indies cannot be viewed only in the light of the monocultural production of sugar by exploited black slave labor. It was also the social, political, economic, cultural, and psychological lifeline of British mercantilism. Although the plantation system was a local creation, its very emergence and continued existence depended on several external factors. One was the development of the continental colonies as the producers and purveyors of foodstuffs and lumber, which freed the plantation system to specialize in sugar production. In the course of the growth of the sugar colonies, Britain's colonial policy shifted from a strict orthodox mercantilist system to a loose imperial structure with its administrative center in Britain. This arrangement explains why the individual islands had only tangential relationships with Britain. On the one hand, they looked to Britain for capital, manufactured goods, the purchase of their major products, and for the supply of African slaves. On the other hand, the sugar colonies relied chiefly on their mainland North American counterparts for the sale of their rum and minor staples, including coffee. But, of greater importance, they depended on the mainland colonies for their sustenance.

In the 1770s the British West Indies received from the mainland colonies approximately one third of their dried fish; almost all of their pickled fish; seven eighths of their oats; almost three quarters of their corn; nearly all of their peas, beans, butter, cheese and onions; half of their flour; quarter of their rice; five sixths of their pine, oak, and cedar boards; over half of their slaves; nearly all of their hoops; most of their horses, sheep, hogs, and poultry; and almost all of their soap and candles.

The British West Indian islands needed food if they were to concentrate on sugar production, to which the economics of the mercantile system had confined them. With limited land, they had no peasant-farmer class which could produce enough food-stuffs for the plantations. Furthermore, sugar was far too profit-able and ratooning too prevalent to permit the planters to divert valuable sugar lands and slave labor to cattle-rearing or food crops. In short, from the earliest period of the relationship, the continental colonies served as bread-baskets for the sugar islands. Thus, in the words of Williams: "only the possession of the mainland colonies permitted this sugar monopoly of the West Indian soil." Consequently, the mainland colonies emerged as the key to the establishment and development of the West Indian plantation system. Any interference with the relationship was likely to be ruinous to the islands.[1]

From the onset of the dispute between Britain and the mainland colonies, the West Indian planters played a low-key role, being sensitive to their tenuous position. Most local colonial officials were convinced that, if the mainland colonists were to carry out their threats to restrict mainland-West Indian trade, the sugar economy would be destroyed. These fears and hopes were ex-pressed by Lord Dartmouth: "The state of affairs in North Amer-ica and particularly in the New England colonies has become very serious. It is to be hoped, however, that nothing will happen to obstruct the commerce that for the mutual interest of both ought to be cherished on both sides." Yet, despite this awareness of the need to maintain close intercolonial commercial ties, Parliament, in response to mainland restrictions on imperial trade, adopted an insensitive and coercive policy. It closed the port of Boston in 1774; it then passed two restraining acts and enacted the Prohib-itory Act in December 1775.[2]

The enforcement of the Prohibitory Act early in January 1776 terminated all commercial intercourse between the mainland and West Indian colonies, except for an illegal trade which operated via the foreign islands, and a small direct trade allowed by a provision permitting British merchants to trade with those colo-nies on the mainland that remained loyal to the Crown and with

1 Eric Williams, *Capitalism and Slavery* (London, 1964; orig. pub. 1944), 110, 111.
2 Ralph Payne to the Earl of Dartmouth, 3 July 1774, Colonial Office (hereafter CO), 152/54; Dartmouth to Payne, 5 Oct. 1774, CO 152/54, 101d.

those areas under the control of British forces. By the beginning of 1776, therefore, the only unencumbered legal trade between the mainland and the sugar colonies was that carried on with Canada, Nova Scotia, and Newfoundland. Bermuda and the Bahamas provided a link between the rebels and the islands.[3]

The importance of the American Revolution to an understanding of the decline of the British sugar colonies has not been fully investigated by historians, who have nevertheless cited it as the watershed period in the economic development of the West Indian islands. Drescher, for example, takes only a cursory look. He writes:

> Although there is no general agreement on when the secular decline in proportionate value begins, the American Revolution is often depicted as the decisive event in the cycle. Some turning point is of course significant for any causal argument, since the decline must be shown to have preceded the major initiatives in the dismantling process.[4]

Furthermore, Drescher fails to examine its economic and political effects on the development of the West Indies. He states only that:

> The departure of the continental colonies is cited by Williams and the others as both a political and economic blow to the sugar colonies, weakening slavery's ability to resist assaults after 1783. While we cannot measure the impact of Independence, our purpose will be amply served if we can show that the American separation did not alter the balance of economic forces against British slavery and, above all, against the slave trade.[5]

The pioneer work setting forth the decline thesis is Ragatz, *The Fall of the Planter Class in the British West Indies*. He dates the economic decline of the British West Indies from as early as 1763, and he also points to the American Revolution as a factor in worsening the economic fortunes of the sugar colonies. Williams

---

3 Richard B. Sheridan. "The Crisis of Slave Subsistence in the British West Indies during and after the American Revolution," *William and Mary Quarterly*, XXXIII (1976), 618.
4 Seymour Drescher, *Econocide: British Slavery in the Era of Abolition* (Pittsburgh, 1977), 15.
5 *Ibid.*, 33.

employed Ragatz's decline thesis in describing the impact of the American Revolution on the economy of the West Indies. He wrote that it was "the greatest disaster for the British sugar planters."

> It left them face to face with their French rivals. The superiority of the French sugar colonies was for the British planters the chief among the many ills which flew out of the Pandora's Box that was the American Revolution.

For Williams, the war itself was probably not the turning point in the fortunes of the sugar colonies; this distinction he reserves for the attainment of American Independence.[6]

Not only did mainland independence, in Williams' opinion, cause the decline of the islands, "it destroyed the mercantile system and discredited the old regime." Williams goes on to point out that the emergence of the United States stimulated "the growing feeling of disgust with the old colonial system which Adam Smith was voicing and which rose to a veritable crescendo of denunciation at the height of the free trade era." Some colonial governors and planters were voicing similar opinions and calling publicly for the dismantling of the mercantilist system. The refusal of the British government to amend the navigation laws forced West Indian planters and merchants to initiate ways to circumvent British commercial policy. At the slightest sign of disaster, applications were normally made to the governors for a relaxation of the restrictions on trade. Mainland supplies thus reached the islands surreptitiously, resulting in little or no benefits to the planters, high food prices, and the drain of specie from the British colonies.[7]

In this essay I argue that the impact of the American Revolution on the British West Indies was traumatic and permanently devastating; the islands never recovered their earlier productive capacity. The revolutionary war, and not American independence, marked the beginning of the "uninterrupted decline" of the sugar colonies. British postwar commercial policy continued wartime

---

6 Lowell J. Ragatz, *The Fall of the Planter Class in the British West Indies* (New York, 1928); Williams, *Capitalism and Slavery*, 120, 122.
7 *Ibid.*, 120.

conditions and thus hindered the recovery of the islands, unlike the pattern after previous eighteenth-century wars.

The outbreak of the fighting between Britain and the mainland colonies threatened the preeminent position of the West Indies in the economic system of the empire. In the earlier wars of the seventeenth and eighteenth centuries the British islands generally fared well. Shipping functioned almost normally under the protection of a strong navy. Supplies of slaves from Africa, and provisions and lumber from North America reached the islands in large quantities. In addition, freight and insurance rates remained relatively low. Indeed, some branches of colonial commerce "even prospered more than in peace." During the revolutionary war, however, Britain lost command of the sea to its European rivals for long periods of time and, with the restrictions on the West Indian trade, there emerged a number of crises that retarded the sugar economy. Food and lumber supplies were reduced to a trickle; the slave trade all but disappeared; many slaves starved and died; and West Indian exports were reduced significantly. Attempts to find alternative external supply sources were only partially successful and the economy never fully recovered, even after the restoration of peace.[8]

From as early as the beginning of 1776, the islands all faced severe shortages of all categories of American foodstuffs and lumber. As a result prices rose significantly. From the middle of 1776, the essential articles of food for the slaves became scarce and prices of various articles rose from between 35 to over 600 percent. By the end of the year, the scarcity of provisions and lumber caused grave concern among many planters, especially at times when outward convoys from Britain and Ireland were delayed.[9]

Shortages worsened in 1777: at times, there was hardly any food for the slaves in the smaller islands of Montserrat and Nevis; in Barbados, Antigua, St. Kitts, and Jamaica conditions were only marginally better. In the following year, the threat of all-out war

8 Richard Pares, *War and Trade in the West Indies, 1739–1763* (London, 1963); Sheridan, *Sugar and Slavery: An Economic History of the British West Indies 1623–1775* (Baltimore, 1973).
9 Captain Benjamin Payne to General Lord Howe, 15 Feb. 1776, CO 5/93, pt. 1, 126–129d; Dalhousie and Stephens to Sir Hugh Smyth, 23 July 1776, Woolnough Papers: Ashton Court Collection AC/WO 16 (27), 89–101.

in the Caribbean worsened conditions as fewer supplies reached the islands. Pinney's comment, "You have no idea of the distressed and unhappy state of this country," describes the situation.[10]

In an attempt to forestall the severe food shortages and other economic hardships that would result from the passage of the Prohibitory Act, the planters had imported larger quantities of provisions at the end of 1775. Food could not, however, be stored in the sub-tropical climate of the islands. Some planters, fearing problems of slave subsistence, devoted more land and labor to the cultivation of provisions. The very nature of the monocultural sugar plantation system made this temporary alternative unworkable and, if the islands were to survive, external sources of supply had to be found.

One of the first legislatures to take any action was that of Jamaica. In November 1775 it initiated a bounty system to encourage the importation of dried fish. As an incentive, it offered £5 per ton and 10s. per barrel of dried fish imported for local sale before mid-December 1776. In order to encourage local shipbuilding, all goods were to be imported in vessels at least half-owned by residents.[11]

Attempts to pass similar legislation in many of the remaining islands met with opposition. In Antigua, for example, the growing shortage of foodstuffs and lumber influenced Richard Burton to introduce legislation to award bounties on provisions and lumber imported for local sale. The bill was rejected because the council felt that if high prices did not motivate the merchants no bounty would. Despite its reluctance to interfere with the economy, as food shortages became more severe and conditions worsened in the latter part of the year, the Antigua legislature in 1780 passed an act imposing a heavy duty on the export of livestock.[12]

The success or failure of these legislative measures cannot be ascertained. The bounty system, however, had facilitated the importation of American provisions and lumber through the free ports of foreign governments. On the whole, the initial response

---

10 John Pinney to William Crocker, June 1778, Pinney Papers, Letter Book 4, 220.
11 *Journal of the Assembly of Jamaica* (J.A.J.), 9 Nov. 1775, CO 140/46, 583.
12 *Journal of the Assembly of Antigua* (J.A.A.), 3, 6 Feb., 14 Apr. 1776, CO 9/33; 7 Dec. 1780, CO 9/41; John Wilkes to Isaac Gouverneur and Joseph Curson, 23 Jan. 1791, CO 239/1, 211.

to the crisis was a frantic search for alternative sources, demonstrating the islands' dependence on external markets. This conclusion is further supported by Governor William Mathew Burt's recommendation that, in order to forestall disaster, the Caribbean islands should be permitted to import lumber, fish, pitch, and tar from Russia and the Baltic countries in exchange for rum, carried in either foreign or British vessels. Such a policy was an infringement of British commercial laws and was impractical because of the costs of shipping and insurance. It was therefore not implemented, although some lumber from the Baltic countries reached the West Indies through Britain.[13]

Thus, with the commencement of the American War of Independence, the "redirection of trade" initiated an expansion of commerce between the West Indies and the United Kingdom. One area which featured in this increased commerce was Scotland. Before 1765, the volume of the Scottish trade had been negligible. After that year, Scottish businessmen made important gains to go along with their significant role in the American tobacco trade, the interruption of which had caused the merchants of Glasgow to extend their West Indian activities.[14]

The cessation of American commerce led to increased demands in the islands for Scottish dry goods, staves, and herrings. Company vessels carried out the goods, returning with tropical products to be sold on commission. In addition to selling directly to the planters, Scottish companies shipped supplies to their commission agents. Orders were requested to be made one year in advance so that they could be filled and sent in the outward-bound sugar ships. The functioning of this trade brought about greater dependence on Britain. In the pre-revolutionary commission business with the mainland colonies, West Indian merchants had played an important role. They decided what goods and how much of them were to be shipped and they also provided the funds for the initial investment. In the Scottish trade the initiative and investments came from the merchant houses and their agents in the islands.[15]

---

13 Mathew Burt to Lord George Germain, 17 Sept. 1777, CO 152/56; "State of Trade" (no date), CO 325/6, 4.
14 Sheridan, "Slave Subsistence," 618; Pares "Merchants and Planters," *Economic History Review*, Supplement 4 (1960), 33.
15 Pinney to Alexander Houston and Co., 3 June 1776, Pinney Papers, Letter Book 4,

The functioning of this system had several disadvantages for the colonists. Because of repeated captures by American privateers, special clauses were written into insurance policies to allow company ships to engage in the inter-island trade. But the danger to shipping during the war made it difficult for planters to collect their goods. At times, orders were substantially reduced and, throughout the war, there were complaints of spoilage. Furthermore, Scottish supplies did not adequately meet West Indian demands, since they too depended on factors such as the success of the fishing season, domestic and foreign demand, and the price and availability of staves for containers in which to ship the goods. In addition, numerous charges such as freight, insurance, lighterage, and commissions made the cost of Scottish herrings very high.[16]

Initially, West Indian exports to Scotland increased to fill the vacuum created by the loss of the tobacco trade. The prospects of increased business from the restrictions on West Indian trade led most Scottish merchant houses to anticipate that the initial boom conditions would continue throughout the war. This optimism was short-lived. The Scottish market collapsed and the ensuing recession reduced prices to 1775 levels. Over-importation of tropical commodities and the destruction of the tobacco trade had depressed the market. Sugar prices fell as the recession deepened and money became scarcer.[17]

In order to lessen the expected hardships in the colonies, Parliament allowed the exportation of all articles of food from Britain to the sugar colonies. Likewise, in order to facilitate Irish

---

46; Houston and Co. to John Herbert, Houston Papers, National Library of Scotland (N.L.S.), ms. 8, 793, 40; Marc Egnal, "The Changing Structure of Philadelphia's Trade with the British West Indies 1750–1775," *Pennsylvania Magazine of History and Biography*, XCIV (1975), 175–179.

16 Houston and Co. to James Smith, 1 Oct. 1776, Houston Papers, N.L.S., ms. 8, 793, 55; Houston and Co. to John Constable, 7 Feb. 1777, *ibid.*, 170; "Invoice of fifty Barrels of Herrings . . . on Account and Risque of William Bryan Esq. of Jamaica," 17 Sept. 1777, Chrisholm Papers, N.L.S., ms. 177:75, 3; ". . . William Bryan Esq. Account Current with Alexander Scott," 17 Feb. 1778; "Invoice of Sundry's shipped by order of Messrs. Peter and James Grant of London . . . Consigned to James Chisholm Esq.," 30 Nov. 1782, and letter dated 12 Dec. 1782, *ibid.*, 35.

17 Houston and Co. to Josias Jackson, 4 Mar. 1776, Houston Papers, N.L.S., 8793, 2; Houston and Co. to James Turner and Robert Paul, 4 Mar., 19 Apr. 1776, *ibid.*, 12; M. L. Robertson. "Scottish Commerce and the American War of Independence," *Economic History Review*, IX (1956), 125–127.

business interests, in 1778 Parliament removed some of the restrictions on trade between Ireland and the West Indies, which
facilitated the export of beef, butter, and herrings to the islands.
In the following year the remaining restrictions were abolished.
As a result larger quantities of beef, pork, and herrings were sent
to the islands and increased amounts of West Indian sugar and
rum were imported into Ireland (Table 1).[18]

On the whole, the British West Indies gained nothing from
increased trade with Ireland. The growth in the quantity of sugar
imported there was negligible. Furthermore, the Irish took very
little additional West Indian rum, which was a great disappoint-
ment to the planters who needed increased sales to compensate
for the loss of the American rum market. The quantity of rum
taken by the Irish declined markedly between 1780 and 1783. The
planters, meanwhile, were forced to purchase the higher grade
Irish beef, pork, and herrings which were normally not fed to
slaves.

The official values of Irish imports from, and exports to, the
West Indies give a relatively clear view of the trade. On the one
hand, the value of goods exported in 1783 increased by 43 percent
over the 1775 figures—from £266,710 to £381,617 (Table 2). On
the other hand, the value of Irish imports from the colonies
declined steadily from £185,216 in 1775 to £118,143 in 1783, with
particularly low levels in 1780 and 1781. In all wars throughout
the seventeenth and eighteenth century, the ships leaving Britain

Table 1   British West Indian Imports from and Exports to Ireland,
1780–1783

	IMPORTS			EXPORTS	
YEAR	BEEF (BBL.)	PORK (BBL.)	HERRINGS (BBL.)	SUGAR (CWT.)	RUM (GAL.)
1780	49,806	42,205	15,004	—	333,489
1781	60,867	29,470	12,304	7,384	69,473
1782	50,222	29,498	24,915	18,681	157,053
1783	48,336	38,292	35,962	33,869	29,074

SOURCE: David MacPherson, *Annals of Commerce, Manufacture, Fisheries and Navigation*
(London, 1805), 4 v.

18   The legislations were 16 Geo. III C. 37; 18 Geo. III C. 55: 20 Geo. III C. 10. See
Ragatz, *Fall of the Planter Class*, 147–149.

Table 2 Value of West Indian Trade with Ireland, 1775–1783 (Official Values)

YEAR	WEST INDIAN IMPORTS	WEST INDIAN EXPORTS
1775	£266,710	£185,216
1776	264,799	167,341
1777	331,377	130,622
1778	301,016	81,700
1779	241,023	71,086
1780	304,251	35,142
1781	347,324	43,276
1782	348,550	67,130
1783	381,617	118,145

SOURCE: MacPherson, *Annals of Commerce,* III, 700, IV, 56–60.

for the West Indies provided few of the plantation supplies for the colonies. During the revolutionary war, however, Britain became the chief supplier of provisions to the sugar islands and determined their levels of subsistence. From the beginning of 1776, many planters or their managers were hard-pressed to find alternative sources of supply and food shortages worsened. They turned therefore to their agents or absentee owners in England, imploring them to send out larger quantities of food for the slaves, lest they starve.[19]

As a result of such ominous forecasts, which were sent repeatedly to Britain throughout the war, increased quantities of some categories of supplies were sent to the West Indies. Beef and pork exports from Britain rose from 2,300 barrels in 1775 to 38,500 barrels in 1782, with an annual average number of approximately 16,210 barrels. The quantity of wheat and flour also increased substantially during the same period, while bread exports rose from 431 cwt. in 1774 to 43,795 cwt. in 1782. Peas and herrings were sent in larger quantities than at any other time (Table 3).

It is difficult to assess the impact of these increased quantities on the level of supplies for the slave population. They did not compensate for the loss of American supplies. They went to feed the large number of troops and loyalists who had expanded the demand for English foods and were generally not used to feed

19 Pares, *War and Trade,* 474–475; Sheridan, "Slave Subsistence," 623–624.

Table 3 Food Supplies from England to the British West Indies, 1774–
1783

YEAR	WHEAT (QT.)	FLOUR (QR.)	BREAD (CWT.)	PEAS (QR.)	HERRINGS (BBL.)	FISH (CWT.)	BEEF/PORK (CWT.)
1774	15	—	431	330	3,482	69	2,597
1775	2,070	3,108	3,071	675	4,141	40	2,324
1776	17,852	20,499	31,255	2,777	10,693	452	11,108
1777	11,699	6,590	18,583	6,061	10,721	1,055	16,434
1778	14,202	6,900	26,947	1,224	9,269	411	16,055
1779	36,832	13,175	34,492	3,967	9,453	242	9,845
1780	10,967	29,157	30,581	1,011	8,893	11,756	17,195
1781	3	35,377	23,832	1,712	9,759	780	15,715
1782	783	41,491	43,795	2,015	14,870	3,019	38,561
1783	108	4,290	6,657	755	17,780	1,407	18,050

SOURCE: "An Account of all Salted Beef and Pork . . . Wheat, Flour Biscuit and Peas Exported from England from 1 January 1765 to 1 January 1784" (no date), Public Records Office, Treasury Papers, T.64/274, fos. 105, 106.

slaves. In terms of the food requirements of the West Indies, supplies from all the sources looked at were mere drops in the bucket and the problem of slave subsistence remained a serious issue.

Throughout the war, the main source of supplies for the slaves in the Leeward Islands was St. Eustatius. Continuing food shortages had tragic results and despite efforts by many planters to provide ample rations, deaths among the slaves caused alarm. Deaths from malnutrition among the slaves numbered several thousands in the Leeward Islands and Jamaica. In Barbados, an estimated 5,000 slaves perished between 1780 and 1781. John Braithwaite, the agent for the assembly, estimated that the slave population declined from 78,874 in 1774 to 63,248 in 1781. The slave population was given as 61,808 for 1784. Conditions in the West Indies had deteriorated to such an extent that in 1777 Pinney asked: "What will become of us?" He went on to explain that "the unhappy contest with America united with our internal distressed situation is truly alarming and will, I am afraid, cause the ruin of every individual." A month later, he added:

> With . . . the low ebb of West Indian credit, united with our present unhappy contest . . . Provisions and all plantations necessaries are so excessively dear, that the expense of supporting our slaves and keeping up our Estates in a proper condition, swallows up the

greatest part of the produce. For these reasons, I want to contract my concerns here and fix a fund in England—not solely to depend upon estates subject to every calamity.[20]

The loss of the American source of foodstuffs and plantation supplies created a vacuum in West Indian trade. Britain's inability to meet West Indian demands is reflected in the statistics giving the official value of British exports to, and imports from, the West Indies for the years from 1769 to 1783 (Table 4). For the first seven years, 1769 to 1775, the average annual value of British exports amounted to roughly £1,395,472. In the next seven years, this amount fell by over £190,000 to £1,202,634. Although the decline may seem minimal, it was nevertheless of immense sig-

Table 4 Value of British West Indian Trade with Great Britain, 1769–1782

YEAR	WEST INDIAN IMPORTS	WEST INDIAN EXPORTS
1769	£1,346,247	£3,002,679
1770	1,313,676	3,418,823
1771	1,209,822	2,972,203
1772	1,433,028	1,465,404
1773	1,328,703	1,848,613
1774	1,420,524	3,622,948
1775	1,706,301	3,675,948
1776	1,602,713	3,329,920
1777	1,247,771	2,794,457
1778	1,151,594	3,057,424
1779	1,127,465	2,811,909
1780	1,675,313	2,450,078
1781	1,031,028	1,860,546
1782	1,289,928	2,217,928

SOURCE: "An account of the Number of Ships, with their Tonnage, which cleared Outwards from Great Britain to the British West Indian Islands, in each Year, from 1780 together with the Total Value of Exports from Great Britain to the West Indies," *Parliamentary Papers,* LXXXIV, Appendix, pt. IV, no. 687.

20 "An account of the Number of Slaves returned into the Treasurer's Office of Barbados from 1780 to 1787 inclusive (1788)," CO 28/62, 204; Pinney to Sarah Maynard, 3 May 1777, Pinney Papers, Letter Book 2, 111; Pinney to Simon Pretor, 12 June 1777, *ibid.,* 114. See also Pares, *A West India Fortune* (London, 1950), 93–94.

nificance. In the wars from 1744 to 1748 and from 1756 to 1763, the volume of British exports did not decrease. On the contrary, both wars "stimulated exports to the West Indies." Similarly, the total annual official value of tropical imports into Britain from the sugar colonies also decreased during the American War of Independence. From 1769 to 1775, the average yearly value was approximately £3,000,000; for the next seven years, this declined to an annual figure of roughly £2,647,000.[21]

The relatively marked decline in the total annual value of West Indian products reaching Britain, in spite of the high prices for sugar on the London market, was partly the result of decreased production in the islands. Earlier wars had little damaging effect on the production of the British sugar colonies. For example, imports increased after the Peace of Aix-la-Chapelle and "continued throughout the Seven Years' War and the years which followed it." The revolutionary war reversed this trend. The cessation of mainland-West Indian trade was the main reason. In addition, the British market was overstocked because of the loss of the re-export trade and there was, at times, little demand for West Indian products. Sugar imports thus declined by almost 1 million cwt., from 2,021,059 cwt. in 1775 to 1,080,848 cwt. in 1781. Imports of rum declined in the same period—from 2,305,808 gallons in the former year to 1,207,421 in the latter. Coffee imports fell from over 54,000 cwt. in 1775 to 6,305 cwt. in 1781. Pimento imports dropped off to 451,880 pounds in 1782 from 2,522,356 pounds in 1775; cocoa exports followed a similar trend declining from 6,536 cwt. in 1776 to 605 cwt. in 1782 (Table 5).[22]

The loss of the American market for West Indian rum and other staples made it necessary that the consumption of, and prices for, these articles remain high in Britain throughout the war. However, this was not the case for rum imports and prices. A close reading of market conditions shows that, after the initial increase in prices at the beginning of 1776, there was a slump

21 Pares, War and Trade, 472–473, 491–493.
22 Houston and Co. to Charles Irvine, 28 Aug. 1777, Houston Papers, N.L.S., ms. 8,793, 259; Houston and Co. to Turner and Paul, 1 Oct. 1778, ibid., 8,794, 53; Rawlinson, Charley, and Grierson to William Eccles, 12 Mar. 1782 in J.A.J., 12 Feb. 1783, CO 140/59, 546; "Account of the Imports between . . . England and the British West Indies . . . from Christmas 1773 to Christmas 1783 (1784)," PRO, Treasury Papers 38/269, 1–11.

Table 5 Quantity of British West Indian Exports to Great Britain, Various Products, 1775–1783

YEAR	SUGAR (CWT.)	RUM (GAL.)	COFFEE (CWT.)	COCOA (CWT.)	PIMENTO (LB.)
1775	2,021,059	2,305,808	54,937	5,334	2,522,356
1776	1,726,507	1,726,507	51,833	6,536	1,589,145
1777	1,416,291	2,068,756	48,636	4,080	1,418,471
1778	1,521,457	2,456,572	38,801	3,494	2,498,192
1779	1,525,833	2,143,055	25,295	3,932	613,247
1780	1,394,559	1,615,841	8,568	1,908	676,076
1781	1,080,848	1,207,421	6,305	1,235	951,262
1782	1,374,269	1,562,327	12,118	605	451,880
1783	1,584,275	1,873,029	19,933	2,853	901,597

SOURCE: Elizabeth B. Schumpeter, *English Overseas Trade Statistics, 1697–1800* (Oxford, 1960), 62.

from 26d. per gallon in March to only 18d. in December. Lower prices resulting from the fall in demand for rum continued throughout the war.[23]

Similarly, sugar prices had also increased at the beginning of 1776. Prices, however, soon fell significantly and remained low for the rest of the year. In 1777 prices again increased 25 percent to 50s. from 40s. for most of the year, except in December when St. Vincent's sugar was sold for 67s. 6d. per cwt. Sugar from St. Kitts fetched between 47s. 6d. and 66s. per cwt. Jamaican and Grenadian sugars were priced slightly lower, at 58s. to 60s. per cwt. After the first quarter of 1778, prices declined markedly. The market quotations for sugar in London in 1778 show that Jamaica brown was sold at 44s. to 46s., with prices as low as 40s. for lesser grades. Sugar of exceptionally high quality fetched prices of 46s. to 52s. per cwt. In a few cases sugars from Antigua and St. Kitts were sold for 51s. and 57s., respectively.[24]

In light of the fact that sugar prices rose significantly during the war, from a range of 31s. 7d. to 43s. 7d. per cwt. in 1776 to roughly 55s. 1d. to 63s. 1d. per cwt. in 1781 (according to figures in the Letter Books of Houston and Company), did the planters

23 Houston and Co. to Turner and Paul, 23 Nov. 1778, Houston Papers, N.L.S., ms. 8,794, 78; "Jamaica Advices," 27 July 1778, British Museum, add. ms. 12,412 1qd.
24 William Cunninghame to Robert Dunmore, 9, 21, 27 July, 3 Aug. 1778; Charles Cowes to Dunmore and Co. 9 July 1778; Robert Colquhoun to Dunmore, 6 Aug. 1778, National Registry of Archives (Scotland), ms. G.D. 247/59/Q.

make enough profits to recoup their losses? Calculations suggest that there was a steady decline in returns to the planters throughout the war, except in the years 1780 and 1781, and there may even have been losses in its last years. Planters and merchants had made significant profits during previous wars, but conditions were different. During the revolutionary war, the costs of provisions, lumber, and other plantation necessities were high. Furthermore, the loss of the mainland markets for rum was catastrophic to the sugar economy, and weakened the planters' ability to bear the expenses of running the estates. In addition, operating and staffing costs rose steeply during the war decade. The salaries of white bookkeepers, overseers, distillers, and carpenters, for example, increased from between 40 to 100 percent; those for skilled workers doubled. Wages for carpenters, earlier estimated at £50 annually, increased to £70 and £80 for ordinary tradesmen and to as much as £100 for those who were highly skilled. Distillers' salaries increased from £20 to £30 a year. Similarly, the cost of hiring slaves, a practice which was increasing, rose appreciably, from under 1s.10d. per day to an average of 2s. 3d. and as high as 2s.6d. daily.[25]

Added to the problem of unstable profits, West Indian planters faced severe shipping shortages during the war. For the entire period, fewer ships reached Caribbean ports than during any previous war. There were several reasons for this: the numerous captures by American privateers; the large number of ships commandeered for government services; and the prohibition of West Indian-mainland commerce, which excluded a significant part of British shipping. Furthermore, ships captured during the war were not replaced because of high labor costs and the shortages and high prices of materials. As the war intensified, with the entrance of France, many planters could not secure freight to Britain. Table 6 illustrates the significant decline in the number of British ships employed in the West Indian trade.[26]

25 Douglas Hall, "Incalculability as a Feature of Sugar Production in the Eighteenth Century," *Social and Economic Studies*, X (1961), 343; "Comparative Prices and Charges attending the Jamaican Planter at and since the commencement of the war" (no date), British Museum, add. ms. 12,413, 45; John Van Keeler to John Foster Barham, 9 Sept. 1782, Bodleian Library, ms. Clarendon Dep. C.357/1, Bundle 1; "Report from the Committee on the Commercial State of the West India Colonies," *British Parliamentary Papers* (1807), II, 32.
26 William Chricton, "A True State of the Explanation of the Causes of the Rise of the

Table 6 Number of British Ships in the West
        Indian Trade, 1775–1783

YEAR	NUMBER OF SHIPS
1775	354
1776	329
1777	299
1778	243
1779	249
1780	261
1781	244
1782	211
1783	217

SOURCE: Minutes of the West Indian Merchants, I, fos. 76, 85,
115, 147, 174; II, fos. 30, 58, 92, 112d.

The shortage of and high risk to shipping sent freight rates
to new heights, increasing costs of the plantations and adding to
the distress of the planters. In September 1776 the outward bound
freight rates for beef to Jamaica rose by over 300 percent from
2s. 9d. to 8s. 6d. per barrel. In the following year, the cost of
shipping goods from Scotland was 6s. per barrel; boards were
£4.10s. per thousand feet; hoops £4.4s. per thousand feet; staves
£5 per thousand; white oak staves and heading £5.10s. per thousand feet, and puncheon packs 5s. each. In 1781 the rates increased
by approximately 50 percent. The cost of shipping a barrel of
beef to Jamaica rose to 14s. in 1782.[27]

The homeward freight rates also increased significantly. The
normal charges from Jamaica to London during peace were 3s.
9d. per cwt. for sugar, 6d. per gallon for rum, and, for other
goods, from 1d. to 1½d. per lb. In 1777 sugar and rum rates from
Jamaica rose by 33 percent. Freight rates from the remaining
islands were 5s. per cwt. for sugar and 7d. per gallon for rum,
except from Barbados where the rate was 6d. In the early part of
1778, shipping shortages forced the rates up to 8s. per cwt. for
sugar. Later that year they rose again, by 1s. per cwt. on sugar

---

Price of Sugar," 6 July 1778, Pinney Papers, Letter Book 4, 191, 262; "Jamaica Advices,"
26 July, 23 Sept. 1778, British Museum, add. ms. 12,412, 6; Van Keeler to Barham, 10
May 1782, Barham Papers: Bodleian Library, ms. Dept. C. 357, Bund. 1.
27 Edward Long, "History of Jamaica," British Museum, add. ms. 12,404, 463; "Invoice
of fifty barrels herrings," 17 Sept. 1777, Chisholm Papers, N.L.S., ms. 188/75, 34.

and 3d per gallon for rum. There were further increases in 1779 and 1780 reaching 10s. 6d. per cwt. for sugar in the previous year and 10d. to 1s. per gallon for rum in the latter.[28]

The devastating impact of the revolutionary war on West Indian commerce may also be assessed by its effect on the slave trade. In previous wars in the Caribbean, the trade was free of any restrictions and was hampered only when no contestant had total control of the sea routes. During the Seven Years' War, when Britain was the dominant naval power in the Caribbean, even though British shipping to Africa decreased, slave imports into the West Indies increased as the ships carried more slaves per ton. There was therefore no significant loss in the number of slaves retained in the islands. There was a dramatic turnaround during the revolutionary war and the number of slaves retained declined markedly. In Barbados, slave imports almost ceased. The decline in slaves retained continued for the next three decades, until abolition; in some years more slaves were re-exported than imported.[29]

The slave trade to Antigua showed a trend similar to that of Barbados. The number of negroes retained on the island declined significantly during the war, from 1,137 in 1775 to 9 in 1779 and 132 in 1781. Despite periodic increases, the trend of slaves retained in Antigua after 1775 is one of decline (Table 7). The slave trade to Dominica showed the same pattern.[30]

As in the case of the other islands, the British slave trade to Jamaica was seriously affected by the American Revolutionary War. Even up to the end of the decade of the 1780s, the trade had not fully recovered the pre-war levels of the years 1774, 1775, and 1776, as indicated by an assessment of the figures of the British slave trade to Jamaica between 1763 and 1791. Yet, Jamaica was probably the only island where the overall imports of slaves increased after 1783 and reached levels approximating those of the prewar years. Edwards, commenting on the effect that the Rev-

28 "Rates of Freight Homewards for 1777," in *Supplement to the Cornwall Chronicles and Jamaica General Advertiser*, 29 Mar. 1777, I, 200–203.

29 Pares, *War and Trade*, 472–473; Phillip D. Curtin, *The Atlantic Slave Trade: A Census* (Madison, 1969), 154.

30 National Record Society, *Private Papers of John, Earl of Sandwich* (London, 1936), I, 260.

Table 7   Number of Slaves Retained, Four West Indian Islands, 1775–1783

YEAR	ANTIGUA	BARBADOS	DOMINICA	JAMAICA
1775	1,127	879	5,687	13,870
1776	476	407	3,032	15,016
1777	286	34	1,996	5,049
1778	144	7	305	4,419
1779	9	No figures	Captured	2,859
1780	73	"	"	3,015
1781	132	138	"	6,755
1782	571	109	"	4,423
1783	910	194	"	9,580

SOURCES: Compiled from *Parliamentary Papers*, LXXIV: Accounts and Papers, XXVI, No. 646 (12), 51; *Parliamentary Papers*, LXXXVII: Accounts and Papers, XXIX (1790), nos. 622 and 677, 2; "Accounts of Negroes retained in Dominica" (no date), CO 318/2, fos. 249, 252; Long, "Statistics of Jamaica" (1789), British Museum, add. ms. 12,435 (no date), CO 319/1, fo. 151; MacPherson, *Annals of Commerce*, IV, 155. MacPherson's figures for 1783 are much lower than those used in the table.

olution had on the slave trade, notes that its decline was "unquestionably due to the American War." Table 7 indicates the decline in the number of negroes retained in four of the major islands between 1775 and 1783, supporting Edward's observation.[31]

In addition to the economic difficulties, there was a psychological blow caused by the war. The revolution broke the spirit of the planters. They lost the resilience so characteristic of the eighteenth-century planters, who were noted for continued sugar production despite the dangers to themselves and their families and the hardships caused by slave rebellions, wars, droughts, and hurricanes. British West Indian trade survived, nevertheless, although it was greatly weakened, as was the imperial tie which fostered it. "Commerce hath suffered an unspeakable injury," wrote a Bristol resident.[32]

The loss of direct trade with the mainland had even more far-reaching results. It forced the merchants and planters to de-

31   Bryan Edwards, *The History, Civil and Commercial of the British Colonies in the West Indies* (London, 1794), I, 57.
32   Fellow Citizens to the Citizens of Bristol, 22 Jan. 1782, Bristol Public Library, Jefferies Collection of Mss., VIII, 94.

pend on the foreign islands for their supplies of provisions and lumber and thus created an extensive illegal trade between West Indians and citizens of the United States in foreign colonial ports. Colonial merchants, in order to supply the planters, sent large sums of money to the French West Indies to purchase lumber and provisions—a tactic which was fraught with problems. Governor John Orde of Dominica best summed up the dilemma of the planters. He wrote: "the difficulties they labour under, in now procuring those supplies with which they formerly abounded, are sensibly felt."[33]

As a result of their wartime experience, most West Indian planters and merchants supported a return to the old commercial connection. They realized that the prosperity of the plantation system was inexorably linked to close commercial ties with the United States. But British policymakers, steeped in the doctrine of imperialism, were in no mood to make any concessions. Supported by Lord Sheffield, several interest groups, including the loyalists in North America, the British shipping industry, and even the West India Society, contended that the exclusion of the United States shipping from the West Indies would automatically expand British shipbuilding and merchant marine, thus enlarging the "nursery for British seamen."[34]

Therefore, on 2 July 1783 an order-in-council framed by William Knox, undersecretary of state, was issued regulating United States commerce with the British empire. It was based on the principles of the navigation acts and banned all American vessels from West Indian ports. In addition, United States salted beef, pork, dairy products, and fish were excluded from the sugar colonies. The monopoly of supplying these products was given to the Canadian and Irish merchants. The West Indians were allowed, however, to import lumber, livestock, grain, flour, and bread from the United States, and they were allowed to send them their tropical products, but only in British ships. This restriction was the most important single blow to the revitalization of the islands' economy after wartime depression. The order created further instability among the planters. It continued wartime

33 John Orde to Lord Sydney, 19 Mar. 1778, CO 71/8, 150.
34 Minutes of the West India Merchants, 25 Feb. 1783, II, 11a–11d; "Extracts from the Minutes of a General Meeting of the West India Merchants," 25 Feb. 1783, CO 137/83, 182.

shortages, thus placing greater strain on the already declining sugar economy.[35]

Sharp price increases followed immediately. The cost of lumber in Kingston increased rapidly from between £10 and £12 to £28 per thousand feet and went as high as £40 in northern areas. The price of lumber in Barbados went from £7 to £25 per thousand feet. In the Ceded Islands (Dominica, Grenada, St. Vincent, and Tobago), prices of American products reached new heights. High costs and instability in food supplies led to a shift of labor and capital from the islands. Only the injection of large sums of money and an increased black slave labor force could have brought new life to the West Indian plantation system. Their absence retarded the economic advancement of the islands and sparked the continuous decline of the sugar economy.[36]

The operation of imperial policy did not function as smoothly as the experts had forecast. Supplies reaching the sugar colonies in imperial ships did not compensate adequately for the loss of direct trade in American vessels. Several governors and some agents in London suggested a change in policy. Governor Thomas Shirley of the Leeward Islands suggested that small American vessels should be allowed in the West Indian trade. Governor David Parry of Barbados went further: he recommended a ban on the importation of French brandy into Britain, the reduction of duties on rum by 50 percent, and the admission of American ships under 100 tons to a free intercourse for three years or until the Canadians were able to supply the islands. Fuller, the agent for Jamaica, made similar suggestions early in 1785, but these were rejected outright.[37]

By the middle of June 1785, the condition of the islands, especially Barbados, was critical and, in a blistering critique of

35 Herbert Bell, "British Commercial Policy in the West Indies, 1783–1787," *English Historical Review*, XXXI (1916), 434–436; Sheridan, "Slave Subsistence," 629–630; Edwards, *History of the West Indies*, II, 382; Thomas Shirley to Lord Sydney, Jan. 1785, CO 152/64, 95; David Makinson, *Barbados: A Study of North American-West Indian Relations, 1739–1789* (The Hague, 1964), 89–90.

36 Minutes of the Committee for Trade, 11 Mar. 1784, Board of Trade (B.T.) 5/1, 10–12; Extract of Letter, 25 Feb. 1787, B.T. 6/77, 208; "Prices of the following are compared with average before . . . and since the War," 11 Nov. 1784, CO 137/85, 115; "Answers to Queries" (1786), CO 152/64; Shirley to Sydney, 30 July 1784, CO 152/63, 81.

37 Parry to the Committee for Trade, 7 Sept. 1784, B.T. 6/84 273d–274d. See CO 28/60, 183–184d; Stephen Fuller to His Majesty's Ministers, 8 Mar. 1785, B.T. 6/83, Part 1, 23d.

the British commercial policy, Parry recommended the abandon-
ment of the Navigation Acts, which he argued had retarded the
commercial development of the West Indies and which only encouraged the establishment of alternative markets for American
trade.[38]

The operation of British policy made the foreign ports en-
trepôts for American goods destined for the sugar colonies. Small
droghers, crewed by blacks, went to the foreign islands where
they purchased American foodstuffs and lumber. These were retailed to the planter at 50 to 100 percent profit. A brief comparison
of the prices of American goods between St. Domingue (Haiti)
and Jamaica shows clearly the marked differences in the costs of
most articles in favor of the sugar planters in the foreign island,
the prime costs of most articles being from 22 to 93 percent higher
in Jamaica than in St. Domingue.[39]

A comparison of the total quantity of all articles imported
into the British islands from the United States, Canada, and the
foreign West Indies from 1785 to 1787 reveals that the quantities
of most articles from the United States and the foreign islands
were much larger than from British North America (Canada).
The only articles for which Canada sent the largest quantities to
the sugar colonies were beef, pork, and fish. Canada sent 17
percent of the fish and 72 percent of the beef and pork. She
exported to the islands only 2 percent of all their corn and rice
and only 3 percent of their flour and bread. A further assessment
of the evidence indicates that British policy had forced the smaller
colonies to rely on the French islands for most of their American
supplies. Table 8 gives the average annual quantity of various
articles entering the sugar colonies.[40]

The illegal trade had an effect on the economies of the sugar
colonies similar to that of the war years. The slave population
still declined as a result of disease caused by malnutrition. In

38 Parry to Sydney, 16 June 1785, CO 28/42, 88d–90.
39 Evan Nepean, "Trade between North America and the British West Indies, 1787,"
British Museum, add. ms. 38,248, 20d; Tench Coxe, *A Brief Examination of Lord Sheffield's
Observation on the Commerce of the American States* (Philadelphia, 1791), 9, 11, 21, 22.
40 "An Account of Ships and their Cargoes entered Inwards in the British Islands, from
the United States, British North America and the Foreign West Indies" (no date), CO
318/1, 142–148. For Dominica, see CO 318/2, 264.

Table 8 Quantity of British West Indian Imports from North American
Sources, Various Products, 1785–1787 (Annual Averages)

	UNITED STATES	FOREIGN ISLANDS	BRITISH NORTH AMERICA (CANADA)	SHARE OF BRITISH NORTH AMERICA IN TOTAL NORTH AMERICAN TRADE
Lumber (m. ft.)	7,918,937	3,694,022	2,566,667	19.8
Staves (no.)	20,425,577	10,109,777	3,492,964	11.4
Hoops (no.)	207,355	281,104	34,554	8.0
Corn and Peas (bus.)	175,516	48,401	5,642	2.6
Flour (bb.)	92,775	21,597	4,281	3.8
Bread (bb.)	17,243	1,437	681	3.9
Rice (bb.)	7,007	153	553	2.0
Fish (hhd.)	161	13	5,874	97.2
Pitch (bb.)	4,062	288	583	12.1
Beef and Pork (bb.)	62	125	375	72.1
Horses (no.)	821	324	109	9.5
Oxen (no.)	91	150	17	8.0
Onions (bu.)	33,819	5,500	7,068	20.9
Oil (bb.)	450	19	496	51.7
Shaken Hhds[a] (no.)	2,520	777	453	13.0

SOURCES: "A comparative State of the Trade between the West Indies and North America
from 1 October 1785 to 1 October 1787" (no date), CO 318/1, fo. 315. For illegal trade
at Cape François between the French and Jamaicans, see Elisha Tyler to Caleb Mumford
(no date), British Museum, add. ms. 38,376, fos. 99–100d.

a Empty vessels.

Barbados, for example, the total number of slaves decreased from
68,270 in 1780 to 62,712 in 1782. Reports from Jamaica in 1786
estimated that eighteen to twenty thousand had died from starvation.[41]

Slave losses were not offset by increased imports. In the
colonial period of the United States, when conditions for economic growth in the West Indies were ideal, a steady reinforcement of the slave population with fresh cargoes was needed. At
least 7 percent annual growth was required to maintain population
and production levels, and to inject new life into the system. The

41 "Number of Slaves returned into the Treasury Office of Barbados from 1780 to 1783"
(1788), CO 28/61, 204. The remaining years are 1783–52,258; 1784–61;808; 1785–62,775;
1786–62,115. Extracts of two letters from Jamaica . . . , 21 Sept. 1786, B.T. 6/76, 1;
Stephen Raester and Co. to Sir John Hugh Smyth, 8 Dec. 1783, Woolnough Papers,
Ashton Court Collection, AC/SO 16(27), 113–122; Edward Brathwaite, *The Development
of Creole Society in Jamaica 1770–1820* (Oxford, 1971), 85–86.

slave trade, however, had declined during the war. It was revived immediately on termination of the fighting, but imports retained show a decline and this continued at below 1784 levels through the end of the period under study (Table 9). The number fell from 23,287 in 1784 to 18,897 in 1791. There was a sharp increase in the number of re-exports, from an annual average of 4,991 in the years from 1784 to 1787 to 10,096 in the years 1788 to 1791. This situation forced up slave prices in Jamaica to approximately £73 sterling on the average—an ominous sign for the plantation system.

The decline in the number of slaves retained was reflected in the quantity of colonial products reaching Britain from the sugar colonies. After previous eighteenth-century wars, production of all staples normally regained and exceeded prewar levels. That this was not so now indicates the nature of the West Indian economy and signals the ultimate downfall of the plantation system based on the monocultural production of sugar with slave labor. To understand the significance of this problem, we can examine the imports of sugar into Britain from 1772 to 1791. The period is divided into five four-year periods for greater clarity. The decrease in sugar imports into Britain between the first four years and 1784 to 1787 amounts to 71,425 cwt.—an annual decline of 3.72 percent. In the last period, 1788 to 1791, sugar imports

Table 9 Number of Slaves Imported, Re-exported, and Retained, British West Indies, 1784–1791

YEAR	IMPORTED	RE-EXPORTED	RETAINED
1784	28,550	5,263	23,287
1785	21,598	5,018	16,580
1786	19,160	4,317	14,843
1787	21,023	5,366	15,657
1788	24,495	11,212	13,283
1789	21,425	8,764	12,661
1790	21,889	7,542	14,347
1791	30,763	12,866	17,897
Annual Average:			
1784–87	22,583	4,991	17,592
1788–91	24,643	10,096	14,547

SOURCE: "Account of Negroes retained in the British West Indies . . . 1783–1788," CO 318/1, fo. 141; MacPherson, *Annals of Commerce*, IV, 228.

into Britain were only about 2,000 cwt. above their level of sixteen years before (Table 10). This was an improvement, but was still short of the normal postwar recovery trend in West Indian production in the eighteenth century.

Further examination of the extant statistics shows that the quantity of minor staples exported from the British West Indies to Britain declined or made no significant growth between 1783 and 1791. Rum imports showed an overall increase after the disastrous war years, but only in one year did the postwar figures

Table 10   British Sugar Imports, 1772–1791

PERIOD AND CONDITIONS	YEAR	RAW SUGAR IMPORTED (CWT.)
	1772	1,829,721
	1773	1,804,080
Years preceding the American Revolution	1774	2,029,725
	1775	2,021,059
ANNUAL AVERAGE		1,921,145
	1776	1,726,507
	1777	1,416,291
First Years of the War: No Hurricanes	1778	1,521,457
	1779	1,525,833
ANNUAL AVERAGE		1,547,833
	1780	1,394,559
	1781	1,080,848
Cultivation during War with Hurricanes	1782	1,374,269
	1783	1,584,275
ANNUAL AVERAGE		1,358,488
	1784	1,782,386
Cultivation—Peace	1785	2,075,909
Hurricanes—Restriction	1786	1,613,965
	1787	1,926,621
ANNUAL AVERAGE		1,849,720
	1788	2,065,847
No Hurricanes—French Revolution	1789	1,936,448
Begins	1790	1,882,106
	1791	1,808,950
ANNUAL AVERAGE		1,923,328

SOURCES: "Account of the quantity of British sugar imported between 1772 and 1791 . . ." (no date), British Museum, add. ms. 12,432, fo. 18; Ragatz, *Fall of the Planter Class*, 189 n.; Pares, *War and Trade*, 471.

exceed those for 1776. This was in 1785, when approximately 7 percent more rum reached Britain from the sugar colonies. With the planters facing stiffer competition in the American market, they needed greater exports to Britain, but this was not achieved.[42]

Although pimentos were not widely cultivated throughout the Caribbean for export, their production was of marked importance to several areas in Jamaica. Exports to Britain declined during the revolutionary war and continued to do so until 1785 when a partial recovery was made. After that year, however, exports declined continuously for the rest of the period. Cocoa exports to Britain came chiefly from the Ceded Islands and Jamaica. Its production, therefore, had a significant impact on the economies of only a few colonies. The decline in exports to Britain began with a revolutionary war and continued unabated into the decade of the 1780s.

Of the minor staples under discussion, coffee was the most important. It was produced in the Ceded Islands and in Jamaica. In the 1770s the legislature of Jamaica gave incentives to producers to improve quality and increase production. The intervention of the American War of Independence shattered this program. Exports to Britain declined as a result of the war, and no recovery was made as late as 1791. The meteoric rise in cotton exports from the British West Indies into Britain, which began with the decline of sugar cultivation during the revolutionary war, continued into the decade of the 1780s until 1790, after which decline was just as rapid. This fall was certainly the result of competition from United States-grown cotton, and its sensational decline demonstrated that Britain's attempt "to sustain an economy whose main staple, sugar, was disturbed" had failed.[43]

Other branches of West Indian trade also showed only limited recovery by 1791. One must be careful not to read too much into this trend since lower sugar prices had led to smaller returns from sugar production. The optimism of the Canadian colonists in believing that they were capable of replacing the United States in importing large quantities of British West Indian products was not realized. Sugar imports into Canada, for example, declined after 1784. Rum imports, however, increased significantly over

---

42 Data on the minor staples presented in the next three paragraphs come from a variety of primary and secondary sources. See Carrington, *British West Indies*, for details.

43 John Ehrman, *The Younger Pitt: The Years of Acclaim* (London, 1964), 382.

those for the years 1770 to 1773, but competition from the French
islands reduced the quantity that would otherwise have been
taken. Local distilleries imported in excess of 167,240 gallons of
French molasses in 1786 for their rum industry. Similarly, the
legal imports of British West Indian products into the United
States declined. Sugar imports fell from 47,595 cwt. in 1784 to
19,921 cwt. in 1787. Rum imports fell from 2,742,277 gallons in
the first year to 1,620,205 gallons in the latter year. It must be
noted that these figures were lower than those taken in the prewar
years, 1770 to 1773 (Table 11).[44]

Table 11   British West Indian Trade with the United States and British
North America (Canada), Various Products, 1770–1773 and
1783–1787

United States

YEAR	SUGAR (CWT.)	RUM (GAL.)	MOLASSES (GAL.)	COFFEE (CWT.)	COCOA (LB.)	PIMENTO (LB.)
1770	65,489	3,250,060	220,450	4,031	120,988	34,529
1771	45,994	2,180,000	101,717	2,305	146,837	30,656
1772	44,456	3,337,750	106,032	4,222	126,794	73,530
1773	38,365	3,049,298	105,432	4,097	131,539	91,971
1783	5,651	679,760	53,600	414	55	57,400
1784	47,595	2,742,271	5,800	573	74	169,500
1785	46,116	2,188,000	43,800	1,202	154	54,300
1786	35,801	1,399,040	1,800	1,874	186	16,900
1787	19,921	1,620,205	4,200	3,246	124	6,400

British North America

YEAR	SUGAR (CWT.)	RUM (GAL.)	MOLASSES (GAL.)	COFFEE (CWT.)	COCOA (LB.)	PIMENTO (LB.)
1770	653	38,310	6,418	4	200	
1771	840	67,588	3,078		5,500	
1772	979	85,715	8,935	5	248	3,266
1773	393	82,505	4,296		6,352	
1783	6,761	564,873	135,636	555	136	7,100
1784	14,744	888,170	54,730	454	24	
1785	12,214	677,412	86,400	786	133	1,000
1786	18,836	953,743	95,260	1,426	79	
1787	9,891	874,580	26,300	575	81	200

SOURCES: "Account of the Number of Ships with their Tonnage, the quantity of produce, trading to
the British Colonies in America and the United States" (no date), *Parliamentary Papers*, LXXXIV, pt.
IV: Appendices nos. 13, 21; Ragatz, *Fall of the Planter Class*, 185–186.

44 "Report of the Committee to enquire into the Present State of Intercourse between
the British West Indian islands and His Majesty's Colonies in North America . . . ," 8
Jan. 1788, B.T. 6/76, 30.

Because trade with the foreign islands was circumventing Britain's monopoly of the commerce of the West Indies, Parliament in 1787 prohibited the entry of flour, bread, rice, wheat, and timber from the foreign West Indies into the British Islands, including the Bahamas and Bermuda, except in emergencies. On occasion, the governors, on advice of their councils, were empowered to permit the importation of United States goods, but for a limited time only. Most governors welcomed the new law, hoping that it would lessen the importance of the French colonies. Yet, they recognized that it would greatly reduce supplies to the islands. Parry recommended a bounty system for British ships trading with the West Indies to ensure a steady and reliable supply of food. Shirley forecast a bleak economic future for the colonies and suggested that alternative markets for rum should be found. Without these, he wrote, "many of the Colonies must feel the prohibitions of the Act to a ruinous degree."[45]

In spite of the documented decline of the West Indies, the British government adhered to its mercantilist doctrine and passed statutes in 1787 and 1788 prohibiting imports from the foreign islands to the sugar colonies. This was Parliament's attempt to close the gaps in its commercial policy "and the navy and local courts were told to deal strictly with offenders. But the remedy only nourished another disease." Intercourse with the United States having thus been restricted, the decline of the economies of the sugar colonies was not arrested, and British policy inadvertently aided the development of the French islands at the expense of her own. In addition, it prevented the British West Indies from adjusting to the new Atlantic commercial system and, thus, their decline was further accelerated.[46]

This article has shown that, beginning with the outbreak of the War of American Independence, the economy of the British West Indies went into a decline from which very little recovery was achieved as late as the early 1790s. This downturn was certainly the result of the American war and was exacerbated by the mercantilist policies to which the British resorted in their attempt to control the economic development of the United States. Britain,

---

45 27 Geo. 111 C.7; Sydney to Parry, 6 Jan. 1787, CO 28/61, 1–1d; Parry to Sydney, 27 May 1787, CO 28/61, 56–56d; Shirley to Sydney, 7 June 1787, CO 152/65, 169.
46 27 Geo III C.7 and Geo. III C.6; Ehrman, *The Younger Pitt*, 337.

by adopting a restrictive and monopolistic policy toward the United States, had undoubtedly set in motion the decline of the British West Indian economy. After 1783 the sugar planters and merchants were restricted from exploiting the Atlantic economic system which the United States was well placed to exploit. The emergence of the cotton plantations in the southern states revived slavery there; the decline of sugar production led to the demise of the slave plantation system in the British West Indies. That end was prolonged by events at the end of the eighteenth century, but the die was cast in the American Revolutionary War. That war was "the greatest disaster for the British sugar planters," not only because it left them face to face with their French rivals, but mainly because the plantation system could not function efficiently and profitably without a reliable external source of supply of foodstuffs and lumber. Indeed, the War of American Independence initiated the continuous "decline of the sugar colonies" despite their apparent reprieve in the decades of the 1790s and the French Revolutionary and Napoleonic Wars.[47]

47 Williams, *Capitalism and Slavery*, 120.

Richard S. Dunn

"Dreadful Idlers" in the Cane Fields: The Slave Labor Pattern on a Jamaican Sugar Estate, 1762–

1831 Ever since Curtin published his seminal study of *The Atlantic Slave Trade*, in which he pointed out the glaring disparity between the massive traffic to the Caribbean and the marginal traffic to North America, historians have been trying to explain the sharp demographic contrast between the two regions. Why did the slaves imported to the West Indian sugar islands die faster than they propagated, while the slaves imported to North America experienced marked natural increase? Four features of the Caribbean slave system are now commonly emphasized: the lethal disease environment, the high proportion of African-born slaves with low fertility, the inadequate slave diet, and the brutal and exploitive labor regimen.[1]

This essay focuses on the last of these factors, and discusses the impact of the Caribbean labor routine upon the enslaved cane workers. My framework was established by Higman, who has used the British slave registration records of 1813 to 1834 to analyze the overall labor pattern in the British West Indian sugar islands during the closing generation of Caribbean slavery, and my methodology is borrowed from Craton, who has used the detailed plantation records at Worthy Park estate in Jamaica to present the first microcosmic account of a Caribbean slave gang in action. Like Craton, I have been scrutinizing the records of a particularly well-documented Jamaican sugar plantation: Mesopotamia estate in the western parish of Westmoreland. The Meso-

---

1 Philip D. Curtin, *The Atlantic Slave Trade: A Census* (Madison, 1969), 86–93. Kenneth F. Kiple discusses the first three factors in *The Caribbean Slave: A Biological History* (Cambridge, 1984). Barry W. Higman stresses the labor factor in his two books: *Slave Population and Economy in Jamaica, 1807–1834* (Cambridge, 1976); *Slave Populations of the British Caribbean 1807–1834* (Baltimore, 1984).

potamian records enable me to reconstruct the individual life history of every single Afro-American who lived and worked on this plantation during the final seventy years of Caribbean slavery. Studied collectively, these life histories demonstrate conclusively that the labor system employed at Mesopotamia had a large and quantifiable impact upon the slaves' health and life expectancy.[2]

The absentee proprietors of Mesopotamia, Joseph Foster Barham and his son, Joseph Foster Barham II, made a systematic practice of cataloging their Jamaican slave gang annually from 1751 to 1831: eighty-five inventories of the Mesopotamia slave force survive among the Barham family papers in the Bodleian Library at Oxford. From 1751 onward the Mesopotamian lists identify each man, woman, and child by name and place of origin. From 1762 onward the inventories supply three especially useful further items of annual information: the age, occupation, and physical condition of each slave. From 1774 on they also identify the mothers of all children born on the estate.[3]

As a data bank for labor historians, these records are particularly informative for the period 1762 to 1831. By correlating the inventories for these years, I have been able to distinguish each of the recorded 1,103 slaves who lived at Mesopotamia during this seventy-year span, and to trace year by year the work experiences of these people individually and collectively. So far as I know, this is the only British Caribbean sugar estate yet discovered where one can trace *all* of the individual workers year by year over a long time span. This rich biographical information documents the impact of demography, of miscegenation, of sex roles, of health conditions, and of patterns of employment upon each and every Mesopotamian slave. And it shows in concrete detail the effect of the ending of the African slave trade upon this particular community of slave workers.[4]

2 See, in particular, *idem, Slave Population and Economy in Jamaica*, 1–17, 121–124, 212–226; *idem., Slave Populations of the British Caribbean*, 158–199, 324–329, 332–336. Michael Craton, *Searching for the Invisible Man: Slaves and Plantation Life in Jamaica* (Cambridge, Mass., 1978).

3 The 85 Mesopotamian inventories are scattered through 5 boxes of the Barham Papers (hereafter identified as Barham): B34-B38, Clarendon Manuscript Deposit, Bodleian Library, Oxford. The earliest inventory is dated 1736. I wish to thank the Earl of Clarendon for permitting me to use these Mesopotamian records.

4 The Mesopotamian inventories are both more numerous and more continuous than at Worthy Park, where Craton drew upon 35 inventories for the years 1783–1796, 1811–

Mesopotamia was situated on the Cabarita River in the West-moreland plain (still the chief sugar growing district in Jamaica), five miles inland from Savanna la Mar, the local port. The estate was laid out about 1700 and was operated by the Barhams from 1728 to 1834, throughout the peak period of slave-based sugar production in Jamaica. Between 1762 and 1831 the slave population at Mesopotamia fluctuated from a low of 238 in 1769 to a peak of 421 in 1820. It was never self-sustaining. As Table 1 shows, nearly twice as many deaths as births were recorded between 1762 and 1831. In order to maintain a viable work force at Mesopotamia (as also at Worthy Park and most other Jamaican sugar estates), the owners had to purchase a great many new slaves. Between 1762 and 1831 the Barhams bought 138 people from the African slave ships and 285 from other Jamaican estates. The elder Barham, who operated Mesopotamia from 1746 until his death in 1789, bought almost all of his new slaves from African ships until 1786, when he purchased forty slaves from Three Mile River estate, a local plantation. His son was repelled by the African trade and stopped buying from the slave ships in 1793, fifteen years before Parliament closed the trade. Instead, he ac-

Table 1   Slave Population Changes at Mesopotamia, 1762–1831

	MALE	FEMALE	TOTAL
Population on 31 Dec. 1761	152	118	270
Increase:			
Recorded Live Births	204	206	410
Purchased from Africa	96	42	138
Purchased in Jamaica	147	138	285
	447	386	833
Decrease:			
Recorded Deaths	429	320	749
Manumitted	4	11	15
Escaped	5	2	7
Sold	4	0	4
	442	333	775
Population on 31 Dec. 1831	157	171	328

1817, 1820–1824, and 1830–1838. However, Craton was able to document the transition from slave to wage labor during the period 1834–1846 at Worthy Park (Craton, *Searching for the Invisible Man*, 275–315), which I cannot do because the Mesopotamian workers disappear from view in 1832 on the eve of emancipation.

quired the new workers he needed from neighboring estates that were closing down or retrenching: 60 from Southfield estate in 1791, 56 from Cairncurran in 1814, and 112 from Springfield in 1820. This policy change by the Barhams was certainly not typical of Jamaican estate management. The African trade to Jamaica reached its peak volume between the years 1790 and 1807. But the fact that the Barhams voluntarily stopped importing from Africa fifteen years before their fellow planters were forced to do so in 1808 means that the effects of this cessation can be measured more fully at Mesopotamia than elsewhere.

The two Barhams took a far greater interest in the physical and spiritual welfare of their black workers than most Caribbean planters. Though they lived (very comfortably) in England, they each visited Mesopotamia as young men, and from the 1760s onward they supported a program of religious instruction on the estate that was conducted by Moravian missionaries. In order to keep close track of conditions at Mesopotamia, they required their business agents in Jamaica to send frequent reports on the slaves. Joseph I instituted the annual inventories. Joseph II voted in Parliament in the 1790s to abolish the slave trade. When he became owner of Mesopotamia on his father's death, he quickly bought many new slaves with the idea that three people could do the work of two in the past, which would "ease the labor of my slaves and make their task light." In another letter to his attorneys, Joseph II remarked: "I carry my ideas a little farther than many on this subject, and think myself obliged to consult not only [the slaves'] health but their happiness." In 1801 he told a new attorney that the slaves' "well-being and happiness is by far the chief object of my concern."[5]

As he looked over the annual slave inventories sent from Mesopotamia, Joseph II frequently complained about the large number of deaths and the small number of births. He asked his attorneys why so many deaths were caused by debility and the flux, and he directed them to give the slaves more rest on the weekends, with special care for pregnant women. Barham's agents responded by sending him statistics from the Westmoreland parish rolls to show that the slaves on neighboring estates

5 Joseph Foster Barham II (hereafter identified as JFB II) to James Wedderburn and John Graham, 16 Oct. 1790; JFB II to Wedderburn and Graham, 8 Sept. 1789; JFB II to Samuel Jeffries, 26 June 1801, Barham C428.

were also decreasing. "No Negroes in the Parish of Westmoreland," they insisted, were "more indulged, better fed or better clothed." Pregnant women were assigned light work recommended by the doctors as positively conducive to their health. The attorneys predicted that as the elderly Africans on the estate died, the Mesopotamian-born creoles would breed and increase. But they warned that problems would continue, because the estate was situated too close to the market town of Savanna la Mar. The slaves were always rambling about and holding balls on Saturday nights, and consequently neglecting their subsistence provision grounds.[6]

Barham's agents were correct in stating that the demographic problems at Mesopotamia were common among the other sugar estates of Westmoreland parish. Inspection of the parish records for the years 1807 to 1834 shows a general pattern of shrinkage within the slave labor force and retrenchment among the Westmoreland plantation owners during this period following the closing of the slave trade. Between 1807 and 1834, the number of estates in Westmoreland with labor gangs of 200 or more slaves fell from thirty-nine to twenty-four, and the number with 100 or more slaves fell from seventy-one to fifty-three. As Higman has pointed out, the sugar planters experienced a greater population loss than the ranchers, who operated livestock pens. The seven large Westmoreland holdings identifiable as livestock pens reported 448 slave births and 419 deaths in the triennial slave registration returns of 1817 to 1832, and claimed compensation in 1834—the year of emancipation—for a collective work force almost the same size as in 1817. But the forty-four identifiable Westmoreland sugar estates reported 3,254 births and 5,334 deaths between 1817 and 1832. Nearly half of these sugar planters made up their losses as the Barhams did at Mesopotamia—by acquiring blocs of replacement workers. But in 1834 they filed compensation claims with the British government for 2,000 fewer slaves than they had registered in 1817—a loss of approximately 18 percent in seventeen years.[7]

6 JFB II to Henry W. Plummer, 6 July 1799; JFB II to James Colquhoun Grant and John Blyth, 6 June 1810; JFB II to Grant and Blyth, 29 July 1815, Barham C428. Grant and Blyth to JFB II, 3 Jan. 1809, 19 Oct. 1812, 13 Oct. 1817; Blyth to JFB II, 9 July 1823, Barham C358.
7 This paragraph is based upon analysis of the following 9 sets of records: the West-

Grim as these parish figures are, the slave population at Mesopotamia was declining faster than on most neighboring estates during the closing years of slavery. Management at Mesopotamia reported 54 slave births for every 100 slave deaths in the triennial returns for 1817 to 1832, as against 65 births to 100 deaths on the ten other sugar estates in the parish of closest equivalent size. Pondering this dismal situation, Joseph II came to believe that the slaves themselves must be responsible for their demographic failure. All of his efforts to increase births and check deaths at Mesopotamia had been frustrated by the slaves' profound moral deficiencies. Accepting the arguments of his Jamaican attorneys, he judged his laborers to be naturally "dissolute" and "dreadful idlers." In 1823, Joseph II published a pamphlet in which he argued that emancipation was a noble objective, but a pointless one until the slaves were morally transformed through a massive program of religious and educational instruction—a program entirely beyond the resources of the Caribbean slaveholders. Therefore Barham called upon the British government to assume the management of all private estates in the sugar islands, compensate the slaveholders for their lost property, and provide the blacks with moral training so that they learn the responsibilities of freedom and the duty of honest labor. Essentially, Barham was abandoning the position he had started with in 1789. As a slaveholder he no longer felt responsibility for his black workers' health and happiness. And he was also expressing disdain for the quality of work performed by several generations of slaves on his estate. "The Negro race," he asserted, "is so averse to labour, that without force we have hardly anywhere been able to obtain it, even from those who had been trained to work."[8]

But Barham's own records supply much evidence to support alternate explanations for the problems at Mesopotamia. The long sequence of slave inventories taken on this estate, designed with the purpose of keeping an annual running check on the status of every man, woman, and child who lived and worked there, pro-

moreland parish tax lists for 1807 and 1814 (Barham B34); the Westmoreland slave registration returns for 1817, 1820, 1823, 1826, 1829, and 1832 (T 71/178–189, Public Record Office, London); and the Westmoreland slave compensation return of 1834 (T 71/723, PRO).

8 JFB II, memorandum on the Negroes at Mesopotamia, n.d., Barham C375; *idem, Considerations on the Abolition of Negro Slavery* (London, 1823), 2–4, 7–10, 14–18, 23, 35.

vides a precisely detailed record of the Caribbean slave labor system in action. By correlating these inventories one can trace the health history and occupational experience of each slave worker, and demonstrate that these two variables were intimately related.

How trustworthy are these Mesopotamian data? In particular, how reliable are the annual age statements for each slave, of crucial importance when correlating one census with another and when interpreting the slaves' individual careers? The ages of all persons recorded as born on the estate between 1751 and 1831 can be verified precisely. The ages of many persons who were imported into the estate can also be verified to some degree. Nearly all of the slaves who were purchased directly from African slave traders were reported as being youthful: 90 percent were listed in the first census after arrival as between ten and twenty-four years old; 50 percent were listed as between ten and fourteen years old. Perhaps the Mesopotamian bookkeepers who entered this information persistently underestimated the ages of these incoming Africans. But teenagers can be tracked with some accuracy by the presence or absence of pubertal developments—the height spurt, voice change in boys, breast development in girls—that even a book-keeper might notice. African pre-adolescents might also be missing the body scars or country marks that were commonly administered to boys and girls during pubertal initiation rites.[9]

The Mesopotamian bookkeepers often revised their age statements for African boys or girls up or down on subsequent lists to correct apparent mistakes. Undoubtedly, the slaves imported from other Jamaican estates possess the most dubious age statements. These people were acquired in large blocs, and arrived at Mesopotamia in family groups. They ranged in age from extreme

9 The Barhams' bookkeepers, employed on modest annual wages, were transients who seldom worked at Mesopotamia for more than two or three years. In preparing new slave lists they seem to have worked from old ones, updating, adding, and deleting entries as needed. Each annual inventory contained a birth and death register. On the question of African tribal scars, when Thomas Thistlewood, a Jamaican planter who lived a few miles from Mesopotamia, bought 10 slaves from an African ship in 1765, he described each of them in his diary by name, sex, tribe, age, height, and country marks. Eight of them, ranging in age from 20 to 13, had country marks, including a Coromante man. The two youngest and shortest children, both Coromantes, were a 10-year-old boy and a 12-year-old girl who had no tribal scars; they had evidently not yet experienced the adolescent initiation rite. Journal of Thomas Thistlewood, 19 June 1765, Monson Manuscript Deposit, 31/16, Lincolnshire Archives, Lincoln.

youth to extreme old age. Their stated ages were supplied by previous owners, who had probably kept less careful records than the Barhams. Yet when the initial age statements in the Mesopotamian inventories for these new Jamaican slaves are studied collectively, they show no detectable distortion, except that too many of the older men and women are heaped at ages thirty-five, forty, forty-five, fifty, and fifty-five. I conclude that the Mesopotamian age statements are defective for the older imported slaves, but are otherwise as accurate as such data can ever be.

The remaining categories of data appear to be consistently and reliably reported. The inventories supply precise exit dates for all slaves who died, were sold, were manumitted, or ran away between 1751 and 1831. I have found no reason to challenge the annual occupational descriptions and health statements—no reason to suspect that the bookkeepers identified carpenters as field workers or vice versa, or that they labelled invalids as able bodied or vice versa.

The following discussion focuses upon those Mesopotamian slaves living on the estate between 1762 and 1831 whose "adult" careers on the estate can be reconstructed completely. I define as "adult" all slaves aged sixteen or older, because young people were customarily assigned to the jobs they would hold during their prime working years at about age sixteen, and bookkeepers generally promoted "boys" to "men" and "girls" to "women" on their lists at age sixteen. But the sixteen-year-old adults at Mesopotamia were definitely not yet adult in a physical sense. Recent research into the stature of Caribbean blacks in the early nineteenth century, as revealed by the slave registration returns, indicates that teenagers began their adolescent growth spurts noticeably later than in modern Western black populations: girls at about age thirteen and boys at about age fifteen. By age sixteen males and females were both approximately the same height, on average just about five feet tall. The girls would grow another inch or so to achieve mature stature, and the boys would grow a median four inches by the time they reached age twenty-two.[10]

10 Higman, *Slave Populations of the British Caribbean*, 280–292, 534–535, 542–546; *idem.,* "Growth in Afro-Caribbean Slave Populations," *American Journal of Physical Anthropology,* I (1979), 377–382; Gerald C. Friedman, "The Heights of Slaves in Trinidad," *Social Science History,* VI (1982), 493–501. The data analyzed by Higman and Friedman are from the registration records in Trinidad, St. Lucia, and Berbice. See also Robert W. Fogel et al.,

By restricting attention to these Mesopotamian slaves whose adult careers on the estate can be traced in full, I have excluded from analysis half of the 1,103 slaves who are recorded as living at Mesopotamia between 1762 and 1831: the 137 children who died before they reached age sixteen; the 100 men and women who turned sixteen before 1751 when systematic annual inventory keeping began; and the 328 people who were still alive in 1831 when the last inventory was taken. This leaves a cohort of 538 men and women—49 percent of the total recorded population— whose adult careers at Mesopotamia began after 1751 and ended by 1831. Of these, 322 or 60 percent were men, and 216 were women; 186 or 35 percent were born at Mesopotamia; 182 or 34 percent were imported directly from Africa; 170 or 31 percent were purchased from other Jamaican estates; and 17 or 3 percent were mulattoes.[11]

Each of these 538 adult slaves was annually listed within one of eight broad occupational categories: (1) the drivers who supervised the several gangs of field laborers; (2) the craft workers, such as carpenters, coopers, blacksmiths, masons, boilers, and distillers; (3) the stockkeepers and transport workers, such as penkeepers, stable hands, mulemen, and carters; (4) the prime field hands, who performed the chief agricultural labor and who were subdivided into two work units, the first gang and the second gang; (5) the domestics who attended the white overseers, bookkeepers, artisans, and missionaries; (6) the marginal workers who held a variety of peripheral jobs, such as grass cutters, dung carriers, jobbers, hog herders, sheep herders, gardeners, fishermen, rat catchers, doctors, midwives, field cooks, fowl keepers, and water carriers; (7) the watchmen and nurses who were always elderly and in broken health; and (8) the nonworkers who were too old or sick for any employment whatsoever.[12]

"Secular Changes in American and British Stature and Nutrition," *Journal of Interdisciplinary History*, XIV (1983), 445–481. Regrettably, neither the Jamaican slave registration returns nor the Mesopotamian inventories supply any information on slave stature.

11 Twelve of these mulattoes were among the 186 Mesopotamian-born slaves, and 5 were among the 170 imported from other Jamaican estates.

12 Unfortunately, the Mesopotamian inventories only start to distinguish between the two field gangs of category (4) in 1801. Before this date, all laborers in this category were simply identified as field workers. Jobbers in category (6) are not to be confused with jobbing laborers who were hired out by jobbers—i.e., by slaveholders who contracted their workers out to perform especially arduous work (such as cane hole digging) on other

The Mesopotamian slaves were routed through this occupational system via a well-established tracking network. Boys and girls were put to work very early, some at age five and on average at age seven. Those who began as field laborers, cutting grass or carrying dung, almost always continued on as field workers when they became adults. Those who began as cattle boys or hog herders generally continued on as stockkeepers. Boys who started work as domestics were usually converted to apprentice craft workers in their early teens, whereas most girl domestics became field workers. Adults were generally kept in the same line of employment until they became too sick or old for prime labor, when they were switched to lighter tasks. The only people who were promoted to higher job categories in mid-career were the drivers, who usually started out as field workers. For example, Cuffee Tippo was an African who came to Mesopotamia at about age ten; he worked for his first six years with the grass gang, then continued as an adult field laborer for thirty-five years before he was promoted to driver at age fifty-one. By this time Cuffee was listed as "infirm," but he served as driver for sixteen years and spent his last three years in retirement as an invalid; he died at age seventy—a ripe old age for a Mesopotamian slave.

The slaves in categories (1), (2), (3), and (4) were valued much more highly by the Barhams and their attorneys and overseers than those in categories (5), (6), (7), and (8). This relative worth is demonstrated by the prices paid for slaves who had already been assigned to adult occupations on other Jamaican estates before they entered the Mesopotamian work force. Among the 156 slaves acquired from Three Mile River, Southfield, and Cairncurran estates, drivers, craft workers, stockkeepers, and field workers consistently fetched the best prices. Drivers exercised the

---

estates. No Mesopotamian slaves were employed in this way, although the Barhams' attorneys hired gangs of jobbing laborers to work at Mesopotamia when the estate labor force was particularly short-handed. The slaves listed as "jobbers" in the Mesopotamian inventories were men in ailing health, retired from field work, who could no longer perform strenuous physical labor.

My classification system agrees with Higman's in *Slave Populations of the British Caribbean*, 158–179, and also with Craton's more elaborate system of 20 categories (*Searching for the Invisible Man*, 141), except that Craton ranks the nurses among the elite workers, whereas at Mesopotamia I find them to be semi-invalids who took on this work late in life after being shifted from more "valuable" jobs. Likewise, the female doctors and midwives at Mesopotamia had generally started out as field workeres.

greatest responsibility, since they kept the field laborers working in unison and on schedule; however, they were not by any means the strongest or healthiest members of the work force, being usually middle-aged or elderly. The craft workers received considerable job training and possessed the most critical skills: boilers and distillers had to know how to brew acceptable sugar and rum; coopers had to construct leak-proof hogsheads and puncheons; and carpenters, masons, and smiths had to keep the plantation buildings and machinery in working order. The stockkeepers and transport workers enjoyed more independence and lighter physical labor than the craft workers.[13]

The prime field hands in category (4), especially the members of the first gang, were the key workers in this system. They performed the hardest physical labor by far, digging the deep square cane holes in which to plant new shoots, and cutting the ripe cane stalks at harvest time. They executed this strenuous manual work in regimented lock step, so that each member of the gang was forced to keep pace with the work of the others. The Barhams paid good prices for field workers: the fifty-nine prime hands acquired from Three Mile River, Southfield, and Cairncurran cost almost as much as the other ninety-seven new slaves. The critical issue was that field workers had to be in sound health. Once they became identified in the annual inventories as "weak," "sickly," or "diseased," they were shifted to easier and less productive work in categories (5), (6), or (7). Thus the managers at Mesopotamia needed to recruit new field hands continuously in order to keep the first and second gangs at strength.

In Table 2 the 538 men and women whose adult careers at Mesopotamia can be traced in full are categorized by primary occupation. A number of male workers held two primary jobs simultaneously. Thus Robin, born on the estate in 1784, had childhood training both in the grass gang and as a cattle boy, and was employed in his late teens as a combined carter/field hand. By his early twenties Robin had become a rebel; he was described

13   The price list of Three Mile River slaves is in Barham B33; the Southfield list is in Barham B36; the Cairncurran list is in Barham B34. Unfortunately I have found no parallel list for the 112 slaves purchased from Springfield estate in 1820. The domestics in category (5) were the favorites of the white managerial staff, and had the least strenuous employment of all the able-bodied laborers, but they fetched lower prices than the craft or stock workers because their jobs were considered more marginal.

Table 2 The Primary Occupations of 538 Adult Mesopotamian Slaves by Gender, 1762–1831

OCCUPATION	MALES	% M	FEMALES	% F	TOTAL	% OF WORKERS
1. Drivers	13	81	3	19	16	3.0
2. Craft Workers	42	100		0	42	7.8
2.5 Craft + Stock	11	100		0	11	2.0
3. Stock Keepers	16	100		0	16	3.0
3.5 Stock + Field	22	100		0	22	4.1
4. Field Workers	177	49	182	51	359	66.7
5. Domestics	3	33	6	67	9	1.7
6. Marginal Workers	26	67	13	33	39	7.2
8. Nonworkers	12	50	12	50	24	4.5
TOTALS	322	60	216	40	538	100.0

in the inventories as a "notorious thief and runaway," and the overseers decided that he was no longer suitable for transport work. From age twenty-one onward Robin worked solely in the second field gang until he died of pleurisy at age twenty-eight. There were twenty-one other Mesopotamian slaves who, like Robin, combined field with livestock work, and eleven who combined craft with stock or transport work. I have placed these people in categories (2.5) and (3.5) in order to distinguish them from the full-scale craft, stock, and field laborers.

Table 2 points up three significant features of the Mesopotamian labor pattern. First and most obvious, the number of privileged workers was small and the number of field workers was large. The chance of becoming a driver was 1 in 33, whereas the chance of becoming a field hand was 2 in 3. Second, relatively few slaves beyond the age of sixteen escaped employment of some kind. Less than 5 percent of these 538 adults did no work at all at Mesopotamia; most slaves in this category were unwanted elderly or incapacitated people who came to Mesopotamia in job lots from other Jamaican estates. Third, the female workers were especially discriminated against at Mesopotamia. Women had very little chance of escaping field labor: 84 percent of the adult females became prime field hands, as against 55 percent of the adult males. Women were excluded from craft work, transport, and all stock work except for fowl keeping. They could be drivers, but only of the grass gang. Even the marginal jobs in category (6) went mainly to the males, who served when they were in failing health as jobbers, gardeners, fishermen, rat catchers, and watchmen. For women of equivalent feebleness, the only job assignments available beyond field work were as domestics, doctors (just one female black doctor was employed on the estate at any given time), midwives, nurses, field cooks, fowl keepers, and water carriers. The female water carriers were always cripples who had lost an arm or a hand in sugar mill accidents; presumably they carried water containers on their heads. Table 2 shows that, whereas males constituted 60 percent of this total group, more than half of the field workers were female. To be sure, the women in the West African societies from where these slaves came were accustomed to doing most of the agricultural work. But they were certainly not accustomed to the gang labor system practiced at Mesopotamia.

Table 3 considers the significance of origin and color in determining the employment pattern at Mesopotamia. As one might expect, the most privileged workers were the locally born slaves of mixed color; the least privileged slaves were African-born immigrants. But this stereotype does not tell the full story. Between 1762 and 1831, there were forty-six mulattoes and six quadroons—sired by the overseers, craft supervisors, and bookkeepers from the white managerial staff—who lived at Mesopotamia, constituting about 5 percent of the total slave population. Of these, nine were manumitted as children, ten died before age sixteen, and another sixteen were still alive in 1831, leaving sev-

Table 3 The Primary Occupations of 538 Adult Mesopotamian Slaves by Origin and Color, 1762–1831

OCCUPATION	MESOPOTA- MIAN-BORN BLACKS		JAMAICAN BLACKS		AFRICAN BLACKS		MULATTOES	
	NO.	%	NO.	%	NO.	%	NO.	%
1. Drivers	7	4	4	3	5	3	0	
2. Craft Workers	12	7	10	6	8	4	12	70
2.5 Craft + Stock	6	4	2	1	2	1	1	6
3. Stock Keepers	14	8	2	1	0		0	
3.5 Stock + Field	16	9	3	2	3	2	0	
4. Field Workers	105	60	99	60	155	85	0	
5. Domestics	4	2	2	1	1	1	2	12
6. Marginal Workers	8	5	27	16	4	2	0	
8. Invalids	2	1	16	10	4	2	2	12
TOTALS	174	100	165	100	182	100	17	100

enteen mulattoes in our cohort of adult workers. They were employed exclusively as craft workers or as domestics. Over the years, the proportion of mulattoes in the Mesopotamian population increased significantly. In 1762, only two mulattoes were members of the adult work force: a mason named John and a carpenter named William. But, by 1831 (when the records close), there were thirteen slaves of mixed color who held adult craft or domestic jobs—leaving just eighteen additional job slots in these categories for the 218 blacks in the adult employment pool. Since privileged positions were in very short supply at Mesopotamia, the mulatto employment pattern must have been noticed and resented by the blacks. Several of the more serious recorded fights among the Mesopotamian slaves were between mulattoes and blacks. In 1806 a black fourteen-year-old apprentice cooper named Tamerlane was kicked in the intestines and killed by an unidentified mulatto boy. In 1826 cooper Robert McAlpine (a mulatto, the son of a white Mesopotamia bookkeeper) maimed distiller Peter (a black) with a handsaw when Peter failed to pay him a debt of "two bits."[14]

In strong contrast to the mulattoes, only eleven of the 182 slaves in our cohort who were purchased directly from the African slave ships became craft workers or domestics; 85 percent were put into the field gangs. But as a group these African newcomers were also the most functional laborers on the estate: 66 percent of them were male, 96 percent of them were assigned to primary jobs, and only 2 percent had to be channeled directly into marginal work, with another 2 percent being nonworking invalids. In all of these respects the Africans compare very favorably with the 165 black slaves who were acquired from other Jamaican estates. Among the Jamaican imports, 53 percent were male and only 74 percent could be assigned to primary jobs. Since many were old and sick on arrival, 16 percent had to be channeled directly into marginal work, and 10 percent did no work at all for the Barhams. The 174 Mesopotamian-born Negroes show still another occupational pattern. Compared with both groups of imported slaves,

14 McAlpine could also have been Tamerlane's assailant in 1806; he was a 13-year-old boy at that time. In punishment for his attack on Peter (who died a few months later), McAlpine was flogged and put into the workhouse for a month. William Ridgard to JFB II, 4 Aug. 1826, Barham C359.

they clearly had easier access to the more responsible and interesting jobs. Table 3 shows that 34 percent of them became supervisors, domestics, craft workers, or stock workers. In particular, they had a virtual monopoly on the stock and transport jobs.

Table 4 considers the impact of occupational assignment upon the health and longevity of the Mesopotamian black workers. This tabulation omits the seventeen mulattoes—who were all either craft or domestic workers, and whose inclusion would skew the findings for these two job categories—and aggregates the amount of time spent in primary and secondary occupations by each of the 521 adult black slaves in our cohort. The distinction between primary and secondary occupations is important, since most workers at Mesopotamia were shifted to employment in categories (5), (6), and (7) only when they became too sick or weak to continue productive labor. As we have already seen in Table 3, sixty-one of these people never held primary jobs at Mesopotamia, and twenty-two did not work at all. To illustrate how the system ordinarily operated, a man named Strephon, imported from Africa at age nineteen, worked as a field hand through age thirty-one, by which time he suffered so badly from

Table 4 The Longevity of 521 Mesopotamian Adult Black Slave Workers by Occupation

	NO.	MEAN YEARS PRIME OCC.	SECOND OCC.	TOTAL OCC.	HEALTH IN % ABLE	SICK	INVALID	MEAN AGE AT DEATH
MALES:								
Drivers	13	15.1	16.0	31.1	65	29	7	56.1
Craftworkers	40	19.0	3.5	22.5	55	37	8	44.6
Stockkeepers	38	20.7	3.8	24.5	59	35	6	43.8
Fieldworkers	177	13.2	7.2	20.4	47	48	5	42.2
Domestics	3	5.7	9.3	15.0	56	34	10	38.3
Marginal	26		10.8	10.8	3	75	22	48.4
Nonworkers	11						100	28.5
TOTALS	308	13.4	6.7	20.1	48	45	7	43.4
FEMALES:								
Drivers	3	14.3	16.3	30.6	29	47	24	59.3
Fieldworkers	182	15.6	5.3	20.9	43	42	15	45.3
Domestics	3	29.3	2.7	32.0	47	51	2	52.0
Marginal	13		10.6	10.6	5	66	29	57.3
Nonworkers	12						100	45.6
TOTALS	213	14.0	5.4	19.4	41	43	16	46.4

internal ruptures that he was made a watchman and fisherman. He continued in this secondary line of employment through age sixty-six, was an invalid for two years, and died at sixty-eight. In Table 4 Strephon is one of the 177 male field workers and is credited with twelve years of primary labor and thirty-five years of secondary labor. Pooling the employment data for all the male field workers from age sixteen onward, Table 4 shows that they averaged 13.2 recorded years in the field gangs and 7.2 years in a variety of secondary occupations, for a total 20.4 years of adult employment. This table also aggregates the annual health reports for each of these workers. Again to use the example of Strephon, during his career at Mesopotamia he was listed as in sound or "able" health in six inventories, as "ruptured," "badly ruptured," or "weak" in forty-one inventories, and as a nonworking invalid in two inventories. Collectively the 177 male field workers were able bodied 47 percent of the time, sickly 48 percent of the time, and nonworking invalids 5 percent of the time. They died at a mean age of 42.2.

The male and female slaves at Mesopotamia experienced somewhat differing patterns of health and life expectancy. Among the black men, the drivers had the longest careers and died at the most advanced ages, which is not surprising since they were elevated to this post in middle life, having been selected at least in part because of their proven durability. The stockkeepers worked longer and stayed healthier than the craft workers, but both groups had long careers by Mesopotamian standards, and two thirds of them stayed in the same line of adult work until they died or retired, without ever switching to secondary employment. A pen keeper named Neptune and a carter named Joe both held their jobs for forty-six years until they were sixty-two years old, and eleven other stock or craft workers served in their prime adult occupations for thirty years or more. The few adult males in domestic service were probably not robust enough for hard manual labor; this frailty would explain their short careers and early deaths. Collectively, the ninety-four comparatively privileged males in Table 4 served as adult workers at Mesopotamia for 24.1 recorded years on average—3.7 more years than the field hands—and died at the age of 44.8—2.6 years later than the field hands. More important from the sugar planter's point of view, the average field worker lasted only 13.2 years in the field gangs—7.5 fewer years of primary labor than the average stock-keeper. Almost all of the field workers were described in the inventories as "able" when they first entered into adult gang labor, but their health broke down rapidly, which surely suggests the deleterious effect of cane planting, weeding, and harvesting upon the strength and health of these slave laborers. The most durable male field worker was an African named Cromwell who toiled in the first or second gang for thirty-four years before being switched to watchman for the final fifteen years of his employment. Only four other males worked in the field gangs for as long as thirty years.

Among the black women, there were only six privileged job holders: three drivers and three domestics. These privileged women had long careers, but so too did a number of the 182 female field workers. Fifteen women toiled for thirty years or more in the fields, a record matched by only five men. Three of them—Bathsheba, Eve, and Priscilla—worked in the cane fields for forty years, a record matched by none of the men. Overall, it appears that the women at Mesopotamia who performed the same gang tasks as the men were tougher than the males and better survived the trauma of sugar field labor. Table 4 indicates that they outlived the men by three years. And among the field hands, the average woman put in 2.4 more years of prime gang labor than the average man. One might suppose that the female field workers were assigned to the second gang while the men performed the heavier tasks in the first gang, but such was not the case at Mesopotamia. From 1801 onward, when the inventories on this estate differentiate between membership in the two prime field gangs, there were always more females than males in the first gang.

The work that these women did in the cane fields clearly affected their health and probably damaged their reproductive capability. As Table 4 demonstrates, both men and women were generally reported to be in poor physical shape; they were sickly or incapacitated for more than half of their adult careers. But the women fared worse than the men, being sick or invalids 59 percent of the time. And although they lived longer, they spent more time in retirement, so that their average working careers were actually shorter than the men's. Fertility was very low among these women. The 504 females who lived at Mesopotamia between 1762 and 1831 produced only 410 recorded live births. Nearly half of the adult women had no recorded live births, and it would appear that gang labor was a contributing factor. The most prolific mother among the six privileged females in our cohort was a Mesopotamian-born seamstress and housekeeper named Minny, who had fourteen children. The most prolific mother among the 182 field workers was another Mesopotamian-born woman named Sally, who had ten children, and she was excused from field labor after the birth of her sixth baby when she was thirty years old, and spent the remainder of her life tending her children. Only five of the other field workers had big families of seven or more recorded children.[15]

Between 1762 and 1831 the labor force at Mesopotamia changed from a male to a female majority. In 1762 the male workers were clearly dominant; the sex ratio among the prime working slaves was 153/100. The managers of the estate did their best to sustain this ratio by introducing new young male laborers via the African trade, and by 1781 the sex ratio among the prime working slaves had climbed to 172/100. But when Joseph II began to recruit his new workers in Jamaica rather than from Africa, the male majority quickly eroded. By 1801 the sex ratio among the prime workers was down to 109/100, and from 1810 onward the female workers outnumbered the males. When the British government took a final slave census in Jamaica in August 1834, the sex ratio among the 316 slaves at Mesopotamia was 88/100 and among the prime workers was 87/100. This shift from male to female was by no means peculiar to Mesopotamia. In Jamaica as a whole the sex ratio changed from 100/100 to 95/100 between 1817 and 1832, and on the other big sugar plantations in Westmoreland parish the ratio changed from 88/100 to 82/100 between 1817 and 1834. Furthermore, by 1834 only one of the field gangs on the twenty-one largest Westmoreland sugar estates had a male majority.[16]

By way of summarizing our findings, Table 5 compares the overall work experience of the 186 slaves who were born on the

15 Some of these childless women may have produced babies who died within a few days of birth; such short-lived infants were generally not reported in the Mesopotamia birth and death registers.

16 For the overall Jamaican pattern, see Higman, *Slave Population and Economy*, 72. I have tabulated the sex ratios on 21 Westmoreland estates with 200 or more slaves in 1817 and 1834 from T 71/178; T 71/723, PRO.

Table 5 The Longevity of 538 Mesopotamian Adult Slave Workers by Gender, Origin, and Color

	NO.	ENTRY AGE	MEAN YRS PRIME JOB	SECONDARY JOB	TOTAL WORK	MEAN AGE AT DEATH
1. All males	322	21.7	13.4	6.5	19.9	43.0
All females	216	23.2	13.9	5.4	19.3	46.3
	538	22.3	13.6	6.0	19.6	44.4
2. Males born at						
Mesopotamia	110	16.0	17.1	5.7	22.8	40.9
Females born at						
Mesopotamia	76	16.0	16.9	5.7	22.6	42.4
	186	16.0	17.0	5.7	22.7	41.5
3. Males imported						
from Africa	121	19.1	14.7	8.7	23.4	43.8
Females imported						
from Africa	61	18.4	18.5	6.8	25.3	48.2
	182	18.8	16.0	8.1	24.1	45.3
4. Males from other						
Jamaican estates	91	31.9	7.0	4.3	11.3	44.6
Females from other						
Jamaican estates	79	34.0	7.4	3.9	11.3	48.7
	170	32.9	7.2	4.1	11.3	46.5
5. Mulatto Males	14	19.4	13.6	0.3	13.9	35.2
Mulatto Females	3	30.3	11.0		11.0	45.7
	17	21.4	13.2	0.2	13.4	37.1

estate with the 182 who were imported directly from Africa, and with the 170 who were purchased from other Jamaican estates. Here the seventeen mulatto laborers, who were excluded from Table 4 because of their skewed occupational distribution, are combined with the black workers (twelve mulattoes are among the Mesopotamian-born slaves and five are among the slaves imported from other Jamaican estates) and are also considered separately as a distinctive subgroup. In Table 5, the base point for analysis is the entry age of each group of slaves into the adult work force. Those born on the estate, as well as those imported to Mesopotamia before the age of sixteen, have entry ages of sixteen; those imported after the age of sixteen have the entry age listed in the first inventory after arrival. The slaves imported from Africa have a collective entry age only 2.8 years greater than the slaves born at Mesopotamia, because they arrived young, the majority as teenagers. But the slaves purchased from other Jamaican estates were collectively more than twice the age of the Mesopotamian-born slaves on entry into adult work; 28 percent of them were listed as age forty or above and 11 percent were listed as age fifty or above. As noted earlier, the stated ages of these older imported slaves must be treated with suspicion, being often rounded and probably inflated; hence both the mean entry age and the mean exit age for the 170 imported Jamaican slaves may well be several years too high. But the length of adult employment for these slaves, as for all the others, can be calculated with precision.

One striking feature of Table 5 is that the seventeen mulattoes, despite their privileged job status, had much shorter adult careers than the black slaves. They worked for only 13.4 years and died at the very early mean age of 37.1. The oldest of these mulattoes was Betty from Southfield, who was blind when she arrived at age fifty-nine and had to be tended to by one of the young children; after eleven years as an invalid she died at age seventy. Only one other mulatto in this group, a carpenter named William, lived to old age; he worked as an adult for forty-three years, was retired for another seven years, and died at age sixty-six. But the mulattoes collectively contributed very little to the Mesopotamian production system.

Table 5 also demonstrates that the 186 Mesopotamian-born slaves and the 182 slaves imported directly from Africa played a far more significant role in the Barhams' work force than the 170 slaves introduced from other Jamaican estates. The Jamaican imports put in only 11.3 adult years of work for the Barhams on average—less than half as much as their Mesopotamian and African counterparts—and they were invalids for 2.3 years before dying at a mean age of 45.3 The other two groups of slaves performed at an almost equal level: Mesopotamian-born workers served longer at their primary jobs, whereas Africans had the longer total employment. Mesopotamian-born workers had the handicap of being exposed to the local disease environment, poor nutrition, and regimented labor throughout childhood before starting adult employment. These people, having spent about ten years apiece as child laborers for the Barhams, worked a mean 22.7 years as adults, were invalids for 2.8 years, and died at age

41.5. The Africans may have been in better physical shape than the creoles when they entered the adult work force, but they had suffered the shock of captivity and compulsory adjustment to a strange and hostile new environment. It is noticeable that the African males lasted in their primary jobs a mean 2.4 years less than the Mesopotamian males. The African men may have lost their health more quickly because 79 percent of them were field hands as compared with 35 percent of the Mesopotamian men. Or they may have lost their spirit more quickly because of the degradation of being forced to perform women's work in the cane fields. In any case, the Africans collectively entered the adult work force at Mesopotamia at a median age of 18.8, labored for a median 24.1 years, were invalids for 2.4 years, and died at age 45.3.

The evidence from Mesopotamia suggests that first generation slaves, imported directly from Africa, endured the plantation work regimen at least as well as the second generation slaves who were born into the system. In particular, African female workers were more durable than the locally born women. On average they put 2.7 more years into adult labor and they died 5.8 years later. However, these African working women produced very few children at Mesopotamia. Evidence on this point is lacking before 1774, when the Mesopotamian inventories begin to identify the mothers of newborn infants, but between 1774 and 1831 the sixty-one African female workers in Table 5 produced only twenty-nine recorded live births; the seventy-six Mesopotamian-born women produced 117 recorded live births. Only twelve of the African women had children during this span, averaging 2.4 births each, whereas twenty-eight of the creole women had children, averaging 4.2 births each. Obviously neither of these records is impressive, but the crude birth rate at Mesopotamia did begin to rise after the Barhams stopped buying slaves directly from Africa. Thus comparison between the African and local workers suggests—from management's point of view—a no-win situation. The Africans tolerated the labor regimen at Mesopotamia well but did not breed, whereas the local slaves did breed but showed less tolerance for the labor system.

From a business point of view, it is clear that Joseph II made a mistake when he stopped buying slaves from Africa and voted in Parliament to abolish the slave trade. Like all the other Jamaican sugar planters he had to have replacement slaves, and—as Tables 3 and 5 have demonstrated—the most functional and durable replacement slaves at Mesopotamia came from Africa, not Jamaica. Had Barham followed the practice of his fellow planters between 1789, when he acquired the estate, and 1807, when the slave trade ended, he would have selected his replacement slaves from the African traders and thereby bolstered his work force as needed with prime young adult males, while largely avoiding the nuisance and expense of maintaining nonproductive children. But Barham broke away from this practice of his fellow planters for moral reasons. He not only rejected the slave trade but he expanded the size of his work force so as to lighten the labor of his slaves. Ironically, Barham's new policy contributed directly to the demographic problems at Mesopotamia that discouraged him so deeply by the 1810s and 1820s. When he added large numbers of overaged and unhealthy slaves from neighboring Jamaican estates to his work force, he unwittingly pushed the death rate at Mesopotamia above the median level for sugar estates in Westmoreland parish.[17]

The Barhams were certainly not solely motivated by altruism. Like any other sugar planters they wanted productivity and profit. In seventy-one crop seasons at Mesopotamia, from 1761 to 1831, their slave laborers produced 14,012 hogsheads of sugar and about 8,100 puncheons of rum shipped to Britain. This sugar and rum grossed approximately £595,000 Jamaican currency. Unfortunately, it is not possible to calculate the Barhams' running expenses during these years nor to reckon their net earnings, because the Mesopotamian accounts are much too incomplete. But it is clear that slave labor costs consumed a modest part of the Barhams' annual budget. Between 1762 and 1831, father and son paid a total of about £33,500 Jamaican currency to purchase 423 new slaves; the surviving accounts indicate that they expended an additional £30,000 to £35,000 in food, clothing, and medical care for the slaves during this period—in all, something like 10 to 12 percent of the gross income that they received from Mes-

---

17 A great many of the replacement slaves that JFB II bought from Jamaican estates had originally come from Africa. The first Jamaican slave registration in 1817 identified each slave by place of birth; according to this registration, 45% of the slaves that JFB II purchased from local estates had been born in Africa.

opotamia. Such figures suggest the rather modest limits of the Barhams' benevolence.[18]

Figure 1 charts productivity and profit at Mesopotamia against the changing size of the Barhams' slave force during the years 1761 to 1831. There were sharp swings in sugar and rum production from year to year, as there were in the market value of the crop. But the correlation between the size and value of the crop was generally close. There was much less correlation, however, between the size of the crop and the size of the slave gang.[19]

Looking at this productivity chart decade by decade, it can be seen that the boom period for output and profits at Mesopotamia was from 1782 to 1816. Thus the performance of this estate very poorly fits Williams' proposition that the British West Indian sugar industry reached its peak in the years before 1783, but fits very well with Drescher's argument that the peak period was from 1783 to 1807. Figure 1 also dramatizes the generational change at Mesopotamia: the elder Joseph in the years 1761 to 1789 operated on a decidedly smaller scale than his son in the years 1789 to 1831. The father had a labor pool averaging 261 men, women, and children; the son had a pool averaging 340.[20]

During the fifteen years before the American Revolution the estate grossed £5,800 annually, which was about the same figure as in the 1740s. The revolutionary war years, 1775 to 1781, constituted a depressed period at Mesopotamia. With the French contesting for naval control of the Caribbean, supplies were reduced and little sugar was exported. But the sale price per hogshead began to rise steeply in the late 1770s, ushering in an era of

18 The rum and sugar crop totals and valuations are compiled from several lists in Barham B34 and B37. The series of annual sugar totals is complete for these years, but one year of rum production (1777) is missing, and crop valuations are missing for 13 years (1777, 1796, 1817, and 1822–1831). I have supplied estimates for these missing years by extrapolating from the data in the Barham Papers and in Higman, *Slave Population and Economy*. Partial expense accounts for the estate can be reconstructed for the following years: 1770–1789, 1795, 1806, 1813–1820, 1830–1831. These accounts are scattered in Barham B33-37, C360, C389, and C428. The prices paid for 390 of the 423 slaves purchased in 1763–1820 can be traced in Barham B33, B36, and B37; I have estimated the cost of the remaining 33.

19 The productivity line in Figure 1 combines the annual totals for sugar and rum exports, reckoning each puncheon of rum as equivalent to ⅕ of a hogshead of sugar. See Barham B34; C389, bundle 8; Higman, *Slave Population and Economy*, 235–236.

20 Eric Williams, *Capitalism and Slavery* (New York, 1966; orig. pub. 1944), 120–127; Seymour Drescher, *Econocide: British Slavery in the Era of Abolition* (Pittsburgh, 1977), 16–25, 65–91.

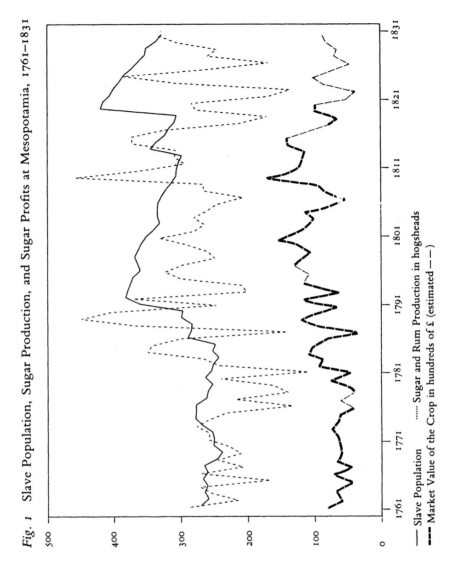

Fig. 1 Slave Population, Sugar Production, and Sugar Profits at Mesopotamia, 1761–1831

—— Slave Population
······ Sugar and Rum Production in hogsheads
▬ ▬ Market Value of the Crop in hundreds of £ (estimated — —)

large exports and high sales averaging nearly £9,000 per annum through Joseph I's final years in the 1780s. It was against this background that young Joseph II augmented his labor force by buying eighty-nine new slaves in 1791/92. Although Joseph II claimed to be lightening the workload of his slaves, a more cynical interpretation of the evidence in Figure 1 (such as Williams might have arrived at) would conclude that he was mainly hoping for bigger crops. With the exception of four bad years, production and profits continued at a high level from 1789 through 1816. During this long period, which was marked by extended naval war in the West Indies between Britain and France, Mesopotamia's sugar and rum exports were valued at nearly £11,000 per annum. In 1810 the estate produced its peak crop—361 hogsheads of sugar and 164 puncheons of rum valued at £16,957. However, the Mesopotamian slave gang was not at peak strength in 1810; with no reinforcements since 1793, the number of prime workers had dwindled from 188 to 146. Joseph II's attorneys unctuously assured him that the bumper crop of 1810 was produced without any extra exertion by the Mesopotamia slaves, who "work well, and go cheerfully, and contentedly through their work."[21]

By this time the African slave trade had closed and Joseph II was in an optimistic mood, looking for reformed management practices by his attorneys, more births and fewer deaths from his slaves, and continuing profits for himself. The attorneys had been nagging him for years to let them buy some additional laborers for Mesopotamia, and in 1814 he approved the purchase of fifty-six new slaves from Cairncurran estate, a coffee plantation in the mountain district of Westmoreland. Immediately after the Cairncurran slaves arrived, the estate produced two more large and profitable crops in 1815/16, which seem to have prompted Joseph II to take an especially bold step in 1819. Without consulting his attorneys, he bought a newly established sugar estate called Springfield in an isolated mountain district of neighboring Hanover parish, and ordered that the entire gang of 112 slaves on this property be removed to Mesopotamia as soon as practicable.[22]

But the Springfield transfer worked out very poorly. This estate was situated only about six miles north of Mesopotamia as

<hr/>

21 Grant and Blyth to JFB II, 11 Aug. 1810, Barham C358.
22 Grant and Blyth to JFB II, 7 Feb. 1814, 28 Jan. 1819, Barham C358; JFB II to Grant and Blyth, 11 July 1814, 9 Dec. 1818, 4 Aug. 1819, Barham C428.

the crow flies, but it was some twelve miles distant by foot via tortuous trails impassable for vehicular traffic. The Springfield slaves did not want to leave their old neighborhood, and when the attorneys ordered them to move to Mesopotamia in 1820 fully half of the gang "skulked in the bushes for a week." They kept returning home on weekends—or absconding for longer periods—to visit family and friends back in Hanover. On hearing about this, Barham complained: "I think it very ungrateful in them towards me to act thus."[23]

Although the Cairncurran and Springfield purchases swelled the Mesopotamian slave population to 420 in 1820, sugar production on the estate was actually lower during the next decade than it had been in the 1810s, and, because sugar prices also fell, Joseph II grossed little more than his father had done in the 1760s. As Figure 1 shows, the Mesopotamian population declined precipitously during this final decade, largely because the Springfield slaves died off quickly. By 1831—just twelve years after their purchase—fifty-three of these people were dead, two had run away, six were nonworking invalids, and twenty-three were in secondary jobs, leaving only twenty-eight Springfield slaves as members of the prime work force.

Between 1805 and 1825, Plummer & Co., Joseph II's sugar broker, deposited £47,583 sterling into his bank account. Receipts for Joseph II's final years are missing, but he cannot have extracted much further income from Mesopotamia. By 1823, after two years of very poor returns, he was becoming openly disgusted with black slave labor. It was in this year that he published his pamphlet calling for the nationalization of the West Indian sugar industry and characterizing the slave workers as "dreadful idlers." By 1829 he was advising his attorneys to warn the Mesopotamian slaves that they had one last chance to reform. Unless they started to produce more children, he would punish them by reducing their food supplies. Or he would form the women who had miscarriages or abortions into a jobbing gang, and hire them out to labor on other estates.[24]

---

23 Grant and Blyth to JFB II, 24 April, 12 June, 3 July, 27 Aug. 1820, Barham C358; JFB II to Grant and Blyth, 7 Dec. 1820, Barham C428. As late as 1826, the Springfield slaves were still absconding to Hanover. William Ridgard to JFB II, 4 March 1824, Barham C358; same to same, 2 May 1826, Barham C359.

24 JFB II's bank books for 1805–1825 are in Barham C389. Some of the deposits from

But if Joseph II lost faith in his workers, they did not lose faith in him. In 1831/32, when a massive slave rebellion broke out in western Jamaica, the Mesopotamian slaves displayed conspicuous loyalty to their absentee master. This rebellion was known as the Baptist War because it was fomented by slave converts to Christianity who were inspired by the Bible to strike for freedom. It started in St. James parish, near Montego Bay, on December 27, 1831, just as our final Mesopotamian inventory was being recorded, and it spread rapidly to Hanover, Westmoreland, and St. Elizabeth parishes. Over 200 plantations were destroyed or damaged, including several within a few miles of Mesopotamia. As the rebellion spread, very few slave gangs refused to join in. But when two rebel agents came to Mesopotamia, Barham's slaves seized them and brought them as prisoners to the militia guardhouse at Savanna la Mar. In early January 1832, when the entire white managerial staff on the estate—the attorneys, overseer, and bookkeepers—were all out on patrol against the rebels, the Mesopotamian slaves started up the sugar mill on their own and during the next month produced fifty-five hogsheads of sugar and ten puncheons of rum.

Moravian missionaries reported to Barham that the Mesopotamian slaves "conducted themselves throughout [the rebellion] in the most exemplary manner," and even Barham's attorneys acknowledged that "at Mesopotamia the Negroes have behaved remarkably well"—although they complained that the rum produced during the rebellion "will be found clowdy it being taken off under the management of the Negroes when all the white people were on militia duty." The two chief loyalist leaders among the Mesopotamian slaves were Samuel Williams, a thirty-four-year-old driver who had spent all his life on the estate, and Richard Gilpin, a thirty-five-year-old mason who had been purchased in 1820 from Springfield. Both of these men were congregants at the Moravian chapel sponsored at Mesopotamia since the 1760s by the Barhams.[25]

Plummer & Co. represent earnings from another Jamaican plantation owned by JFB II—Island estate in St. Elizabeth parish. JFB II to Duncan Robertson and Ridgard, 2 Sept. 1829, Barham C428.

25 Ridgard and Robertson to JFB II, 10 Feb., 16 March 1832, Barham C389; John H. Buchner, *The Moravians in Jamaica, 1754–1854* (London, 1854), 86–88; Mary Turner, *Slaves and Missionaries: The Disintegration of Jamaican Slave Society, 1787–1834* (Urbana, Ill., 1982),

Contrary to Williams' argument that the West Indian blacks rebelled at the first opportunity of freedom, the Mesopotamian slaves refused to torch their master's property when they had the chance in 1831/32. Contrary to Joseph II's allegation that they had to be forced to work, the Mesopotamian slaves voluntarily started up the strenuous sugar harvesting process on their own. And contrary to my contention that they were brutally exploited, the Mesopotamian slaves behaved toward their owners and managers with touching loyalty. No doubt the two Moravian missionaries who stayed on the plantation throughout the six week rebellion did their best to school the slaves in passive obedience. Yet surely the Mesopotamian people acted as they did in 1831/32 because they felt well treated, and because they believed that the Barhams were good masters, more benevolent and humane than most other Jamaican slaveholders. Such a conclusion gives our story a final ironic twist, for, however well intentioned the Barhams may have been, the evidence from their estate records plainly demonstrates that the labor system practiced at Mesopotamia sentenced the slave workers to broken health and early death.

148–178; Craton, *Testing the Chains: Resistance to Slavery in the British West Indies* (Ithaca, 1982), 291–321; Ridgard and Robertson to John Barham, 31 Jan. 1833, Barham C360. Barham sent Gilpin a watch as a reward, but the attorneys were afraid that the other Mesopotamia slaves would be jealous of Gilpin, so the watch went to the head driver at Barham's Island estate in St. Elizabeth parish who had risked his life to stop the rebels from firing the Island sugar works.

Part IV. The Basis of Abolition and Emancipation

Seymour Drescher

Paradigms Tossed: Capitalism and the Political Sources of Abolition

Appearing in 1944, *Capitalism and Slavery* was a comprehensive attempt to explain the rise and fall of British colonial slavery in relation to the evolution of European world-capitalism.[1] For the final stages of British slavery, Eric Williams developed a two-pronged argument linking its demise to changes in the British imperial economy. The first prong emphasized changes in the economic balance between the metropolis and the colonies. Down to the American Revolutionary War, concluded Williams, British slavery and the British Atlantic slave trade were growing and complementary elements of the imperial economy. The slave system provided an ever-increasing amount of tropical staples, a protected market for British manufacturers, and a main source of British metropolitan capital. In a number of ways the slave economy helped to fuel the Industrial Revolution. Williams's second prong related the political economy of Caribbean slavery to an economic ideology designated as mercantilism. Mercantilism theoretically rationalized the multiple linkages of the system by assuming the need for a protected imperial zone in which British manufacturers, trade, and maritime skills could develop.

For Williams, the American Revolutionary War dramatically changed the economic and ideological relationship that had hitherto sustained and nurtured the slave system. British colonial production, under increasing competition from its French counterpart, ceased to provide what was needed by the Empire amply or cheaply enough. According to *Capitalism and Slavery*, 1776 began the "uninterrupted decline" of the British West Indies as a

This chapter was prepared under a grant from the Woodrow Wilson Center for Scholars, where the author was a Fellow in 1983–84.
I wish to express my gratitude to the Bellagio conferees for their helpful comments.
1 Eric Williams, *Capitalism and Slavery* (New York, 1966).

producer of British staples, as a consumer of British industrial output, and as a contributor to British capital.[2] The very capitalism that had been nurtured by slavery now destroyed the fetter on its own further development. At precisely the same moment a new political economy was adumbrated, in Adam Smith's *Wealth of Nations*. It viewed the protected colonial trade as a brake on the creation of national wealth. The demise of slavery was thus perfectly entwined with the rise of laissez-faire.

At a less global level *Capitalism and Slavery* also provided a detailed set of rigorous economic motivations for the short-run surges and stalemates in the process of British abolition. The failure of the British West Indies to recover its rate of profitability after the American war combined with the growth of foreign staple sources to set the stage for the rise of abolitionism in the 1780's. The Saint-Domingue revolution momentarily stemmed the abolitionist tide, but colonial overproduction induced abolition of the slave trade in 1806–07 and emancipation in 1833. All of this was set against the background of a continuous decline in West Indian profits, imperial significance, and metropolitan economic support. One by one those interests which had once supported slavery turned against it.[3] Each and every tightening of the noose could be explained by reference to the interplay of economic patterns and motives. *Capitalism and Slavery* also contained two interesting post-scriptural chapters on the roles of the abolitionist "Saints" and of the colonial slaves, but the main story was carried along by economic determinants.

In the generation after the appearance of *Capitalism and Slavery* a number of objections were raised to some of Williams's short-run interpretations, but all his major structural arguments became deeply entrenched in the historiography of British slavery: the rise of abolitionism was closely correlated with the rise of laissez-faire and the decline of the British West Indies. The first of these elements rested on a tradition of imperial history that regarded the American Revolution as having divided the "old" mercantilist from the "new" laissez-faire British Empire. The second element rested on the work of a number of historians of the Caribbean, above all Lowell Ragatz's massive *Fall of the Planter*

2 *Ibid.*, p. 120
3 *Ibid.*, p. 154.

Class in the British West Indies, 1763–1833. The striking novelty of *Capitalism and Slavery* lay in Williams's lively fusion of these two historiographical streams.

The systematic discussion of *Capitalism and Slavery* is in fact little more than a decade old. Apart from Roger Anstey's initial foray in the *Economic History Review* (1968),[4] *Capitalism and Slavery* was either praised in passing or summarily dismissed, both without extended analysis. It therefore percolated, rather than flowed, into historiographical discourse for reasons which would make an interesting study in its own right.[5] By the mid-seventies, the Williams decline theory was being described by some historians as the new orthodoxy.

A major challenge appeared with the publication of two works. In *The Atlantic Slave Trade and British Abolition* (1975), Roger Anstey attacked some of Williams's short-run interpretations, especially the motives for British abolition in 1806–07. In *Econocide* (1977) I challenged both the long- and short-term premises of *Capitalism and Slavery*. Employing the very data used by both contemporary actors and by Williams to show the "amazing value" of the British West Indies before 1775, I argued that there was no decline in the value of the British slave system until well after the abolition of the slave trade.[6] There was, in other words, a disjuncture between the dramatic rise of political abolitionism around 1790 and the economic decline of its target only 30 years later.

I also took sharp issue with the premise that there was a major shift in the political economy of the British Empire following the American Revolution. Here too, I found that the change required by the Williams thesis was not tangibly operative until

4 2nd Series, XXI (1968), no. 2, pp. 307–320. See also his "A Re-interpretation of the Abolition of the British Slave Trade, 1806–07," *Economic History Review*, LXXXVII (1972), no. 343, pp. 304–332.

5 Cf. Cecil Gutzmore, " 'The Continuing Dispute over the Connections between the Capitalist Mode of Production and Chattel Slavery,' presented at the Sesquicentennial of the Death of William Wilberforce and the Emacipation Act of 1833," pp. 2–6.

6 *Capitalism and Slavery*, pp. 52–54, 225–226, tables; *Econocide: British Slavery in the Era of Abolition* (Pittsburgh, 1977), pp.16–25. See also S. Engerman and D. Eltis, "Economic Aspects of the Abolition Debate" in Christine Bolt and Seymour Drescher, eds., *Anti-Slavery, Religion, and Reform: Essays in Memory of Roger Anstey* (Folkestone, England, and Hamden, Conn., 1980), pp. 272–293; and S. Engerman, "Slavery and Emancipation in Comparative Perspective: A Look at Some Recent Debates," *Journal of Economic History*, XLVI, no. 2 (June 1986), pp. 317–339.

at least three quarters of the age of British abolitionism (1788–1838) had expired, if then. The thrust of my argument was quite clear. If British slavery was economically expanding at the moment that its growth was decisively inhibited by political action, its economic decline was contingent upon, not determinative of, abolition. Relative economic decline may well have eased the late stages of destruction, but a structural change in imperial political economy could not have been determinant at either the beginning or the middle of the abolition process.

Since *Econocide* appeared, it is clear that the factors most important to Williams, a coalescence of antagonistic economic interests and a shift in political economy, have not been documented by further research as playing their allotted role in the decline and fall of slavery. Just as *Capitalism and Slavery* may have exaggerated the importance of the West Indies to the imperial economy before 1775, so it appears to have exaggerated the diminution of its importance to Britain after 1783. It is more likely that at least until 1815 two growing, if unequal, economic systems faced each other, rather than a rising one and a declining one.

Most of those who accept the main critique of the Williams thesis as valid, are nonetheless still attracted by his relocation of the source of abolition. They therefore seek alternative explanations somehow grounded in fundamental economic development. Even if my book overturned most of the factual grounding of Williams's argument, there still "remains something unassailable in this thesis concerning the connection between economics and abolition."[7]

Embodied in this reaction are two fundamental propositions. The first of these is a historiographical presumption that it is surely no accident that abolition coincided with the Industrial Revolution. The second and more recent premise, however, is that the abolition of slavery cannot be explained by direct extrap-

---

7 P.C. Emmer, review in *Belgisch Tijdschrift voor Filologie en Geschiedenis*, LVII, 3 (1979). For subsequent discussion see Walter Minchinton, "Williams and Drescher," *Slavery and Abolition* 4:3 (September 1983), pp. 81–105; S. Drescher, "The Decline Thesis of British Slavery since *Econocide*," *ibid.* 7:1 (May 1986) pp. 3–24; Selwyn Carrington, " 'Econocide'—Myth or Reality—The Question of West Indian Decline, 1783–1806," and my reply, "Econocide, Capitalism and Slavery: A Commentary," both in *Boletin de Estudios Latinoamericanos y del Caribe*, 36 (June 1984), pp. 13–67.

olation from pure economic motives or mechanisms any more than from pure moral consciousness. Most of the alternative approaches thus far lean toward an attempt to find an indirect economic cause for emancipation in a new ideological base for abolitionism. The principal target of scholarly concern has become the antislavery "ideology"—some combination of economic and noneconomic ideas that called forth the abolitionist crusade and permitted it to triumph. There has also been a renewed search for an ideological combination which will include both the abolitionist spokesmen and the political economists of industrializing Britain.

One line of argument, exemplified by Howard Temperley, assumes the empirical weakness of the Williams thesis but focuses on the assumption of free labor's superiority as the significant variable that carried abolitionism to victory. Temperley is less concerned with the economic sources of abolitionism than with its ideological conformity to British political economy as interpreted by Adam Smith.[8]

David Brion Davis's *Problem of Slavery in the Age of Revolution* (1975) similarly focuses on the ideological significance of antislavery as a response to the rise of capitalism.[9] In Davis's study, colonial slavery, whether in decline or not, is not of fundamental concern. The primary social function of abolitionism lay not in the subversion of an overseas economic class (the slaveowners), but in the deflection of metropolitan working-class antagonism. Davis therefore gives an interesting twist to William Cobbett's assertion that the labor of slaves had "been converted into the means of making us slaves at home."[10] For Davis it is not the West Indians, but their abolitionist antagonists, who indirectly converted antislavery into a vehicle for social control, and who strengthened the invisible chains being forged at home. Davis, like Temperley, also clearly suggests the importance of examining the intended and unintended consequences of antislavery. Its ideology was an elastic lens that could transmit more than one

8 Temperley, "Anti-Slavery as a Form of Cultural Imperialism," in Bolt and Drescher, eds., *Anti-Slavery, Religion, and Reform*, pp.335–350; and "The Ideology of Antislavery," in D. Eltis and J. Walvin, eds., *The Abolition of the Atlantic Slave Trade: Origins and Effects in Europe, Africa and the Americas* (Madison, Wisc., 1981).
9 Davis, *The Problem of Slavery in the Age of Revolution, 1770–1823* (Ithaca, N.Y., 1975).
10 Williams, *Capitalism and Slavery*, p. 133.

vision of social priorities. If he emphasizes that abolitionism helped primarily to clear an ideological path for British industrialists, he notes that it also stimulated a new sensitivity to social oppression, although not specifically among abolitionists.[11]

In contrast to Temperley, antislavery ideology for Davis is less an extrapolation from the successes than from the stresses of the metropolitan Industrial Revolution. Reacting to the emergence of wage labor in an industrial society, abolitionists deflected attention away from the final demolition of paternalistic restraints on the labor market. (Along similar lines, Duncan Rice sees *The Scots Abolitionists* as similarly afflicted by the shortcomings of early industrialism, and as achieving similar respite from their anxieties over domestic social conditions.[12]) In Davis's paradigm, Temperley's "free and willing" laborers become E. P. Thompson's wage slaves, hegemonized away from class struggle. I would like, however, to emphasize the common problem to which they address themselves. In both cases the ground has shifted sharply back from the direct clash of imperial economic forces to battles for the minds and hearts of metropolitans.

Underlying this new historiographical focus is an assumption that the history of abolition can best be treated as a new politico-ideological history. The dispute between Williams and the Coupland school, between the primacy of humanity and of economics, is resolved or dissolved with the observation that the "free labor ideology" identified slavery as both immoral and inefficient.[13] The manifest content of antislavery as a coherent at-

---

11 Davis, *Problem of Slavery*, pp. 337–379, 455–456. This work concludes that British abolitionism was elastic enough to breed "sensitivity to social oppression" as well as to help the conservative social disciplinarians win the battle of the Industrial Revolution (*ibid.*, pp. 461–468). However, Davis's major spokesmen for abolitionism are all designated as defenders of the political status quo and social control. Before the mid-1820's abolitionism's putative power to sensitize is exemplified by those who were either venomously anti-black or West Indian apologists. Aside from these, the latent domestic conscience of British abolitionism is represented only by a revolutionist who arrived in Britain after colonial slave emancipation (*ibid.*, pp. 467–468). For the greater part of the age of British abolition, then, the moral vision of the "initial abolitionists" was seemingly inelastic. Domestic sensitivity was extrinsic to their vision, the preserve of anti- or nonabolitonists. See also Drescher, "Cart Whip and Billy Roller: Antislavery and Reform Symbolism in Industrializing Britain," *Journal of Social History* 15:1 (Fall, 1981), pp. 3–24; and the chapter by David Brion Davis in this volume.

12 *The Scots Abolitionists, 1833–1861* (Baton Rouge and London, 1981), pp. 34–35.

13 Engerman and Eltis, "Economic Aspects," p. 285; Eltis, "Abolitionist Perceptions of Society After Slavery," in J. Walvin, ed., *Slavery and British Society 1776–1846* (London, 1982), pp. 195–213.

tack on injustice is reanalyzed as a metropolitan "false conscious-ness" or a displacement of metropolitan realities.

The historians of ideology, accepting Williams's premise that humanitarian ideals cannot alone explain the emergence and triumph of antislavery, look toward the convergence of those ideals with those of emergent capitalist ideologues and assume a conscious or unconscious alliance between the capitalist ruling class and the Saints. Their response to the old question of how humanitarian ideology was converted into political victory is, basically, to search for additional capitalist ideological strata. That is, in addition to humanitarianism they have uncovered addi-tional levels of contemporary thinking about society, especially elite assumptions about free labor in a capitalist society. The question of just how these ideological strata functioned among the abolitionists is somewhat obscure.

This still poses the problem of accounting, not just for the capitalists' sense of free labor's superiority, but precisely why "reformers in metropolitan societies should have invested so much energy in securing its removal."[14] As Temperley notes, the com-mercialized Italian Renaissance city-states made no effort to im-pose antislavery values either at home or in their overseas colo-nies. It strikes me that it is not enough merely to contrast the Renaissance city-states with the polities of late eighteenth-cen-tury Europe and their colonial networks which encircled the globe. For the fact is that there were far more eighteenth- and nineteenth-century "free labor" metropolises in which virtually no antislav-ery energy was expended than those in which it was. Against the Anglo-American areas one must set the virtual absence of met-ropolitan abolitionism in Denmark, Sweden, the Netherlands, and Portugal, the belated movement in Spain, and the sputtering combustibility of France. Almost *all* of these nineteenth-century metropolises had colonies and trading posts spread over three oceans. Nor did abolitionism require far flung possessions. There was more abolitionist mobilization in the United States than in any continental European polity.[15] Abolitionism clearly did not develop ubiquitously in societies with free labor at home and overseas slave colonies.

14   Temperley, "Ideology of Antislavery," p. 30.
15   S. Drescher, "Two Variants of Anti-Slavery: Religious Organization and Social Mobilization in Britain and France, 1780–1870," in Bolt and Drescher, *Anti-Slavery*, pp. 43–45.

The question of geographical and temporal specificity is therefore legitimately posed by those skeptical of ideological history: why abolition, and why in Anglo-America at the end of the eighteenth century? One can grant that people mobilize for, or are directed toward, social ends with a very limited range of general ideas about the way the world is going. Historians of antislavery ideology rightly draw attention to the fact that the world view of the abolitionists was embedded in a vision of development which made obvious sense to the overwhelming majority of their politically articulate contemporaries. If these historians have occasionally overemphasized the "labor" component in the ideology of liberty, the superiority of free societies seemed verified by the experience of metropolitan people and the power of metropolitan states.

But if certain ideas about civilization were necessary before the abolitionist takeoff could begin they hardly seem sufficient. One need only survey how intellectuals perceived the balance of power on the eve of abolitionism to conclude that they expected no rapid change in the way that slave labor was distributed throughout the world. One must therefore also develop a convincing scenario of how—and why—abolitionist ideas became translated into action and into abolitionist policies. At some point historians must therefore reunite economic and ideological with political history in order to present a convincing analysis of the abolition of British slavery. Otherwise the ideological history of the hundred years' war against chattel slavery remains a history of antislavery's general staff.

If overseas slavery was one of the requisites of abolitionism, a highly articulated political life in the metropolis was another. It was more difficult for British abolitionists to rouse the natives of continental Europe to sustained abolitionist fervor in the nineteenth century than it was to convert the slaves beyond the line.[16] The Swedish abolition society held one meeting and rejected public petitioning in favor of a private appeal to the king. The Netherlands offered a case of "abolition without reform," following a stolid path to emancipation 30 years after the British. Emmer characterizes Dutch abolition in a line drawn from Heinrich Heine:

16 Drescher, *Capitalism and Antislavery: British Mobilization in Comparative Context* (London and New York, 1986), chapter 3.

"If the world were to come to an end, I would to go to Holland, where everything happens 50 years later."[17] Slow-growing metropolises with dynamic slave sectors delayed even longer in conforming to the British example. The Spanish government resisted rigorous suppression of the Atlantic slave trade for almost two generations. British hegemony over Portugal in the early nineteenth century did not bring about the early elimination of slavery in Portuguese Africa.

The Iberian cases also remind us that the slave sector was not always the more "dependent" sector of the metropolitan-colonial relationship. Historians who make the ultimate question of abolition rest on the balance of military and political power between slave and nonslave areas must also take note that the Brazilian plantocracy was demonstrably equal to the task of guaranteeing both its self-perpetuation as a ruling class and its independence from Portugal.[18] It was ultimately Great Britain that played the principal role of abolition metropolis to Brazil.[19]

In most metropolitan cases a low level of abolitionism seems to have been linked to a generally low level of popular political mobilization. France provided another variant, in which metropolitan mobilization, coming in two great revolutionary surges, was not internally channeled in the direction of sustained abolitionism. Revolutionary France was of course the first metropolitan area to abandon its colonial slave system (1794). But France also had the distinction of restoring slavery and the slave trade in 1802 and again in 1814. Its definitive termination of the slave trade did not occur until a generation after Britain's.[20] French colonial slavery was not abolished until 1848, 15 years after the British initiative. Each major French thrust occurred without a popular abolitionist mobilization in the metropolis.

It was in Britain where the diffuse and often ambivalent ide-

17 P. C. Emmer, "Anti-Slavery and the Dutch: Abolition without Reform" in Bolt and Drescher, eds., *Anti-Slavery*, pp. 80–98, Introduction.
18 See the general argument in E. Fox-Genovese and E. D. Genovese, *Fruits of Merchant Capital: Slavery and Bourgeois Property in the Rise and Expansion of Capitalism* (New York, 1983), pp. 41–43.
19 Leslie Bethell, *The Abolition of the Brazilian Slave Trade* (Cambridge, 1970). For Cuba, see David R. Murray, *Odious Commerce: Britain, Spain and the Abolition of the Cuban Slave Trade* (Cambridge, 1980).
20 See Drescher, "Two Variants of Anti-Slavery," pp. 43–63; and *Capitalism and Anti-slavery*, chapter 3.

ology of antislavery became rooted as a national social movement at the cutting edge of the Industrial Revolution. It was British public opinion that launched the great "takeoff" of abolitionism in the winter of 1787–88.[21] And it was the abolitionists of the booming, industrializing North of England, who, quite independently of the London Saints, made the mass abolition petition the principal new weapon of abolitionism. Manchester converted a London society that was little more than another low-key lobby like the Quakers into the first social reform movement.

Lancashire had not been particularly active in the reform movements of the 1760's and 1770's. The mid-eighties however, witnessed an extraordinary burst of capitalist development in Lancashire and Manchester in particular. Immediately after 1783 Britain's imports of raw cotton increased at a faster rate than in any other period of its dramatic history.[22] Meanwhile, a government coping with vastly increased indebtedness sought to enhance its revenues by tapping into this extraordinary development. When the government attempted to tax the fustian manufacturers, Manchester organized a massive repeal petition in the name of tens of thousands of Lancastrians whose livelihood depended upon the cotton industry.[23] Significantly, the Prime Minister backed down, explicitly acknowledging that his action was in direct response to the overwhelming popular reaction. Lancashire manufacturers also played a leading role in the petition campaign against a proposed customs union with Ireland. In that campaign Manchester interests were linked up with broader regional interests. Thomas Walker, the leader of the fustian campaign, joined forces with Josiah Wedgwood of the potteries to bring maximum extra-parliamentary pressure to bear upon the government.[24]

The result of these interest-oriented battles of the mid-eighties was to create the organizational expertise that could tap popular enthusiasm despite the still narrow constraints on popular

21 See Drescher, *Capitalism and Antislavery*, chapter 4; and E. M. Hunt, "The North of England Agitation for the Abolition of the Slave Trade, 1780–1800," M.A. thesis, University of Manchester, 1959.
22 Based upon B. R. Mitchell and P. Deans, *Abstract of British Historical Statistics*, (Cambridge, 1962) pp. 177–178.
23 See John Ehrman, *The Younger Pitt: The Years of Acclaim* (New York, 1969), pp. 208–209, 253.
24 *Ibid.*

expression in the 1780's. Manchester lacked both a corporate local government and a representative member in Parliament. There was little sense of division between those with specific electoral qualifications and those without.

Thus a portion of Manchester's elite, with Thomas Walker at their head, launched the abolition petition campaign in 1787 independently of London's leadership. Significantly, they aimed from the outset at a maximum enrollment of the male inhabitants. In the context of the late eighteenth century this was the largest legitimate target group for signatures. The almost 11,000 who signed the Manchester abolitionist petition formed just over 20 percent of the total population of the city. Even if adult males, swollen by migration, represented 30 percent of the city's population, more than two-thirds of Manchester's eligible male population, including the bulk of its workingmen, must have signed. The social depth of the Manchester petition campaign made a deep impression even on hostile contemporaries.[25]

The new social reform movement also moved smoothly along the channels provided by another eighteenth-century economic development. Britain's uniquely dense network of provincial newspapers, with their expanding advertisements, had led to a nationalization of the market by innovative entrepreneurs in the second half of the eighteenth century.[26] The abolitionists of Manchester innovatively decided to use subscription funds to advertise their own petition in every major newspaper in England, calling for similar petitions. At one stroke they placed Manchester on the national map as the pacesetter in abolitionism, and gave their own petition meeting the same ubiquitousness as though it had been a Parliamentary debate.

Manchester, rather than the Clapham Saints or the Quaker religious network, thus pushed Britain across the psychological and political threshold into the abolitionist era. It undermined the policy/morality dualism that had characterized the response to

25 Drescher, *Capitalism and Antislavery*, chapter 4. See also James Walvin, "The Rise of British Popular Sentiment for Abolition, 1787–1832," in Bolt and Drescher, *Anti-Slavery*, pp. 149–162; and S. Drescher, "Public Opinion and the Destruction of British Colonial Slavery," in J. Walvin, ed., *Slavery and British Society 1776–1846* (London, 1982); pp. 22–48.
26 Neil McKendrick et al., *The Birth of a Consumer Society* (Bloomington, Ind., 1982), pp. 77–99.

the first Quaker petition of 1783, and indeed to all previous suggestions to alter the British Atlantic slave system. Manchester was, after all, a hard-nosed manufacturing town, not a sect that could be politically discounted for its long tradition of tender conscience and sectarian isolation.

Manchester's economy was certainly not insulated from the African or the colonial trades. Some of its greatest manufacturers, including the Peels, were able to produce *anti*-abolitionist "interest" petitions from Manchester for another 20 years. The slave interest could accuse the abolitionists of being indifferent to the interests of fellow capitalists. But it could not credibly accuse the citizens of Manchester of making high moral pronouncements in total ignorance of commercial realities. When England's most successful boom town of the 1780's came down overwhelmingly on the side of abolition, and the inhabitants of dozens of cities and towns also petitioned against the trade, a repetition of Lord North's worldly-wise dismissal of the earlier Quaker petition in 1783 could no longer be regarded as inevitable.

It was not any ideological novelty about the superiority of freedom or free labor, but this new combination of elements drawn from the everyday political and economic activity in the 1780's that carried Britain into the age of abolition. It could not have been done so casually in the 1680's or even the 1740's. Manchester's catalytic role in the takeoff of 1787–88 should not therefore overshadow the national aspect of the initial and later campaigns. A closer reading of the descriptive evidence demonstrates that Manchester was part of a broad base of popular petitions from the very first campaign of 1787–88.

Abolitionism was also engrafted onto other everyday practices of commercial capitalism. For Josiah Wedgwood, slavery, after 1788, was no less promising an object for ceramic commemoration than the peace treaty with France, John Wesley, or Captain Cook.[27] So while the pottery workers of Staffordshire were signing up against the African traffic, their principal employer was trafficking in a new line of jasper medallions (with a generous seeding of free samples) depicting a kneeling slave asking "Am I not a man and a brother?" What was unusual about the slave medallion was the anonymity of the figure—an every-

27 *Ibid.*, p. 122.

man of a mass age. The printing press also produced the most famous pictorial representation of the slave-trade campaigns: the plan of a loaded slave ship, far less expensive to buy than even Wedgwood's medallion. If we may credit the cartoonist's instincts for background realism, slave-ship prints soon hung in homes throughout Britain.[28]

By 1791 another abolitionist technique emerged, again without the instigation of the London committee. As a weapon of consumer capitalism, a nationwide slave-sugar boycott achieved some initial successes. It also brought women directly into the orbit of the campaign. The abstention was as closely related to Britain's consumer revolution as Wedgwood's shrewd blending of philanthropy and production. Indeed, it made the proprietary abolitionist elite uncomfortable. They hesitated to sanction a movement launched not merely as a symbolic means of pollution avoidance, but as a weapon of the marketplace.

There is no way of knowing just how many people participated in the abstention movement at its height in 1791–92. Clarkson claimed that 300,000 families were involved. In light of my own rough estimate of petition signers in the second slave-trade campaign of 1792, this is not at all an unreasonable figure. The movement reached the main urban centers of Scotland and even beyond the petition zone to Ireland and Wales. Since it was a family-oriented strategy, special appeals were directed toward women. Some specifically emphasized women's otherwise excluded status from the political arena.[29]

How much weight should one assign to the unprecedented and unmatched British popular mobilization in the destruction of British slavery? Historians have often been skeptical about the short-run impact of popular petitions. The fate of the great radical petitions of the post-Napoleonic and Chartists eras casts doubt on the efficacy of the petition as a sufficient weapon in effecting

28 See caricatures in M. D. George, *Catalogues of Political and Personal Satires in the . . . British Museum*, 11 vols. (London, 1978), no. 8074, "AntiSaccharites, or John Bull and his family leaving off the use of sugar," by Gillray (March 27, 1792); and no. 8081 "The Gradual Abolition" (April 15, 1792).
29 On female initiatives, see the *Newcastle Courant*, January 7, 1792. There were advertisements for "free" sugar in Edinburgh in 1792, and calls for abstention in Glasgow and in Belfast. The first known advertisement in Welsh was published in 1797. Specific accounts of female-initiated abstentions and canvassing were published in Newcastle, Norwich, and Chester.

Parliamentary acquiescence. Yet even in short-run terms abolitionist petitioning was able to elicit an impressive record of legislative responses. Unlike Parliamentary and religious reform between the 1780's and 1820's, abolitionism did manage to obtain positive governmental action in the wake of all major waves of public mobilization.

For 40 years, from 1788 to 1838, the short-term record of abolitionist petition campaigns was in fact far superior to that of any other major social movement in unreformed Britain. To achieve this record abolitionism was probably condemned to ever more massive displays of support. In the late 1780's a total of 170 public petitions a year was the norm. Abolition made its mark by accounting for more than half of all those submitted in 1788. In the 1810's 900 petitions a year was the norm. Abolition responded by alone almost equaling that annual average in 1814. By the critical years 1828–33, petitioning had increased fivefold over the 1811–15 rate. The number of emancipation petitions increased *more* than fivefold. In 1831 and again in 1833 more petitions for immediate emancipation were sent up to Parliament than the annual average for *all* petitions for 1828–33. To put it another way emancipation petitions single-handedly increased the total number of public petitions by fully *50 percent* between 1828 and 1833.[30]

The case of France may reveal how much even a fraction of British mobilizations could achieve in a smaller pond. The average number of petitions to the French Chamber of Deputies in the six years before the second French slave emancipation was about 500 per year. This was about one-tenth the volume sent up to Parliament in 1828–33. The first mass slave emancipation petition submitted to the French Chamber of Deputies in 1844 was signed by about 7,000 Parisian workers. This was probably less than a ninth or a tenth of those who signed even the first British petition in 1788. Minuscule by British standards, it nevertheless sparked new, if minor, French legislation to regulate master–slave relations and conditions of manumission.

The second and last French abolitionist petition totaled only 10,700 names. Yet even the petition of 1847 produced a psycho-

---

30 Rates calculated on total petition figures given in *Parliamentary Papers* 1852–53, vol. LXXXIII, pp. 104–105: "Return of the Number of Petitions Presented in each of Five Years ending 1788–89, 1804–05, 1814–15 . . . [plus each year from 1828–52]."

logical debacle for the French colonial interest in the Chamber of Deputies. The Minister of the Colonies was forced to resign after an attempt to shield the colonies. The colonial agents were demoralized and broke ranks. Some threw themselves at the feet of the more conservative Parliamentary abolitionists in an attempt to introduce a pre-emptive emancipation plan of their own. All this came to pass in the wake of a petition campaign that had delivered no more signatures in 1847 than the city of Manchester alone six decades before with a population base of less than 0.2 percent of France's 35 million. The French petition did not appreciably advance legislation on slavery and the flurry subsided within a few months. But if 11,000 signatures alone could even momentarily break down 15 years of indifference in the French Chambers, we may have some inkling of the impact of more than a hundred times as many signers to the British petition of 1833.

More important than each immediate success was the long-term impact of such recurrent mobilizations. The creation of a climate of political opinion was the most important residue of renewed petitions. It became part of the consciousness of all those who played a role in shaping British policy regarding Atlantic slavery. Unlike most earlier eighteenth-century contentious gatherings, the abolitionist crowd was acting directly on the imperial legislature. It was not seeking a local rectification of a deviation from a traditional moral order, but demanding increasing overseas conformity to an emerging metropolitan moral order. An abolitionist petitioner was assured that he was part of a cumulative collective force both spatially and temporally. "Though for a time . . . unsuccessful," the Baptist Magazine assured potential petitioners; "the voice of the people could not be continually lifted up in vain."[31] The abolitionists therefore not only mobilized temporary opinion. Initial dismissal of abolitionism in 1788 as a "five-days fit of philanthropy" quickly yielded to the sense that a permanent change in the standards of overseas trade and labor relationships had occurred.

Abolitionism was more dependent upon petitions than other

31 *The Baptist Magazine for 1823*, XV, p. 283, cited in Drescher, "Public Opinion," p. 47. See also J. Walvin, "The Public Campaign in England against Slavery, 1787–1834," in D. Eltis and J. Walvin, eds., *The Abolition of the Atlantic Slave Trade: Origins and Effects in Europe, Africa and the Americas* (Madison, Wisc., 1981), pp. 63–79.

major movements to maintain its salience in Parliament. It usually lacked the immediacy of personal gain or loss, which most MP's perceived in Parliamentary or religious reform. It also lacked the ingredient of potential metropolitan upheaval, a "reserve army of violence," which played so great a role in the passage of Catholic emancipation and the Great Reform Bill. On the other hand, abolitionism's petition record over the period 1780–1838 as a whole was much better than those of political or religious reform. Out of doors, abolition was at the top of its ability to gather signatures in the 1780's, the 1790's, the 1810's, the 1820's, and the 1830's. It rose from 100 petitions and perhaps 60,000 to 75,000 signers in 1788, to over 5,000 petitions and almost 1,500,000 signers in 1833.[32] It was probably also unmatched in its ratio of metropolitan support to opposition. The cumulative petition canvas on slavery probably was on the order of 99.5 percent pro-immediatist in 1833. It is difficult to imagine that any other major campaign, including that for the Reform Bill itself, surpassed antislavery's petition ratio of more than 250:1.

Finally, if abolitionism did not possess a reserve army of violence, after 1815 its targets faced the threat of slave resistance occurring in tandem with metropolitan abolitionism. In comparative terms it is clear that in some other systems slave uprisings were of greater significance in determining the pace, or even the decision for, emancipation. The great Saint-Domingue slave revolution of 1791 played a central role in eliciting the French Republic's emancipation decree in 1794. The less famous rising in Martinique, in 1848, probably ensured that the new French Constituent Assembly would not move to reconsider or postpone Victor Schoelcher's French emancipation decree. Danish emancipation was also certainly accelerated by a Caribbean slave uprising in 1848.

Yet the dependence of French emancipation on overseas events in the 1790's showed how easily slavery could be revived by a metropolis when the balance of military power changed. Napoleon decreed the re-establishment of French colonial slavery immediately after the Peace of Amiens in 1803. The role of slave

32 Drescher, "Public Opinion," p. 28, figure 2; see also G. I. T. Machin, *The Catholic Question in English Politics* (Oxford, 1964), pp. 144–148.

resistance in British slave emancipation, while probably more significant than in the American case, was not as decisive as in the French and Danish cases.

The issue was efficacy rather than courage. Slaves demanding much less than freedom in the British islands risked far more than any metropolitan abolitionist. It was the political leverage of the British metropolitan masses that gave them the decisive advantage over the most heroic of Caribbean rebels.

The 10,000 Manchester petitioners who launched the popular movement to end the slave trade in 1788 probably exercised greater influence in placing abolition on the British political map than the ambivalent musings of the philosophers of the eighteenth century, and certainly more than the equivocal conclusions of political economists of the early nineteenth century.[33] And the more than 15,000 social events—to refer only to British abolitionist petitions which permeated the world of high politics for the next 50 years—were the most obvious indicator of a collective activity that differentiated the context of British overseas slavery from the slaveries of Mediterranean antiquity, medieval northern Europe, Renaissance Italy, and early modern Russia.

What is the import of this analysis on the general historiography of British antislavery outlined at the beginning of this chapter? As the role of Williams's putative grand coalition of capitalist interests proves increasingly difficult to document, those who are uncomfortable with ideological history or hegemonic paradigms have to consider the metropolitan free masses as a critical new variable in the history of slaves. They are the measurable, empirical fact—the new social force that differentiated Anglo-American mobilizations from 1780 to 1860 from those of continental Europe in scale and duration.

Stimulated by Eric Williams, the deeper understanding of the ecology of British slavery and antislavery dissipated the splendid moral isolation of antislavery so dear to the old Whig interpretation.[34] Historians could never again so casually reiterate the mid-Victorian invocation of the British antislavery crusade as

---

33 See D. B. Davis, *The Problem of Slavery in Western Culture* (Ithaca, N.Y., 1966), chapters 13 and 14; and Drescher, *Capitalism and Antislavery*, chapters 6–8.

34 S. Drescher, "The Historical Context of British Abolition," in David Richardson, ed., *Abolition and its Aftermath in the West Indies* (London, 1985) volume I, chapter 1.

among the "three or four perfectly virtuous pages comprised in the history of nations."[35] But they sometimes fall into the opposite trap and confuse the banality of most human actors, whether for good or evil, with their collective human achievements.

35 W. E. H. Lecky, *A History of European Morals* (London, 1869), 6th edition (1884), volume I, p. 153.

David Brion Davis

Capitalism, Abolitionism, and
Hegemony

Attention is turning once again to the almost simultaneous appearance of industrial capitalism and antislavery sentiment in Great Britain. Since the publication of Eric Williams's *Capitalism and Slavery,* more than a generation ago, the relation between these two broad forces has provoked considerable debate. As Howard Temperley demonstrates in his essay in this volume, the issues have acquired high ideological voltage in the Third World as well as in Britain and the United States.

Williams and his many followers have sought to portray Britain's antislavery measures as economically-determined acts of national self-interest, cynically disguised as humanitarian triumphs. Roger Anstey, who led the way in undermining Williams's case for economic motivation, viewed Christianity's role in abolitionism as nothing less than "a saving event within the context of Salvation History."[1] While few of Williams's opponents have shared this explicit faith in slave emancipation as a step toward historical redemption, it has been difficult to find a middle ground that rejects Williams's cynical reductionism but that takes account of the realities of class power. A historian who scrutinizes the moral pretensions of the abolitionists or who observes, to borrow a phrase C. Vann Woodward has applied to the American Civil War, that West Indian emancipation enabled Britain to add an immense sum to the national "treasury of virtue" and to bank on it for "futures in moral credit," runs the risk of being classified as a follower of Eric Williams. Yet national pride is especially dangerous and deceptive, as Reinhold Niebuhr re-

---

1 Roger Anstey, "Reflexions on the Lordship of Christ in History," *Christian,* 3/1 (Michaelmas, 1975), 69–80. See also David Brion Davis, "An Appreciation of Roger Anstey," in *Anti-Slavery, Religion, and Reform: Essays in Memory of Roger Anstey,* ed. by Christine Bolt and Seymour Drescher (Folkestone, England, 1980), pp. 11–15.

minded us, when it is based on the highest achievements of human history.[2]

In 1975, in *The Problem of Slavery in the Age of Revolution, 1770–1823,* I suggested that British abolitionism served conflicting ideological functions but that it helped, in this initial period, to reinforce the hegemony of capitalist values. This view has recently evoked fruitful criticism from Seymour Drescher, Thomas L. Haskell, and Betty Fladeland, among others.[3] Since I bear some responsibility for the misinterpretations that have been given to my "thesis," I would like to take this opportunity to restate and clarify my argument and to assess some of the criticisms.

I should first emphasize that my hegemonic argument fills only a few pages in a 570-page volume and that it applies only to British history in a limited period from the 1790's to 1823, with some brief speculations reaching ahead to the 1830's. In this volume I did not extend the concept of hegemony to America or France, where abolition movements emerged in wholly different contexts. Certainly I advanced no general theory of abolitionism per se as an instrument of hegemonic control. I have never meant to suggest that abolitionism can best be understood as a device for deflecting white working-class discontent or that it was not part of the wider egalitarian and liberalizing movement I described in *The Problem of Slavery in Western Culture* (1966).

It is important to distinguish the *origins* of antislavery sentiment, a subject I discussed at length in the first volume, from the *conditions* that favored the widespread acceptance of antislav-

2   C. Vann Woodward, *Thinking Back: The Perils of Writing History* (Baton Rouge, 1986), p. 112; Richard Wightman Fox, *Reinhold Niebuhr: A Biography* (New York, 1985), p. 181.
3   See especially Seymour Drescher, "Cart Whip and Billy Roller: Antislavery and Reform Symbolism in Industrializing Britain," *Journal of Social History,* 15/1 (Sept., 1981), 3–24; Drescher, *Capitalism and Antislavery: British Mobilization in Comparative Perspective* (New York, 1987); and Drescher's essay in this volume; Thomas L. Haskell, "Capitalism and the Origins of the Humanitarian Sensibility," Part 1, *The American Historical Review,* 90/2 (April, 1985), 339–361; and Part 2, *The American Historical Review,* 90/3 (June 1985), 457–566; Betty Fladeland, *Abolitionists and Working-Class Problems in the Age of Industrialization* (Baton Rouge, 1984). David Eltis's *Economic Growth and the Ending of the Transatlantic Slave Trade* (New York, 1987) and Robert William Fogel's forthcoming *Without Consent or Contract* extend my own arguments and show that they are not incompatible with the main empirical findings of Drescher and Fladeland. I am grateful to Professors Eltis and Fogel for allowing me to read early versions of their own extremely important manuscripts. I am also much indebted to Christopher Lowe, a Yale graduate student, whose seminar paper on "Ideology, Hegemony and Class Rule in *The Problem of Slavery in the Age of Revolution"* helped to clarify my own thinking.

ery ideology among various governing elites. This is a distinction that Thomas Haskell continually blurs. In all my work I have taken pains to emphasize the importance of religious sources of antislavery thought and the religious transformations that made slave emancipation a symbolic test of the efficacy of Christian faith. In *The Age of Revolution* I do not say, and here Haskell misquotes me, that the "origin" of the new humanitarian sensibility lay in "the ideological needs of various groups and classes."[4] I do maintain that "the continuing evolution" of antislavery opinion "reflected the ideological needs of various groups and classes."[5] I had in mind the ideological needs generated by the French Revolution and the early Industrial Revolution, by war, nationalism, and religious revivalism. At issue are the uses made of antislavery doctrine and rhetoric as the movement pulled away from the Painite radicals of the early 1790's, won legitimacy from government ministries in 1806–07, was appropriated by the aristocratic African Institution, and was then reshaped by wealthy merchant philanthropists.

In *The Age of Revolution* I had to deal with Britain in the period from 1793 to 1823, decades of reactionary politics and domestic repression that should not be confused with the era of social ferment and reform that accompanied West Indian slave emancipation and the abolition of apprenticeship. The crucial question, therefore, was not why groups of enlightened Britons, Frenchmen, and Americans attacked slavery from the 1760's to the 1780's, but why this single reform cause, which attracted significant radical support in the early 1790's and which some conservatives denounced as a Jacobin-front movement, won growing acceptance in the early nineteenth century from British political and social elites otherwise obsessed with the fear that social reform would open the gates to revolution.

During the long period from the late 1790's to 1823, the British public showed little interest in the slavery issue except at the end of the Napoleonic wars. In 1814 an eruption of petitions expressed outrage at the prospect that the government would allow France to resume the Atlantic slave trade, which Britain had earlier renounced on moral grounds. This brief popular outburst

4 Haskell, "Capitalism," Part 1, p. 344.
5 Davis, *The Problem of Slavery in the Age of Revolution, 1770–1823* (Ithaca, N.Y., 1975), p. 42.

drew on nationalistic pride and was orchestrated by abolitionist leaders who were eager to demonstrate to the courts of Europe that "with a single voice" the English people demanded international suppression of the slave trade. The cause served the purposes of Wellington and Castlereagh, who actively cooperated with the abolitionists. Castlereagh even requested a digest of anti-slave-trade evidence that could be translated into French in preparation for the Congress of Vienna. It was a notably reactionary and repressive British government that tried to influence French public opinion and bribe Spain and Portugal into ending or restricting the Atlantic slave trade.

Historians have often exaggerated the continuity of popular antislavery agitation from the late 1780's to the 1830's. The crucial antislavery measures from 1800 to 1823 were not the result of public pressure. Government leaders and a few influential abolitionists were responsible for the decisions to curtail and then stop the flow of African slaves to Guiana and other foreign colonies conquered by Britain, and then to prohibit the British slave trade to all foreign nations and colonies. The successful abolition bill of 1807 originated in the House of Lords; the prevailing public apathy and ignorance of the question prompted Wilberforce to publish and widely circulate *A Letter on the Abolition of the Slave Trade; Addressed to the Freeholders and Other Inhabitants of Yorkshire.* The later campaign to establish a central registry of all colonial slaves aroused little public interest, though it was seen as an essential preparatory step toward emancipation. Even in 1823 and 1824, when an organized emancipation movement got under way, the abolitionists who solicited petitions and organized auxiliary societies were surprised by the general public ignorance concerning West Indian slavery. Yet the governing elites had become increasingly committed to colonial labor reform. Why should colonial slavery have seemed so repugnant to such groups?

In pursuing this question I should have made it clearer that by "ideology" I did not mean a fixed set of ideas and doctrines used to promote concrete class interests. When referring to an ideology as a "mode of consciousness," I was thinking of a perceptual lens, a way of viewing social reality that helps to define as well as to legitimate class, gender, or other collective interests. Keeping this elasticity in mind, it is important to draw a distinction between the motives of individual reformers and the ideological context that gave hegemonic meaning to their rhetoric and influence.

When in 1786 Thomas Clarkson published his prize-winning Cambridge University essay on the horrors of the African slave trade, he clearly had no intention of condoning British child labor in factories and mines. But Clarkson's proslavery opponents like Gilbert Francklyn and Jesse Foot immediately contrasted the alleged comfort and security of West Indian slaves with the oppression of English workers and the plight of English children exposed to the "pestilential vapour" of factories. Francklyn pointedly asked why the universities did not offer prizes "for the best dissertation on the evil effects which the manufactures of Birmingham, Manchester, and other great Manufacturing towns, produce on the health and the lives of the poor people employed therein?" He proceeded to show how Clarkson's rhetorical techniques could be applied to the specific consequences of the early Industrial Revolution.[6]

Such antibolitionist counteroffensives had appeared even earlier and they would become a dominant theme of British and later American proslavery writing. Similar points were made by radical labor spokesmen who were in principle opposed to all forms of economic and political bondage. Given the venom of the debate, no abolitionist could plead ignorance of the charge that moral outrage was being directed against oppression overseas while similar or worse oppression was complacently tolerated at home. In 1818, for example, Sir Francis Burdett asked why William Wilberforce could be shocked by the enslavement of Africans and yet support in Parliament a seditious meetings bill and the suspension of habeas corpus, measures that allowed Englishmen to be seized and treated like African slaves.

Theoretically, abolitionists faced by such challenges could condemn all forms of social oppression and simply give priority to the slave trade or chattel slavery as the most flagrant and remediable crimes against humanity. This course would entail a disavowal of the proslavery writers' claims and at least a private expression of regret over the unintended consequences of extolling free wage labor. As a second alternative, exemplified by some

---

6 Cited in Davis, *Problem of Slavery in the Age of Revolution*, pp. 462–463. Since I am responding to misreadings of this book, I will draw most of my examples from it.

of the later Garrisonians and labor reformers, the abolitionists could claim that both distant and nearby evils arose from a common cause. As a third choice, they could deny any comparability between black slaves who were subjected to constant physical coercion and English workers who faced merely the threat of starvation, which was termed a "liberal motive" and a "rational predicament" by the reformer who drafted the 1833 slave emancipation act.[7]

In response to proslavery indictments of the wage-labor system, most abolitionists accentuated the moral contrast between what they conceived of as the free and slave worlds. Their greatest hope, after all, was to end the involuntary shipment of Africans to the New World and to transform black slaves into cheerful, obedient, and grateful laborers whose wants could be satisfied only by working voluntarily for wages. This hope rested on the assumption that the British system of labor had achieved a reasonable balance between freedom and order and could serve as a norm against which harsher regimes should be measured. I am not suggesting that early abolitionists were mostly conservatives who accepted the status quo and opposed domestic reforms, though some of them fit this description. But the sharp contrast they drew between British and colonial society had ideological meaning, especially at a time when there was a growing need to valorize wage labor as a universal norm, when the Industrial Revolution was introducing new forms of exploitation and suffering, and when it was by no means clear that the British working class was less victimized than West Indian slaves.

For example, early in 1807 at a depressing stage in Britain's war against Napoleon, James Stephen the elder, who was the abolitionists' master strategist, singled out British depravity in Africa and the West Indies as the cause for God's vengeance. Stephen specifically excluded domestic sins and proceeded to marvel over the "social happiness [that] has been showered upon us with singular profusion." "In no other part of the globe, are the poor and helpless so well protected by the laws, or so humanely used by their superiors. . . . If it be as the protector of the poor and destitute, that God has entered into judgment with us, we must,

7 Davis, *Slavery and Human Progress* (New York, 1984), p. 218.

I repeat, look to Africa, and to the West Indies, for the causes of his wrath."[8]

Stephen was a deeply religious man who was genuinely concerned with collective guilt and retribution. We can be almost certain, from what we know of him, that he did not consciously intend to use his abhorrence of slavery and the slave trade, which he had observed first-hand in the West Indies, as a means of diverting attention from domestic suffering. Though as a boy he and his mother had lived in debtors' prison, he honestly believed, at least after marrying into the Wilberforce family and allying himself with paternalistic Tories, that Britain's treatment of the poor could not be a cause for divine displeasure. Later in 1807 Stephen played an important role in securing the abolition of the British slave trade, a law hailed by political leaders as the most altruistic act since Christ's crucifixion and as proof that Britain waged war for human brotherhood.

From the time of the Mosaic Exodus, slavery and redemption have been extremely powerful paradigms involving the ultimate questions for both individual and collective life: the passage from present misery and degradation to a land of Canaan. Apart from their religious meanings, these paradigms are capable of being extended to a wide range of social experiences with oppression and liberation, or of being confined to the historical sufferings of a particular people. According to Rousseau, "man is born free—and everywhere he is in chains." But since Rousseau, at least, there has always been a tension between such generalizing proclamations and attempts to dramatize the horrors of a special instance of human bondage.

For James Stephen, Wilberforce, and the government leaders who deplored the African slave trade and who moved toward gradualist antislavery policies, it was essential to maintain a sharp distinction between the evils of the colonial slave world and the ostensibly free institutions that had been imperiled both by French tyranny and English Jacobins. The constant comparisons in abolitionist literature between the agony of black slaves and the smil-

---

8 Quoted in Davis, *Problem of Slavery in the Age of Revolution*, pp. 366–367. Wilberforce also warned in 1807 that Britain's afflictions might be a prelude to much worse divine punishment if the nation persisted in the criminal slave trade (*Letter on the Abolition of the Slave Trade* [London, 1807], pp. 4–6).

ing, contented life of English "husbandmen" was not fortuitous. Abolitionists repeatedly reminded Britons that the Somerset decision of 1772 had outlawed slavery in England. At a time when many of the peoples of Europe were said to be "enslaved" by French despotism, it was crucial to define England as a "free" nation—both in the sense of having no slaves and of having successfully resisted foreign domination. With the growth of nationalism in the Napoleonic era, *freedom* increasingly signified membership in a nation that had resisted or thrown off foreign tyranny. When national leaders were perceived as the protectors of liberty in this collective sense, it was more difficult to accuse them of fostering various forms of domestic oppression.

If the slave colonies helped England to define itself as free soil—much as Communist countries enable the United States to define itself as the leader of the free world—they also helped to specify the nature of freedom. The African slave trade defined, by negative polarity, the conditions necessary for consensual and acceptable labor transport. It was unacceptable for an employer to claim ownership of the person of an employee, to sell husbands apart from their wives, or children apart from their parents. It was acceptable, on the other hand, to buy the labor of adults or children even under conditions that led to the separation of families and that made a mockery of the worker's supposed consent.

British selectivity, as I suggested in *The Age of Revolution,* must be understood in terms of historical context. The government's first interventions in the colonial labor system coincided with an urgent domestic problem of labor discipline and labor management—not yet the problem of an industrial proletariat but of an immense rural labor force that had been released from traditional restraints and controls but not yet deprived of the independence of preindustrial village culture. Many Britons, including abolitionists, felt ambivalent toward the changes accompanying early industrialization. Tensions mounted between the advocates of hard-headed utilitarianism and the defenders of traditional paternalism or evangelical benevolence. The issue of slavery provided a meeting ground for these diverse groups and for members of different propertied classes who longed to ensure stability while benefiting from the economic changes underway.

Because the slave system was both distinctive and remote, [I wrote,] it could become a subject for experimental fantasies that assimilated traditional values to new economic needs. An attack on the African slave trade could absorb some of the traditionalist's anxieties over the physical uprooting and dislocation of labor. . . . By picturing the slave plantation as totally dependent upon physical torture, abolitionist writers gave sanction to less barbarous modes of social discipline. For reformers, the plantation offered the prospect of combining the virtues of the old agrarian order with the new ideals of uplift and engineered incentive. Abolitionists could contemplate a revolutionary change in status precisely because they were not considering the upward mobility of workers, but rather the rise of distant Negroes to the level of humanity. . . . British antislavery provided a bridge between preindustrial and industrial values; by combining the ideal of emancipation with an insistence on duty and subordination, it helped to smooth the way to the future.[9]

I have quoted at length from this passage because I have sometimes been interpreted as arguing that British abolitionism was a "screening device" designed to distract attention from metropolitan exploitation.[10] In actuality, I was trying to suggest a far more complex model in which the colonial plantation system served as a projective screen or experimental theater for testing ideas of liberation, paternalism, and controlled social change that were prompted in part by domestic anxieties. As one might expect in a society as deeply divided as early industrial Britain, different audiences drew contradictory conclusions from the experiments in overseas reform. But it is difficult to deny that the abolition cause offered both national and local ruling elites an increasingly attractive opportunity to demonstrate their commitment to decency and justice.

In the passage quoted above I was also concerned with the implications of sharply separating slavery from other kinds of coerced labor and social domination. It is noteworthy that even Thomas Clarkson, who retained much of the liberal spirit of the late 1780's and early 1790's, found nothing inequitable about coerced labor. Any state, he said, might legitimately use convicts

9 Davis, *Problem of Slavery in the Age of Revolution*, pp. 466–467.
10 See especially Drescher, "Cart Whip and Billy Roller," p. 4.

to work in mines or clear rivers. What outraged Clarkson and
other early abolitionists was the claim of personal proprietorship
that justified arbitrary and unlimited authority. The slave owner's claims contrasted sharply with those of the idealized British
squire, whose authority was constrained by law and custom; and
with the rights of the rising capitalist, who was content to purchase labor in the market like any other commodity.

Above all, the slave system came to epitomize an inherent
and inescapable conflict of interest, a kind of warfare sublimated
or suspended from the time the original captive was subdued.
For a time the more moderate abolitionists searched for means to
ameliorate this conflict, hoping that an end to further slave imports, for example, would persuade masters to promote their
slaves' welfare as part of their own long-term self-interest. Yet
the continuing negative growth rate of the West Indian slave
population seemed to show that the system itself was unreform-
able and would lead to eventual genocide. This impression was
reinforced by the slaveholders' truculent resistance to missionaries, moral uplift, the abolition of Sunday markets, restrictions
on the flogging of women, and other benevolent measures. The
whole thrust of the British antislavery movement, by the early
1820's, was aimed at creating a natural harmony of interests between planters and black workers, a relation similar to the assumed mutuality between British landlords and tenants.

In arguing that antislavery mirrored the needs and tensions
of a society increasingly absorbed with problems of labor discipline, I was not saying that such needs and tensions are sufficient
to explain the emergence and ultimate direction of antislavery
thought. While emphasizing the importance of class and social
context, I specifically warned against "the simplistic impression
that 'industrialists' promoted abolitionist doctrine as a means of
distracting attention from their own forms of exploitation."[11] My
main theme was that antislavery cannot be divorced from the
vast economic changes that were intensifying social conflicts and
heightening class consciousness; that in Britain it was part of a
larger ideology that helped to ensure stability while accommo-
dating society to political and social change.

Even in Britain, where the cause won significant support from

11 Davis, *Problem of Slavery in the Age of Revolution*, p. 455.

the governing elites, there were both conservative and radical aspects to abolitionist thought. Some readers have focused exclusively on the first part of my argument, in which I claimed that the abolitionists' acts of selectivity "helped to strengthen the invisible chains being forged at home." But I also emphasized that abolitionism "bred a new sensitivity to social oppression," "that it provided a model for the systematic indictment of social crime," and that it "ultimately taught many Englishmen to recognize forms of systematic oppression that were closer to home."[12] To illustrate the radical potentialities of antislavery thought I quoted from Friedrich Engels precisely because he showed how abolitionist perceptions and locutions had become universalized by the 1840's; even a resident alien, with no roots in the abolitionist movement, appropriated the language and perspective of Anglo-American abolitionists when he exposed the "slavery" of Manchester's working class. As early as 1817, when Wilberforce and his friends in the Liverpool cabinet feared that England was on the verge of revolution, another radical alien pointed to the connections between the oppression of West Indian slaves and the oppression of England's poor. Iain McCalman has recently discovered that Robert Wedderburn, a Jamaican mulatto whose slave mother was born in Africa, edited a London periodical, *Axe Laid to the Root,* which called for a simultaneous revolution of West Indian chattel slaves and English wage slaves. Associated with Thomas Spence, Thomas Evans, and other London radicals, Wedderburn popularized a plebeian antislavery rhetoric in the taverns and hayloft chapels of London's underworld.[13]

Social movements often serve opposing or contradictory functions, especially if they endure for any length of time. As I have already indicated, slavery and emancipation have long been

12 *Ibid.,* pp. 455, 467–468. Seymour Drescher has greatly amplified these themes, which do not contradict my position, as he seems to think. No doubt I should have cited more varied examples of the linkage between denunciations of colonial slavery and wage slavery, and I was unaware of the language in petitions that Drescher has discovered. It was my intention to explore this subject in a succeeding volume on the "Age of Emancipation." Drescher does not seem to deny that Wilberforce, Stephen, Macaulay, Clarkson, Cropper, Buxton, and the other national leaders of the early period were unsympathetic to the wage-slavery argument, which they associated with their enemies

13 Iain McCalman, "Anti-Slavery and Ultra-Radicalism in Early Nineteenth-Century England: The Case of Robert Wedderburn," *Slavery and Abolition,* 7 (September 1986), 99–117.

extraordinarily complex paradigms, since they are capable of almost infinite extension to both material and spiritual states. Even in the 1820's antislavery agitation led American radicals like Langton Byllesby and Thomas Skidmore to the conclusion that black slavery was not only the quintessential American crime but that it revealed deep structural flaws that enabled a fortunate few to live off the labor of the so-called free majority. On the other hand, when radical American reformers later contended that the wage system was slavery, that conventional marriage was slavery, and that submission to any government using coercion was slavery, their rhetoric surely diluted the charge that Negro slavery in the South was a system of exceptional and intolerable oppression. As Christopher Lasch has observed with respect to our own time, the language of radical protest was impoverished when it was appropriated by fat people, short people, old people, and other such groups who claimed that they were as much oppressed as racial minorities: "Since interest-group politics invites competitive claims to the privileged status of victimization, the rhetoric of moral outrage becomes routine, loses its critical edge, and contributes to the general debasement of political speech."[14]

While acknowledging that abolitionism was always double-edged and set precedents for attacking practices and institutions that most abolitionists condoned, we should remember that even in America it was the Tappan brothers and their associates, not Thomas Skidmore, who shaped the basic character of the antislavery movement, at least in the 1830's. For their part, spokesmen for the radical labor movement in New York City had concluded by 1850 that it was essential "to abolish Wages Slavery before we meddle with Chattel Slavery." Faced with the workers' hatred for middle-class moralizers and with their persistent racial prejudice against free black competitors, labor leaders wished to postpone emancipating slaves "who are better off than to be let loose under the present Competitive System of labor. . . ."[15] The abolition movement was neither monolithic nor unchanging; in the United States, in contrast to Britain, it presented a fundamental challenge to economic, political, and religious estab-

14 Christopher Lasch, "The Great American Variety Show," *New York Review of Books*, Feb. 2, 1984, p. 36.

15 Sean Wilentz, *Chants Democratic: New York City & the Rise of the American Working Class, 1788–1850* (New York, 1984), pp. 162–168, 183–190, 382.

lishments. Yet it also served various hegemonic functions, particularly by promoting a free-labor ideology as the antithesis of the Slave Power it attacked.

The concept of hegemony is easily discredited by misconstruction or misunderstanding—by attacking the argument, for example, that a discrete capitalist class imposed a form of false consciousness upon a passive populace, duping people with antislavery propaganda designed to divert attention from the women and children in the mills and mines. It is now clear that by the early 1830's, in both England and the United States, the movement attracted significant support from artisans and other skilled workers; that in England the swelling "pressure from without" ran ahead of the elite antislavery leadership, embarrassing Thomas Fowell Buxton in his negotiations with government ministers; and that a few reformers moved from an apprenticeship in the abolitionist campaign to more radical activism as Chartists or labor reformers.[16] But these facts in no way invalidate the hegemonic argument when properly understood.

Hegemony, as Eugene D. Genovese has written, implies no more than the ability of a particular class to contain class antagonisms "on a terrain in which its legitimacy is not dangerously questioned."[17] Ideological hegemony is a process that is never complete or total; it can be understood in different ways by opposing groups or classes as long as it limits the terms of debate, heads off more fundamental challenges, and serves to reinforce the legitimacy of the ruling groups and existing order. Obviously antislavery agitation had very different meanings in 1814, 1833, and 1838, and a detailed analysis would be required to show the degree to which abolitionism stabilized or destabilized Britain's social and political order at a particular moment in time. But a few preliminary points can be made in response to the common view of an expansive, one-directional surge of democratic consciousness.

16 For a discussion of the pressure exerted on Buxton and the Parliamentary abolitionists, see Davis, *Slavery and Human Progress*, pp. 195–202. Seymour Drescher's *Capitalism and Antislavery* emphasizes the broad-based, popular character of the antislavery movement. For abolitionist Chartists, see Betty Fladeland, " 'Our Cause being One and the Same': Abolitionists and Chartism," in *Slavery and British Society, 1776–1846*, James Walvin, ed. (Baton Rouge, 1982), pp. 69–99.
17 *Roll, Jordan, Roll: The World the Slaves Made* (New York, 1974), p. 26.

No doubt many British workers empathized with colonial slaves and understood abolitionist principles in ways that would have deeply troubled Wilberforce, Buxton, and Zachary Macaulay. But rank-and-file abolitionists could not escape the fact that the governing classes had appropriated the cause and defined the terms of the debate. Britain's landlords, merchants, and manufacturers had made it clear that there were varieties of exploitation that would no longer be tolerated in England or on the high seas; that there were forms of labor, even in the distant colonies, that would have to be brought more in line with metropolitan standards. This affirmation of moral standards helped to legitimate both the existing system of class power and the emerging concept of free labor as an impersonal marketable commodity. The 1833 emancipation act gave assurance to Britons of various classes that there were limits to the rapid socioeconomic changes taking place: workers could not literally be reduced to chattel slavery; owners of even the most questionable form of private property could not be deprived of their capital without generous compensation.

While the politics of slave emancipation were extremely complex, the act of 1833 fostered the illusion that the newly reformed Parliament had become an almost democratic assembly that would respond to the voice of a moral majority. The succession of antislavery victories and official commitments, beginning with the order-in-council of 1805 restricting the slave trade to conquered colonies, vindicated trust in the government's basic sense of justice. It is no wonder that when various British groups wanted to dramatize their own oppression or lack of freedom, they complained that their condition was at least as bad as that of West Indian slaves. Defenders of colonial slavery had opened this door, and the argument implied two propositions: first, that to receive attention one had to meet the "slavery test" by enumerating horrors equivalent to those in abolitionist literature; second, that since Parliament and the middle-class public were attuned to this language, the same techniques that had brought Parliament to bestow liberty on West Indian slaves would also bring freedom and justice at home.

In effect, the antislavery radicals were addressing the governing classes as follows: wage labor under present conditions leads to even worse misery than chattel slavery; since you responded to moral arguments in abolishing the slave trade and in freeing the colonial slaves, you should now relieve the distress of England's poor. But this reinforcement of ruling-class standards is precisely what is meant by ideological hegemony. Denunciations of "wage slavery" were a way of expressing outrage and resentment over working conditions in industrial Britain and America. But as Christopher Lowe points out, there could be no lower standard than to ask that free laborers be treated better than slaves.[18] Everyone knew that white workers were not really slaves. The analogy, whatever its emotive power, invited a rhetorical response celebrating the benefits of the market and the inestimable privilege of being free to change employments. The dichotomous terms of this debate forced radicals to prove that in some fundamental respects wage earners were no freer or better off than slaves.

There can be no doubt that abolitionism contributed to more radical kinds of social criticism. Especially in the United States, where slavery was abolished in a cataclysm of violence, radical labor leaders and socialists found that parallels between black and white slavery retained resonance well into the twentieth century.[19] But analogies with chattel slavery may also have retarded the development of a vocabulary that could depict more subtle forms of coercion, oppression, and class rule. To be a free worker was to be as unlike a Negro slave as possible. Most opponents of slavery equated unjust domination with a legalistic conception of property rights in human beings. This absolutist approach often made it difficult to distinguish the forms of domination concealed by voluntary contracts and the "bundle of powers" that could be exercised over nominally free workers.

I have already responded implicitly to many of the criticisms of my hegemonic thesis, but Seymour Drescher's forceful arguments deserve some further comment.[20] There is a seeming disjunction between Drescher's attacks on the hegemonic thesis (especially in "Cart Whip and Billy Roller") and his substantive findings on popular political mobilization. In his essay in this

18 Lowe, "Ideology, Hegemony and Class Rule," p. 7.
19 Barry Herbert Goldberg, "Beyond Free Labor: Labor, Socialism and the Idea of Wage Slavery, 1890–1920," Ph.D. dissertation, Columbia University, 1979.
20 I address some of Thomas Haskell's arguments in "Reflections on Abolitionism and Ideological Hegemony," *The American Historical Review*, 92/4 (Oct. 1987), part of which replicates this essay.

volume, he accuses me and other "historians of ideology" of "accepting Williams's premise that humanitarian ideals cannot alone explain the emergence and triumph of antislavery. . . ." But this premise has been accepted by Reginald Coupland, Roger Anstey, and virtually every historian of the antislavery movement, including Drescher himself. Even the abolitionists never presumed that humanitarian ideals could alone account for their triumphs.

In a number of statements Drescher also seems to question those historians who accept his main critique of the Williams thesis but who continue to seek "alternative explanations somehow grounded in fundamental economic development." He cites Peter C. Emmer's conclusion that even if Drescher's *Econocide* overturned most of the factual grounding of the Williams thesis, there still "remains something unassailable in this thesis concerning the connection between economics and abolition." Since Drescher never reveals his own stand on this issue and moves on to expose the deficiencies of the "ideological historians" who have sought to find indirect links between abolitionism and economic change, many readers may assume he rejects any connection between humanitarian ideals and economic or ideological interests. Yet Drescher affirms that British abolitionism became "engrafted onto other everyday practices of commercial capitalism." He refers to the slave-sugar boycott as "a weapon of consumer capitalism." It was only in Britain, he tells us, that antislavery ideology "became rooted as a national social movement at the cutting edge of the Industrial Revolution." Drescher seems positively exuberant when he finds that the petition campaign of 1787 originated not in London but in Lancashire and was launched by "a portion of Manchester's elite," the same manufacturing interests that had led the petition campaign against a proposed customs union with Ireland. What are we to make of these links between capitalism and antislavery? One need not doubt Thomas Walker's sincerity as a radical abolitionist to suspect that antislavery and capitalist enterprise formed part of a coherent world view.

Drescher's research on petitioning and popular mobilization has greatly enriched our understanding of British abolitionism. Historians were long aware that the abolitionist leaders were eager to advertise their cause as emanating from the voice of the united people. Although some of the more conservative London abolitionists feared that popular agitation would get out of hand, no pains were spared to circulate petitions at public meetings and in taverns and workshops as well as churches. We can never know the motives of most petition signers, but Drescher has demonstrated with graphic new detail the extraordinary popularity of the cause. One should add that in 1833 slave emancipation was no less popular in the House of Commons, where the final bill passed by an overwhelming majority. But why should so many Britons of different rank and background be concerned about Negro slavery, an institution thousands of miles away across the Atlantic?

Drescher never quite confronts this question. He does note that "the abolitionist crowd" "was not seeking a local rectification of a deviation from a traditional moral order, but demanding increasing overseas conformity to an emerging metropolitan moral order." This is precisely the argument that I and other "ideological historians" have made. But why should so many Britons *care* about overseas conformity? Why should Manchester's capitalists and artisans want to extend their "everyday political and economic activity" to a campaign that would bring them no tangible political or economic rewards? When there were so many competing human rights and humanitarian causes, why should colonial slavery take center stage? Free-labor ideology— which Drescher wrongly sees as somehow inconsistent with his own approach—provides a plausible answer. The anti-slave-trade petitions, Wedgwood's medallions, the slave-ship prints, the innovations in public communication—all symbolized the "progressive" spirit of Lancashire's labor system and cotton boom.

Drescher pictures British abolitionism as part of a larger liberating, modernizing process. I accept this view with one crucial reservation: the process was also oppressive, exploitive, and controlling. Drescher frames the debate in binary terms of either this or that. It is inconceivable that a social movement could both inspire working-class reforms and provide the moral capital to legitimate a new alliance of elites. Yet the evidence suggests that abolitionism served different social functions and had different meanings for various groups and classes. As Drescher has shown, the antislavery petitions of 1823 and 1824 stimulated petitions for political reform and other domestic causes. But Thomas Clarkson, who canvassed the country for many months soliciting antislavery petitions and organizing nearly 200 antislavery societies, emphasized that only the daily flow of petitions from all parts of the country would support the *government* as it withstood the "threats and clamor of interested persons." Clarkson also reassured Lord Liverpool that the petitions were "respectable beyond all precedent" and showed a complete unity of Whigs and Tories, of Churchmen and Dissenters, of supporters and opponents of Liverpool's administration.[21] No one could make this claim for the petitions calling for domestic reform.

The theory of ideological hegemony presupposes continuing conflict over the meaning of shared beliefs and commitments. The key question is not whether abolitionism "hegemonized" the working class, as Drescher puts it, but the degree to which the movement encouraged other forms of protest or reinforced the moral authority of local and national elites. When Clarkson traveled through England, Wales, and Scotland, he sought out chief magistrates, vicars, curates, bankers, solicitors, industrialists, and dissenting clergymen. Some of these "leading men" opposed organizing a local antislavery society and argued that the matter should be left entirely to the government. Others seized the opportunity to lead a local meeting. Some groups favored immediate emancipation and a boycott of all slave produce. In Carlisle, however, an antislavery committee expressed the fear that a consumer boycott would be most injurious to the slaves, who would either starve or "retire into the woods and lead there a *savage* life."[22] It would require a detailed study of numerous towns and districts to sort out the local meanings of antislavery and to determine the degree to which the movement destabilized local structures of power.

Drescher's most valuable contribution is his elucidation of the distinctive political culture that enabled the people to exert pressure on the British government. His discussion of Continental countries suggests that a "highly articulate political life" was a necessary precondition for a successful antislavery movement. One should note, however, that the United States had not only met that test but had moved far beyond Britain in devising institutions for the expression of popular sovereignty. American ab-

21 Thomas Clarkson to John Gibson (?), March 7, 1824, Howard University Library; Clarkson to Lord Liverpool, May 3, 1823, British Library Add. MS 38,416, fols. 391–392.
22 Thomas Clarkson, MS Diary, 1823–1824, National Library of Wales.

olitionists tried to follow Britain's example of popular political mobilization, but with extremely disappointing results. Drescher does not seem to appreciate how weak and isolated the American abolitionists were, at least until the rise of the Republican party. Even by the late 1850's there was no groundswell of opinion demanding slave emancipation.

Surely the British people were not morally superior to the Americans; there must have been as many humanitarians per capita in the United States as in Britain, and evangelical Christianity reached a larger proportion of the American population. But in the United States, unlike Britain, slave emancipation threatened vital metropolitan interests. In Britain, where Drescher notes that abolitionism "lacked the ingredient of potential metropolitan upheaval," the governing elites could tolerate and even encourage reforms that redeemed the national character and enhanced their own authority. In contrast, Drescher finds that French antislavery was "distinguished by an inability to combine a stable élite leadership with a mass appeal."[23] That is what I meant by hegemony.

23 Drescher, *Capitalism and Antislavery*, p. 53.

Howard Temperley

Eric Williams and Abolition: The Birth of a New Orthodoxy
When, on August 1, 1984, Prime Minister Forbes Burnham told a rally of 5,000 people in Georgetown, Guyana, that Britain did not abolish slavery in 1834 for humanitarian reasons but because the system had become "unprofitable, risky and expensive" it is unlikely that it came as news to most members of his audience.[1] Certainly no surprise was registered when Mrs. Marilyn Gordon, Minister of Sports, Culture, and Youth Affairs, addressed similar remarks to a gathering at the Institute of International Relations of the University of the West Indies at St. Augustine, Trinidad, two days earlier.[2] However revolutionary such comments may have seemed in Oxford, or indeed elsewhere, in the 1930's or 1940's, they were, so Elsa Goveia tells us, "already orthodox at the UCWI in the 1950's" and were penetrating large numbers of schools all over the West Indies.[3]

Professor Goveia was, of course, referring specifically to the views of Eric Williams. As a politician, Williams, one suspects, would not have been displeased at the frequency with which his ideas were cited in connection with the 150th anniversary of the abolition of slavery in the West Indies, although whether, as a scholar, he would have approved of all that was said in this regard we can be less sure. To anyone familiar with the full range of his writings, and with the way his ideas changed over the years, it is plain that the public pronouncements made on this occasion do not adequately reflect the subtlety, complexity, and also, it must be confessed, sheer contrariness of his argument.

1 As reported in *The Times of London*, August 3, 1984.
2 Mrs. Gordon was opening a conference, sponsored by the University of the West Indies Extra-Mural Studies Unit, St. Augustine, at which the author was present.
3 Elsa V. Goveia, "New Shibboleths for Old," *Social and Economic Studies*, 10, no. 2 (1964), p.53.

In no respect are these characteristics more revealingly displayed than in his treatment of one of the phenomena singled out for particular mention by Mr. Burnham, namely British humanitarianism. "The British humanitarians," so Williams tells us in *Capitalism and Slavery* (1944), his principal published work on the subject, "were a brilliant band." They were "the spearhead of the onslaught which destroyed the West Indian system and freed the Negro." It was, after all, their "humanitarianism which destroyed that system." Nevertheless "their importance has been seriously misunderstood and grossly exaggerated." Some, like Clarkson, personified "all the best in the humanitarianism of the age," but others did not measure up to his pristine standards. They were conservative, inconsistent, and easily deflected. Compared to Clarkson and Ramsay, "Wilberforce with his effeminate face appears small in stature. . . . As a leader, he was inept, addicted to moderation, compromise and delay. . . . He was a lobbyist, and it was a common saying that his vote could be safely predicted for it was certain to be opposed to his speech." Buxton, Wilberforce's successor, was naive and easily swayed. There is even a possibility that in some instances antislavery zeal was sharpened by expectations of pecuniary gain. The case for this is difficult to prove but the circumstances are suggestive and the suspicions thereby aroused did harm to the cause. And finally they simply abandoned the Negro. "The Emancipation Act marked the end of the abolitionist efforts. They were satisfied. It never dawned on them that the Negro's freedom could only be nominal if the sugar plantation was allowed to endure." Even Clarkson's support proved less than unwavering. In the end we are left wondering if, indeed, they were brilliant at all.[4]

Whether, on the basis of this assessment, one would be justified in drawing the kind of conclusions reached by Mr. Burnham and Mrs. Gordon is uncertain, but what is clear is that at first sight at least Dr. Williams's views appear somewhat contradictory. Few today, of course, would wish to identify themselves with every aspect of the case as presented by the abolitionists during their long campaign, still less with their views on other questions. They were men of their time and the arguments they

---

4 Eric Williams, *Capitalism and Slavery* (Chapel Hill, N.C., 1944), Chapter 9. References to this work are hereafter given in the text.

used were not necessarily those we would use. More important, they were engaged in a struggle that demanded the exercise of political skills which, in turn, imposed powerful constraints on the freedom with which they expressed their views. Often what they said, for example in the course of parliamentary debates, reflected not their fundamental beliefs but the political needs of the moment. These, needless to say, were matters over which the abolitionists themselves often disagreed. In some ways they were an oddly-assorted group. Many of their disagreements were, in practice, over matters of tactics but frequently they extended to more basic issues.

Such disagreements do not, however, fully explain the apparent contradictoriness of Williams's account. Was it humanitarianism that in the end conquered slavery or was slavery discarded for other reasons altogether? Were the abolitionists true friends of the slave who fought a long and arduous battle for his emancipation or were they vacillating incompetents who in the end let the Negro down? At different points Williams's writings appear to lend support to each of these contentions.

One way of throwing light on these matters is to look first at the way in which Williams's ideas developed and then at the larger context within which, as he came to see it, the antislavery struggle took place.

Eric Williams was born in 1911, the eldest son of a minor post office official in Port-of-Spain, Trinidad. The family was large and times were hard. Simply finding somewhere to live, he tells us, was difficult. As the eldest child he in due course became his parents' principal assistant in making ends meet, a problem that became progressively harder to solve as the family grew faster than the funds available. "The descending family fortunes," he recalls in his autobiography, "were reflected in the descent from the water closet to the cesspit and in one bad case the bailiff appeared. The ordeal of removal, the horror of the cesspit, the dread of eviction were only the external aspects" of an existence that included inadequate clothing, diet, and medical care.[5]

Williams never forgot the bitterness of these early experi-

5 Eric Williams, *Inward Hunger: The Education of a Prime Minister* (London, 1969), pp. 26–28.

ences or the political and economic circumstances that occasioned them. The Trinidad of his youth, he later wrote, was "a government unrepresentative of the people and not responsible to it; an economy almost exclusively in non-native hands; and a native population which were hewers of wood and drawers of water for its foreign overlords." Yet, compared to many, the Williams family was privileged; at least they had a regular income and access to education. Most Trinidadians had neither. British imperialism in the nineteenth century had justified its expansion with the slogans " 'We must educate our masters' and 'Open a school and close a jail.' British rule in Trinidad, on the other hand, was marked by the denial of education to the masses and the priority of jails and their appurtenances over schools."[6] Altogether the people of Trinidad had little cause to feel overjoyed at what British rule had done for them.

Nevertheless, it was to school rather than to jail that Eric Williams went. From Queen's Royal college, Trinidad, he won a scholarship that took him to Oxford where he gained a First in History and, in due course, a doctorate. Yet Williams's memories of Oxford were far from happy. His tutors thought sufficiently well of him to suggest that he try for a prize fellowship at that most elite of British institutions, All Souls College. In the written examinations he was placed ninth out of sixteen candidates. Nevertheless the episode, to which he devotes three pages in his autobiography, left him feeling bitter. "I was very angry. It was not that I felt I had won the fellowship. I knew I had not. But I knew I could never win one." The lesson he drew from this experience was that "No 'native,' however detribalized, could fit socially into All Souls" or indeed into any other Oxford senior common room. Tutors hastened to assure him that he was mistaken and that, at Oxford at least, race was irrelevant, but he remained unpersuaded. One tutor whom he later encountered was, he noted, "a man of my own age, who had got the best first in Philosophy the very year I got the best first in History. Being white, however, he had landed a Fellowship even without examination." Despite its liberal protestations and all that he had done to win its approval, Oxford, it transpired, was unwilling to take him to its bosom.[7]

6 *Ibid.*, pp.11, 18, 21.
7 *Ibid.*, pp.30–31, 43, 45–47.

These were Williams's later recollections, although whether they are a fair reflection of the way he felt at the time we cannot be sure. In particular we cannot be certain how exactly he viewed the Oxford History School, for the inadequacies of which, especially with reference to its treatment of West Indian matters, he was to reserve his most severe strictures. In *British Historians and the West Indies* (1966), he characterized Britain as "an old, tired, tiresome world, whose historian representatives, adorning the greatest of the metropolitan universities, have sought only to justify the indefensible and to seek support for preconceived and outmoded prejudices."[8] Apart from Thomas Carlyle, to whom he devoted a whole chapter (and who, incidentally, did not hold a university chair), the figure he singles out for special criticism is Reginald Coupland, in Williams's day Beit Professor of Colonial History at Oxford and, as it happens, a fellow of All Souls. Coupland was, among other things, Wilberforce's biographer and also the author of *The British Anti-Slavery Movement* (1933).[9] His views on these, as indeed on most other matters, were characteristic of those held by liberal intellectuals between the wars. His credentials, both as a Whig historian and as a pillar of the liberal establishment (he was ultimately awarded a knighthood for his services) were impeccable.

Yet, in Williams's later estimation, Coupland's work "was distinguished, at least where the West Indies were concerned, by a total contempt of the fundamental sources which ought to be used by a historian."[10] The prevailing view, expounded by Coupland and by British historians for a century and more, was that

> a band of humanitarians—"The Saints," they had been nicknamed—had got together to abolish slavery, and had after many years succeeded in arousing the conscience of the British people against man's greatest inhumanity to man. Britain had repented and given an earnest of her contribution by voting twenty million pounds sterling to the slave-owners for the redemption of their slaves.[11]

8 Eric Williams, *British Historians and the West Indies* (London, 1966), p.12.
9 Reginald Coupland, *Wilberforce* (London, 1923); *The British Anti-Slavery Movement* (London, 1933).
10 *British Historians*, p.199.
11 Williams, *Inward Hunger*, pp.49–50.

It is easy to see why, if these were indeed Coupland's views, they would have appeared to Eric Williams, or indeed to any West Indian, as inadequate. C.L.R. James, a fellow Trinidadian and a former teacher of Williams at Queen's Royal College, writing at the time Williams was working on his dissertation, commended Coupland's volumes to his readers as "typical for, among other vices, their smug sentimentality, characteristic of the official approach of Oxford scholarship to abolition. As the official view, they can be recommended for their thorough misunderstanding of the subject,"[12] This certainly accords with Williams's own later opinions. After all, the dominant theme in British imperial history had been the pursuit of national interest. It was the search for profits that had created the West Indian slave system and there was no lack of evidence to show that such motives had continued to operate since its demise. One had only to think of the introduction of indentured coolie labor, the abolition of the preferential sugar duties, and the brutal suppression by Governor Eyre of the Jamaican rebellion. Was it really possible that this one episode was as totally "clean" as Coupland claimed? Even if it was, to focus on that episode alone created a totally false impression of the nature of the metropolitan–colonial relationship. The trouble with Coupland and the spokesmen of the Whig School generally was that they actually believed the "twaddle" put out by the British government about constitutional rights and democracy which, as any West Indian Negro could testify, bore little relation to the realities of existence in those impoverished and cruelly exploited colonies. West Indians had little to be grateful for. By celebrating the achievements of the "Saints" and holding them up for emulation as examples of disinterested benevolence, liberal intellectuals were acting as unconscious apologists for policies undertaken for quite other and altogether more mercenary motives. "The British historians," Williams was to conclude, "wrote almost as if Britain had introduced Negro slavery solely for the satisfaction of abolishing it."[13]

In fact, this is a very misleading representation of Coupland's views. Not only does Coupland take full note of the part Britain played in building up the West Indian slave system but

12 C. L. R. James, *The Black Jacobins: Toussaint L'Ouverture and the San Domingo Revolution* (2nd edn., New York, 1963), p.386.

13 *British Historians*, pp.173–74, 197, 199, 202, 205–208, 233.

he is peculiarly harsh (more harsh, indeed, than Williams) in his moral condemnation of the influence it exerted on masters and slaves alike.

> If in other fields of human relationship the world was moving forward, in that field it was going back, restoring to a new and unnatural life the dead wrongs of the past; and, though historians must hesitate to judge their ancestors by the standards of their own day, it is difficult not to regard this treatment of Africa by Christian Europe, following Moslem Asia, as the greatest crime in history.[14]

Nor does *The British Anti-Slavery Movement* by any means ignore the economic influences that contributed to abolition, although its treatment of these, given the overall scope of his work and the space allotted to him by the editors of the Home University Library Series, is necessarily brief.

> The loss of the American colonies accentuated the economic value of the "sugar islands" and intensified, as the conduct of the war with France was soon to show, the desire to acquire more of them. But, so far from implying any change in the relations between whites and blacks, this rendered the mainenance of the slave-system more of an economic "necessity" than ever.[15]

Nevertheless, the "inevitable decline of the British 'sugar islands' had already begun by 1807" and no amount of economic tinkering by Parliament was capable of allaying it. Soil exhaustion, the competition of foreign sugar from Cuba and Brazil, and the challenge posed by East Indian producers—some of whom, he noted, were supporters of the Anti-Slavery Society—inevitably undermined the influence of the West India lobby in Parliament.

> Lost causes are apt to be unpopular; and, though the cause of Slavery was not yet quite lost, the steady impoverishment of its upholders in the islands was bound to cool the sympathies of anyone

14 Coupland, *The British Anti-Slavery Movement*, p.35; see also pp.21–22, 28–34. Williams, curiously, has little to say regarding the horrors of slavery; Coupland, on the other hand, dwells on them at length and plainly finds them deeply shocking.

15 *Ibid.*, p.63; see also pp.62, 64, 82, 105–106. Coupland speculates interestingly (pp.62–63) about what might have happened to the antislavery cause if Britain had managed to retain her North American colonies.

who doubted the expediency, in politics as in finance, of "throwing good money after bad."[16]

Apart from the fact that he saw West Indian economic decline as beginning before rather than after 1807, Coupland's account stands up remarkably well to modern criticism and, as we will see, was not much out of line with what Williams himself was to argue in his doctoral thesis.

Thus Williams's later characterization of himself as a rebel against the prevailing views of the Oxford of his day needs to be treated with caution. Certainly there was nothing particularly rebellious about the title of his thesis, "The Economic Aspect of the Abolition of the West Indian Slave Trade and Slavery."[17] That abolition had economic aspects had never been denied. The most notable work in the field at the time Williams was writing was Lowell J. Ragatz's *The Fall of the Planter Class in the British Caribbean, 1763–1833* (Washington, D.C., 1928), a massive, statistically based study which set out to chronicle the economic and social decline of the British West Indies from the American Revolution onward. It was to Ragatz that Williams later dedicated his own *Capitalism and Slavery*. But although Ragatz included a chapter on the abolitionists he has nothing new to say on this subject or, for that matter, about abolition. In the main he was happy to endorse the prevailing idealistic interpretations of these events. The principal thrust of his work was to show the way in which, from the time of the American Revolution onward, the economic basis of the once-prosperous planter class was eroded as a result of mismanagement, soil exhuaustion, imperial tariff policy, foreign competition, and war, and it was upon these findings that Williams based his own interpretation of events. It stood to reason that if the West Indies were in process of continuous decline this must have been taken note of in the mother country and have influenced thinking on the abolition question. No less suggestive was the fact that these changes coincided with the beginnings of a period of rapid economic transformation and unprecedented industrial growth within Britain itself. It was hard to believe that these three developments were not in some way

16 *Ibid.*, p. 123; see also pp. 122, 124.
17 Eric Williams, "The Economic Aspect of the Abolition of the West Indian Slave Trade and Slavery" (Ph.D. thesis, Oxford University, 1938).

related. It was, then, to tracing these connections that Williams turned his attention.

Williams's Oxford dissertation differs from *Capitalism and Slavery* in a number of important ways. As its title suggests, it covers a more limited time span. Essentially it picks up the story in the 1780's and ends with emancipation in 1833. Nothing is said about the role of British capital in building up the West Indian slave system or the way in which profits deriving from that system contributed to Britain's own economic growth. Nor, although there are some references, is much attention paid to the actions of the slaves themselves or the impact that the fear of rebellion had on British policy-making. On the other hand, the issues he *does* cover are treated at much greater length. The dissertation is divided into twelve chapters plus an epilogue and three appendices as compared with the five corresponding chapters in *Capitalism and Slavery* and, running to some 100,000 words, is roughly three times longer. Not surprisingly, many of the ideas used in the later work are foreshadowed, but the prevailing tone of the argument is more cautious and reference to particular events more specific. In part this is because issues are dealt with in the main chronologically. For example there are frequent references to the problems of monopoly and overproduction, but in each case it is evident from the context what forms of monopoly and overproduction he is referring to. Most striking of all is the omission of those broad statements concerning the dominance of economic forces which were to characterize his later work. Far from requiring abolition, economic developments merely created a context within which abolition became a practical proposition. Moreover he continually warns readers against the danger of seeing history as merely the interplay of neatly packaged economic interests. "Men," he tells us, "do not act absolutely in accord with economic tendencies which, a hundred years later, when they have run their course, we can distinguish with a clarity impossible at the time. If that were so the writing of history would be a matter of geometrical deduction and very simple."[18] Economics was a factor but it was not the only factor or, in most cases, even the overriding one.

So far as the humanitarians are concerned, his comments,

18 *Ibid.*, p.152.

although not adding greatly to what was already known, are on the whole perspicacious and judicious. He makes full allowance for the political circumstances in which they were obliged to operate. "It must be reiterated," he states, "that it was imperative for the abolitionists to try to win over hostile forces thinking fundamentally in terms of economics,"[19] and in an extended analysis that takes up the greater part of his first chapter, he shows how they set about making out just such a case. He does not, it should be emphasized, claim that they themselves were economically motivated although there are incidental references to the writings of Arthur Young and Adam Smith and the fact that "at the beginning of the Industrial Revolution the bourgeoisie established the principle of the superiority of free labour over slave."[20] He also refers to the fact that many who spoke up for abolition had invested heavily in East Indian stock.[21] These lines of argument, however, are not fully developed. In general, he goes along with the prevailing idealistic interpretation with regard to the behavior of both the antislavery activists and the general public. By 1833, the opposition to slavery outside Parliament "had become a settled religious feeling."[22] It was also, he notes, a by-product of a widely diffused reform impulse that, for reasons largely unconnected with economics, was sweeping not only Britain but France too:

> In the midst of the humanitarian ardour . . . came the successful French Revolution of 1830 to increase the pressure of the reform movement in Britain. The agitation for emancipation was postponed until the Reform Bill was passed. . . . [The] powerful reform movement in Britain gave a great impulse to that demand for the reform of all abuses of which slavery was the greatest and most obvious. In the humanitarian and religious excitement there was nothing in any way savouring of economic considerations. The people were spontaneously moved by the conviction that slavery was a disgusting and immoral system, and therefore it had to go.[23]

Neither here, nor elsewhere in his dissertation, is there any hint of economic determinism. Looking simply at Williams's disser-

19 *Ibid.*, p.12.
20 *Ibid.*, p.59.
21 *Ibid.*, pp.387–391.
22 *Ibid.*, p.240.
23 *Ibid.*, p.237.

tation one would be justified in concluding that the author's intention was to supplement rather than to challenge the then prevailing interpretation. Williams himself noted that Reginald Coupland, who was one of his examiners, admitted that "if he had to revise his own work he would have to make fundamental changes."[24] Just how fundamental these would have needed to be one is entitled to wonder. Evidently Coupland had not read Ragatz, which may be regarded as a serious oversight, for which Williams was later to take him to task.[25]

Meanwhile, disappointed in his hopes of obtaining an Oxford fellowship, Williams had gone to Howard University in Washington, D.C., where, for the next nine years, he was engaged in teaching politics. He also traveled to Cuba, Haiti, and Puerto Rico where he made the acquaintance of leading Caribbean intellectuals, including Dr. Fernando Ortiz and Hermino Portell Vila of Cuba.[26] The influence that these, his associates at Howard and the United States black community, in whose circles he now moved, exerted on his thinking can only be guessed. That his ideas were in process of radical change is evident from his first book, *The Negro in the Caribbean* (New York, 1942), which is, among other things, an outspoken condemnation of white colonialism. In it he acknowledges a particular intellectual debt to three of his Howard colleagues, Alain Locke, Ralph J. Bunche, and W.O. Brown.[27] It was during these same years that he wrote the first six chapters of *Capitalism and Slavery*, which cover the period up to the American Revolution, together with the last chapter, "The Slaves and Slavery." So far as the abolition period is concerned, however, there is nothing to suggest that he had extended his research into new areas. For example, he never got around to looking at what happened to the British antislavery movement after 1833, which was already fairly well covered in the works of Coupland and Mathieson.[28] What he did do was to reorganize and redraft his dissertation materials and to present them in a new and highly condensed form. This involved, among

24 *Inward Hunger*, p.51.
25 *Ibid.*, pp.49–50; and *British Historians*, pp.197–208.
26 *Inward Hunger*, p.64.
27 *The Negro in the Caribbean*, "Acknowledgments."
28 Coupland, *The British Anti-Slavery Movement*; W. L. Mathieson, *British Slavery and its Abolition, 1823–1828* (London, 1926), *Great Britain and the Slave Trade, 1839–1865* (London, 1929), *British Slave Emancipation, 1838–1849* (London, 1932), and *The Sugar Colonies and Governor Eyre* (London, 1936).

other revisions, abandoning the narrative structure of the earlier work in favor of a series of portraits or collages: "The Development of British Capitalism, 1783–1833," "The 'Commercial Part of the Nation' and Slavery," "The 'Saints' and Slavery," and so on. The other major change was the insertion of those broad claims that have since attracted so much attention and for which the book is principally remembered.

Unlike the dissertation, this new version represented a clear break with the prevailing historiographical views of the day. The Williams approach is, if nothing else, bold. One consequence of this is that *Capitalism and Slavery* achieves an effect, rare among works of modern historical scholarship, of being aesthetically pleasing. The sense that he is addressing himself to the major economic and social issues of the day, his confident assertions regarding the motives which at different times swayed public policy, the adroit marshalling of detail, above all the broad sweep of his argument carry the reader along in a way achieved by few works of history.

Like many innovators, however, Williams was not averse to the use of hyperbole. This is much in evidence in *Capitalism and Slavery,* which, as the reader is soon made aware, goes further than his modestly entitled doctoral thesis and is, in fact, no less than an economic *explanation* of abolition.

> When British capitalism depended on the West Indies, [the capitalists] ignored slavery or defended it. When British capitalism found the West Indian monopoly nuisance, they destroyed West Indian slavery as the first step in the destruction of West Indian monopoly. (P. 169)

In short, it was the same forces that had built up the slave system—self-interest, greed, and the lust for power—that ultimately combined to destroy it. If dependent slave colonies had appeared advantageous in the age of mercantilism they had, in the new age of mature capitalism, become a hindrance. He states his case forcefully:

> The attack falls into three phases: the attack on the slave trade, the attack on slavery, the attack on the preferential sugar duties. The slave trade was abolished in 1807, slavery in 1833, the sugar preference in 1846. These three events are inseparable. (P. 136)

But in what sense, we may wonder, were they inseparable? Although at first sight the Williams thesis, as it has come to be known, appears strikingly simple, on closer examination it turns out to be nothing of the kind. At one level it sets out to show how, from the American Revolution onward, the economic and political interests which supported the colonial slave system were progressively weakened and replaced by the emerging forces of industrial capitalism. At another level it purports to show that these new interests were inherently hostile to slavery. And at yet other levels it is a statement about the relative importance of economic as opposed to other sorts of motive and, closely bound up with this, the extent to which selfless idealism, such as that attributed to the abolitionists, contributed to the eventual outcome.

Like all reductionist accounts, however, it has its problems. One of these was that of deciding what weight, if any, to give to the work of the humanitarians. In the dissertation this was easily handled: it was there accepted that economic considerations were only one factor among many. But if, as was now being claimed, they were the only or at all events the overriding factor it necessarily followed that the humanitarian contribution would have to be correspondingly reduced. In short, to substantiate this new argument, it was necessary not merely to show that economic influences were important but—and this was a good deal more difficult—that humanitarian influences were unimportant.

Before considering how he went about solving this problem, however, it is necessary to look at Williams's own version of events.

In choosing to base his study on Ragatz's findings Williams was building on insecure foundations. Ragatz, it is now clear, took the planters' perennial complaints too literally and as a result saw the beginning of West Indian decline as having occurred more than a generation earlier than it did. As Seymour Drescher has since shown,[29] up to 1807, and indeed for some years thereafter, the British slave system continued to expand its share of world sugar and coffee production, its proportion of British trade in

29 Drescher, *Econocide: British Slavery in the Era of Abolition* (Pittsburgh, 1977).

terms both of exports and imports, and the supply of virgin land available to it. Far from being in process of decline, the sugar colonies were, whatever forms of economic measurement one cares to use, actually becoming more important to the mother country. This, as we have seen, is closer to what Coupland had assumed.[30] It thus follows that economic decline could not have been a causative factor at least so far as the abolition of the slave trade was concerned. That decline did set in subsequently is not in dispute, but the effect of Drescher's work has been to suggest a causative pattern which is the exact opposite of the one that Williams proposes, namely that economic decline, instead of being the cause, was actually the consequence of abolition.[31]

Yet even supposing that Ragatz's theory was correct it is hard to make sense of the arguments Williams uses. According to Williams there were two reasons why slavery had to be got rid of: monopoly and overproduction. Let us begin with monopoly.

The monopoly to which, in Williams's account, British capitalists so vehemently objected was, of course, the privileged access to the British market that West Indian sugar producers enjoyed by virtue of paying lower tariffs. It was, as we have seen, to get rid of this monopoly that the capitalists were supposed "as the first step" to have "destroyed West Indian slavery" (p. 169). But why, we may ask, bother with slavery at all, why not simply abolish the preferential tariffs? More to the point, however, is the question of why capitalists should have objected to the West Indian monopoly in the first place since it was not, in the sense of giving colonial producers control over the pricing of their product, a monopoly at all. The fact is that the West Indies produced more sugar than the British market could absorb and the surplus had to be sold on the world market in competition with sugar from elsewhere. It was thus the world price which, at least up to 1833, largely determined the renumeration which West Indian producers received. This is evident from Table 1.

30 *The British Anti-Slavery Movement,* p. 63.
31 For a brief summary of Drescher's findings and their relation to the Ragatz and Williams theses see Seymour Drescher, "Capitalism and the Decline of Slavery: The British Case in Comparative Perspective," *Annals of the New York Academy of Sciences, 292* (1977), pp. 132–42.

Table 1   Comparative Sugar Prices (per cwt.), Exclusive of Duty, on the London Market, 1823–47

YEAR	BRITISH WEST INDIES		BRAZIL		CUBA		YEAR	BRITISH WEST INDIES		BRAZIL		CUBA	
	s.	d.	s.	d.	s.	d.		s.	d.	s.	d.	s.	d.
1823	32	11	28	9	32	10	1836	40	10	27	11	33	2
1824	31	6	24	2	26	10	1837	34	7	21	3	27	10
1825	38	6	35	3	37	6	1838	33	8	21	3	27	3
1826	30	7	28	9	32	8	1839	39	2	22	1	26	8
1827	33	9	29	9	37	0	1840	49	1	21	6	25	4
1828	31	8	27	10	34	8	1841	39	8	20	9	21	6
1829	28	7	21	8	30	8	1842	36	11	18	4	20	1
1830	24	11	18	11	24	2	1843	33	9	17	2	21	2
1831	23	8	17	11	23	10	1844	33	8	17	0	21	8
1832	27	8	21	5	24	10	1845	32	11	20	6	26	4
1833	29	3	22	5	24	9	1846	34	5	19	11	24	6
1834	29	5	23	3	25	11	1847	28	3	21	2	25	10
1835	33	5	27	5	31	4							

SOURCES: *Parliamentary Papers:* 1841, XXVI (290), p.281; 1847–48, LVIII (422), p.535; 1852–53, XCIX (461), p.569.

These figures do not, of course, include the additional costs paid by British consumers on account of the tariff. These rose sharply during the Napoleonic Wars and by 1805 effectively doubled the price at which sugar was retailed.[32] This, however, was a quite separate issue. Had foreign sugar been admitted at the same rate of duty as West Indian sugar it would not have affected the price at which sugar was retailed by more than a few percentage points.

So where, it may be asked, does Williams's evidence of opposition to monopoly come from? The answer is that it came initially from Mauritian and East Indian producers who, until 1825 and 1836 respectively, were obliged to import their sugar into Britain at less favorable rates than those enjoyed by the West Indians. But as Williams's own endnotes make plain,[33] there was no general outcry until after 1838 when, as a result of abolition,

32 For a graph showing the steep rise in tariffs after 1796 see L. J. Ragatz, *The Fall of the Planter Class,* p.380.
33 See endnotes to Chapter 8, "The New Industrial Order," *Capitalism and Slavery,* pp.243–245.

production declined below Britain's own requirements, allowing colonial producers, for the first time, to charge prices significantly above the world average. Thus, as with the West Indian decline thesis, the developments cited by Williams—in this case a marked discrepancy in price between British and foreign sugar—postdated the events they are supposed to explain and are, in reality, consequences and not causes.

The second motive for abolition cited by Williams is "overproduction." As always, he states his case boldly: "Overproduction in 1807 demanded abolition; overproduction in 1833 demanded emancipation" (p.152). Again, one is entitled to enquire whether, if overproduction was indeed the problem, the government could not have found less drastic ways of curtailing it. The obvious way would have been to lower the tariff, thereby decreasing the price and encouraging consumption. It was certainly not a problem that need have troubled British capitalists who, if what they wanted was cheap sugar, had every reason to welcome the price cutting which was the inevitable consequence of a glutted market. If, as a result, West Indian producers went bankrupt this was no concern of theirs.

What also needs to be pointed out is that the two sets of motives cited are mutually incompatible; monopoly favors producers at the expense of consumers whereas overproduction has precisely the opposite effect.[34] On whose side, then, was the British government acting? Assuming, as on the basis of the general thrust of Williams's argument we must, that it was acting on the side of British consumers (who included, of course, "the capitalists"), its policies would seem to have been wholly counterproductive. As Table 2 shows, sugar prices were notably low in 1807 and 1833 and rose thereafter.

---

34 Williams confuses the issue by referring in this connection to "subsidies" on the re-exportation of sugar from Britain to the Continent: "The West Indian planters were being paid, in fact, to enable them to compete with people . . . who were some of Britain's best customers. . . . To the capitalists this was intolerable" (p.152). In reality the "subsidies" were merely drawbacks on the amounts paid in the form of tariffs when the sugar entered the country. Similarly, the so-called bounties were payments made in respect of sugar refined in England which, having been substantially reduced in volume, qualified for an additional sum. It is hard to see why capitalists, or indeed anyone else, should have objected to this. Drawbacks were, in any case, discontinued in 1819 with the result that re-exports, far from being subsidized, were actually being taxed. This, not surprisingly, drew many complaints from the West India Committee. See Ragatz, *The Fall of the Planter Class*, p.336.

Table 2   Price Range of Raw Sugar in London (in shillings per cwt.)
and Sugar Consumption in the United Kingdom
(in lbs. per capita per year), 1790–1849.

YEAR	PRICE	CON-SUMPTION	YEAR	PRICE	CON-SUMPTION	YEAR	PRICE	CON-SUMPTION
1790	38–46		1810	43–54		1830	23–25	
1791	47–65		1811	35–45		1831	23–25	
1792	48–76		1812	42–49		1832	23–30	
1793	41–73		1813	51–75		1833	26–31	
1794	32–67		1814	54–97		1834	31–33	
1795	42–75	13.0	1815	57–75	17.0	1835	30–38	17.8
1796	61–78		1816	49–60		1836	38–45	
1797	52–75		1817	44–54		1837	33–37	
1798	59–83		1818	47–55		1838	33–42	
1799	26–87		1819	36–51		1839	39	
1800	32–70		1820	34–37		1840	49	
1801	32–75		1821	29–35		1841	40	
1802	26–55		1822	28–34		1842	37	16.4
1803	30–58		1823	27–37		1843	37	
1804	44–66	18.0	1824	30–34	17.6	1844	33	
1805	48–59		1825	32–41		1845	33	
1806	39–49		1826	30–39		1846	33	
1807	32–38		1827	32–36		1847	27	22.6
1808	32–50		1828	32–38		1848	26	
1809	36–51		1829	26–30		1849	22	

SOURCE: Noel Deerr, *The History of Sugar* (2 vols., London, 1949–50), 2, pp. 531–532.

Most striking of all, however, is the fact that, between 1760 and 1939, the only times that per capita sugar consumption in Britain actually fell were in the years 1810–19 and 1840–44.[35] In the first instance this was caused by high prices due to increasing taxation and the vicissitudes of war, but in the second case it was the direct result of the shortfall of production that followed abolition. For a time at least the British found themselves having to pay for their philanthropy. If emancipation was the result of a capitalist demand for cheap sugar it would appear to have been remarkably wrong-headed.

35   These figures are given in Noel Deerr, *The History of Sugar* (2 vols., London, 1949–50), 2, p. 532. But perhaps the best source for judging the accuracy of Williams's economic arguments is *Parliamentary Papers*, 1852–53, XCIX (461), *Tabular Return showing the Quantities of Sugar of the several Sorts Imported into the United Kingdom . . . from 1800 to 1852, followed by a Comparative Statement of the Average Prices of British Plantation and Foreign Sugar (ordinary Yellow Havannah) for the same Series of Years*, pp. 568–569.

It thus transpires that the economic explanation of abolition is altogether less persuasive than Williams would have us believe. In particular, he fails to demonstrate any plausible connection between the interests of British capitalists and the destruction of the West Indian slave system, still less how these supposed "interests" were translated into legislative action. It is notable that Ragatz, from whom he draws much of his data, made no such connection. What makes the case Williams presents appear compelling is not the evidence he cites, which singularly fails to support the large claims he makes, or the logic of his arguments, since these on closer examination turn out to be incompatible, but the power of the rhetoric with which it is presented. Far from being a straightforward work of history as it might at first sight appear, *Capitalism and Slavery* is, in fact, a polemical work of great subtlety and passion.

Nowhere is this more in evidence than in its treatment of the abolitionists, who, insofar as they were humanitarians, as plainly they were, and acted from humanitarian motives, as plainly they did, could not be readily fitted into the book's overall scheme. As already noted, Williams saw little cause to celebrate the way in which the West Indies had been treated by the British. Like other West Indian intellectuals he resented the manner in which, as if it were Britain's principal legacy to her black subjects, historians had sung the abolitionists' praises. To all of which must be added the fact that, in Williams's own case, these abolitionists could be seen to represent that genteel liberal culture to which Coupland and the fellows of All Souls belonged and by which he himself had been rejected.

His characterization of his own work in *British Historians and the West Indies* is in these respects revealing.

> Exclusively West Indian in his outlook and interests . . . Williams sought to illuminate the West Indian scene by international experience. His *Capitalism and Slavery* was an explicit attack on the conventional British thesis on the abolition of the slave system; he saw abolition as the logical outcome of an economic development which, having outgrown its foundations, abolished the very system of slavery which had given it its head start in the world.

Other West Indian writers had fallen foul of the British establishment,

> But the full force of British hostility was reserved for Williams, himself a product of Oxford, as a rebel against the British historical tradition which Oxford had done so much to develop. The darkest threats were issued about his historical analysis. His *Capitalism and Slavery*, greeted with high praise in the United States when it was published in 1944, failed to attract the attention of British publishers before 1964.[36]

What these "dark threats" were is not revealed. The British had other matters to preoccupy them in 1944, with the result that the appearance of *Capitalism and Slavery* largely escaped notice.[37] The refusal to publish his work, however, he attributes to an attitude typified by the comment of an English publisher to whom, in 1939, he had offered his then still unrevised Oxford thesis: "I would never publish such a book. It is contrary to the British tradition!"[38]

But if Williams could not celebrate the abolitionists and their achievements, he could not ignore them either. Only one of his 13 chapters, " 'The Saints' and Slavery," was devoted to the abolitionists specifically, but there are frequent comments about them and their activities in four of his other chapters. Indeed, much of the evidence he uses to illustrate the attitudes of British capitalists derives from abolitionist sources. This is most clearly exemplified in his chapter on "Capitalism and the West Indies," where he cites evidence of abolitionist activity in the various British regions as indicative of the attitudes and interests of those who controlled the major industries in those areas (pp. 154–67). This is essentially impressionistic and, as such, is characteristic of his technique generally. In none of these chapters does he attempt a chronological account of the events he is describing.

36 *British Historians*, p.210.
37 The American responses, from which he quotes in his autobiography, were mostly glowing. It is notable, however, that Elizabeth Donnan, reviewing *Capitalism and Slavery* for the *American Historical Review* of April, 1945, thought that "Mr. Williams in his zeal to establish the primacy of the economic forces is somewhat less than fair to the humanitarians whose voices were raised against the slave trade and later against slavery." *Inward Hunger*, p.71.
38 *British Historians*, p.211.

One result of this is that he leaves himself free to roam backwards and forwards in time, selecting material to illustrate the arguments he is advancing. A second consequence is to make it extremely difficult to refute his arguments, for even if it can be shown beyond doubt that the particular pieces of evidence he cites do not support the large claims he makes, the possibility remains that there may be evidence somewhere else that does.

What is most notable about Williams's treatment of the abolitionists, however, is not the details—although some of these, as we will see, are striking—but the rhetorical strategy he adopts. Of particular interest in this respect is the way he forestalls criticism by paying tribute to the abolitionists—they were "a brilliant band"—and at the same time seeks to minimize their achievement—"their importance has been seriously misunderstood and grossly exaggerated." Like Mark Antony's funeral oration in *Julius Caesar,* Williams's chapter on the abolitionists, which begins with Clarkson and ends with Thomas Carlyle, is a deliberate exercise in denigration. Like Antony's speech, it is very subtle in that it relies on suggestion and implication rather than on forthright statement and for that reason is difficult to refute. It is only *compared to others* that Wilberforce "appears small in stature" (p.181). He does not actually *say* that Cropper, with his East Indian interests, had ulterior motives for supporting abolition but the implications are obvious (pp.186–87).[39] Nor does he specifically *tell* us that the East Indian sugar the abolitionists were intent on importing was slave-produced (his dissertation assumes that it was not) but again the reader is left to draw his own conclusions (p.184).[40] And each time it might appear that he has gone too far he reassures the reader that defamation is not his intention and that, on the contrary, the abolitionists were a splendid group.

Finding material with which to denigrate the abolitionists is not difficult. The planters provided plenty of it and this, as in the case of Cropper, Williams does not hesitate to use. What is

39 For a detailed account of Cropper's motives see David Brion Davis, "James Cropper and the British Anti-Slavery Movement, 1821–1823" *Journal of Negro History,* 45 (1960), pp.241-258.

40 Williams, "Economic Aspects," ch. 3. There is no evidence that British East Indian sugar was slave-produced. Certainly it was the assumption of both British and American abolitionists, as well as of the British government, that it was free-grown. For an account of abolitionist efforts to substitute East Indian for Brazilian and Cuban sugar see Howard Temperley, *British Antislavery, 1833–1870* (London, 1972), pp.165–66.

lacking, however, is any clear indication of what the abolitionists could have done to win Williams's approval. "Wilberforce was familiar with all that went on in the hold of a slave ship but ignored what went on at the bottom of a mineshaft" (p.183). Ought he, then, to have spent more time in mineshafts? Had he done so it is unlikely that he would have gained higher marks, for almost immediately we find Williams taking Professor Merivale to task for claiming that slavery was merely "a great social evil differing in degree and quality, not in kind, from . . . pauperism, or the overworking of children" (p.194). Clarkson's final "betrayal" of the cause related, as Williams must well have known, to his opposing a legislative provision that encouraged British men-of-war to seize slaving vessels after rather than before they had loaded their cargoes.[41] Williams's concluding peroration (pp.193–96), designed to illustrate Britain's change of heart after 1833 ("Slavery was now regarded in a different light. . . . Even the intellectuals were engulfed") mixes quotations spanning the entire period from the 1790's to the 1840's.

All this would, of course, have been much clearer if he had actually spelled out for the benefit of his readers what the principal concerns of the British humanitarians after 1833 were: supporting the cause of the West Indian freedmen, suppressing the Atlantic slave trade by means of naval intervention and international treaty, sponsoring schemes for African civilization, encouraging abolitionist activity in the United States and on the Continent, and opposing the introduction into Britain of slave-grown sugar from Brazil and China.[42] In the absence of such an account much of what he says is confusing and a good deal simply misleading. For example, he devotes three pages (pp.172–75) to the opposition put up in the 1840's by "the capitalists" to Britain's "noble experiment" of suppressing the foreign slave trade without explaining what this policy was, describing the successes it achieved, or mentioning that the opposition to it proved, in

---

41 *Capitalism and Slavery,* p.194 and endnote 104. The latter refers to Mathieson, *Great Britain and the Slave Trade,* pp.34–35, where the reasons for Clarkson's action are made quite clear.

42 An account of these activities will be found in the Coupland, Mathieson, and Temperley volumes already cited. Among the organizations whose activities he overlooks are the Central Negro Emancipation Committee (1837–40), Thomas Fowell Buxton's African Civilization Society (1839–43), Joseph Pease's British India Society (1839–43), and Joseph Sturge's British and Foreign Anti-Slavery Society (1839–present).

the event, unsuccessful. Similarly, he has Lord Brougham, in 1843, "still looking forward with sanguine hope to the abolition of slavery in India" (p. 186), but fails to mention that slavery in India was, after much abolitionist agitation, abolished in that very year.[43] Joseph Sturge is introduced (p. 158) as a representative of the new capitalist class that in the 1830's was turning against the West Indies. Did Sturge have the destruction of the West Indian monopoly in mind? Plainly not. Who would imagine from Williams's account that during the 1840's he was to lead the national antislavery organization in a prolonged campaign against the acceptance of "blood-stained sugar" and in favor of *retaining* the preferential tariffs?[44] Such examples bear out Roger Anstey's claim that "Dr. Williams too often uses evidence misleadingly, makes too large claims on only partial evidence, or ignores evidence."[45]

All historians, of course, make mistakes and not a few change their minds. This is commonly the case with innovators and it would be an act of gross injustice to dismiss a new and striking interpretation merely because it contained a number of factual errors or appeared to claim more than the evidence cited would readily permit. Yet it is hard to apply generous criteria to *Capitalism and Slavery,* not least because Williams himself had already produced, in his Oxford dissertation, a very different and, it must be admitted, more accurate account. Again, allowance must be made for the way he condensed this earlier version. Even so, it is hard to suppose that he actually *believed,* as he states in *Capitalism and Slavery,* that "The Emancipation Act marked the end of the abolitionist efforts" (p. 191). If he did it would be an extraordinary statement. Coupland's *The British Anti-Slavery Movement* had devoted three of its eight chapters to the period after 1833 and W. L. Mathieson had written three whole volumes on the subject. These are works Williams cites.[46] Yet to have stated that the British antislavery crusade continued on into these later

---

43 Temperley, *British Antislavery*, Chapter 5, esp. p. 107.
44 *Ibid.*, pp. 137–167.
45 Roger Anstey, "Capitalism and Slavery, A Critique," *Economic History Review*, 21 (1968), pp. 307–320. See also G. R. Mellor, *British Imperial Trusteeship, 1783–1850* (London, 1951), pp. 54–57, 118–120, 443–447. Mellor concludes his account of *Capitalism and Slavery* with the observation that "unless those who are engaged in research are very careful they will find what they are looking for."
46 Mathieson, *Great Britain and the Slave Trade, 1839–1865; British Slave Emancipation, 1838–1849;* and *The Sugar Colonies and Governor Eyre.*

years would have meant acknowledging that it not only had an independent life of its own but wielded considerable political power. This would have undermined Williams's own essentially economic thesis. It is easy to see why, despite the urging of Henry Steele Commager,[47] he never turned his attention to American abolitionism, which plainly did have a life of its own and wielded great political power.

Williams never responded to his critics, nor, after *Capitalism and Slavery*, did he modify his views in any essential respects. In his 1970 book *From Columbus to Castro: The History of the Caribbean, 1492 to 1969*, he reproduces the same arguments, often word for word.[48] His tone, however, is more overtly polemical. He is writing now as Prime Minister and his judgments are appropriately *ex cathedra*. There are, however, changes. Britain's 50-year struggle to secure the suppression of the Atlantic slave trade is here dealt with, although only cursorily. The "fundamental" object of this policy, we are told, was to "protect the British West Indian planters, denied annual slave imports, from competition with sugar producers like Cuba and Brazil, which continued the slave trade."[49] Unlike Coupland, he was never one to dwell on the horrors of the slave trade or the iniquity of the slave traders, nor, plainly, does he feel any sympathy for those who were attempting to suppress this traffic. On the other hand he does note that capitalists objected to this misuse of Britain's resources and quotes extensively the comments of foreigners who objected to what they saw as an infringement of their sovereign rights. As always, the British were high-handed; and yet, it would also appear, they were not high-handed enough, for

> The campaign against the foreign slave trade failed because British capitalism was heavily interested in trade with Latin America, particularly Brazil and Cuba. It could not kill the goose that laid the golden eggs—that is, it could not oppose the introduction of the slaves who produced the sugar and coffee that made possible the purchase of British textiles and provided freights for British ships.[50]

47 *Inward Hunger*, pp.71, 77, 79.
48 Eric Williams, *From Columbus to Castro: The History of the Caribbean, 1492 to 1969* (London, 1970). Compare, for example, pp.269, 289, 293, 297, and 318–319 of this work to pp.174–175 and 193–195 of *Capitalism and Slavery*.
49 *From Columbus to Castro*, p.311.
50 *Ibid.*, p.310.

Britain's right hand, it would appear, did not know what its left hand was doing. That, despite all the criticism, the suppression policy was maintained, that it substantially reduced the volume of the traffic, and that by armed intervention, it effectively ended the trade to Brazil, are not mentioned.[51]

In dealing with emancipation, and treating the topic more briefly, Williams comes close to contradicting his own argument. To mount an attack on monopoly at a time when markets were glutted was, he points out, "the height of illogicality."[52] Why British capitalists, whom he had earlier presented as being so hard-headed, failed to realize this and proceeded, by means of abolition, to reduce the supply and thereby double the price of sugar is glossed over. More surprisingly, the prevalence of antislavery activity in industrial areas, which he had earlier used as evidence of capitalist interest, is now cited as proof that "the emancipation of the slaves was part of the general movement of the European industrial proletariat towards democracy."[53]

To square these observations with the historical record is not easy. They can, however, be readily understood if we argue that the search for objective truth about the past is not the only, or necessarily the principal, reason for writing history. In his foreward to *British Historians and the West Indies,* Williams tells us that his own work

> is not inferior, in terms of his responsibility to his discipline, to that of the majority of historians whose work he . . . seeks to analyse. And even if he is over sanguine in this respect, in the final analysis it is the heart that matters more than the head. The author seeks principally to emancipate his compatriots whom the historical writings he analyses sought to deprecate and to imprison for all time in the inferior status to which these writings sought to condemn them.[54]

---

51 For an account of these policies and their results see Christopher Lloyd, *The Navy and the Slave Trade: The Suppression of the Slave Trade in the Nineteenth Century* (London, 1949). The political aspects are dealt with more fully in Mathieson, *Great Britain and the Slave Trade.*

52 *From Columbus to Castro,* p.289.

53 *Ibid.,* pp.292–293.

54 *British Historians,* p.12. For a critique of this work see Elsa V. Goveia, "New Shibboleths for Old," pp.48–51.

It is, then, to free his fellow West Indians from the "servile mentality" encouraged by "intellectual concepts and attitudes worked out by metropolitan scholars in the age of colonialism" that he is writing.[55] This, as Alan Bullock notes in his preface, is an entirely laudable aim.[56] There is everything to be said for looking at history from new and, in particular, since most history has been written in the metropolis, from nonmetropolitan points of view. Williams sees his own writings as specifically addressed to the needs of the newly independent nations. "The old intellectual world is dead. . . . The new world of the intellect open to the emerging countries has nothing to lose but the chains that tie it to a world that has departed."[57] Yet to reconcile these aims with the strict requirements of scholarship is not always easy. As another West Indian, Arthur Lewis, founding Vice-Chancellor of the University of the West Indies (and subsequently a Nobel prizewinner for his work on development economics), reminded his audience in a Graduation Address at Mona, Jamaica, "When we abandon the pursuit of truth for any reason, whether because it is dangerous or because we are lazy or for any other reason, then we became parasites. . . . This is why academic people have always to be so hard on one another."[58]

So what are we to make of Williams's account of abolition? Let us suppose that it could be shown that prior to emancipation British West Indian sugar prices were never significantly out of line with world prices. Let us also suppose that the two major pieces of antislavery legislation, the abolition of the slave trade in 1807 and the emancipation of the slaves in 1833, each occurred at a time when British West Indian sugar prices were low and British per capita sugar consumption was high. And let us suppose further that each was followed by a dramatic rise in the price of sugar on the British market and a corresponding decrease in consumption. And finally let us suppose that, in the second instance at least, this rise was the direct and clearly foreseen result of the

55 *British Historians*, pp.12, 13.
56 *Ibid.*, pp.7–8.
57 *Ibid.*, p.13.
58 Quoted in E. C. Richardson, *The Scholarship of Eric Williams* (Port-of-Spain, Trinidad, 1967), p.24.

policies adopted. How much would then be left of the Williams thesis?

As we have noted, all these things can be shown. Certainly, they are there in Ragatz. What is perhaps most striking here is that Ragatz, who deals exhaustively with tariff policy and the debates it occasioned, fails to make the connections between these and abolition in the way Williams does. Nor did the participants themselves. But then neither did Williams, at least not in his doctoral dissertation.

He did, nevertheless, secure a place for himself in the annals of historiography by becoming the first scholar to explore, in any purposeful way, the relationship between abolitionism and the emergence of modern industrial capitalism. In this respect, however, his work is more important for the questions it raises than for the answers it gives. Williams's error was to look for a solution in the form of a cash nexus. It was what, on the basis of his assumptions about British policy toward the West Indies in other periods, he expected to find. It was a type of explanation much in favor in the Depression years. It also explains why, to those of a particular political persuasion, *Capitalism and Slavery* continues to be regarded as a definitive work. In the event, he was not able to find the evidence he was looking for, at least not of a kind that would allow him to make out a straightforward case in traditional narrative form. Instead, he did what seemed the next best thing, which was to paint a portrait of a society, in process of rapid economic transformation and much preoccupied with financial matters, within which the fragmentary and often conflicting items of information he had collected could be accommodated. His method was part impressionist, part pointillist, consisting of broad general statements followed by brief, heavily footnoted particulars, not all of which, as closer examination discloses, bear on the point at issue.

As a piece of historical rhetoric, *Capitalism and Slavery* is superb, as its reappearance in successive reprints reveals. For the light it throws on abolition, however, his Oxford dissertation is a great deal more subtle, open, and suggestive. In part this is because he had not yet locked himself into the position of having to choose between idealism and interest, a position into which his claims about the predominance of the latter inevitably forced him. He was thus able to show, often with considerable insight, how the two interacted. Humanitarians were fully aware of the need to marshal economic arguments in favor of their cause, although it by no means follows that they were themselves economically motivated or even that this was the case with those whom they were addressing. They simply had to demonstrate, in response to the essentially economic arguments of their opponents, that they too could argue in economic terms and that the final result of their policies would not be as bad as was being claimed and might even, in some respects, be in the national interest.

How far they themselves were actually persuaded by such arguments is hard to ascertain. In such cases it is always difficult to draw a line between belief, wishful thinking, and an understandable desire to put the best possible face on matters. The obvious answer is that it depended very much on circumstances and the individual. That there were those who took economic arguments literally was demonstrated when letters began arriving at the offices of the British and Foreign Anti-Slavery Society enquiring why, contrary to expectation, the price of sugar had gone up rather than down.[59] Most abolitionists, however, would probably have accepted Thomas Fowell Buxton's 1833 dictum "that if justice were incompatible with the cultivation of sugar, he would prefer justice to sugar."[60] Whether those Parliamentarians who voted for abolition accepted this view is another matter, but then no one expected that the British would have to go without sugar. What is plain is that there are no grounds for adopting a double standard by assuming that while idealism might be used as a cloak for economic interest, economic interest could not equally readily be used as a cloak for idealism.

Most recent commentators, it is worth noting, have explicitly rejected such simple dualisms. While accepting that abolition and the economic changes that were simultaneously occurring in Britain and elsewhere were intimately connected, they have been more concerned with analyzing the way in which these developments gave rise to attitudes hostile to slavery than with attempting to document the interplay of economic interests. One such approach has been to show that the Industrial Revolution

59 Temperley, *British Antislavery*, pp. 147–48.
60 *Hansard's Parliamentary Debates, Third Series, 18* (June 10, 1833), 538.

itself, by requiring as it did greater flexibility in the use of labor, and by opening up new vistas of economic progress, gave rise to an ideology—exemplified in the writings of Adam Smith—that was fundamentally hostile to slavery.[61] Much of the grassroots support for abolition, it has been demonstrated, came from small independent entrepreneurs whose personal experiences within the burgeoning metropolitan economy made them highly receptive to such notions.[62] Others have explored the wider implications of the issue by pointing out that abolitionism, far from being an isolated phenomenon, was part of a much broader humanitarian movement that swept through the societies of the Western world during these years and led to the adoption of new attitudes toward the relief of the poor, the treatment of criminals, care of the insane, and a host of other institutions and practices.[63] How people regarded slavery in the colonies had much to do with how they felt about questions involving freedom and social discipline at home.[64] Accounting for abolition has thus become part of a much larger enterprise that involves tracing the relationship between changes in the economic sphere and evolving notions about progress, social institutions, and individual moral responsibility within Western society generally.

To the extent that he was prepared to consider these broader aspects of the problem, as in his Oxford dissertation to some degree he was, Williams's approach was very much in line with modern historical thinking. The space devoted to abolition was, of course, much greater in the dissertation than in any of his later

61 Howard Temperley, "Capitalism, Slavery and Ideology," *Past and Present*, 75 (May, 1977), pp.94–118; "Anti-Slavery as a Form of Cultural Imperialism," in Christine Bolt and Seymour Drescher, eds., *Anti-Slavery, Religion and Reform: Essays in Memory of Roger Anstey* (Hamden, Conn., and Folkestone, England, 1980), pp.335–350; "The Ideology of Antislavery" in David Eltis and James Walvin, eds., *The Abolition of the Atlantic Slave Trade: Origins and Effects in Europe, Africa and the Americas* (Madison, Wisc., 1981), pp.21–35; and "Abolition and the National Interest," in Jack Hayward, ed., *Out of Slavery* (London, 1985).

62 Seymour Drescher, *Capitalism and Antislavery: British Mobilization in Comparative Perspective* (London, 1986).

63 See the two-part article by Thomas L. Haskell, "Capitalism and the Origins of the Humanitarian Sensibility," *American Historical Review*, 90 (April and June, 1985), 339–361, 547–566.

64 David Brion Davis, *The Problem of Slavery in the Age of Revolution* (Ithaca, N.Y., 1975).

published works. It is a pity that the publisher to whom he apparently offered it in 1939 did not agree to take it.[65]

In the event, as we have seen, he published the fruits of his research in the United States and in a quite different form, abandoning the cautious narrative approach of the dissertation in favor of a more impressionistic and polemical one. Precisely why he did so is a matter for future biographers to unravel. It was itself, however, an act of some historical moment in that it not only provided the Caribbean with what many have since come to regard as a historical declaration of independence—as the comments of Mr. Forbes Burnham and Mrs. Marilyn Gordon indicate—but also constituted an important stepping stone in what was to become a notable political career.

That events took the turn they did is a matter about which scholars should have mixed feelings. The defection of Eric Williams, first to the Secretariat of the Caribbean Commission and then to politics, was a notable loss to the profession. *Capitalism and Slavery,* the work for which he is principally remembered and which he published while he was still only in his early thirties, is, at least in its treatment of abolition, deeply flawed. Today it is remembered in this respect, by those outside the Caribbean, principally because it marks one of the extreme poles in an ongoing debate, the other pole being W. E. H. Lecky's much-quoted remark about the British antislavery crusade being "among the three or four perfectly virtuous pages comprised in the history of nations."[66] It is, of course, a misleading polarization since even in his later writings Williams never went so far as to claim that the abolitionists were lacking in idealism, still less that they were unvirtuous, nor did Lecky say that abolition was without its economic aspects. The solution, as modern historians are well aware, and as the young Eric Williams went some way toward showing, hinges on finding ways of relating the two.

---

65 *British Historians,* p.211.

66 W. E. H. Lecky, *A History of European Morals from Augustus to Charlemaigne* (7th edn., London, 1886), I, p.153. It was simply a passing comment. Lecky was concerned with morals rather than economics, also with a much earlier period of history.

Michael Craton

What and Who to Whom and What: The Significance of Slave Resistance

The essence of *Capitalism and Slavery* for most of its readers—what is commonly termed "the Williams thesis"—is the book's concern with the degree to which the origins, the nature, and, most of all, the ending of formal slavery were determined by global economics. The twelfth and last chapter of *Capitalism and Slavery,* however, does not fit comfortably into this restricted view of Williams's ideas, and therefore tends to be ignored.

Unlike the rest of *Capitalism and Slavery,* Chapter 12 deals almost exclusively with the colonies rather than the metropolis, to show the ways in which "the colonists themselves were in a ferment which indicated, reflected, and reacted upon the great events in Britain."[1] In broad terms, it concentrates on questions of political power and expediency rather than on economics and abstract humanitarianism. In Chapter 12, Eric Williams argues that, quite apart from economic or moral considerations, metropolitan legislators became concerned with the way that both slave unrest and plantocratic recalcitrance jeopardized the very fabric of British imperialism in the West Indies. As the slavery debate intensified in the metropolis, it exacerbated the existing tension between masters and slaves within the colonies. Planters tightened their repressive system and openly threatened secession if slavery were decreed abolished, while the slaves responded by an escalating series of plots and open rebellions, climaxing in the Jamaican Christmas Rebellion of 1831–32. "In 1833, therefore, the alternatives were clear," concludes Williams: "emancipation from above, or emancipation from below. But EMANCIPA-TION."[2]

---

1 Eric Williams, *Capitalism and Slavery* (London, 1964), 197.
2 *Ibid.,* 208.

The purpose of the present essay is twofold. Its longer part will test the validity and strength of Williams's arguments in Chapter 12 of *Capitalism and Slavery* against the historical evidence. Then, having decided that Williams's arguments are at least plausible, it will more briefly and tentatively address the more difficult task: deciding whether questions of power politics, particularly the active role of the slaves themselves, are, or even can be, reconciled with the familiar understanding of the Williams thesis.

With remarkable brevity and brilliant illumination through selective quotation, Eric Williams shows in Chapter 12 how rapidly change came to the British West Indies after the French Revolution and the Napoleonic Wars. The West Indian planters responded first to the Registry Bill of 1815 and then to the proposed amelioration measures from 1823 to 1832 with a panicky rearguard action. Even more serious to them than the threat of losing their fortunes was the prospect of losing power over their slaves and all nonwhites, a system of control that they feared would be undermined if legislation were ever imposed upon the colonies by a metropolitan government fallen under the sway of meddling ideologues.[3]

For its part, the growing community of free coloreds was for the first time threatening to exercise an influence proportionate to its size. Feeling superior to the enslaved blacks, the free coloreds sought civil rights hitherto denied them by a plantocracy that they already outnumbered. More respectable than either slaves or the white elite, however, they threatened neither rebellion nor secession. Unlike the mulattoes of Saint-Domingue, they were not fired up by a partial interpretation of the ideals of the French Enlightenment. Their interest, indeed, was to keep the slaves to heel, while professing extreme loyalty to a Crown that might yet use them as counterweights to an overweening plantocracy. From the historians' privileged perspective they were thus the men of the future. But for the present, they were too preoccupied with short-term gains and personal security to pose a radical threat.[4]

3 *Ibid.*, 197–201.
4 *Ibid.*, 201.

For Eric Williams it was the mass of the black slaves who constituted the most dynamic force for change in the British West Indian colonies. "Not nearly as stupid as his master thought him," he writes with residual condescension, "the slave was alert to his surroundings and keenly interested in discussions about his fate." Williams slights the effect upon the British slaves' group consciousness of the events in Saint-Domingue between 1791 and 1804, making far more of the effect of the subsequent "economic dislocation and the vast agitations which shook millions in Britain," as relayed to the slaves through the distorting lenses of their masters' unguarded conversations. "The consensus of opinion among the slaves whenever each discussion arose or each new policy was announced" (or each new governor was sent out), writes Williams confidently, "was that emancipation had been passed in England but was withheld by their masters. . . . No state of the Negro mind was so dangerous as one of undefined and vague expectation."[5]

Whether or not one agrees with Williams that such invariable rumors and exaggerations could have been unintentionally circulated, rumor certainly did play a significant role in the sequence of slave revolts in British slavery's last decades, indicating a causal connection between metropolitan debates and colonial revolts. Williams argues a direct connection between abolition in 1807 and an alleged revolt in British Guiana in 1808 (which in fact never occurred), between the Registration dispute and the Barbadian revolt of 1816, between the first Bathurst Amelioration Circular and the Demerara revolt of 1823, and between the news of wide-ranging political reform in England between 1829 and 1831 and the Jamaican Christmas Rebellion of 1831–32.[6]

With his less than ideal view of the slaves' intelligence and his failure to identify any coherent leadership among the rebellious slaves, Williams could not see the late slave revolts as being anything but spontaneous reactions to ill-founded rumors, bound to fail in their immediate objects. Yet, in the long run and indirectly, he claims, they did succeed. On the strength of the rumor syndrome, the planters were able to attach blame to false philan-

5 Ibid., 201–206.
6 Ibid., 204–207. For the alleged revolt in British Guiana in 1808, Williams cited Governor Nicholson to Lord Castlereagh, June 6, 1808, C.O. 111/8, which clearly refers to a plot rather than an actual outbreak.

thropists, pernicious bureaucrats, and misguided missionaries working on the minds of ignorant blacks—and thus justify their tactics of propaganda, obstructionism, threats of secession, and the extension of repression from slave to nonconformist missionaries. On their side, the legislators at Westminster gradually came to believe, with Lord Brougham, that the colonial whites were a self-interested rabble, indifferent alike to Christian principles and the larger imperial issues, whose behavior in provoking the slaves and threatening secession was jeopardizing the very integrity of the British Empire.[7] Thus, argues Williams, by 1833 a majority came to believe that only by freeing the slaves could the West Indian colonies be made safe within the Empire—a sixth and clinching argument for emancipation.[8]

Williams's chief concern in Chapter 12 is to assess the influence of purely colonial events and forces upon imperial decisions. Just as he had earlier dealt with the crescendo of debate in England, now he describes a parallel tide of colonial unrest. His argument is that the relationship was reciprocal. Yet, whereas he makes much of the effect that the various phases of the antislavery campaign had upon colonial masters and their slaves, he does not integrate successive colonial events into the metropolitan debates with sufficient precision to prove the countervailing influence convincingly.

Williams almost ignores the ways in which the question of slave rebellion conditioned the metropolitan debate almost from the beginning, and this leads him to underplay the way that changes in the nature of slave resistance crucially shaped the course of debate. Also, by understating the horror felt by most imperial legislators for any form of popular rebellion, he fails to convey the way in which most West Indian slave rebellions were counterproductive to the antislavery cause. There was a fundamental difference—in effect as in form—between the earlier "Af-

7 Henry Lord Brougham, *Speeches on Social and Political Subjects,* 2 vols. (London, 1857), II, 93–190.

8 "Economic change, the decline of the monopolists, the development of capitalism, the humanitarian agitation in British churches, contending perorations in the halls of Parliament, had now reached their completion in the determination of the slaves themselves to be free." *Capitalism and Slavery,* 208.

rican" and the later "Creole" forms of slave resistance. While slave revolt could be termed the product of "African savagery," the antislavery lobby could argue that the process of "civilization"—including abolition, amelioration, and even emancipation, as well as the insensible process of creolization—could lessen the chances of colonial insurrection and disturbance. Thus, the evidence that it was the elite, most creolized, even most Christianized, of slaves who were instrumental in the later slave rebellions, was to be a serious blow to the emancipationists of Wilberforce's generation, calling for new attitudes and tactics.

Long before Bryan Edwards, the greatest of British plantocratic writers, made his famous admission that slaves would always rebel when they could because their enslavement was unnatural, depending as it did upon "that absolute coercive necessity which, leaving no choice of action, supercedes all questions of right,"[9] it was taken for granted by abolitionists such as Wilberforce that uncivilized Africans were particularly prone to rebel, since law and order—and their acceptance—were concomitants of civilization. This belief could even be used as an argument against the African trade, particularly once the abolitionist debate came under the shadow of the French Revolution and the terrific slave revolt in Saint-Domingue, which began in 1791.

In a great speech on April 2, 1792, William Wilberforce tried to meld his fellow legislators' beliefs and fears to abolitionist ends. Citing Edward Long, a plantocratic writer altogether cruder than Bryan Edwards, he pointed out that after the 1760 slave rebellion, the Jamaican planters had attempted to place a prohibitive duty on the importation of Coromantine (that is, Gold Coast, Akan-speaking) slaves. "Surely," he declared,

> when gentlemen talk so vehemently of the safety of the islands, and charge us with being so indifferent to it; when they speak of the calamities of St. Domingo, and of similar dangers impending over their own heads at the present hour, it ill becomes them to be the persons who are crying out for further importations. It ill becomes them to charge upon us the crime of stirring up insurrections—upon us who are only adopting the very principles which

9 Bryan Edwards, *The History, Civil and Commercial, of the British Colonies in the West Indies,* 3 vols. (London, 1793), III, 36.

Mr. Long—which in part even the legislature of Jamaica itself—laid down in the time of danger, with an avowed view to the prevention of any such calamity.[10]

Wilberforce disavowed any intention of damaging the plantation economy. On the contrary, abolition should aid the plantations by obviating insurrections. "Why should you any longer import into those countries that which is the very seed of insurrection and rebellion?" he asked.

Why should you persist in introducing those latent principles of conflagration, which, if they should once burst forth, may annihilate in a single day the industry of a hundred years? Why will you subject yourselves to the imminent risk of a calamity which may throw you back a whole century in your profits, in your cultivation, in your progress to the emancipation of your slaves?[11]

Whatever short-term penalties the planters might incur, claimed Wilberforce, would be as nothing to the grander, long-term socioeconomic, political, and moral advantages. "It amounts but to this," he argued,

the colonies on the one hand would have to struggle with some few difficulties and disadvantages at the first for the sake of obtaining on the other hand immediate security to their leading interests; of ensuring, Sir, even their own immediately commencing that system of progressive improvement in the condition of the slaves which is necessary to raise them from the state of brutes to that of rational beings, but which can never begin until the introduction of these new disaffected and dangerous Africans into these same gangs shall have been stopped.[12]

These arguments were reiterated and refined in the debate that finally led to the ending of the British slave trade, 15 years later

---

10 *Parliamentary Debates*, XXIX, 1055–1158, Commons, April 2, 1792, excerpted in Eric Williams (ed.), *The British West Indies at Westminster, Part I, 1789–1823* (Port-of-Spain, 1954), 23. The fact that Eric Williams selected this and the subsequently quoted speeches by Grenville, Howick, Wilberforce, and Pallmer in his 1954 anthology might indicate that he himself saw the need to augment and refine the material in *Capitalism and Slavery* (originally published in 1944).

11 *Ibid.*, 23.

12 *Ibid.*, 24.

and three years after the black republic of Haiti came into existence. "The abolition of the trade is the only way of avoiding, in your islands, the horrors which have affected St. Domingo," Lord Grenville told his fellow peers in February 1807.

> I look forward to the period when the negroes in the West Indian islands, becoming labourers rather than slaves, will feel an interest in the welfare and prosperity of the country to whom they are indebted for protection, and of the islands where they experience real comforts, and when they may be called upon to share largely in the defence of those islands with a sure confidence in their loyalty and attachment.[13]

To this, Lord Howick added a rider in the subsequent Commons debate, in response to a suggestion that the cutting of the African link might incite the remaining slaves. "The prohibition to import fresh negroes could not be fairly adduced as a motive why the old ones should revolt," he claimed. "It was proved by experience and fact that in those islands where there was no regular supply of fresh negroes no insurrection ever took place."[14] This confident assertion, however, was very soon proved false.

Once the Napoleonic War was over, Wilberforce and his allies returned to the attack, stressing the civilization of the slaves as a necessary corollary to the preservation of the prosperity and tranquility of Britain's West Indian colonies. In June 1815, during the debate on the Registry Bill, Wilberforce spoke of "the duty of parliament to provide for the moral and religious instruction of the negroes." "Above all other circumstances," he was reported as saying,

> he had looked to the encouragement of marriage among the slaves as a necessary and most beneficial consequence of the abolition of the trade. . . . How desirable would it be to convert the slaves into a free and happy peasantry, capable of defending the islands which they inhabited, instead of endangering them by their presence.[15]

---

13 *Parliamentary Debates*, VII, 657–661, Lords, February 5, 1807, in Williams, *British West Indies at Westminster*, 37.
14 *Parliamentary Debates*, VII, 946–994, Commons, February 23, 1807, *Ibid.*, 41.
15 *Parliamentary Debates*, XXXI, 772–785, Commons, June 13, 1815, *Ibid.*, 71.

Besides the inadvertent but telling use of the verb "convert," it should be noticed that, by implication, Wilberforce had come round to the belief that it was not just African but all unsocialized slaves who were likely to rebel. In this respect he was almost prophetic, for in May 1816 came news of the stunning slave rebellion in Barbados, where well over 90 percent of the slaves were island-born.

Involving some 20,000 slaves from more than 75 estates, the Barbados rebellion occurred a whole generation after the Haitian Revolution, in a colony where not even a plot had ruffled the planters' complacency for 115 years. Though the planters also implicated a handful of disaffected free coloreds, the revolt in fact was led by a vanguard of slave drivers, rangers, and craftsmen, some of whom were literate, though very few formally Christian, and only two African-born. The mass of the rebels almost immediately took over the southeastern third of Barbados, chasing the whites to town but committing no immediate bloodshed and remarkably little property damage. Setting up defensive positions, they fully expected the regime to negotiate, but were soon disillusioned, being savagely suppressed by regular troops and militia. Some 120 slaves were slaughtered in the field at the cost of one white and one black soldier killed, with 144 slaves executed later and 132 deported to Honduras.[16]

Once the Barbados revolt was suppressed, the plantocracy was at pains to exculpate itself. They argued that since the slaves were not badly treated, and in any case were incapable of organization or even rational thought, the revolt must have been generated by outside forces, namely the English emancipationists and those at Westminster whom they were encouraging to impose an imperial slave registration act upon proudly self-legislating British West Indian colonies. "The general opinion which has persuaded the minds of these misguided people [the slaves] since the proposed Introduction of the Registry Bill," summed up the official report of the Barbados House of Assembly in 1818, "[is] that their Emancipation was decreed by the British Parliament. And the idea seems to have been conveyed by mischievous persons, and the indiscreet conversation of individuals."[17]

16 Michael Craton, *Testing the Chains: Resistance to Slavery in the British West Indies* (Ithaca, N.Y., 1982), 254–266.
17 Codd to Leith, April 25, 1816, in Leith to Bathurst, April 30, 1816, C.O. 28/85.

For his part, William Wilberforce—who in 1815 had supported the Corn Law ostensibly in return for government support of the Registry Bill, and had his windows broken by the mob in consequence[18]—was desperate to disavow blame for the rebellion, or any intention of undermining the Barbadian plantocracy. He vehemently denied that he had ever advocated immediate emancipation—rather, simply, abolition of the slave trade followed by amelioration, with emancipation as an eventual natural consequence. He further disclaimed any intention to abrogate the local planters' legislative rights; rather, he argued, the Barbadian plantocracy was undermining itself. "The insurrection, which all lamented," he was quoted as saying in the Commons on June 19, 1816, "had proceeded from the intemperance of the colonists themselves, and was to be attributed to the imprudence of their language and conduct. Whatever had happened had no reference to himself or his friends; he had no share in creating the explosion that had been felt; he washed his hands clean of the blood that was spilt."[19]

Unfortunately for Wilberforce, the very next speaker was the proslavery MP, C. N. Pallmer, who referred obliquely to the news recently brought to England by "Monk" Lewis that rebel slaves in Jamaica were invoking Wilberforce's name, along with God's, in their struggle for freedom against their masters. "Persons had been found," asserted Pallmer,

> assuming the sacred office of religious instructors, making their way into the interior of the islands, instilling into the minds of the negroes doctrines subversive of the public tranquillity, mixing with the truths of Christianity the dreadful principles of insubordination and insurrection. . . . It had appeared that nightly assemblies had been held at which a sort of religious ceremony was performed, and a hymn was sung, the purport of which was to return thanks to Providence, that their good friend, naming the hon. gentleman, had made them free, but that their masters would not allow them to be so.[20]

18 The Registry Bill had got as far as a first reading in 1815, but was withdrawn for that session. See Robert I. Wilberforce and Samuel Wilberforce, *The Life of William Wilberforce*, 5 vols. (London, 1838), IV, 282–286.
19 *Parliamentary Debates*, XXXIV, 1154–1220, Commons, June 19, 1816, in Williams, *British West Indies at Westminster*, 78.
20 *Ibid.*, 79.

This quite clearly referred to the subversive slave ditty recorded by Lewis on March 22, 1816, though not published until 1834, which, while neatly encapsulating the Creole slaves' new ideology of resistance, challenged two of Wilberforce's most dearly held tenets: that Christianized slaves would not rebel, and that he himself was at least as concerned as the West Indian planters to maintain the social order.

> Oh me good friend, Mr. Wilberforce, make we free!
> God Almighty thank ye! God Almighty thank ye!
> God Almighty make we free!
> Buckra in this country no make we free:
> What Negro for to do? What Negro for to do?
> Take force by force! Take force by force![21]

Not surprisingly, this was the juncture at which Wilberforce decided that the emancipationists had better "rest on their oars" awhile, going so far as to risk a breach with his brother-in-law James Stephen for his pusillanimity.[22] Wilberforce never forsook his belief that slavery was incompatible with civilization, but the idea of popular insurrection was anathema to him, in England even more so than in the West Indies. In the period 1817–19, indeed, he spent almost as much effort in supporting the government's repressive measures at home as he did on the West Indian

---

21 Matthew Gregory Lewis, *Journal of a Residence Among the Negroes in the West Indies* (London, 1845 edition), 114–116. The rumored conjunction between Wilberforce's campaign and political unrest among British slaves was not new in 1816; this was merely the most convincing case to date. As early as December 1791, the attorney Thomas Barritt wrote to his absentee employer about the fears of disturbances among the Jamaican slaves "in consequence of what has happened in Hispaniola etc." "These fears are not groundless," he added, "for some weeks ago (say 5) a body of Negroes in Spanish Town who call themselves the Cat Club, had assembled drinking King Wilberforce's health out of a Cat's skull by way of a cup, and swearing secrecy to each other. Some of them were taken up and put into the workhouse, but will not divulge the business. In Trelawney or thereabouts, some Negroes have been detected making the Cartridges and fire arms found in their houses, so that my Dear Sir, you see the Effects likely to take place in the West Indies by our Worthies at home." Thomas Barritt to Nathanial Phillips, St. Thomas in the East, Jamaica, December 8, 1791, National Library of Wales, Aberystwyth, quoted in Clare Taylor (ed.), *West Indian Planter Attitudes to the American and French Revolutions* (Aberystwyth, 1977), n.p. Slebech Papers MS 8386.
22 Wilberforce and Wilberforce, *Wilberforce*, IV, 286–295, 307; Sir George Stephen, *Anti-slavery Recollections, in a Series of Letters addressed to Mrs. Beecher Stowe* (London, 1854), 26.

cause, and he was never more than a figurehead of the antislavery campaign thereafter.[23]

The second generation of emancipationists, led and epitomized by Thomas Fowell Buxton, were clearly men of a different, more pragmatic stamp, living in a subtly different age. In contrast to the antirevolutionary panic triggered by the Jacobin Terror in France, and the counterrevolutionary overreaction that followed the downfall of Napoleon, British politics entered a new phase of inoculative liberal reform—the era ushered in by Canning in the Commons and Huskisson at the Board of Trade. In the dozen years after the suicide of Castlereagh in 1822—which saw the achievement of Catholic Emancipation and the troubled passage of the Great Reform Bill—a turning point occurred in the perennial political dialectic between expediency and principle, in which the former (though never previously absent) firmly took over from the latter.

In due course, in response to what was essentially a new constituency, Buxton and his colleagues were not only able to turn the blame for slave rebellions from godless slaves to their ungodly masters, but to suggest that slavery threatened both Britain's reputation and her imperial mastery. This position was already close to the Victorian liberal precept that if Empire were to prevail (as prevail it must), it should be just.[24]

The transition, however, was far from sudden. The next major episode in the West Indian process, in 1823–24, almost replicated the events of 1815–16, though with significant advances on both colonial and metropolitan sides. Moderate liberal reforms, promulgated in response to widening emancipationist

23 Robin Furneaux, *William Wilberforce* (London, 1974), 358–383. What must have been particularly distressing to Wilberforce was the involvement of the Jamaican "Black" Davidson in the Cato Street conspiracy in 1819, and the activities of other blacks in the radical underground in England, such as Robert Wedderburn, pastor of a "Christian Diabolist" church and plotter of a Haitian-style revolution in Jamaica. See Iain McCalman, "A Radical Underworld in Early Nineteenth Century London: Thomas Evans, Robert Wedderburn, George Cannon and their Circle, 1800–1830," unpublished Ph.D. dissertation, University of Melbourne, 1983.
24 This is the position developed, with specific reference to Frederic Harrison in 1866, in Michael Craton, *Sinews of Empire; A Short History of British Slavery* (London and New York, 1974), 315–316.

activity, triggered a stunningly coordinated slave revolt, which in turn led to overreaction from the colonial regime and, successively, dismay, caution, and a reshuffled policy on the part of the antislavery lobby.

In January 1823, buoyed up by the growing moral and political fervor in the country, the new Anti-Slavery Society was founded and T. F. Buxton took over leadership from the ailing William Wilberforce. In response to Buxton's demand for gradual emancipation, Canning and Bathurst cannily substituted an ameliorationist policy clearly designed to promote Wilberforce's ideal of a civilized, Christianized laboring class. A six-point program, including the promotion of religious instruction, the banning of Sunday markets, the encouragement of marriage and families and the setting up of savings banks, as well as some easing of the restrictions on manumission and the banning of the flogging of female slaves, was to be experimentally imposed on the Crown Colonies and only strongly recommended to the self-legislating colonies.[25] But even such a moderate program was too radical for the Guianese planters who, powerless to reject it, dragged their feet over implementation. This provoked the Guianese slaves, 30,000 of whom, from over 60 estates on a 30-mile stretch of eastern Demerara, rose up on Monday, August 18, 1823.[26]

As in Barbados in 1816, the rebels committed little property damage, contenting themselves, for the most part, with placing captured whites in the slave punishment stocks. When, on the first morning, Governor Murray met a spearhead of rebels and asked them what they wanted, they replied simply, "Our rights." However, when Murray tried to satisfy them with details of the forthcoming Bathurst reforms, they became more specific. "These things were no comfort to them," Murray reported them as saying. "God has made them of the same flesh and blood as the whites, that they were tired of being Slaves to them, that their good King had sent Orders that they should be free and they would not work any more."[27]

25 Lord Bathurst to Colonial Governors, Downing Street, July 9, 1823, *Parliamentary Papers*, 1824, XXIV, quoted in Michael Craton, James Walvin and David Wright, *Slavery, Abolition, and Emancipation, A Thematic Documentary* (London, 1976), 300–303.
26 Craton, *Testing the Chains*, 267–290.
27 Governor Murray to Lord Bathurst, August 24, 1823, C.O. 111/39; *ibid.*, 283.

Such strike action elicited as savage a response from the plantocratic regime as in 1816, with some 120 slaves butchered in the fighting—compared with three whites killed and a handful wounded—with another 60 shot out of hand and an equal number more ceremonially executed after military trials. Outweighing these 250 black victims in the minds of the British public, however, was the fate of the Congregationalist missionary John Smith, whose chapel had been the focus of the slaves' discussion and planning. Smith was tried for complicity, found guilty, and condemned to death (with a recommendation for mercy). He died in prison in February 1824.[28]

The news of the Demerara revolt, which reached England early in October 1823, disappointed the antislavery lobby and gave strength to its opponents. The fact that, unlike Barbados in 1816, missionaries had been active in Demerara and a majority of the rebel leaders had not only been elite slaves but also Christian converts, was particularly embarrassing to the metropolitan "Saints." Even they regretted the timing, if not the contents, of the Bathurst instructions, Zachary Macaulay going so far in his attempt to reassure Buxton and Wilberforce as to claim that the revolt was "the work of Canning, Bathurst and Co. and not of your firm."[29]

No one dared, at least in public, to defend the actions of the Demerara slaves. Yet an alternative line of attack presented itself to the antislavery forces over the next few months, as the disgraceful details of Smith's trial reached England, along with news of the concurrent wrecking of Shrewbury's Methodist chapel in Barbados, and the Jamaican planters' overreaction to a threatened revolt in Hanover parish. Clearly, the blame could be laid on the West Indian planters even more directly than in 1816. Not only had they agitated the slaves by repression, resistance to reform, and loose threats of secession, but they had also demonstrated a lawless godlessness in attacking the Christian Church and its adherents. This was the core of Lord Brougham's marathon attack

---

28 *Ibid.*, 288–289. Smith died of galloping consumption in Georgetown, just a week before George IV, in London, signed a reprieve with an order for deportation.

29 Zachary Macaulay to William Wilberforce, November 11, 1823, in Wilberforce and Wilberforce, *Wilberforce*, V, 202. Macaulay was countering the reported remark of Chinnery, private secretary to Canning, that the Demerara revolt was instigated by "Wilberforce, Buxton and Co."

on the colonial plantocracies on June 1, 1824; a speech that Charles Buxton claimed "changed the current of public opinion."[30] Two weeks later, in his last ever Parliamentary speech, William Wilberforce argued that such an ungodly body as the Guiana planters would never voluntarily reform, and helped win the minor concession that the Bathurst measures would be imposed on British Guiana and the other Crown Colonies despite the Demerara revolt.[31] In a parallel move, moreover, the Canning government in 1824 instituted the first two Anglican bishoprics in the West Indies, in Jamaica and Barbados, with the express intention of pushing forward the ideal of amelioration under the safe aegis of the established church.[32]

The period between 1824 and 1833, as Eric Williams suggests, saw events accelerate toward an ultimate crisis and resolution. The gulf between the metropolis—Colonial Office, public, and even Parliament—and the colonial plantocracies rapidly widened. As their support throughout Britain increased, the emancipationists made the critical transition from gradualism to immediatism in May 1830.[33] At the same time, unrest increased in the West Indies as the slaves became increasingly adept at taking advantage of developing conditions. All colonies were affected. But, not surprisingly, it was in the richest, most populous, most plantocratic colony, Jamaica, that the climactic slave revolt erupted around Christmas 1831, spreading over an area of 750 square miles and involving perhaps 60,000 slaves from over 200 estates.[34]

Besides having one of the harshest regimes and the most turbulent history of slave resistance, Jamaica was by 1831 the colony in which Christianity had most firmly taken root. This was a development over which the planters were perilously ambivalent. Some had encouraged the resolutely regime-supporting

30 Charles Buxton (ed.), *Memoirs of Thomas Fowell Buxton, Bart.* (London, 1849), 78; Brougham, *Speeches*, II, 113–190.
31 Wilberforce and Wilberforce, *Wilberforce*, V, 223.
32 Sehon S. Goodridge, *Facing the Challenge of Emancipation; A Study of the Ministry of William Hart Coleridge, First Bishop of Barbados, 1824–1842* (Bridgetown, Barbados, 1981), 5–6.
33 William Law Mathieson, *British Slavery and its Abolition, 1823–1838* (London, 1926), 130–150; David Brion Davis, "The Emergence of Immediatism in British and American Anti-Slavery Thought," *Mississippi Valley Historical Review*, XLIX, 1962, 209–230.
34 Craton, *Testing the Chains*, 291–321.

sects, such as the Moravians, Presbyterians, or even Methodists, in the belief that they might usefully socialize the slaves, and in recent years there had even been cautious proselytizing by the established Anglican Church. Yet what slave converts made of Christianity was rarely what planters intended or missionaries recognized. By far the most popular Nonconformist Church was the Baptist, which owed its vitality as much to its foundation by "native" black preachers who had come to Jamaica with their Loyalist masters over 25 years before the first white missionaries arrived from England, as to its encouragement of popular participation.[35]

The Jamaican rebellion of 1831 occurred in the center of "native Baptist" activity, and so many black deacons and their congregations were involved that the uprising was popularly known as the Baptist War. Without doubt there were politically explosive—even millenarian—elements in the rebels' preferred type of Christianity. Yet Christianity was by no means essential to the slaves' resistance. As in Demerara, the chapels and the slaves' more or less authorized Sunday activities provided cover for organization and planning, chapel services contributed to rebel rhetoric, and contact with missionaries even provided a sense that the slaves were linked with sympathetic allies overseas. As the reported speeches of Sam Sharpe, the Baptist deacon who was the slaves' chief leader, indicate, the revolutionary message in 1831 was only marginally religious. One condemned rebel described how Sharpe

> referred to the manifold evils and injustices of slavery: asserted the natural equality of man with regard to freedom. . . . that because the King had made them free, or resolved upon it, the whites . . . were holding secret meetings with the doors shut close . . . and had determined . . . to kill all the black men, and save all the women and children and keep them in slavery; and if the black men did not stand up for themselves, and take their freedom, the whites would put them at the muzzles of their guns and shoot them like pigeons.

The slaves, counseled Sharpe, should therefore be prepared to fight, but merely to use the threat of force as the backing for

35 Ibid., 241–253.

what was essentially strike action, binding "themselves by oath not to work after Christmas as slaves, but to assert their claim to freedom, and to be faithful to each other."[36]

Once again, these tactics of strike action, with force only used to counter force, proved ineffectual in the face of an implacable and overwhelmingly well-armed local regime. Some 200 slaves were killed in the fighting and "pacification" process (for less than a dozen killed by them), while no less than 340 were executed, including more than 100 after civil trials once martial law was lifted in February 1832. Beyond this, the local whites, largely under the cover of an Anglican organization called the Colonial Church Union, carried out a veritable pogrom against the Nonconformist missionaries and their congregations, burning down virtually every chapel in the rebel parishes.[37]

The response of the Jamaican plantocracy was traditional, but this time it was undoubtedly a case of overkill, tending to speed the ending of the very institution it was desperate to preserve. The news of the Jamaican rebellion reached England in mid-February 1832, at a time when the complex struggle for the reform of Parliament itself was approaching its climax. This phase found the Lords fighting a desperate rearguard action, as mobs stoned the houses of unpopular Tories, radical workingmen's associations armed and drilled, and the petty bourgeois were being encouraged, in the slogan recorded by Francis Place, "To stop the Duke, go for gold."[38]

The proslavery forces responded to the news from Jamaica with a campaign designed to outmatch that of the antislavery Agency Committee, with their public meetings still able to attract up to 6,000 people. Many converts to antislavery wavered,

---

36 Henry Bleby, *The Death Struggles of Slavery* (London, 1853), 128–129; Craton, *Testing the Chains*, 300.

37 *Ibid.*, 316–319.

38 Graham Wallas, *The Life of Francis Place, 1771–1854* (London, 1928), 295–313. For the interaction between the antislavery movement and the general process of reform, see Seymour Drescher and Christine Bolt (eds.), *Anti-Slavery, Religion, and Reform* (Folkestone, England, and Hamden, Conn., 1980); David Eltis and James Walvin (eds.), *The Abolition of the Atlantic Slave Trade* (Madison, Wisc., 1981); James Walvin (ed.), *Slavery and British Society, 1776–1846* (London, 1982), The best work on the direct relationship between the Jamaican revolt and the political process in the metropolis is now Mary Turner, "The Baptist War and Abolition," *Jamaican Historical Review*, XIII, 1982, 31–41.

with those most terrified of insurrection at home and abroad deserting the camp, and many others, convinced of the involvement of converted slaves in the rebellion, retreating to a gradualist position.[39] Yet, after much agonizing, T. F. Buxton and his staunchest allies chose a bolder and, in the event, more strategic line, propagating the notion that only by immediate and complete emancipation could a disastrous conflagration be averted. "If the question respecting the West Indies was not speedily settled," Buxton warned the Commons as early as March 7, 1832, "it would settle itself in an alarming way, and the only way it could be settled was by the extinction of slavery."[40] Two weeks later, strengthened by reports from Jamaica about the whites' attacks upon missionaries and slave Christians, and planters' threats of revolt and secession from the Empire, Buxton was able to place the blame for slave unrest and rebellion firmly on the regime.[41]

Between April and May 1832, Buxton's resolve was transferred to the antislavery movement at large. Governor Belmore's revelations about the destruction of sectarian chapels were underlined by the arrival in England of refugee missionaries. The Anti-Slavery Society held its annual meeting on May 12, in the middle of what William Cobbett called "The Days of May"—the tumult occasioned by the obstructionism of the Lords, the King's refusal to create reformist peers, and the consequent resignation of the Whig Prime Minister, Earl Grey. The Anti-Slavery Society members were spurred on by the elder James Stephen, one of the earliest advocates of immediate emancipation, who, through his son and namesake, was ideally placed both to understand the obduracy of West Indian planters and to influence imperial policy. But the keynote speaker was Buxton himself, who stated that it was now "unquestionable that only by the interposition of Parliament [that] any hope can be entertained of peacefully terminating [slavery's] unnumbered evils, or any security afforded against the recurrence of those bloody and calamitous scenes that have recently affected Jamaica." As a result, the Anti-Slavery Society almost unanimously voted that Parliament be pressed to

39 David J. Murray, *The West Indies and the Development of Colonial Government, 1801–1834* (Oxford, 1965), 191; Buxton, *Memoirs*, 238.
40 *Parliamentary Debates*, 3rd. ser., X, March 7, 1832.
41 *Ibid.*, XI, March 23, 1832.

fulfill without delay the promise to end slavery made, in the vaguest possible terms, by Canning in 1823.[42]

The ultraconservative Wellington failed in his attempt to form a government, and Grey's Whigs returned to power on May 19 with a commitment to reform. Taking advantage of the change, Buxton made a crucial speech in the Commons less than a week later, calling for the appointment of a select committee "to consider and report upon the measures which it may be expedient to adopt for the purpose of effecting the Extinction of Slavery throughout the British Dominions, at the earliest period compatible with the safety of all Classes in the Colonies."[43] Buxton's motion, which was aimed to supplant the Lords' mere committee of inquiry, was outvoted 136 to 90. But a Commons committee was appointed nonetheless, if with an ostensibly milder mandate, and the antislavery momentum was maintained. The evidence heard by the committee over the following months, coupled with the cresting wave of antislavery campaigning throughout the country and the growing number of Members in the newly constituted House of Commons pledged to reform, made the passage of an Emancipation Act by the Whig government within 18 months seem—at least in retrospect—almost inevitable.

The refugee missionaries were key figures in this final phase of the emancipation campaign, particularly the Baptist William Knibb, whose evidence before the Parliamentary committee covered 40 pages, and whose highly colored lectures drew hisses and boos from the Jamaican planters up and down the country. Perhaps significantly, the British public, as in 1823, was far more easily moved by the maltreatment of white missionaries than by the wholesale slaughter of black rebels. True Christians, it was felt, were bound to be innocent of insurrection, and even Knibb was at pains to argue that neither he nor his parishioners were

42 Mathieson, *British Slavery and its Abolition*, 223–224; George Spater, *William Cobbett; The Poor Man's Friend*, 2 vols. (Cambridge, 1982), II, 496–499. The wording of the 1823 resolution was, perhaps, significant; emancipation "at the earliest period that shall be compatible with the well-being of the slaves themselves, with the safety of the colonies, and with a fair and equitable consideration of the interests of private property." (Public Record Office, London.) C.O. 320/1, 209.

43 *Parliamentary Debates*, 3rd. ser., XIII, May 24, 1832; Buxton, *Memoirs*, 245–246; Craton, *Testing the Chains*, 323. Buxton's wording can be significantly compared with that in the Canning resolutions of 1823, cited above.

involved in actual rebellion, conveniently ignoring the fact that he would scarcely have had a case were it not for the rebel slaves' initiative.

The attitude of Parliament itself was far more pragmatic. Neither slaughtered rebels nor martyred Christians were as effective at Westminster as the real threat perceived to the Empire at large by the catastrophic breakdown in relations between West Indian masters and their slaves. For a majority of Parliament, the question was essentially political, not moral. It was a matter of morality only in the limited sense that in liberal ideology empire can only be sustained if its morality is justified. Thus, the crux of the debate was probably Buxton's speech of May 24, 1832, in which he brilliantly argued the coincidence of slavery's corrupting immorality with its political unwisdom. "Was it certain," he asked,

> that the colonies would remain to the country if we were resolved to retain slavery? . . . How was the government prepared to act in case of a general insurrection of the negroes? . . . a war against a people struggling for their rights would be the falsest position in which it was possible for England to be placed. And did the noble Lords think that the people out of doors would be content to see their resources exhausted for the purpose of crushing the inalienable rights of mankind?[44]

That Buxton's words were no mere parliamentary rhetoric or debating point is borne out by his private correspondence at that time. Immediate emancipation was vital, he argued in response to a radical critic a few months later, "for I know *our* power of emancipating in one way or another is fast drawing to a close. I mean they [the slaves] will take the work into their own hands."[45] Whether or not Buxton's speech of May 24, 1832, was instrumental in swaying Parliament, the decisive watershed certainly occurred during the next six months. In November 1832, the government privately invited Buxton to present a specific plan for freeing the slaves, and so confident did the emancipationist leader feel of the outcome that he counseled a less militant cam-

44 *Parliamentary Debates*, 3rd. ser., XIII, May 24, 1832. See also Buxton, *Memoirs*, 201; Mary Turner, "Baptist War and Abolition," 40–41.
45 Buxton to Mr. East, October 15, 1832, Buxton Papers, III, 31–32, quoted in David Brion Davis, *Slavery and Human Progress* (New York, 1984), 203.

paign for fear of alarming conservatives, especially in the Lords. In the event, such expediency proved, once more, wise. In effect, only the timing and details of emancipation remained to be debated and resolved, though since the agenda included the mechanics of imposing a transitional phase of compulsory labor and the amount by which the owners should be compensated for their forfeited slave property, as well as the means of ensuring "the safety of all classes in the colonies," it was to be more than a year before the first Emancipation Act became law, and fully six years before, on August 1, 1838, the three-quarters of a million British West Indian slaves became "fully free."[46]

In sum, Eric Williams's subordinate thesis in Chapter 12 of *Capitalism and Slavery* is broadly consonant with the historical record. Slave revolts and plantocratic unrest in the last decades of British slavery were interrelated, and the degenerating sociopolitical climate in the colonies did contribute to slave emancipation in 1834–38. Most of the elements in Williams's analysis at which criticism can be levelled are simply the result of the type of compression inevitable in such a work. As in much of the rest of the book, further detail does little more than flesh out and refine the revisionary groundwork originally laid some 40 years ago.

As we have indicated, more detail of the effect of the Haitian revolution on slaves, their masters, and the imperial government, would simply have shown that the threat of slave rebellion conditioned the antislavery debate almost from the beginning. More information than Williams provided on the terror felt by emancipationists such as William Wilberforce for any form of popular unrest, would merely have strengthened the theme that emancipation was the culmination of a civilizing and socializing process aimed at preventing such manifestations. Similarly, the discovery that imperialist concern for the injudicious, even barbaric, behavior of the colonial planters came much earlier than previously thought, actually reinforces the theme that contradictions be-

---

46 For detailed descriptions of the final emancipation debates, see Lowell J. Ragatz, *The Fall of the Planter Class in the British Caribbean, 1763–1833* (New York, 1928), 149–152; W. L. Burn, *Emancipation and Apprenticeship in the British West Indies* (London, 1937); Murray, *Colonial Government*, 193–202; Craton, *Sinews of Empire*, 277–280; William A. Green, *British Slave Emancipation: The Sugar Colonies and the Great Experiment, 1830–1865* (Oxford, 1976), 112–125; Davis, *Slavery and Human Progress*, 160–217.

tween imperial policy and plantocratic behavior were as dangerous as actual slave rebellions.

Rather more damaging to a balanced evaluation is the way
in which Williams's 12-page treatment ignores the process by
which the emancipationists' attitudes and tactics changed, as it
was progressively realized that not only the mass of ignorant Africans, but also elite Creole and, finally, Christian slaves were
likely to make a bid for freedom through rebellion. Williams's
assumption was that slavery was so obnoxious that all slaves were
likely to rebel, but the fact that this truth only gradually dawned
upon the imperial master class greatly refines our understanding
of the emancipation process—the way in which a naive civilizing
mission, promoted by an idealistic minority, gradually shifted to
a more sophisticated, even cynical, pragmatism, eventually endorsed by a Parliamentary majority.

Even more remarkable in the work of one at pains to argue
the slaves' contribution to their own emancipation through resistance and rebellion, is Eric Williams's almost complete silence
about the precise ideology, aims, and tactics of the slaves, and of
the ways these subtly changed in the shift from "African" to
"Creole" forms of resistance. Unfriendly critics might blame this
upon an ignorance stemming from an indifference to, even contempt for, mere human aspirations and endeavors in the face of
larger, mechanistic forces. Rather, we would see it as an over-
simplifying generalization. The objective reality that slaves consistently sought their freedom and repeatedly rebelled, and that
colonial slave resistance rose to a climax in intimate conjunction
with the emancipation process, were sufficient facts for Williams's revisionist purposes in Capitalism and Slavery.

Finally, then, how well does Eric Williams's twelfth chapter fit
into the rest of Capitalism and Slavery? However convincingly he
shows that metropolitan decisions over the ending of slavery were
accompanied and influenced by slave revolt and planter reaction
in the colonies, how well can such political dynamics be integrated into an analysis that is primarily concerned with the artic-
ulation of West Indian plantation slavery into the world economy?

Despite the author's later deviations as a practical politician,
and whether or not, as C. L. R. James has alleged, Eric Williams

simply adopted whatever imperfect ideology the book contains from sitting at his former schoolmaster's feet in London in the late 1930's, *Capitalism and Slavery* must be regarded—and itself analyzed—as essentially a work of Marxian analysis. Besides a resolute economic determinism, Williams explicitly adopts in *Capitalism and Slavery* at least the structural center of the Marxist historical framework: the shift from feudal to mercantile and then to industrial capital phases and modes of production and social relations. Reinforcing this Marxist structure are his peculiar contributions to the analysis of the process: his emphasis upon the opening up of the West African coast as a vital influence in the switch from the Middle Ages to the age of mercantilism, and his stress on the contribution of the profits of the Triangular Trade to the next great transition in the development of capital, the British Industrial Revolution.

Slavery and plantations, indeed, loom larger in Williams's work than in Marx's, where the crucial difficulty lay in deciding the degree to which they constituted a feudal mode.[47] By implication, Williams saw slave plantations as comprising those elements of feudal ownership and socioeconomic relations that conveniently spanned the expansive phase of European merchant capital. These feudal elements, in Williams's view, became outmoded once industrial capital demanded a different mode and scale of production and a changed set of relations of production—that is, demanded a wage-earning proletariat rather than a servile, dependent laboring class.

This analysis underpins and illuminates the relationships described in Chapter 12 of *Capitalism and Slavery*. The continuance of empire depended upon a new phase of industrial capital that made both slavery and the quasi-feudal attitudes of the West Indian planter class dangerously *démodé*. While the achievement of British West Indian slave emancipation in 1834–38 was only the first stage in a 50-year process of legislated emancipation in the Americas as a whole, it was speeded by Britain's primacy in the industrializing process, the unique concurrence in Britain of practical secular and idealistic liberal ideas, and by the peculiar nature of British slave resistance.

---

47 Karl Marx, *Grundrisse*, (Penguin edition, London, 1973), 471–514; *Pre-Capitalist Economic Formations* (J. Cohen, ed., London, 1964).

Complex circumstances decreed that the Haitian slaves achieved a revolutionary overthrow of the industrializing process between 1791 and 1804, while, at the other extreme, in Cuba, Brazil, and the United States, a catastrophic confrontation was long delayed and, in due course, easily defused. The case of the British West Indies was intermediate. Slave resistance was endemic and rebellions frequent, reaching, indeed, a climax in the period 1815–32. Imperial and colonial forces, however, remained sufficient, and sufficiently coordinated, to suppress even the most widespread of the slave revolts. Moreover, when these occurred they were no longer truly revolutionary.[48] Led by Creolized, and eventually Christianized slaves, they no longer aimed at the annihilation of the whites or the total destruction of the economic system. Rather, the British West Indian slaves in slavery's last phase demanded a form of freedom that might rationally include free wage labor on the plantations as well as peasant farming. This, of course, was the "part peasant–part proletarian" lifestyle that was, in fact, substituted for slavery in most of the British West Indian colonies after 1838, though the terms of relationships remained resolutely in favor of the landowner/employer master class.[49]

Thus, while Eric Williams's analysis, in *Capitalism and Slavery* and his subsequent works, concurred with the neo-Marxism of C. L. R. James and Herbert Aptheker in respect of slave resistance—seeing it as part of a perennial undercurrent of resistance by the underclass—it is also, at least by implication, attuned to the hegemonic interpretations of the greatest of all neo-Marxists, Antonio Gramsci.[50] Although the Italian theorist did not specifically address the case of the British West Indian slaves and their allegedly free descendants, undoubtedly he would have used the evidence adduced by Williams—in the twelfth chapter of *Capitalism and Slavery,* in the postemancipation chapters of *From Columbus to Castro,* and in the brilliant short analysis of neocolonialism

48 On this, compare Craton, *Testing the Chains,* 161–171, 241–253, with Eugene Genovese, *From Rebellion to Revolution: Afro-American Slave Revolts in the Making of the Modern World* (Baton Rouge, La., 1979).
49 Richard Frucht, "A Caribbean Social Type: Neither 'Peasant' nor 'Proletarian'," *Social and Economic Studies,* XIII, 1967, 295–300.
50 Antonio Gramsci, *Selections from the Prison Notebooks* (Quintin Hoare and Geoffrey Nowell Smith, eds., London, 1971), 161, 188–189, 365–366.

included in *Inward Hunger*—as a perfect illustration of the hegemonic principle: the subtle way in which a ruling class can maintain its domination by apparently adopting liberal changes, thereby recruiting a willing underclass into a new, and initially unrecognized, form of subordination.[51]

A Gramscian analysis, moreover, would perfectly integrate the matter treated in Chapter 12 with the rest of *Capitalism and Slavery*. At different levels, imperial and plantocratic hegemony in the seventeenth and eighteenth centuries stemmed from the control of the Triangular Trade and the system of social controls that defined Negro slaves as chattel. In the later eighteenth and early nineteenth centuries, conflict threatened between an industrializing metropolis and a less progressive planter class, as well as between planters and their slaves, as theorists and humanitarians edged the imperial government toward liberal policies of free trade and free wage labor. Yet, at both levels, disastrous conflicts were avoided and hegemony maintained. At the imperial/ colonial level, this was achieved by engineering a peaceful transition from slavery to wage labor through the apprenticeship system, by generous compensation to ex-slaveowners, and by the introduction of new measures of social control aimed at sustaining hegemony in a liberal guise. At the purely colonial level, it could be argued, hegemony was facilitated more subtly still, and over a longer period, through the very process of Creolization and Christianization which, as Wilberforce dreamed, came close to creating a respectable, hard-working, thrifty, long-suffering— and only nominally free—black wage-laboring class.

51 Williams, *Capitalism and Slavery*, 197–208; *From Columbus to Castro: The History of the Caribbean, 1492–1969* (London, 1970), 328–515; *Inward Hunger: The Education of a Prime Minister* (London, 1969), 338–343.

Part V. *Capitalism and Slavery* in Historical Perspective

Gavin Wright

Capitalism and Slavery on the Islands: A Lesson from the Mainland

In selecting a title for his now-classic book, Williams chose to relate one of the most palpable realities of Western economic history to one of the slipperiest abstractions of the Western intellectual heritage. With a rather different set of specific concerns, the same association has been at the heart of the debate over slavery in the United States, for the past two decades if not longer. Aroused primarily by the analysis set forth by Genovese in *The Political Economy of Slavery* and subsequent works, the mainland discussion has focused on the social identity and economic motivations of the slaveholding classes. Historians of British abolition have been more concerned with the motives and politics of the abolitionists in relationship to industrial capitalism. But there is a bedrock economic question common to both histories: was abolition facilitated by a decline of the slave economy? On close examination, there are many other thought-provoking parallels between the West Indian and North American cases. Yet, with a few significant exceptions, they have been treated separately. This essay takes an unorthodox historical approach. It first sketches a reasonably well-developed analysis of capitalism and slavery for the American South in the nineteenth century, and then carries the suggestions formulated by this exercise back to the eighteenth-century British West Indies to see what light they shed on the earlier experience.[1]

This essay does not concern itself with confirming or refuting the "Williams thesis." *Capitalism and Slavery* was a product of its times in more ways than one, and any modern restatement would

The author thanks Carl Degler, David Galenson, and Barbara Solow for comments on the first draft of this article.

1 Eric Williams, *Capitalism and Slavery* (Chapel Hill, 1944); Eugene Genovese, *The Political Economy of Slavery* (New York, 1965).

require extensive editing and translation. At this historical distance it does a book more honor to be read for inspiration and a sense of direction. So guided, we may then go on to develop our own formulations, more consistent with modern thinking and with what we have learned about history and about the world since 1944.

SLAVERY AND THE SLAVE ECONOMY IN THE SOUTH   There is a basic difference between investment in slaves on the one hand, and investment in land and most forms of industrial capital on the other: slaves are movable, most other investments are not. It was the movability of slaves that made the Atlantic slave trade possible, but that movability did not end with the crossing of an ocean. Even for a slave who may have spent a lifetime in one locality, *potential* movability determined value, because a buyer could carry the slave anywhere that slavery was legal. This characteristic is the economic essence of the distinction between real and personal property, slaves almost always being clearly classified as the latter. Whereas free labor markets were often localized and imperfect, constrained by geographical, ethnic, and family loyalties and by social norms, slave labor markets were bounded only by profit calculations and legal barriers.

The implications of this simple distinction are pervasive. It influenced population growth, private investment patterns, farming practices, mineral exploration, and politics. The unifying element is the consideration that the value of investments in slaves was completely independent of local development. Planters whose wealth consisted mainly of slaves had relatively little to gain from improvements in roads and marketing facilities in a particular area. They had little stake in community life generally, and no particular desire to attract settlers by building schools, villages, and factories. Since immovable land was a small part of their investment, they had no great interest in spending time and money looking for precious metals or even coal and iron deposits. In short, slavery generated a lesser and looser connection between property holders and the land that they occupied.

This formulation offers a unified explanation for features of the southern economy stressed by both sides in the continuing debates over the capitalist versus the pre-bourgeois character of American slavery. The debate has centered, unfortunately, on the question of whether or not the slaveholding planters were acquisitive, calculating profit-seekers, rather than on the real economic issue: did the incentives and interests of slaveownership lead the southerners to behave in the same ways and support the same programs as did farmers and industrialists in the free states? Clearly not. Genovese and Fox-Genovese observe: "The southern leaders themselves built their transportation system colonial-style: it bound the staple-producing plantation districts to the ports and largely bypassed the upcountry," almost as though they were built by absentee landlords. The canal boom of the 1830s virtually bypassed the South, although it occurred during one of the most vigorous decades of cotton expansion. A railroad network of sorts was built after 1840, but as of 1860 it had only one third of the density of the northern system. It was "generally inferior in construction, rail, motive power and rolling stock," and it featured much longer stretches between stopping points. Wiener cites the example of the north-south Alabama line which was given state funds in 1850 to connect the Tennessee River with Mobile, but was "not located, except incidentally, to develop the coal trade."[2]

Oakes, however, a vigorous critic of Genovese, stresses the extremely low rates of geographical persistence (i.e., high rates of geographical turnover) among wealthy planters in some of the richest counties of Georgia and Alabama: "In Jasper County, Georgia, at the heart of that state's cotton belt and long past its frontier days, nearly sixty percent of the 1850 slaveholders were gone ten years later." Wiener reports similar persistence rates for the wealthiest planters in five Alabama counties. Although his object was to determine whether the planters had survived the Civil War, he demonstrated inadvertently that that question was not meaningful, because the majority of wealthy planters had not persisted in the same county for a decade even before the war.[3]

Oakes points out that these rates of geographical mobility are comparable to those of the poorest classes of unskilled laborers in the North. It is an important point, but Oakes takes it to mean that the southern planters were merely acquisitive commercial

2 *Idem* and Elizabeth Fox-Genovese, *Fruits of Merchant Capital* (New York, 1983), 50; John F. Stover, *Iron Road to the West* (New York, 1978), 89–90; Jonathan Wiener, *Social Origins of the New South* (Baton Rouge, 1978), 141.
3 James Oakes, *The Ruling Race: A History of American Slaveholders* (New York, 1982), 77; Wiener, *Social Origins*, 10.

farmers like those of the North. Wealthy property holders in the North, however, did not behave in this way at all. Homeownership significantly reduced the likelihood of moving, and most of the very rich had stable, long-term connections with an urban or regional business community.[4]

The issue is not acquisitiveness or calculating behavior, but over what geographical horizon the calculations are performed. A study by Schaefer, which actually traces observations within the entire South between 1850 and 1860, finds that slaveowners were slightly less likely to move than nonslaveowners, but that the distances moved (and the deviations from a straight east-west migration path) were substantially greater for slaveowners. Wealthy and ambitious planters like James Henry Hammond not only considered moving west, but made detailed comparative cost calculations for cotton growing on farmland hundreds of miles away. Significantly, only after deciding to stay in the east (for reasons as much personal and political as economic) did Hammond turn his attention to "scientific agriculture." For Charles Tait, another Georgian planter-politician, not even a seat in the United States Senate deterred him from forsaking his constituents (though not the office until his term expired) to join the migration to the southwest.[5]

The most striking and significant contrast between the economies of the free and the slave states was in the rate of growth of population. Modern economists, accustomed to analyzing national income trends on a per capita basis, have disseminated the notion that the antebellum southern economy enjoyed high rates of growth compared to the rest of the country. But this claim is *only* true on a per capita basis; the total size of the southern economy grew much more slowly. Population in the two regions was virtually equal at the time of the Revolution, yet, by the time of secession, the North had twice the numbers of the South (Table 1).

This difference was mainly attributable to foreign immigration, which went northward almost exclusively. The patterns of

4 Oakes, *Ruling Race*, 78.

5 Donald F. Schaefer, "A Statistical Profile of Frontier and New South Migration, 1850–1860," *Agricultural History*, LIX (1985), 563–578; Drew Gilpin Faust, *James Henry Hammond and the Old South* (Baton Rouge, 1982), 109–113; Ulrich Phillips, *Life and Labor in the Old South* (New York, 1929), 274. For the example of Charles Tait, I am grateful to Everett Lee.

Table 1 Population Growth, North and South, 1790–1860

	POPULATION (in thousands)							
	1790	1800	1810	1820	1830	1840	1850	1860
SOUTH	1,961	2,622	3,461	4,419	5,708	6,951	8,983	11,133
NON-SOUTH	1,968	2,687	3,779	5,219	7,152	10,112	14,210	20,310
Northeast	1,968	2,636	3,487	4,360	5,542	6,761	8,627	10,594
North Central		51	292	859	1,610	3,351	5,404	9,097
West							179	619

SOURCE: *Historical Statistics of the United States* (Washington, D.C., 1975), 22.

immigration may in turn be directly linked to the behavior of the property holders just described. In the North a whole range of strategies served to encourage immigration in the hopes of raising land values. The desire for capital gains was a main motive behind canal and railroad promotions, which mobilized public and private funds and showered the country with publicity. Town-building schemes proliferated, with schools, stores, and roads offered up to attract settlers. Local farmers, aptly described by Veblen as "cultivators of the main chance as well as of the fertile soil," were more often than not enthusiastic backers of these projects.[6]

The position of industrial capital was similar. Threatened by outmigration to the west, northeastern manufacturers welcomed and encouraged immigrants from abroad. The landowner may perceive value explicitly as a potential sale price for land, whereas the owner of industrial capital may focus on the value which he will extract in production. But for present purposes, these two methods of realizing value from ownership amount to the same thing: both recruited the variable factor (labor) to the site of the fixed factor (land or physical capital) as a way of increasing the value of the latter. The net aggregate effect of all these activities by all those owners of stationary property was to turn the North into a veritable demographic vacuum cleaner.

6 Thorstein Veblen, *Absentee Ownership and Business Enterprise in Recent Times: The Case of America* (New York, 1923), 135. Veblen's words on country towns are also quotable: "The location of any given town has commonly been determined by collusion between 'interested parties' with a view to speculation in real estate, and it continues through its life-history . . . to be managed as a real estate 'proposition.' Its municipal affairs, its civic pride, its community interest, converge upon its real estate values" (142).

By contrast, the South had little activity of this sort, had few interior towns, and remained isolated from outside labor flows. In a recent study of antebellum demography, McClelland and Zeckhauser have uncovered the remarkable fact that the South was a region of net white outmigration throughout the period, even at the height of the cotton booms and in the most prosperous sections of the southwest. They observe that "the South was continually viewed by its own inhabitants—at least by those who left—as promising less economic opportunity than did the North. This in turn raises doubts about those accounts that portray in glowing terms the southern economic performance in the 1840s and 1850s." But the presumption that prosperity should be associated with in-migration is one which reflects the thinking of a free-labor economy. In the slave South, even the proposal to reopen the African slave trade was successfully blocked by the opposition of slaveholders.[7]

This recital by no means exhausts the inventory of differences between the free and slave economies, but in the present context it should serve to show that there was a basic contrast in resource allocation and dynamic tendencies. The best indication that the institution of slavery was at the root of the matter is that many of the specific features of the southern economy changed abruptly with emancipation. Interior towns sprang up, new mineral resources were discovered, railroad projects were undertaken, and in a relatively short time the South was a high-population-growth region. It took a much longer time, however, to undo the fundamentals of the regional economic structure which the slave economy had built.[8]

PERSPECTIVES ON THE NORTH–SOUTH DEBATE   Northern observers in the late antebellum years had little doubt that the slave South was backward and stagnant. This view was not just based on remoteness and poor information; eyewitness visits produced some of the most negative impressions. William H. Seward went South in 1835, 1846, and 1857, for example, and reported each

7 Wright, *The Political Economy of the Cotton South* (New York, 1978), 150–154. Peter McClelland and Richard J. Zeckhauser, *Demographic Dimensions of the New Republic* (Cambridge, 1982), 7.
8 The transition in economic structure after emancipation is covered in more detail in *idem, Old South, New South: Revolutions in the Southern Economy since the Civil War* (New York, 1986).

time on the "exhausted soil, old and decaying towns, wretchedly-neglected roads, and, in every respect, an absence of enterprise and improvement." He wrote that on every trip he wished that "at least one northern man from every town could be with me to see the practical workings of slavery." Such comments were reiterated and accepted many times over.[9]

But what exactly was it that these people were observing? They were certainly not looking at modern statistical aggregates like per capita income: average southern incomes for the entire population (including slaves) grew as fast or faster than the national average in the antebellum period, and per capita incomes for the *free* population were about equal to those in the rest of the nation. Nor were they looking at the net worth of typical slaveholders. The average wealth of adult male southerners was nearly double that of the average northerner; the average *slaveowner* was more than five times as wealthy as the average northerner. These differences are not what caught the attention of northern travelers. They were looking for what they took to be the overt signs of progress—canals, towns, schools, factories, and machines in the fields. Emerson declared in 1844:

> Slavery is no scholar, no improver; it does not love the whistle of the railroad; it does not love the newspaper, the mail-bag, a college, a book or a preacher who has the absurd whim of saying what he thinks; it does not increase the white population; it does not improve the soil; everything goes to decay.

Objectively, it would be hard to prove him wrong.[10]

Recent articles by Temperley develop the theme of "antislavery as cultural imperialism" which has much to offer in understanding these perceptions. Northerners tended to attribute their economic success to their own system, and specifically to the hard work which their own system had encouraged. Assum-

9 Eric Foner, *Free Soil, Free Labor, Free Men* (New York, 1970), 40–48, from which the Seward quotations are taken.
10 Ralph Waldo Emerson, "Address Delivered in Concord on the Anniversary of the Emancipation of the Negroes in the British West Indies, August 1, 1844," quoted in David Brion Davis, *Slavery and Human Progress* (New York, 1984), 110. Stanley L. Engerman, "A Reconsideration of Southern Economic Growth, 1770–1860," *Agricultural History*, XLIX (1975), 343–361; *idem*, "Some Economic Factors in Southern Backwardness in the Nineteenth Century," in John F. Kain and John R. Meyer (eds.), *Essays in Regional Economics* (Cambridge, Mass., 1971), 279–306; Lee Soltow, *Men and Wealth in the United States* (New Haven, 1975), 65; Wright, *Economy of the South*, 35–36.

ing that free institutions were responsible for their economic success, northerners sought to impose the same institutions on the slave areas after the war, honestly believing that the result would be an accelerated growth of production (in which expectation they were to be severely disappointed, as were the British abolitionists). I differ with Temperley, however, when he writes: "The overall effect of taking economic measurements, therefore, has been to suggest that economics had little to do with the matter." This statement may be literally true, but only because economists have focused on a narrow set of economic indicators. From the analysis developed here we can go even farther than Temperley: the northerners not only *associated* their economic success with their free institutions, but they came to *define* economic success in a way that only made sense in a free-labor society. For a society of landlords, population growth is a natural yardstick of success, because it is closely associated with the measure of preeminent concern: land values. When it came to the growth of land values, the North outstripped the South decisively.[11]

Table 2 shows that in the value of farm land alone the North had doubled the South by 1850. On a per acre basis, the northern advantage was even greater. Even in 1860, after the most prosperous decade ever for the cotton economy, land values in the

Table 2 Land Values, North and South, 1774–1860

| | VALUE OF FARM LAND AND BUILDINGS ($000,000) | | | VALUE OF FARM LAND AND BUILDINGS PER ACRE ON FARMS | |
	1774	1850	1860	1850	1860
SOUTH	133	1,056	2,323	$6.18	$10.32
NON-SOUTH	156	2,216	4,322	18.02	23.75
Northeast	156	1,455	2,122	26.45	34.79
North Central		752	2,130	11.94	19.72
West		9	70	1.80	5.38

SOURCES: *Historical Statistics of the United States* (Washington, D.C., 1975), 460–462; Alice Hanson Jones, *Wealth of a Nation to Be* (New York, 1980), 37, 90. 1774 pounds sterling converted to dollars at $4.80.

11 Howard Temperley, "Capitalism, Slavery and Ideology," *Past & Present*, 75 (1977), 94–118; *idem*, "Anti-Slavery as Cultural Imperialism," in Christine Bolt and Seymour Drescher (eds.), *Anti-Slavery, Religion and Reform* (Folkestone, Eng., 1980), 340.

South lagged far behind the North. This difference is not a reflection of intrinsic land quality (a concept which economic theory rightly eschews): at the time of the Revolution the value per acre of farmland in the South was greater than in the New England and Middle Colonies, and the natural geographical advantages of cotton growing under antebellum demand conditions had no match anywhere in the North. The regional contrast does, however, have much to do with differences in the speed of land improvement, population growth, transportation, cities, and towns—in short, all of the indicators that northerners took to be self-evident signs of southern backwardness.[12]

Thus the northerners were right to associate northern progress with free land and free labor since fee simple property rights in land were basic to the whole process. Where they went wrong was in their assumption that the difference lay in the sphere of *productive effort,* the incentives to exertion which they took to be absent under slavery. This was more an assumption than an observation, the logical corollary to the belief held by most successful people that their success has come from their own hard work. The regional contrasts in population density, transportation, and population growth were obvious to every visitor and to every knowledgeable person, but the level of effort by slaves was not something about which they would have any reliable knowledge, as is clear from Foner's survey of Republican opinion. Speakers were emphatic about the disastrous economic effects of slavery, he writes, but "they did not always make clear what it was in slavery that caused the impoverishment of the South. Often they were content to draw the comparison between free and slave states and let their listeners draw their own conclusions." Lacking evidence, and lacking an alternative conceptualization of the issue, they took a supply-side view of the matter, and this is the interpretation which was handed down from Benjamin Franklin to Adam Smith to John Elliott Cairnes to Ulrich Phillips to Eugene Genovese.[13]

In *Political Economy of Slavery,* for example, Genovese presented strong evidence about soil exhaustion and the limited progress of fertilization in the southeast, but he attributed the problem

---

12 Jones, *Wealth of a Nation to Be,* 109.
13 Foner, *Free Soil,* 44–45.

to, among other factors, "the poor quality of the implements that planters could entrust to slaves" and the "carelessness of slaves [which] made all attempts at soil reclamation or improved tillage of doubtful outcome."[14] This is a supply-side view: the planters were trying to achieve these results, but they were constrained by the poor quality of slave labor. The fact that this hardy belief has recently been restated by a distinguished economic historian (lacking empirical support, however) does not make it any less dubious.[15]

Where we do have direct evidence on work performance and technology, the opposite is often found. Scott finds that the large slave plantations in Cuba were *more* mechanized and technologically advanced than the operations where slavery was declining. When it comes to southern fertilization, however, we can explain the observations more readily from the demand side: the bulk of the wealth of southeastern planters was in slaves and was thus completely unaffected by fertilization of the soil. They managed to accumulate huge personal fortunes, all the while ignoring the advice of the scientific agriculture reformers and struggling along with their careless slaves. Fertilization is a good example of a technique which in itself is neither "advanced" nor "backward." Lebergott has recently calculated that investment in fertilizer in either the South or the East had a lower return in the 1850s than an investment of the same funds in Western land. What the calculation demonstrates, however, is that the real trade-off was between *mobility* and fertilization. Under slavery, mobility was high and the horizon for such calculations was wide. But the southern Piedmont began a fertilizer revolution almost immediately after emancipation, a development which I doubt was caused by an overnight improvement in the quality of the labor force.[16]

14 Genovese, *Political Economy of Slavery* (New York, 1865), 89.
15 Stefano Fenoaltea, "Slavery and Supervision in Comparative Perspective: A Model," *Journal of Economic History*, XLIV (1984), 635–668. Fenoaltea argues that slavery is suitable for "effort intensive" but not for "care intensive" activities. This claim is directly refuted by the example of North American tobacco, which is more care-intensive than virtually any other major American crop. Yet, before the nineteenth century, North American slavery was overwhelmingly concentrated in the tobacco-growing regions.
16 Rebecca Scott, "Explaining Abolition: Contradiction, Adoptation, and Challenge in Cuban Slave Society, 1860–1886," *Comparative Studies in Society and History*, XXVI (1984), 83–111; Stanley Lebergott, "The Demand for Land: The United States, 1820–1860," *Journal of Economic History*, XLV (1985), 189–192.

But if the analysis offered here gives new support to some older observations about the economics of slavery, it also discredits the venerable contention that slavery was aggressively expansionist in territorial terms. Slaveowners were certainly aggressive in politics and in the righteous defense of their institutions, and as individuals they were footloose and highly mobile. But as a collectivity, the slave South was far less expansionist geographically than the North, which filled up the continent at twice the speed. While southerners were inching into east Texas, John C. Fremont had already seized California for the free soil forces.

If the movability of slaves was their most decisive economic feature, why was the South so much slower than the North at settling territory? Statistically, the main reason that southern expansion was slower was simply that southern population growth was slower. Behind this statistical fact, however, lie some basic elements of political economy. Individually, slaveowners moved often and moved quickly; but collectively their economic interest in rapid territorial expansion was far from clear. The advantages of higher production in the southwest had to be set against the disadvantages of lower cotton prices from increased supply. Southern votes on land policy reflected these divided interests. Thus, some slaveowners had an economic interest in slowing down the pace of geographical expansion. More important than land policy, however, was the interest of slaveholders in slowing the rate of growth of the slave population, reflecting a collective interest in high slave prices, which they all shared.[17]

No misconception is both more persistent and more inaccurate than the belief that southern slaveowners were divided on the African slave trade issue: that there was a basic cleavage between (in Namier's words) the "saturated planters" and the "planters on the make." In Harrison County, Texas, the mean value of real property per household in 1860 was $3,189. The

---

17 Peter Passell and Wright, "The Effects of Territorial Expansion on the Price of Slaves," *Journal of Political Economy*, LXXX (1972), 1188–1202. Subsequent discussion may be found in Lawrence J. Kotlikoff and Sebastian E. Pinera, "The Old South's Stake in the Inter-regional Movement of Slaves, 1850–1860," *Journal of Economic History*, XXXVII (1977), 434–450; Susan Lee, "Antebellum Land Expansion: Another View," *Agricultural History*, LII (1978), 488–502. The most recent exercise finds that the effects were mildly positive on balance. Mark Schmitz and Schaefer, "Paradox Lost: Westward Expansion and Slave Prices before the Civil War," *Journal of Economic History*, XLI 41 (1981), 402–407.

mean value of personal property, almost entirely slaves, was $9,585, three times as much. The typical slaveholding household (60 percent of the total) had over $10,000 in slave property, a fortune not dependent in any way on developments in Harrison County. These people had no significant economic stake in Texas or in slave expansionism, but they certainly cared about keeping the slave trade closed. Sam Houston was elected governor in large part because of a rumor that his opponent might not be utterly unshakable on the African slave trade issue.[18]

The absence of a strong constituency for the geographical extension of slavery is equally reflected in the inability of Texas to raise private capital for internal improvements. There were numerous proposals to improve the navigability of the rivers, but the river counties (the slaveholding planters of which were among the wealthiest men in the country) "had no money for the work." Railroad promoters made enthusiastic speeches about the need for a great southern rail link to the Pacific, but "few of the many companies formed were able to raise the necessary capital." An editorialist observed in 1854: "What now, for instance, is more threadbare than a railroad speech in Texas?" Three years later the governor acknowledged that he had lost faith in the effectiveness of land grants as inducements to construction. The whole situation was in marked contrast to the North, where railroads were pulled westward by farmers engaged in "anticipatory settlement," by land speculators, by small town merchants, and by town builders.[19]

Here then are the grains of truth in the perception that the South was falling behind economically, and that this lag was related to a deterioration of their political strength in the union. By modern measures of performance the South was far from stagnant or declining, nor was slavery unviable economically. One can make a case that an infrastructure of cities, roads, markets, and universities and a well–educated labor force are essential

18 Lewis Namier, *England in the Age of the American Revolution* (London, 1930), 322. These phrases are quoted by Richard Pares in *War and Trade in the West Indies, 1739–1763* (Oxford, 1936), who then writes: "I am not sure that this is quite right" (220). Randolph Campbell, *A Southern Community in Crisis* (Austin, 1983), 26.

19 Charles Ramsdell, "Internal Improvement Projects in Texas in the Fifties," *Proceedings of the Mississippi Valley Historical Association*, IX (1915–1918), 100–106; Albert Fishlow, *American Railroads and the Transformation of the Ante-Bellum Economy* (Cambridge, Mass., 1964), 163–204.

to sustained economic progress in the modern era, but in the nineteenth century slaveowners fared well enough. It is not surprising that they were attracted to anti-bourgeois ideologies and that they were able to see through the hypocrisies and injustices of northern society more clearly than most northerners. But these attitudes had roots in their property interest and reflected the kind of economy which that property interest had created. By slowing the growth of the regional population, both free and slave, that property interest also retarded territorial expansion and political weight. Since this political weight was a factor in secession, and since sheer manpower was a factor in the South's military defeat, in these ways we may say that the economics of slavery contributed to its own demise.

ANALOGIES TO THE BRITISH WEST INDIES   At first glance, the situation in the West Indies may seem to be so different that one could not possibly transfer many lessons from the later mainland example. Certainly the contrasts are not minor. World demand for the products of slave labor was altogether different in the two cases; British West Indian sugar had nothing like the dominant market position of United States cotton in the nineteenth century. Basic underlying demographical circumstances were different, the high natural rate of slave population growth on the mainland being virtually unique among slave systems. The political relationships also differed, with nothing in the West Indies analogous to free soilism and the territorial issue. Even the main topic of debate is not the same, since the American literature focuses on the late antebellum period when the slave trade had been long closed, whereas the issues raised by Drescher relate mainly to the circumstances leading up to the abolition of the slave trade in 1807. For that matter, the whole historical era was different, and the United States experience was surely not independent of the prior West Indian history.

Yet a host of differences need not preclude all comparisons if some of the underlying principles are the same. The basic conception that slavery was a form of production which did not foster ties between the planter and his land would seem to apply to the West Indies even more forcefully than to the mainland. As one looks more closely, other tempting analogies appear. Although the role of slave trade profits in financing the Industrial

Revolution is not a topic covered in this article, it is still notable that Williams could have made an even stronger case for this idea in the United States: it is well known that early New England manufacturing capital came from merchants who not long before had engaged in the slave trade or in commerce related to the slave trade.[20]

There are also parallels in the legal and political histories. In both cases, critical court decisions concerned the transportability of slave property into free-labor areas: the Somerset case of 1772 and the Dred Scott decision of 1857. And like the southeastern planters who had to balance gains from territorial expansion against losses from intensifying cotton competition, the West Indian planters faced conflicting pressures in 1764, when the British empire faced a choice between Canada and Guadeloupe. Concerned about competition in the protected British sugar market, the planters successfully pushed for Canada. Similarly, there were periodic signs of planter ambivalence on the slave trade issue itself.

There are also remarkable parallels in the historical literature. In both cases we have an "economic interpretation" handed down to us from the 1930s in which "industrial capitalism" destroys slavery, yet we are unable to identify specific economic benefits or motives. In both cases we seem to have decline in the midst of expansion. Williams described the planters as "an outworn interest, whose bankruptcy smells to heaven in historical perspective," and declared that "any impartial observer, if such existed, could have seen that their time was up," but he never said why. He did write early in his book that "slave labor is given reluctantly, it is unskillful, it lacks versatility," but he footnoted this statement to Cairnes, and neither Cairnes nor Williams ever looked any further into actual conditions of production. On the question of decline, Williams relied heavily on Ragatz' *Fall of the Planter Class*. Ragatz followed Phillips in attributing problems to racial traits rather than slavery, but he too never examined production and he too never really said why. Ragatz and Williams were like the northern Republicans who, in Foner's words, "did

---

20 Lance Davis, "Sources of Industrial Finance: The American Textile Industry," *Explanations in Entrepreneurial History*, IX (1957), 189–203. Caroline F. Ware, *The Early New England Cotton Manufacture* (Boston, 1931), 15–16, 60–62. Douglass North also argued that the inflow of cotton earnings between 1816 and 1840 was a critical stimulus to northern and western growth, but this interpretation is now largely discounted: *The Economic Growth of the United States, 1790–1860* (New York, 1961), 66–121.

not always make clear what it was in slavery that caused impoverishment."[21]

But if there is an interpretation implicit in the Ragatz-Williams account, as I believe there is, it is that the problem lay not in work effort or versatility, but in the decadence of the planters, reflected most strikingly in absenteeism. Many of the wealthiest representatives of the West Indian interest had little West Indian identity at all, but were more English than the queen. They had no interest in developing West Indian resources: a British newspaper correspondent wrote that "if the finest geologist of Europe were to . . . state that indications of coal were evident in the formations of the neighboring mountains . . . no effort would be made to obtain it." No wonder Williams believed the profits might have financed the Industrial Revolution: they certainly were not being plowed back into the West Indies.[22]

The indictment of slavery was as much a matter of social cohesion as economics: the absence of local pride, lack of quorums in island assemblies, multiple office-holding, and constant departures for Europe. One of Drescher's most telling points is that the severe economic decline of the islands in the aggregate came *after* the abolition of 1807 and was clearly a *result* of that political step. But neither Ragatz nor Williams showed the slightest interest in this distinction, freely invoking events from the post-abolition period as illustrations of decline. Does this mean that they were manipulating the evidence, or does it mean that, as they must have been conceiving the issue, the spinelessness which led the planters to accept abolition in the midst of a temporary overproduction crisis was itself one of the chief symptoms of decay and decline?

In the interests of concreteness and in the hopes of suggesting new ways of approaching the subject, I reason here by analogy to the United States case and offer the following specific propositions on the economics of slavery, decline, and abolition:

First, slavery discouraged the growth of white population in the islands. As early as the 1670s, fears of white depopulation were severe enough to lead to passage of "deficiency laws" on

21 Williams, *Capitalism and Slavery*, 211, 6; John Elliott Cairnes, *The Slave Power* (New York, 1969; orig. pub. London, 1862); Lowell J. Ragatz, *The Fall of the Planter Class in the British Caribbean* (New York, 1928); Phillips (ed. Genovese), *The Slave Economy of the Old South* (Baton Rouge, 1968).
22 Ragatz, *Fall of the Planter Class,* 63.

many of the islands—attempts to require or encourage white settlers. Although complaints about heat, insects, and hurricanes were undoubtedly genuine, slavery itself discouraged settlement, first by filling up the land that white settlers might hope to acquire, later through distaste for the customs of the Africans, and increasingly from fear of slave insurrections. Behind the specific motives on the part of potential settlers, however, lies a deeper reason: the absence of a strong landed interest actively working at attracting them. As Dunn notes, the economic successes of the British in the Caribbean were not widely publicized; he counts no more than eight or ten promotional tracts in a century, numbers exceeded almost every year in colonies like New Jersey and Pennsylvania. The deficiency laws were never given sufficient authority or resources to make them effective. Although this problem was of long-standing, a number of islands did begin to experience absolute depopulation of whites in the 1770s. According to Ragatz, the white population began to decline in Barbados from 1773, in Jamaica from 1778, in Dominica from 1773, and in Montserrat from 1772.[23]

Second, there was a life-cycle trajectory to the island slave economies. Initially slavery accelerated settlement and the growth of production, by providing *elastic* supplies of labor which had no legal right to depart upon arrival. Over time, however, slavery retarded further growth by discouraging white immigration, and by fostering absenteeism and reinvestment in other locations. According to Davis, it was part of the "accepted public geography" of the mid-eighteenth century that older slave societies had "the image of social and cultural wastelands blighted by an obsessive pursuit of private profit," as slavery moved toward "always more promising frontiers." This was the essence of what Williams called the "law of slave production." But whereas he attributed the absence of soil intensive adaptation to problems of managing slave labor, the argument proposed here is that owners did not pursue such strategies because they had no lasting attachment to the land which they owned. As Galenson's recent study

23 David Galenson's econometric work shows that servants bound for the West Indies received shorter terms (by as much as 8 to 9 months) than those going to the mainland, indicating that the mainland was strongly preferred: *White Servitude in Colonial America: An Economic Analysis* (New York, 1981), 110. Richard S. Dunn, *Sugar and Slaves* (Chapel Hill, 1972), 23; Ragatz, *Fall of the Planter Class*, 30.

shows, high turnover among estate owners and managers was a phenomenon which *emerged over time* on particular islands, and was not a climatically determined condition from the beginning.[24]

Third, a self-interest in restricting slave imports emerged cumulatively over time. Demographically and economically the West Indies were not like the mainland, but it was still the case (according to the figures of Ward) that investment in slaves and other movables was substantially higher than the investment in land. For Jamaica in fact, the ratio of the two was at an all-time high from 1799 to 1819. As slave prices began to rise above the African supply price, some slaveholders were tempted by the appeal of restricting new imports as a way of raising prices further or protecting themselves against price declines. There are indications that many planters on the older islands were ambivalent about the slave trade by the late eighteenth century, and this has to be considered a factor in the success of the abolition movement.[25]

These planters, however, did not get the kind of abolition they wanted: specifically, the restrictions on the interisland trade made abolition much less attractive than they might have hoped.

24 Evidence on the high elasticity of slave labor supply in the seventeenth century is summarized in Henry A. Gemery and Jan S. Hogendorn, "Elasticity of Slave Labor Supply and the Development of Slave Economies in the British Caribbean," in Vera Rubin and Arthur Tuden (eds.), *Comparative Perspectives on Slavery in New World Plantation Societies* (New York, 1977), 72–83. Their concept is the elasticity of supply to the British Caribbean as a whole. The supply elasticity to any one island or colony was virtually infinite, as argued by Galenson in *White Servitude in Colonial America*, 141–157. The implications of an elastic labor supply to the *individual firm* are explored by Heywood Fleisig, "Slavery, the Supply of Agricultural Labor, and the Industrialization of the South," *Journal of Economic History*, XXXVI (1976), 572–597. Davis, *Slavery and Human Progress*, 79–80. Williams, *Capitalism and Slavery*, 113; Galenson, "Population Turnover in the English West Indies in the Late Seventeenth Century," *Journal of Economic History*, XLV (1985), 227–235.

25 J. R. Ward, "The Profitability of Sugar Planting in the British West Indies, 1650–1834," *Economic History Review*, XXXI (1978), 203. Ward's profitability estimates unfortunately do not resolve the debate between Drescher and Selwyn Carrington about the specific timing and future expectations of profits on the different islands. Drescher, *Econocide: British Slavery in the Era of Abolition* (Pittsburgh, 1977); Selwyn H. H. Carrington, review of *Econocide*, *Journal of Caribbean History*, XVIII (1984), 110–114. One problem is that Ward lumps 1799–1819 into one period, when the issue turns on the timing within this period. Another is that Ward defines profit in such a way as to factor *out* changes in implicit land rents, thus extracting the one component which would provide location-specific information about current profits and future expectations. Expectations are critical because the actual profit experience during 1793–1815 was so heavily influenced by political and military history.

I do not mean to deny Drescher's contention that the main pressure behind abolition was a British public determined to end the trade. But what sort of a socioeconomic system would flirt with self destruction in response to a short-term crisis? When Williams wrote that "the withdrawal of the thirteen colonies considerably diminished the number of slaves in the empire and made abolition easier than it would have been had the thirteen colonies been English when the cotton gin revivified a moribund slave economy in the South," he apparently forgot that the "revivified slave economy in the South" accepted the same abolition in the same year without significant protest.[26]

Fourth, the slaveowners of the sugar islands were not politically aggressive in expanding slave territory. In 1763 the sugar interest pressed the empire to retain Canada and return Guadeloupe, preferring to limit their own potential space to admitting a "dreaded rival" into the British sugar market. In 1772 the West Indian planters opposed a proposal to advance money to develop the new sugar islands that had been obtained in the Seven Years' War. The West Indian interest did not favor taking St. Domingo in 1793, at the time of the Haitian revolution, much to the consternation of advocates of conquest and imperial expansion. Like its mainland counterparts two generations later, the sugar interest was heavy on the volume of political rhetoric, but its objective interests did not lead it to support policies which would strengthen its long-run position. Drescher rightly stresses that at the time of abolition there were ample new opportunities for expansion of slave territory within the empire; Williams himself wrote that "the new colonies, crying out for labor, full of possibilities . . . were permanently crippled by abolition." But it was their own policies in the recent past which led them into such an isolated and vulnerable position.[27]

Fifth, abolition and emancipation did not hurt the British economy. In one of the clearest statements of a very old perception, Parker describes a broad shift in the sources and character of European economic growth between the eighteenth and nineteenth centuries. The "Age of Adam Smith," in which growth

---

26 Williams, *Capitalism and Slavery*, 123–124.
27 *Ibid.*, 115, 113, 149; Ragatz, *Fall of the Planter Class*, 228–229.

was dominated by expansion of trade and commerce and by exploitation of the gains from trade and the market, gave way to the "Age of Schumpeter," as entrepreneurship moved into the search for innovation in technology and improvements in the process of production. The resemblance to Williams' conception is not hard to see. Slavery encouraged commerce by accelerating the production of exotic commodities in far-off places. As entrepreneurial energies moved into home-based production of manufactured goods, the sugar islands came to seem more remote and irrelevant to the important things in economic life, as indeed they were.[28]

Drescher's powerful *Econocide* forces us to confront the fact that abolitionism and anti-slave sentiment emerged early in this whole process, before the British capitalist self-image crystallized into the ideological package of free trade, free labor, and free market. What Drescher forces us to acknowledge is that the abolition movement and its success was part of the ideological learning process which led to this crystallization. But there *was* a learning process. With the American Revolution, the British learned that they could lose a major colony without disrupting their economic progress. With abolition, they learned that they could give up the slave trade without disrupting economic progress, indeed without significantly increasing the price of sugar. When emancipation did temporarily cause a rise in the price of sugar in the 1840s, they learned that there was a convenient remedy in free trade. It is not always inappropriate to reason backwards from later consequences to prior causes, since if any of these lessons had been seriously wrong, the anti-slavery momentum might have slowed down early.[29]

---

28 William N. Parker, *Europe, America, and the Wider World: Essays on the Economic History of Western Capitalism* (New York, 1984). The importance of slavery in facilitating long-distance trade is the main theme of Barbara Solow's articles, "Caribbean Slavery and British Growth: The Eric Williams Hypothesis," *Journal of Development Economics*, XVII (1985), 99–115, and "Capitalism and Slavery in the Exceedingly Long Run," in this volume.

29 Drescher, *Econocide*. Adam Smith pre-dates the abolition campaign, but Drescher argues persuasively that free-trade principles did not begin to influence *policy* until well after 1807, whereas the principle argument of the slave-merchants between 1788 and 1806 was "an appeal to the ethos of capitalism." Drescher, "Capitalism and Abolition: Values and Forces in Britain, 1783–1814," in Roger Anstey and Paul E. H. Hair (eds.), *Liverpool, the African Slave Trade, and Abolition* (Liverpool, 1976).

The victors record the histories, and when Williams wrote that "mature industrial capitalism" destroyed slavery he was recording a version of the victor's account, although obviously not the most friendly or charitable version. But the sort of subtle interactive process described here is surely within the scope of his conclusion:

> Great mass movements, and the anti-slavery mass movement was one of the greatest of these, show a curious affinity with the rise and development of new interests and the necessity of the destruction of the old.[30]

The "affinity" between anti-slavery and industrial capitalism was considerably more curious than Williams himself understood; yet there is more wisdom and subtlety in his underlying argument than recent scholarship has acknowledged. This essay has tried to show that the "curious affinity" was not merely ideological but also a reflection of basic differences in the internal economic logic of slave and non-slave regimes. Such contrasts are not timeless and eternal, but they had great power and visibility in an era when capitalist firms had well-defined geographical location and national identity, and economic progress was closely associated with national strength and cohesion.

30 Williams, *Capitalism and Slavery*, 211.

Hilary McD. Beckles

"The Williams Effect": Eric Williams's *Capitalism and Slavery* and the Growth of West Indian Political Economy

In spite of persistent and penetrative criticisms of Eric Williams's *Capitalism and Slavery* in the past four decades, the book has continued to exert an overwhelming intellectual influence over scholars researching the Caribbean dimension of colonial American political economy. In the main, criticisms have come from European and American scholars, but the work survives with an almost unblemished reputation among most Caribbean-based historians. The refusal of these historians to formulate lengthy and substantial criticisms of this work, though some Marxists have made minor theoretical critiques, results from a deep-rooted acceptance of, if not admiration for, its research quality and theoretical incisiveness.[1] Recently, a regional economic historian has attempted to protect and defend this work from one of its most formidable opponents, and by doing this, he spoke, no doubt, for many of his colleagues.[2] This fundamental academic respect that *Capitalism and Slavery* enjoys within the Caribbean has brought scholars, not only in historical studies but also within the disciplines of economics and political science, under its considerable influence. G. K. Lewis, the Caribbean's leading and most prolific political-

[1] Eric Williams, *Capitalism and Slavery* (Chapel Hill, N.C., 1944); H. McD. Beckles, "Capitalism and Slavery: The Debate Over the Williams Thesis," *Social and Economic Studies*, 33 (1984), pp. 171–190; F. Taylor, "Review of Capitalism and Slavery," *Bulletin of Eastern Caribbean Affairs*, 8, No. 2 (1982), pp. 509–510; W. K. Marshall, "A Review of Historical Writing on the Commonwealth Caribbean Since c. 1940," *Social and Economic Studies*, 24 (1975), pp. 272–273.

[2] S. Carrington, "Econocide—Myth or Reality? The Question of West Indian Decline, 1783–1806," *Boletin de Estudios Latinoamericanos Y Del Caribe*, 36 (1984), pp. 13–67. At the conference on Caribbean slavery and British capitalism held at Bellagio, Italy, May 21–25, 1984, Carrington was the only scholar who systematically defended the Williams "decline" thesis in its original form. He, like Williams, is from Trinidad and Tobago.

intellectual historian, noted that "it is testimony to the essential correctness of that thesis that the attempt of a later scholarship to impugn it has been unsuccessful."[3] But nowhere outside of the historical field is this influence more evident than in the development of West Indian political economy.

In a methodological critique of what West Indian political economists refer to as the theory of plantation economy and society, Benn noted that Williams's analysis provided much of the "intellectual inspiration" for its adherents, and that the logic of the overall analysis of plantation America within this theoretical construct follows very closely Williams's conceptions of the Atlantic slave economy.[4] Benn also recognized the influence of Latin American dependency theorists, notably Furtado and the prolific Andre Gunder Frank, upon West Indian political economy. But in his most clearly articulated work, Frank pays tribute to Williams's book and integrates its analysis into the core of his theory of capitalist underdevelopment in agrarian plantation/hacienda/latifundia America.[5] This chapter, then, is an overview of the methodological and conceptual relationships between postwar West Indian political economy and Williams's *Capitalism and Slavery*.

During the 1960's and early 1970's, a body of economic thought, generally referred to among West Indian political economists as the plantation economy school, was formulated almost exclusively by a small group of young radical economists at the University of the West Indies. Particularly prominent within this forum, which became known as the New World Group, were economists Lloyd Best, Norman Girvan, C. Y. Thomas, and George Beckford.[6] Their new and radical political economy had emerged partly from a critical appraisal of the perceived limited

3 G. K. Lewis, *Main Currents in Caribbean Thought: The Historical Evolution of Caribbean Society in its Ideological Aspects, 1492–1900* (London, 1983), p. 95.
4 D. Benn, "The Theory of Plantation Economy and Society: A Methodological Critique," *Journal of Commonwealth and Comparative Politics*, 12 (1974), pp. 249–260. See also P. O'Brien, "European Economic Development: The Contribution From the Periphery," *Economic History Review*, 35 (1982), pp. 1–19; and J. Mandle, "The Plantation Economy: An Essay in Definition," *Science and Society*, 36 (1972), pp. 49–62.
5 A. Frank, *On Capitalist Underdevelopment* (Delhi, 1975), pp. 15–16; *Dependent Accumulation and Underdevelopment* (London, 1978), p. 15.
6 See N. Girvan and O. Jefferson (eds.), *Readings in the Political Economy of the Caribbean* (Kingston, Jamaica, 1971). These Essays on the Caribbean economy were written and published by the New World Group. See also G. L. Beckford (ed.), *Caribbean Economy* (Kingston, Jamaica, 1975).

usefulness to the region of traditional Keynesian and neoclassical economic theory as presented by their internationally eminent colleague, Professor Arthur Lewis.[7]

The early 1960's had brought new intellectual challenges to the region. The politics of territorial federation had forced these radical economists to examine the theory of customs union and related integrationist economic institutions, in addition to the common overall structural problems associated with economic underdevelopment. It was argued that the Lewis paradigm could not account fully for the causes of regional economic backwardness since it was not cast within an historical dialectical mold. That is, his theories were not rooted within the dynamic socioeconomic processes associated with slavery and the postslavery realities. Furthermore, the radicals were politically located within the black nationalist anticolonial traditions, and needed an account of the historical reality that identified and specified the forces of colonial domination and exploitation. Recently, three young Jamaican economists noted in evaluating this conceptual departure that "the radical thinkers identified with the historical struggles of the Caribbean people—the Maroon wars, the fight against slavery, the revolts of the 1930s and the nationalist movement which emerged thereafter."[8] Eric Williams's *Capitalism and Slavery* was conceived as providing that historical ammunition needed by these radical social scientists. With Williams's powerful statement of West Indian economic and political history in hand, Beckford noted, they were determined from the outset to fashion the tools of economics to the new needs of the Caribbean environment. Hence an intensive search was launched for what he referred to as a "relevant economics" based upon, and always sensitive to, historical forces.[9]

The objective of the group was to present an interpretation

7 L. Best and K. Levitt, "Character of the Caribbean Economy," in Beckford (ed.), *Caribbean Economy*, pp. 34–36.

8 R. Bernal, M. Figueroa, and M. Witter, "Caribbean Economic Thought: The Critical Tradition," *Social and Economic Studies*, 33 (1984), p. 35. This very extensive paper was first presented at the 21st Anniversary Celebration Conference of the Faculty of Social Science, University of the West Indies, Mona, Jamaica, March 20–24, 1983. It is a detailed survey, written from the Marxist perspective, of the development of West Indian political economy. Though the authors emphasize the critical role of the *Capitalism and Slavery* methodology and conceptions of the political economists of the 1960's and 1970's they make no specific mention of Williams.

9 G. L. Beckford, "The Struggle for Relevant Economics," *Social and Economic Studies*, 33 (1984), pp. 47–57.

of the Caribbean economy and society so as to facilitate structural change. Beckford noted that Williams's focus upon the plantation system and its historical legacy set the stage for the subsequent formalization of a theory of Caribbean society. Though in some cases the influence of *Capitalism and Slavery* is not explicitly stated, but confirmed by oral evidence, sensitive readers, especially those familiar with the intellectual conjuncture, can in fact make firm statements concerning the relationship. Beckford began his analysis of underdevelopment in the Caribbean with the following statement, which is clearly a conceptual extraction from Williams:

> Modern Caribbean economic history begins with the slave plantation. European capital and management combined with African slave labour provided the basis for utilizing the fertile lands of the region to produce agricultural raw materials for trans-shipment to Europe. Caribbean economy during that era was totally dependent on Europe (and Africa), and underdevelopment was at a peak during that era of total dependency. . . . The raw sugar from each plantation was then consigned to metropolitan merchant-bankers for sale in the metropole. Supplies of capital goods for plantation use came back from the metropole to supplement the capital stock which the plantation could build from its own resources.[10]

This conception of the Caribbean economy is followed by a detailed account of the unequal exchange relationship that characterized colonial-metropolitan trade, and here the Williams influence is pervasive. Not only do Best and Beckford show, like Williams, how the terms of trade consistently favored the metropolis, hence the accumulation of the surplus there, but they illustrate the negative socioeconomic impact upon the colonial structures. This was critical to their understanding of the problems of dependency and underdevelopment. Best, for example, states that Williams's *Capitalism and Slavery* was a "monumental

10 G. L. Beckford, "Caribbean Rural Economy," in Beckford (ed.), *Caribbean Economy*, p. 80. During the early 1960's, Eric Williams was hailed by most Caribbean academics as a principal spokesman for intellectual decolonization within the region, and his *Capitalism and Slavery* was generally accepted as gospel. Even the late Professor Elsa Goveia of the UWI, who viciously criticized Williams's later *British Historians and the West Indies*, accepted the earlier work as a classic study of the highest standard. See E. Goveia, "New Shibboleths for Old: A Review of Eric Williams's *British Historians and the West Indies*," *Caribbean Quarterly*, 10 (1964), pp. 42–50.

attempt to trace out significant linkages between the slave economy and the development of British capitalism without the aid of a systematic quantitative framework."[11] As an economist, he intended to provide such a framework, but first he sought to outline his conceptual parameters:

> We have sought to study contemporary economic problems in the perspective of the past performance of Caribbean economy. To this end, employing the method of "histoire raisonée" we have constructed a series of models. As an interpretation of economic history, these models may be conceived of as successive stages in the evolution of plantation economy. We must emphasize, however, that our primary interest lies in isolating the institutional structures and constraints which the contemporary economy has inherited from the plantation legacy. . . . Our major argument is that the study of the character of the plantation sector and its relation both with the outside world and with the domestic economy provides the single most essential insight into the mechanism of Caribbean economy.[12]

For Best, then, the primary value of *Capitalism and Slavery* lies in the manner in which Williams outlines in detail the ways in which the West Indian islands, after having absorbed large quantities of foreign resources (European capital, European and African labor) in the formative stages, soon became self-financing, and then emerged as a net exporter of capital. In addition, he was attracted by Williams's formulation of the subsequent dependency of the islands upon the metropolis for "reinvestments," markets, technology, and, probably most damaging of all from the points of view of Creole society, political administration. These were the variables with which the plantation-economy theorists were preoccupied.

Williams showed how the region's dependency upon British capitalism was carefully constructed through a series of proprietary-assisted merchant companies, navigation laws, naval and military operations, and royal-chartered monopoly organizations. He also illustrated how economic subordination was reinforced by the existence of well-placed political and legislative

11 L. Best, "The Mechanism of Plantation-Type Economies: Outline of a Model of Pure Plantation Economy," *Social and Economic Studies*, 17 (1968), p. 305, footnote 39.
12 Best and Levitt, "Character of the Caribbean Economy," pp. 37–38.

machinery that ensured sociopolitical and cultural acceptance of most, or all, things "English." Thus, as all economic activity in the colony had to be sanctioned by the metropolis, social, intellectual, and political thought also had to gain imperial approval before it could be legitimately disseminated—hence Best's use of the concept of "total exploitation" within the region's plantation system.[13]

In addition, the plantation economy theorists stressed fundamental continuity rather than change in the economic history of the region. It was not particularly difficult to illustrate that with market-determined legalistic emancipation in the English West Indies in 1838, the central structural features of the slave-plantation economy and society were further entrenched, rather than undermined; and that the emergent use of money wages was essentially a minor adjustment in the relations between capital and labor. After the 1820's, the metropolitan financial institutions may have diminished their interests in the region, but the plantations and their owners (and managers) still remained overwhelmingly the determining forces within the new socioeconomic order. For the laborers throughout the region, wages remained unsatisfactory. In Jamaica, wage levels of between 1s. 6d./day and 2s. 5d./day were not acceptable to most laborers and the decades after emancipation were characterized by continuous industrial unrest. In the Leeward islands, Barbados, and the Windwards, wages were lower, ranging from 6d./day to 1s. 5d./day. Malnutrition was reported widespread among the freed workers, and many found that their material living standards had not improved since the slavery days. The freed workers' continuing inability to dictate the pattern of economic activity, and the marginalization of peasant activity in most territories, led the plantation–economy theorists to refer to the postemancipation period as "capitalism and neo-slavery"—the conceptual continuation of the Williams's model. This analytic approach was central to G. L. Beckford's study of the post-emancipation West Indian plantation economy.[14]

13 *Ibid.*, pp. 40–43.
14 G. L. Beckford, "Socio-Economic Change and Political Continuity in the Anglophone Caribbean," *Studies in Comparative International Development*, Spring, 1980, pp. 3–14. See also Beckford, *Persistent Poverty: Under-development in Plantation Economies of the Third World* (Oxford, 1972).

A more specific manipulation of *Capitalism and Slavery* can be found in Best's model of the "pure plantation economy," an attempt to identify the forces generating capitalist underdevelopment in the region. Best, like his colleagues, accepted Williams's view that the plantation economy of the region was capitalist by inception, structure, and function. The objective nature of the region's economy, therefore, was not one of *un*development, but capitalist *under*development. Williams had shown how economic activity in the plantation economies was structurally geared toward the satisfaction of mercantile interests—hence the characteristic foreign trade bias and metropolitan-market determinism within the region. Best, therefore, reformulated Williams's argument and designated the islands "export-propelled economies"—subtypes of the wider North Atlantic capitalist mode of production. In order not to be accused of vulgar structural reductionism or economism, as Williams has been by his critics, the plantation theorists borrowed heavily from the historical sociology of M. G. Smith and Elsa Goveia and constructed the corresponding superstructures of these plantation economies. As a result, therefore, they went beyond Williams and provided a more complete conceptualization of the plantation system.[15]

Best's attempt to present a typology of the West Indian economy within a historical framework was theoretically pathbreaking.[16] He noted, following Myrdal and Seers, that his analysis rests upon the view that economic theory in the underdeveloped regions can profit only by relaxing its unwitting preoccupation with the special cases of North Atlantic countries and by proceeding to a typology of structures, each having characteristic laws of motion. Plantation economy, the type selected, Best noted, falls within the general class of hinterland or periphery externally propelled sub-economies. At this stage Williams's presentation of the structures of the mercantile system was invoked in order to separate the monoculture economies of Barbados and the Leewards from the more diversified economies, such as Jamaica's.[17]

In addition, within the typology presented by Best, the fol-

15   E. Goveia, *Slave Society in the British Leeward Islands* (New Haven, Conn., 1975); M. G. Smith, *The Plural Society in the British West Indies* (Berkeley, 1965).
16   C. Y. Thomas, "A Model of Pure Plantation Economy: A Comment," *Social and Economic Studies*, 17 (1968), pp. 339–348.
17   Best and Levitt, "Character of the Caribbean Economy," pp. 38, 41.

lowing central features of the slave economy under matured mercantilism were identified: (a) muscovado bias, (b) monopolistic metropolitan exchange mechanism, (c) Navigation Laws and exclusive trading, and (d) imperial preference.[18] He made references to the important work of Ragatz and Pares, but his model is based largely upon the cyclical movement of the British West Indian plantation economy between 1650 and 1838, as presented by Williams. He notes:

> The cycle can be divided into a foundation period, a golden age, and a period of maturity and decline. Maturity and decline tends to be a chronic condition, terminated by the total collapse of the system or the arrival of a new staple.[19]

By the end of the eighteenth century, Best notes,

> the metropolitan economy is undergoing far reaching change. Merchant enterprise has been organising industry, activating agriculture, and transforming the economy. Increasing commodity production both in the hinterland and in the metropolis, reduces the scarcity value of the imperial luxuries. In the course of time, the expansion of production and the extension of the market erodes mercantile profits, and with that, mercantile influence. . . . Capital shifts from trade to production. . . . The exclusivist structure erected to protect the profitability of mercantile economy is seen by rising industrial interest as a brake on further expansion. This we describe as the "Williams' Effect."[20]

This is clearly a restatement of the "decline thesis," which was also conceptualized by Ragatz but was originally presented in *Capitalism and Slavery.*

Furthermore, Best analyzed within his typology the many characteristics of the cyclical movements in the slave-plantation economy studied by Williams. In the first phase of the construction of plantations, Best noted, because most supplies and capital facilities were imported from the metropolis, the Keynesian multiplier effects of colonial expansion were experienced there. In addition, since most successful merchants and planters were ab-

18 Best, "The Mechanism of Pure Plantation-Type Economies," pp. 283–284.
19 Best and Levitt, "Character of the Caribbean Economy," p. 44.
20 Best, "The Mechanism of Pure Plantation-Type Economies," p. 291.

sentee, their domestic consumption patterns gave the plantation economy no opportunity to become diversified. The overall result was that any dynamic in the plantation economy must then have been infused by the surviving small settlers and manumitted slaves, insignificant groups in terms of numbers and resource ownership.

Also characteristic of the "pure plantation economy" was the form of adjustment to fluctuating earnings. Market conditions, though favorable in general, varied from time to time in response to temporary overexpansion, changes in weather, outbreak of war, and the like. A wide range of production rigidities resulted from the muscovado bias within the mercantile regulations, and the deployment of capital within the economy did not effectively respond to short-term market trends. The third feature relates to the size and distribution of the product. The closed character of the business rewards and profits were marked by what Douglas Hall refers to as incalculability. These features, also identified by Williams, and to a lesser extent by Pares and Ragatz, continued into the post-emancipation period, Best argues, and became the structural obstacles to economic development within the region.

Beckford's analysis of the region's contemporary economy also borrows significantly from the description of the mercantile system found in *Capitalism and Slavery*. His

> underlying theses . . . are that contemporary Caribbean economy and society maintain certain basic structural features rooted in slavery and the plantation system. . . . The economies of the West Indies are a passive part of the international capitalist system. As such, they demonstrate a high degree of dependency on the metropolitan economy for trade, capital, technology and management. The region itself provides only natural resources and labour. This represents an advance in relation to the slave plantation economy, which depended on imported labour.[21]

During the postslavery period, Beckford argues, the planter class survived. In fact, it was not seriously threatened at the levels of production and exchange by the growing black peasantry. The plantation continued to dictate the internal and external relations

---

21 Beckford, "Socio-Economic Change," p. 3.

of the economies, and the mercantile system became Creolized rather than undermined. The formation of an indigenous merchant class out of the colored, Jewish, Chinese, and other minority ethnic groups, continued to perpetuate the traditional mercantile dominance of the economy. Importation of commodities for distribution took precedence over diversified production of manufactures—hence the entrenchment of a neomercantilism in the twentieth century. Williams had elaborated on these points, not in *Capitalism and Slavery,* but in his 1970 book, *From Columbus to Castro: The History of the Caribbean.*[22]

An important comparative argument by Williams in *Capitalism and Slavery* stressed the differences found in the economic policies of the Spanish mercantile system and those of the English, in so far as they relate to industrialization in the colonies. In Cuba and Puerto Rico, for example, the Spanish imperial government assisted colonists in the development of local industry—particularly in the manufacture of consumer goods and in shipping facilities. As a result, during the eighteenth and nineteenth centuries, these economies were significantly diversified and largely self-reliant. The English policy toward the Indies, however, was different; it specified that "not even a nail" was to be manufactured in the colonies, Williams noted. At best, the colonists were allowed to assemble and modify English manufactures, but never to make their own. Industrialization was meant to be an imperial monopoly, and this was the central explanation for economic backwardness within the region into the twentieth century. Beckford, then, following Williams, stressed the argument that the mercantile arrangement and its ideas and institutions continued after slavery to place considerable pressures upon the allocation of capital within the region, hindering the growth of the domestic economy by starving the nonstaple sectors of resources. He notes:

> Contemporary Caribbean economy is essentially a modification of slave plantation economy. It is more diversified, as a result of peasant activity. But, by and large, the bulk of the resources of the

22 E. Williams, *From Columbus to Castro: The History of the Caribbean, 1492–1969* (London, 1970). See also W. A. Green, "The Planter Class and British West Indian Sugar Production, Before and After Emancipation," *Economic History Review,* 26 (1973), pp. 448–463.

economy are owned and controlled by foreign-owned producing units which maintain the character of total economic institutions directly tied to the metropolitan economy through the component subsidiaries and parent company of the multinational complex. These present-day resource-based enterprises create dependency relationships between the Caribbean and the metropole not far different from the slave plantation case.[23]

Williams did not pay specific attention to the evolution of the "proto-peasantry" in *Capitalism and Slavery,* but implied that the marginal economic activities of non-elite whites were an integral part of the plantation system, complementing rather than contradicting its interests. Logically, therefore, Beckford argued that a radical, if not revolutionary, restructuring of the plantation system was a necessary prerequisite for self-sustained economic development in the region.

Whereas Best's analysis represents a direct and static theoretical formulation of what he called the Williams effect, Beckford's presentation illustrates how the continuing decline of the plantation economy into the twentieth century has ensured underdevelopment structures and systems within the region. In his critique, Benn writes,

> Beckford, in fact, attempts to preserve his totalistic conception of the plantation system by arguing that the peasant sector is a mere sub-sector of the overall plantation sector. But even if this could be justified on purely economic criteria, it serves to obscure the independent dynamism of the peasant sector in providing the material base for the emergence of a new class formation within the society during the 19th century, the development of which Beckford's theory of plantation society seeks to explain by almost exclusive reference to the development of the plantation sector.[24]

This particular theoretical problem, Benn suggests, emerged specifically from the historical analysis as presented by Williams and Ragatz. The integration of the *Capitalism and Slavery* methodology into the economic models of the plantation theorists was probably too wholesale, and should have been subject to more critical tests.

---

23 Beckford, "Caribbean Rural Economy," p. 257.
24 Benn, "The Theory of Plantation Economy," p. 257.

Twentieth-century adjustments to the plantation economy were incorporated into the Beckford typology. Each West Indian economy came to be dominated by one or two sectors. All these economies, Beckford notes, share the common feature of traditional dependence. The economic typology looks as follows:

Pure Mineral Exports	Trinidad and Tobago
Pure Tourist	Bahamas, Cayman Islands, Virgin Islands, Antigua, Montserrat
Pure Plantation	St. Kitts, Belize
Peasant Exports	Dominica, St. Lucia, St. Vincent, Grenada
Mixed Economies	Jamaica, Guyana, Barbados

In Jamaica, the mixture is mineral exports, tourism, plantation, and peasant exports; in Guyana, mineral and plantation sectors dominate; while in Barbados, it is tourism and plantation.[25] Beckford notes in addition:

> Overall, the rate of economic growth in the postwar period has been most rapid in the economies dominated by minerals and tourism and slowest in those dominated by plantation and peasant production. But there are no significant differences in pattern of economic diversification. With the exception of peasant export, production in the areas identified is controlled by metropolitan-owned multinational corporations. These vertically integrated enterprises developed few linkages within the regional economies in which they operated. . . . The economy is divided into two broad components, the "overseas" and "residentiary," with the former being the more dynamic.[26]

The economic image that emerges is one of deep-rooted dependency—an extension of the system of relations outlined in *Capitalism and Slavery*.

Within the mining and tourist sectors are therefore to be found the continuation of the basic features of mercantilism. Girvan's research on the mineral economy of the region is conceptually in unison with Beckford's work on the rural economy.[27] He also employs the hinterland-metropolitan concept, and found within

25 Beckford, "Socio-Economic Change," p. 5.
26 *Ibid.*
27 N. Girvan, "Caribbean Mineral Economy," in Beckford (ed.), *Caribbean Economy*, pp. 92–130.

this sector the plantation-type characteristics of foreign owner-ship, metropolitan-market determinism, and terminal production processes. Mines and the modern hotel strips are conceived of as the "new plantations," and like old King Sugar, are subject to revised but essentially traditional laws of neomercantilism. Benn remarks that "in keeping with this macro-theoretical perspec-tive," Beckford sees "the new foreign-owned multi-national cor-porations, based on mining and manufacturing, as operating es-sentially within the institutional framework of the traditional plantation sector."[28] The critical difference between the old and new plantation sectors, for Beckford and Girvan, lies in their corresponding impact upon the social structure and political organization in the region.

During the 1970's, most of these radical economists became either advisors to regional governments or leaders of public-sec-tor institutions committed to policies of economic transforma-tion. There was, therefore, an applied dimension to this revolu-tion in economic thought. Its impact has been felt in the adoption of policies of nationalization, localization of resource ownership, and land reform programs. In addition, Girvan states, it can probably be said to have been associated at least to some extent with the nationalization policies pursued by the Burnham gov-ernment in Guyana since 1970, the Manley democratic-socialist government in Jamaica between 1972 and 1980, the Williams government of Trinidad and Tobago between 1970 and 1980, and Bishop's People's Revolutionary Government in Grenada be-tween 1979 and 1981.[29]

It is difficult, then, to refute the assertion that the plantation-economy school borrowed heavily, both empirically and concep-tually, from Williams's *Capitalism and Slavery*. That these links are not always explicitly stated but are sometimes subliminal in nature, is due essentially to the overwhelming presence of *Capi-talism and Slavery* as the historical point of departure. Invariably it was assumed that Williams's economic history and Goveia's social history were the bedrock of the new analyses, and hence there was no need to make the traditional supportive citation. As

28 Benn, "The Theory of Plantation Economy," p. 257.
29 N. Girvan, "The Impact of Caribbean Economic Thought on Development Policy," paper presented at the 21st Anniversary Conference of the Social Science Faculty, Uni-versity of the West Indies, Mona, Jamaica, March 20–24, 1983.

a result, and criticisms apart, *Capitalism and Slavery* underwent a renaissance during the late 1960's and 1970's in the hands of these radical political economists within the region, particularly those at the University of the West Indies. The black nationalist characteristics attributed to Williams's approach, born out of a powerful intellectual rejection of what he regarded as the condescending arrogance of British liberal historiography on the West Indies, were retained by his academic progeny. Most of these scholars were concerned with, if not angered by, the perceived role of imperial mercantilism in perpetuating economic backwardness and sociopolitical instability within the region. In this context, certain technical and empirical details of *Capitalism and Slavery* that continue to exercise the minds of Euro-American scholars were not seen as critical to its validity. It was the macro-theoretical thrust of the work that was uncritically accepted and reprocessed at the levels of radical economic theory. It would not be an exaggeration to say that its conceptual framework has remained productive and inspiring, if not enshrined, within the full panorama of the West Indian intellectual world.

Richard B. Sheridan

Eric Williams and *Capitalism and Slavery:* A Biographical and Historiographical Essay

We are met here to honor the achievements of the late Dr. Eric Williams and to discuss current research on outstanding issues in British West Indian history. In recent months I have reread much of *Capitalism and Slavery,* together with Williams's other books and articles, critiques of his work, and especially his autobiography, *Inward Hunger: The Education of a Prime Minister.* In this essay I will attempt to present a biographical and historiographical study of Williams, including a sketch of the man and his time and how he was influenced by different schools of historiography. I plan to look at his sources, methods, and findings, and, in greater detail, to show how his work has been assessed by historians and others. In short, I intend to show how various conditioning circumstances helped to mold the historical mind and work of Eric Williams, and how scholars in both the First and Third Worlds have reacted to *Capitalism and Slavery.* More attention will be given to the reactions of British scholars than their counterparts in the West Indies, Africa, and the United States.

Eric Eustace Williams was born in Port-of-Spain, Trinidad, September 25, 1911, the oldest of twelve children of Thomas Henry Williams, a clerk in the Port-of-Spain post office, and Eliza (Boissiere) Williams. He was a precocious child, taking to his studies with exceptional talent and determination under the encouragement and guidance of his father, but not to the exclusion of active participation in sports and part-time help with his mother's bakery business. He was educated in Port-of-Spain at Tranquillity Intermediate School and Queen's Royal College, where he held a government scholarship, graduated with honors, and won the Island Scholarship in 1931. One of Williams's tutors was Cyril Lionel Robinson James, who became a leader in the

Pan-African movement, and is widely known among Caribbean historians for his book, *The Black Jacobins: Toussaint Louverture and the San Domingo Revolution* (London, 1938). George Padmore was another Trinidadian in Williams's generation who became a leader in the Pan-African movement in London and Ghana.[1]

In 1932 Williams left Trinidad to take up his Island Scholarship at Oxford University. There he elected to read for an honors degree in modern history. At the end of three years he came to the final examination, which he described as "a gruelling ordeal of eleven papers lasting three hours each for five and a half days." He was awarded a first-class degree. After receiving his bachelor's degree, Williams went on to the postgraduate study of philosophy, politics, and economics. But after a year he switched to historical research. Here he was fortunate to have Vincent Todd Harlow as his tutor. "Notwithstanding the general contempt for research in colonial history," Williams wrote, "Harlow had already done some valuable work on seventeenth century West Indian history."[2]

For his postgraduate research Williams selected as his topic the abolition of slavery in the British Empire. With the conscientious and sympathetic guidance of Vincent Harlow, his working life for two years was spent in the Public Record Office, among the Additional Manuscripts of the British Library, and among the Parliamentary Papers and the records of Hansard. Williams's disssertation, entitled *The Economic Aspects of the Abolition of the West Indian Slave Trade and Slavery*, was, as he described it, "an important contribution to research on the subject." He was awarded the Doctor of Philosophy degree in December 1938.[3]

Lack of money and no prospects for an appointment to an academic post in England turned Williams's attention to America, where he secured a job as an Assistant Professor of Social and Political Science at Howard University in Washington, D.C. Besides his teaching duties, he entered upon an ambitious program that included research in West Indian history and colonial

1 Ivar Oxaal, *Black Intellectuals Come to Power: The Rise of Creole Nationalism in Trinidad and Tobago* (Cambridge, Mass., 1968), 65–76.
2 Eric Williams, *Inward Hunger: The Education of a Prime Minister* (London, 1969), 39–49.
3 *Ibid.*, 49–51.

questions of contemporary concern, a lecture program on West Indian affairs, and a proposal for a West Indian university. He was delighted to make the acquaintance of historians with kindred interests, especially Lowell Joseph Ragatz and Frank Wesley Pitman, who were leading authorities on the history of the British West Indies. With the help of Ragatz, Harlow, and others, Williams was awarded a Julius Rosenwald Fellowship which enabled him to make a research trip to Cuba, Haiti, and the Dominican Republic. The immediate result of his Caribbean trip was the publication in 1942 of his first book, *The Negro in the Caribbean.*[4]

"The stage was set," Williams later wrote, "for my major work—*Capitalism and Slavery,* the elaboration and expansion of my thesis on the British abolition movement. Having demonstrated the fall of slavery as a part of the movement of mature British capitalism, I proceeded to trace the association of slavery in its heyday with the rise of British capitalism."[5] He drew heavily on American scholarship in the field which he found quite remarkable, emphasizing that "the first half of *Capitalism and Slavery* was entirely new research on the period antecedent to that selected for my doctoral dissertation."[6] The book was published in November 1944 by the University of North Carolina Press at Chapel Hill; it contained 285 pages and sold for $3.00. A second printing appeared within one year of the first. Subsequently, the book was twice republished in New York, by Russell and Russell in 1961 with a second printing in 1967, and by Capricorn Books in 1966. In 1964 Andre Deutsch published a London edition with an introduction by D. W. Brogan. French, Japanese, and Russian editions have also appeared.[7]

Reviews of *Capitalism and Slavery* appeared in numerous American newspapers and learned journals and several British periodicals. Writing in *The American Historical Review,* Elizabeth Donnan felt that "in his zeal to establish the primacy of economic forces, Williams had been somewhat less than fair to the humanitarians whose voices were raised against the slave trade and later against slavery."[8] Carter Woodson, who reviewed *Capitalism and Slavery* in *The Journal of Negro History,* said that all the important archives of the British Empire yielded material for this essay,

4   *Ibid.,* 51–69.   5   *Ibid.,* 69.
6   *Ibid.,* 70.   7   *Ibid.,* 70.
8   Elizabeth Donnan's review in *The American Historical Review,* 50 (1945), 782–783.

which marked the beginning of the scientific study of slavery from the international point of view. He predicted that the book would "make a strong appeal to those who now array themselves against the British Empire because of its present policy of grabbing all of the universe which it can find any excuse for taking over."[9] In the *American Sociological Review,* Wilson Gee wrote that while Williams's treatment of his subject was carefully and well done in a scholarly fashion, he nevertheless exaggerated the role of slavery by claiming that it was almost the indispensable foundation stone in the establishment of modern capitalism.[10]

Frank Tannenbaum, the Latin American historian, wrote the most lengthy and critical review of *Capitalism and Slavery* for the *Political Science Quarterly.* He regarded it as a good book and a serious study but one that was flawed by bending the argument to prove an irrelevant theme and by Williams's acrid vehemence in deriding his teachers and attacking those who disagreed with him. Tannenbaum affirmed that while black slavery was a fact and a tragedy, it had many causes rather than one. He felt that by adhering to a single-minded economic determinism, Williams had repudiated all the values of human life, all traditions, ideals, and beliefs that men had stood and died for. In particular, Tannenbaum thought it erroneous for Williams to argue that whites historically had functioned as well as blacks in the tropics. He thought it better to accept the greater fitness of blacks for the tropics. However, Tannenbaum failed to distinguish between what he termed "the present physical thriving of the Negro" and his inferior political and socioeconomic status.[11]

Three reviews of Williams's *Capitalism and Slavery* appeared in British periodicals. In *The Times Literary Supplement,* D. W. Brogan noted that Williams adhered to a Marxian interpretation and that some of the sections of the book were more brilliant guesses than complete demonstrations of incontestable chains of cause and effect. Notwithstanding these and other criticisms, Brogan affirmed that *Capitalism and Slavery* was "an admirably

9 Carter G. Woodson's review in *The Journal of Negro History,* 30 (1945), 93–95.

10 Wilson Gee's review in the *American Sociological Review,* 10 (1945), 466–467.

11 Frank Tannenbaum, "A Note on the Economic Interpretation of History," *Political Science Quarterly,* 61 (1946), 247–253. See also Eric Williams, "Race Relations in Caribbean Society," and Frank Tannenbaum's "Discussion," in Vera Rubin, ed., *Caribbean Studies: A Symposium* (2nd edition, New York, 1960).

written, argued and original piece of work."[12] W. L. Burn, author of *Emancipation and Apprenticeship in the British West Indies* (London, 1937), reviewed Williams's book for *The English Historical Review*. Burn wrote that by pushing his economic argument too far, Williams had neglected to give sufficient weight to the political and moral arguments in favor of abolition and emancipation, and thus oversimplified the issues.[13] J. F. Rees reviewed the book for *The Economic History Review*. He praised Williams for the care he took in sifting authorities, both primary and secondary, and for providing a valuable guide to the literature on the subject. On the other hand, he questioned the author's inclination to stress the economic motive to the exclusion of all other motives and thought that some of Williams's generalizations should have been presented more guardedly.[14]

Stanley Engerman has observed that Williams presents two quite separable theses in his *Capitalism and Slavery*. The first, which I plan to discuss chiefly in this essay, concerns what Williams's preface calls "the economic study of the role of Negro slavery and the slave trade in providing the capital which financed the Industrial Revolution in England." The second is the role "of mature industrial capitalism in destroying the slave system."[15]

Although Williams was a diligent and able archival scholar, the analysis and interpretation of the data he collected from manuscript and printed primary sources was influenced by the schools of historiography that were prominent at the time he wrote *Capitalism and Slavery*. In this respect I plan to investigate briefly the mercantilist writers and Adam Smith, their chief critic; the free trade imperialists, especially Edward Gibbon Wakefield and Herman Merivale; the British Imperial School of Sir John Seeley and others; the American Imperial School of Charles M. Andrews and his students; and the Toronto School of Harold A. Innis. Moreover, Williams drew on secondary works on the In-

---

12 D. W. Brogan's review in *The Times Literary Supplement*, May 26, 1945, p. 4. See also the excerpts from other reviews in Williams, *Inward Hunger*, 70–71.
13 W. L. Burn's review in *The English Historical Review*, 62 (1947), 111–112.
14 J. F. Rees's review in *The Economic History Review*, 17 (1947), 77–78.
15 Stanley L. Engerman, "The Slave Trade and British Capital Formation in the Eighteenth Century: A Comment on the Williams Thesis," *Business History Review*, 46 (1972), 431; Eric Williams, *Capitalism and Slavery* (Chapel Hill, N.C., 1944), vii–viii.

dustrial Revolution in Britain authored by Sir John Clapham, Paul Mantoux, Thomas S. Ashton, and others. Among the historians who cannot be linked to any school are C. L. R. James and Richard Pares. To my knowledge, Dr. Williams was a pioneer in developing an analytical framework for what Philip Curtin calls the South Atlantic System, or what Williams calls the Triangular Trade. I shall attempt to run down the sources used to develop this system and make some attempt to assess its merits and demerits.

That Eric Williams drew heavily upon the economic writers of the seventeenth and eighteenth centuries is evident from a perusal of the endnotes of *Capitalism and Slavery*. "The writings of the leading mercantilists, Postlethwayt, Davenant, Gee, Sir Dalby Thomas, Wood, have been carefully examined; so has *The Wealth of Nations,* the anti-mercantilist classic," he wrote in the bibliography.[16]

As an undergraduate at Oxford, Williams offered British colonial history from 1830 to 1860 as a special period of history for the first-class degree. In preparation for this paper he said he read Edward Gibbon Wakefield's *A View of the Art of Colonization* (1849) and Herman Merivale's *Lectures on Colonization and Colonies* (1861). From these economists, and especially Merivale, Williams learned much concerning the economics of slavery and the operation of the mercantile system in the British West Indies. In Wakefield's view, it had been slavery that had made possible the combination of labor, division of employments, surplus produce of different sorts, and a great increase of capital—a chain of causes and effects suggestive of the Williams thesis.[17]

The leading figure in British imperial historiography in the mid-Victorian period was John Robert Seeley, who in 1883 published two series of his Cambridge lectures under the title, *The Expansion of England*. In contrast to the planned colonial empire envisaged by the mercantilists, Seeley taught that England had "conquered and peopled half the world in a fit of absence of mind." Asserting that the British Empire was bound together by a community of race and religion, Seeley stressed the need for an im-

16 Williams, *Capitalism and Slavery*, 266.
17 Williams, *Inward Hunger*, 41; Bernard Semmel, *The Rise of Free Trade Imperialism: Classical Political Economy, the Empire of Free Trade and Imperialism 1750–1850* (Cambridge, 1970), 76, 98–99, 111.

perial federation of the colonies of white settlement in temperate-zone regions, at the same time that he neglected the tropical colonies of mixed races and coerced labor.[18] In his *British Historians and the West Indies,* Williams set out to emancipate his compatriots from what he regarded as the detestable view of certain British historians whose writings sought to depreciate and imprison the West Indian people for all time in the inferior status to which they had been condemned. His special targets of attack were Thomas Carlyle, James Anthony Froude, and Reginald Coupland.[19]

Meanwhile, an American school of imperial history was emerging. From about 1910 until his death in 1943, Charles McLean Andrews of Yale University was the foremost historian of the American colonial period and the founder of a school of imperial history. Andrews was influenced by numerous currents of thought, including the "scientific" history of Leopold von Ranke, the Social Darwinism of Spencer and Sumner, the environmental determinism of the anthropogeographers, the Anglo-Saxon cult, and the rise of imperialism. The new school of American imperial history emphasized the basic unity of the Anglo-Saxon race and its mission to govern so-called backward races.[20]

Since the West Indies had played such an important role in Anglo-American colonial relations, it was to be expected that the Andrews school should apply its tools of "scientific" history to the Caribbean area. After exploring the vast treasure house of the Public Record Office, Andrews began to urge his students to use these and other sources to study the island colonies of Britain as well as the continental ones. Taking up the challenge was Frank Wesley Pitman. He wrote in the preface of his *The Development of the British West Indies, 1700–1763* (New Haven, Conn., 1917): "The West Indies have attracted, in recent years, an increasing interest from students of American colonial society." Pitman was concerned to point out the significance of the West Indies in the development and also the disruption of the old British Empire.

18 C. A. Bodelsen, *Studies in Mid-Victorian Imperialism* (New York, 1925), 149–160, 168, 173–175, 205; Deborah Wormell, *Sir John Seeley and the Uses of History* (Cambridge, 1980), 154–158, 166, 176–177.
19 Eric Williams, *British Historians and the West Indies,* with a preface by Alan Bullock (London, 1966), 7–8, 12–13, 59–75, 166–187, 197–208.
20 A. S. Eisenstadt, *Charles McLean Andrews: A Study in American Historical Writing* (New York, 1956), 163 ff.

Following in the footsteps of Pitman were other American historians, foremost of whom was Lowell Joseph Ragatz, author of *The Fall of the Planter Class in the British Caribbean, 1763–1833* (New York, 1928), and a monumental guide to the study of Caribbean history. Williams referred to Ragatz and Pitman as "the two principal scholars on the history of the British West Indies prior to emancipation." Williams dedicated *Capitalism and Slavery* to Ragatz, "the master in the field," who had recommended him to the press at Chapel Hill and who had later congratulated him "upon a corking good volume, one which makes a great and very real contribution to the literature of Colonial History."[21]

Harold A. Innis, the University of Toronto economic historian and creator of the "staples thesis," published his *The Cod Fisheries: The History of an International Economy* in 1940, which Williams cited in *Capitalism and Slavery*. As a tool of analysis, the staples thesis brought unity to Canadian economic history by its emphasis on the study of total situations in terms of resources, technology, markets, and institutions—economic, political, and social. Innis contended that staple exports were the leading sector of the Canadian economy and that economic development was a process of diversification around the export base. American and West Indian economic historians have found the staples thesis useful in showing how such staples as furs, fish, tobacco, rice, and cotton contributed to economic growth in North America, whereas the sugar export economies of the Caribbean have remained in a condition of chronic underdevelopment.[22]

Williams was drawn to the growing literature of what we now call the First Industrial Revolution. He regarded the books by Paul Mantoux and John H. Clapham as providing the best general treatment of the development of capitalism in England. Williams wrote that Clapham's "essay on 'The Industrial Revolution and the Colonies, 1783–1822' in Vol. II of the *Cambridge History of the British Empire* shows a more intelligent understanding of the abolition movement and the destruction of West Indian slavery than is to be found in all the works of the 'official' British historians." For modern studies of the Triangular Trade

21 Williams, *Inward Hunger*, 70; Williams, *Capitalism and Slavery*, 267–268.
22 Donald Creighton, *Harold Adams Innis: Portrait of a Scholar* (Toronto, 1957); Melville H. Watkins, "A Staple Theory of Economic Growth," *Canadian Journal of Economics and Political Science*, 29 (1963), 141–158.

and its relationship to industrial growth in Liverpool and Bristol and their hinterlands, he relied heavily upon Alfred P. Wadsworth and Julia DeL. Mann, *The Cotton Trade and Industrial Lancashire 1600–1780* (Manchester, 1931), and C. M. MacInnes, *Bristol, A Gateway of Empire* (Bristol, 1939). The latter book, which was based on unpublished materials in the Bristol archives, was described by Williams as "a healthy departure from emotional to scientific history."[23]

No recital of Williams's debt to others can diminish the importance of his own achievement. He wove together the separate strands of thought that he had found and in the process transformed their significance. What he brought to the study of imperial history were motives and attitudes that had been shaped by the experiences of his Trinidad boyhood. He wanted to confront the educated class of Britain and the wider English-speaking world with the sins of omission and commission of their forefathers and use this weapon to achieve racial, political, and social justice. In his *Inward Hunger,* he told of the conditions that prevailed in Trinidad in 1911, the year of his birth. These included the island's dependence on external trade, the crown colony legislature which fostered and promoted British interests, the lack of medical and educational advantages, a low standard of living, and widespread poverty and indigence. The Williams family itself was caught up in the culture of poverty and racism. Dr. Williams said that his father had been denied a promotion in the civil service because he lacked the necessary social qualifications of color, money, and education. Like his father, Williams became embittered by racial slurs and the obstacles he encountered in pursuing his career. He said he could not ignore the racial factor involved in his search for funds at Oxford to complete his research. In sum, Williams sought to achieve educational excellence and power as a means of compensation against deprivations. However, his motives do not serve as proof that the arguments he advanced in his scholarly books are incorrect.[24]

As Philip Curtin has noted, the South Atlantic System was a crucial factor in European competition for overseas empire in the seventeenth and eighteenth centuries. He means by this sys-

23 Williams, *Capitalism and Slavery,* 268–269.
24 Williams, *Inward Hunger,* 1–54.

tem the "complex economic organism centered on the production in the Americas of tropical staples for consumption in Europe, and grown by the labor of Africans."[25] In the first half of *Capitalism and Slavery,* Williams sought to show how this South Atlantic System, or, as he termed it, the Triangular Trade, made an enormous contribution to Britain's industrial development. Indeed, he argued that the profits of this trade fertilized the entire productive system of the country.[26]

In his bibliography Williams calls attention to two studies that present in a general way the relationship between capitalism and slavery. The first is a thesis submitted for the master's degree at Howard University in 1938 by Wilson E. Williams, entitled *Africa and the Rise of Capitalism.* Like Dr. Eric Williams, Wilson Williams is concerned with the African trade chiefly as "the apex of the triangular trade . . . which served to stimulate English manufactures, at the same time constituting a source of tremendous profits." But the Howard University thesis is a slim typescript volume of 48 pages which draws only on printed primary and secondary sources.[27]

The second and more important work to demonstrate the relationship between capitalism and slavery is C. L. R. James's *The Black Jacobins.* Williams wrote in this connection: "On pages 38–41 the thesis advanced in this book is stated clearly and concisely and, as far as I know, for the first time in England."[28] In his analysis of these two Trinidadians and their influential books, Ivar Oxaal writes: "Both studies stressed the decisive role of class conflict in history. Williams attacked the moral complacency associated with Britain's understanding of its slave-owning past; James sought to demolish the historical lie of Negro passivity under slavery. Both were radical works of scholarship written from the perspective of a marginal, black intellectual whose personal experiences had made him aware of the hypocrisy behind the metropolitan country's pious self-congratulation over its dealings with the colonies."[29]

25 Philip D. Curtin, *The Atlantic Slave Trade: A Census* (Madison, Wisc., 1969), 3.
26 Williams, *Capitalism and Slavery,* vii, 52, 105.
27 Wilson E. Williams, *Africa and the Rise of Capitalism.* Howard University Studies in the Social Sciences, Vol. 1, No. 1 (Washington, D.C., 1938), 9–10.
28 Williams, *Capitalism and Slavery,* 268.
29 Oxaal, *Black Intellectuals Come to Power,* 75–76.

As might be expected, the reaction to the Williams thesis has been generally positive in Third World countries, especially in the West Indies and Africa, and generally negative among scholars of the present generation in Europe and North America. That the Williams thesis should have had a highly positive reception in the West Indies is explainable, in part, by the author's leadership in the writing and teaching of history, even after he became Prime Minister of Trinidad and Tobago. Williams not only wrote *Capitalism and Slavery*, which inaugurated the modern period of West Indian historiography, but he also edited *The Caribbean Historical Review*, the first professional journal to provide a medium for historical writing of and within the area. Moreover, he edited and published historical documents, revived the Historical Society of Trinidad and Tobago, lectured widely on historical topics, promoted historical research and the teaching of West Indian history at all levels, and, at carnival time and other intervals, isolated himself from his people and political duties to write scholarly works, of which the most outstanding, perhaps, is *From Columbus to Castro: The History of the Caribbean 1492–1969* (London, 1970).[30]

Although the European and North American reaction to the Williams thesis has been generally negative on the part of scholars, the almost monolithic opposition has been challenged in recent years by new research, analysis, and interpretation. In part, this activity can be attributed to the intellectual and moral ferment generated by the revolt against colonialism and the rise of new nations and the civil rights crusade, together with the bitter memory of the slave trade and slavery. Writing in 1981, Stanley L. Engerman observed that "The recent outpouring of scholarly work on slavery and abolition has added much to our knowledge of the specifics of the rise, nature, and fall of the slave system and its impact on Europe, Africa, the Americas, and Asia."[31] However, there are no easy answers and resolutions to complex historical issues. Media for the dissemination of scholarly work

30 Williams, *Inward Hunger*, 108–111, 269–273, 327–331; Woodville K. Marshall, "Review of Historical Writing on the Commonwealth Caribbean since c. 1940," *Social and Economic Studies*, 24 (1975), 271–307.
31 Stanley L. Engerman, "Some Implications of the Abolition of the Slave Trade," in David Eltis and James Walvin (eds.), *The Abolition of the Atlantic Slave Trade: Origins and Effects in Europe, Africa, and the Americas* (Madison, Wisc., 1981), 3.

on the slave trade and slavery include dissertations, monographs, and periodicals. Moreover, papers have been presented at numerous conferences. Indeed, at least seven international conferences, seminars, and symposia concerned with different aspects of the transatlantic slave trade and slavery were convened in the decade of the 1970's: a conference at the University of Rochester, New York, in March 1972;[32] a seminar at the University of Liverpool, England, in May 1974;[33] the Sixth International Conference for Economic History in Copenhagen, Denmark, in August 1974;[34] a conference at Colby College in Waterville, Maine, in August 1975;[35] a conference in New York City in May 1976;[36] a symposium at the University of Aarhus, Denmark, in October 1978;[37] and a conference at the University of Waterloo, Canada, in March 1979.[38]

In this section I intend to identify the leading proponents and opponents of the Williams thesis, with special reference to the relationship between the Triangular Trade and the rise of capitalism, to summarize very briefly the arguments and counterarguments advanced, and to show how the range of issues has broadened over time. These issues include the volume, profitability, and disposition of the profits of the Atlantic slave trade, the profits of West Indian plantation production and trade and their disposition, the profits of the Triangular Trade and their disposition, the extent to which triangularity prevailed, the causes and consequences of the abolition of the slave trade and emancipation of the slaves in the British Empire and elsewhere, and the

32 Stanley L. Engerman and Eugene D. Genovese (eds.), *Race and Slavery in the Western Hemisphere: Quantitative Studies* (Princeton, 1975).
33 Roger Anstey and P. E. H. Hair (eds.), *Liverpool, the African Slave Trade and Abolition: Essays to illustrate current knowledge and research. Historical Society of Lancashire and Cheshire Occasional Series*, Vol. 2 (Bristol, 1976).
34 Pieter Emmer, Jean Mettas, and Jean-Claude Nardin (eds.), *La Traite des Noirs par l'Atlantique: Nouvelles Approches*, special number of *Revue Française d'Histoire d'Outre-Mer*, Tome LXII, Nos. 226–227 (Paris, 1975).
35 Henry A. Gemery and Jan S. Hogendorn (eds.), *The Uncommon Market: Essays in the Economic History of the Atlantic Slave Trade* (New York, 1979).
36 Vera Rubin and Arthur Tuden (eds.), *Comparative Perspectives on Slavery in New World Plantation Societies. Annals of the New York Academy of Sciences*, Vol. 292 (New York, 1977).
37 Eltis and Walvin, *Abolition of the Atlantic Slave Trade*.
38 Michael Craton (ed.), *Roots and Branches: Current Directions in Slave Studies* (Toronto, 1979).

impact of the slave trade and slavery upon Africa and the Americas.

In the decade of the 1950's only one scholarly critic of the Williams thesis has been identified. In his *British Imperial Trusteeship 1783–1850*, George R. Mellor singled out Williams for challenging the "humanitarian" interpretation of the abolition of the slave trade and slavery. Mellor faulted Williams on points of fact and felt that abolition, while it was facilitated by economic factors, was achieved by the application of principles of justice and humanity that far overshadowed any economic factors. More than two decades later, F. O. Shyllon published *Black Slaves in England*, in which he claimed that Mellor had attempted to come to Reginald Coupland's rescue, but in an incompetent and lamentable manner. Williams, on the other hand, was praised by Shyllon for presenting his central theme in a lucid and clearly reasoned manner.[39]

Brief but highly critical notices of Williams and his book appeared in the *Economic History Review* in the early 1960's. K. G. Davies wrote a review article on the work of the late Richard Pares, who was described as a "historian of empire" who made notable contributions to imperial and maritime history. By contrast, no merit could be found in Williams's contention that the great profits of the slave and sugar trades financed the Industrial Revolution. D. A. Farnie was even more critical, contending that *Capitalism and Slavery* had provided Williams's "own community with the sustaining myth that 'capitalism' was responsible for their condition, a view that has not found favour in western Europe, where history has been separated from its taproot in myth, but has been found highly acceptable to the educated elites of Africa and Asia."[40]

In 1964 Sir Reginald Coupland's *The British Anti-Slavery Movement* was reprinted with a new introduction by J. D. Fage. Fage sought to mediate between the interpretations of Williams and Coupland, explaining Williams's underlying lack of sympathy and understanding as perhaps "inevitable in the late 1930s

---

39 George R. Mellor, *British Imperial Trusteeship 1783–1850* (London, 1951), 24, 118–120; F. O. Shyllon, *Black Slaves in Britain* (London, 1974), ix–x, 156, 170, 230–231, 239.
40 K. G. Davies, "Essays in Bibliography and Criticism. XLIV. Empire and Capital," *Economic History Review*, 2nd ser., 13 (1960), 110; D. A. Farnie, "The Commercial Empire of the Atlantic, 1607–1783," *ibid.*, 15 (1962), 212.

and early 1940s, when a young Negro radical from the colonies, still more one from the bitterly depressed West Indies, found himself working in the shadow of the school of imperial history that Coupland had established within the calm walls of Oxford University." Fage suggested that the truth lay somewhere between the interpretations of Coupland and Williams.[41]

The following year saw the publication of my article, "The Wealth of Jamaica in the Eighteenth Century," in the *Economic History Review*. Based largely on the probate records in the Archives of Jamaica, this article lent support to the Williams thesis that substantial profits were derived from the sugar plantations of the British Caribbean colonies, and that much of the planters' wealth and income eventually came to reside in Great Britain. In a critique of my article in 1968, Robert Paul Thomas noted my omission of the administrative and military overhead costs of empire and the monopolistic sugar market in Britain, which taxed consumers to the benefit of planters and merchants. In my rejoinder I likened the modern debate to that between Edmund Burke, who contended that "this colony commerce is a new world of commerce in a manner created," and Adam Smith, who believed that the benefits of empire existed only in the imagination and that colonial policies, if continued, were "likely to cost immense expence, without being likely to bring any profit."[42] J. R. Ward, in an article in the same journal in 1978, calculated that the profits of sugar planting in the British West Indies averaged about 10 percent, a figure somewhat higher than the calculation I arrived at in my article and rejoinder. Ward suggests that a discussion of the social profitability of the British West Indies could usefully be reopened.[43]

Meanwhile, in 1966 M. W. Flinn published his book *The Origins of the Industrial Revolution,* which makes brief mention of the Williams thesis. Finding only one real example of slave traders and sugar importers who turned their profits into industrial

41 J. D. Fage, Introduction to Sir Reginald Coupland, *The British Anti-Slavery Movement* (London, 1964), xvii–xxi.

42 R. B. Sheridan, "The Wealth of Jamaica in the Eighteenth Century," *Economic History Review*, 2nd ser., 18 (1965), 292–311; and "A Rejoinder," *ibid.*, 21 (1968), 46–61; R. P. Thomas, "The Sugar Colonies and the Old Empire: Profit or Loss for Great Britain?" *ibid.*, 21 (1968), 30–45.

43. J. R. Ward, "The Profitability of Sugar Planting in the British West Indies, 1650–1834," *Economic History Review*, 2nd ser., 31 (1978), 197–213.

capital, he concluded that "obviously *some* industrial capital came from this source, but it must remain questionable whether it ever rose to very significant levels."[44]

Roger Anstey began his attack on the Williams thesis in 1968, in a critique published in the *Economic History Review*. Observing that wartime distractions had perhaps muted the immediate formal reception of *Capital and Slavery* in Britain, Anstey proposed "to offer some comments on a book whose continuing influence is suggested by the appearance of no less than three reissues between 1961 and 1966." The book had gained considerable favor among historians, he said, "and also amongst many English-speaking West African intellectuals who saw it as a bed-rock statement of Afro-European relations before the colonial period." Anstey chose to comment on the second half of Williams's book. With reference only to that part of his book where he sought to demonstrate the role of mature capitalism in destroying the slave system, the Trinidad historian was said to have too often used evidence misleadingly, made too large claims on partial evidence, or ignored evidence. Anstey concluded that "the initial impulse for abolition of the slave trade came from newly awakened Christian conviction strengthened by the 'reasonableness' and philanthropy of the Enlightenment."[45]

Anstey continued to publish papers and eventually a book that criticized the Williams thesis in its several parts. At the University of Rochester conference in 1972, he presented a paper on the volume and profitability of the British slave trade. After estimating the volume of slaves loaded and landed between 1761 and 1807 to be 10.3 percent higher than the estimate of Philip Curtin, Anstey proceeded to calculate the average net profit (about 9.5 percent) and the contribution of slave-trade profits to capital formation in England (0.11 percent), which he found "derisory enough for the myth of the vital importance of the slave trade in financing the Industrial Revolution to be demolished." In the first part of his book *The Atlantic Slave Trade and British Abolition 1760–1810* (1975), Anstey devotes three chapters to the Atlantic slave trade, its profitability, and its impact upon Africa. Trading methods in West Africa, treatment of slaves on the Middle Passage,

44 M. W. Flinn, *The Origins of the Industrial Revolution* (London, 1966), 45–46.
45 Roger T. Anstey, "Capitalism and Slavery: A Critique," *Economic History Review*, 2nd ser., 21 (1968), 307–320.

and their sale in the West Indies are themes that the author investigates in some depth. As with his previous papers, Anstey attempted to prove that Eric Williams was wrong to contend that the Triangular Trade made an enormous contribution to Britain's industrial development.[46]

Stanley Engerman also criticized the Williams thesis. In his article of 1972 which was published in the *Business History Review*, he sought to place the slave trade in perspective by concentrating upon an estimate of the profits of the slave trade and its contribution to investment in seventeenth- and eighteenth-century Britain. He calculated that the contribution of slave-trade profits to capital formation ranged for the years 1688–1770 from 2.4 percent to 10.8 percent, concluding that his estimates "should give some pause to those attributing to the slave trade a major contribution to industrial capital formation in the period of the Industrial Revolution."[47]

By contrast with Anstey's and Engerman's refutations of the Williams thesis, my book *Sugar and Slavery* (1974) tended to support Dr. Williams. I argued that "the economic growth of Great Britain was chiefly from without inwards, that the Atlantic was the most dynamic trading area, and that, outside the metropolis, the most important element in the growth of this area in the century or more prior to 1776 was the slave-plantation, chiefly of the cane-sugar variety in the islands of the Caribbean Sea."[48]

In the 1948 issue of *History, The Journal of the Historical Association*, there appeared a short notice of the publication of Williams's *Capitalism and Slavery*. "Dr. Williams," the notice went on to say, "is a West Indian, and it is encouraging to note that other non-European students from these islands are now coming to this country to undertake research into Caribbean history. Moreover, a few Africans are doing likewise, and as university

---

46 Roger Anstey, "The Volume and Profitability of the British Slave Trade, 1761–1807," in Engerman and Genovese, *Race and Slavery*, 3–31; Curtin, *Atlantic Slave Trade*; Roger Anstey, *The Atlantic Slave Trade and British Abolition 1760–1810* (Atlantic Highlands, N.Y., 1975).

47 Engerman, "The Slave Trade and British Capital Formation," 430–443.

48 Richard B. Sheridan, *Sugar and Slavery: An Economic History of the British West Indies 1623–1776* (Baltimore, 1974), 475.

institutions develop at Ibadan, Achimota and Makerere the flow may be expected to increase."[49]

Foremost among the West Indians who came to study in England and make notable contributions to African and Caribbean history before his tragic and untimely death in June 1980 was Walter Rodney. In his seminal study, *How Europe Underdeveloped Africa* (Tanzania, 1972), Rodney is concerned primarily with the negative impact of the Atlantic slave trade upon Africa. The European slave trade is said to have been the stimulus for a great deal of social disruption and violence among different African communities. Conditions became unsettled: warlike activities and kidnapping disrupted agricultural activities, labor was drawn off from agriculture, and the spread of contagious diseases was facilitated. The slave trade removed millions of youth and young adults who were the human agents from whom inventiveness springs. It also led to the influx of firearms and other trade goods by which means the African economy was diverted away from its previous line of development and became distorted. And the exploitation of Africa created a growing gap between Africa and capitalist Europe. Regarding *Capitalism and Slavery*, Rodney said that Dr. Williams had given "a clear picture of the numerous benefits which England derived from trading and exploiting slaves, and he identified by name several of the personalities and capitalist firms who were the beneficiaries."[50]

J. E. Inikori is a West African economic historian who has contributed to and commented on the debate on the Williams thesis. Inikori has discovered data that suggest a substantial upward revision in Curtin's estimates of the volume of the transatlantic slave trade; he has written on the volume and impact of the British gun trade to Africa in the era of the slave trade, and in a recent article he has criticized the widely accepted views on market structure and the profits of the British African trade, which he contends make the trade look much less profitable than it actually was. Although the subject of slave-trade profits is not without significance, Inikori believes that "the contribution of

49 Anonymous, "Recent Research in the Light of the Above Observations," *History, The Journal of the Historical Association*, New Series, 33 (1948), 80–81.
50 Walter Rodney, *How Europe Underdeveloped Africa* (Washington, D.C., 1982; first published in Tanzania, 1972), 85.

the slave trade and slavery to the expansion of world trade between the fifteenth and nineteenth centuries constitutes a more important role than that of profits." In his view, the repeated attacks on the Williams thesis since the 1950's indicate that the critics are not convinced that their attacks have been effective.[51]

A. G. Hopkins is an economic historian of West Africa who has commented on the Williams thesis. With reference to the views of Coupland and Williams, he maintains that "the general thesis put forward in *Capitalism and Slavery,* though it requires modification, comes much closer to understanding the problem than does Coupland's book." Although Hopkins believes that African and Atlantic commerce brought substantial gains to individuals and to certain regions, he does not agree with Williams that the Triangular Trade made an enormous contribution to Britain's industrial development. "Eric Williams's thesis may require qualifications," Hopkins writes, "but it must be acknowledged that in originality of argument and liveliness of presentation his book set standards which few historians attain, and for this reason it will continue to command respect."[52]

Among American authorities on slavery, W. E. B. Du Bois summarized Williams's thesis on the relationship between the Triangular Trade and industrial development of Great Britain in his general history of Africa. John Hope Franklin makes brief mention of Williams's work in his *From Slavery to Freedom.* He says that *Capitalism and Slavery* is significant for an understanding of the role played by the slave trade in the growth of capitalist enterprise. American sociologist E. Franklin Frazier also makes brief mention of Williams's work in at least one of his books. Apart from certain economic historians, few if any American authorities on slavery have given any extended treatment of *Capitalism and Slavery* in their publications, perhaps because Williams was primarily interested in showing how the slave trade and

---

51 J. E. Inikori, "Measuring the Atlantic Slave Trade: An Assessment of Curtin and Anstey," *Journal of African History,* 17 (1976), 197–223; J. E. Inikori, "The Import of Firearms into West Africa (1750–1807): A Quantitative Analysis," *ibid.,* 18 (1977), 339–368; J. E. Inikori, "Market Structure and the Profits of the British African Trade in the Late Eighteenth Century," *Journal of Economic History,* 41 (1981), 745–776.
52 A. G. Hopkins, *An Economic History of West Africa* (New York, 1973), 113–119, 122–123.

plantation slavery provided the capital to finance the Industrial Revolution in Great Britain.[53]

Turning to the West Indies, we find that a "new" school of political economy associated with the Caribbean New World Group emerged in the decade of the 1960's. Consisting of certain academic economists attached to the University of the West Indies, the Group has developed a theory of plantation economy and society in an attempt to explain why the Caribbean and other similar societies have been characterized by monocrop production, rigid class lines, ethnic heterogeneity, and persistent poverty for the masses. It is of interest that while the theory of plantation economy and society has a varied and intricate intellectual pedigree, much of the intellectual inspiration has come from Eric Williams's historical analysis in *Capitalism and Slavery* of the structural links between the colonial and metropolitan economies in the eighteenth and nineteenth centuries. According to the analysis of George Beckford, a member of the Group, the Caribbean economy became an appendage or "hinterland" of North Atlantic capitalism. "The bulk of the region's resources," he writes, "came to be owned by North Atlantic capitalists. Correspondingly, the peoples in the region have been forced to exist on what meagre resources were not alienated by the foreign capitalist. Because Black people gained least access to the left-over resources, theirs has been a lot of persistent poverty."[54]

Another "new" school that emerged in the decade of the 1960's is variously called the structuralist, dependency, and world economy school. Though differing in the emphasis they give to various factors, the leaders of this school focus attention on the relations between powerful capitalist countries and underdevel-

53 W. E. Burghardt Du Bois, *The World and Africa: An Inquiry into the Part which Africa has Played in World History* (New York, 1965), pp. 58–59, 64–65; John Hope Franklin, *From Slavery To Freedom: A History of American Negroes* (New York, 1956), pp. 48, 347–348, 547, 610; E. Franklin Frazier, *Race and Culture Contacts in the Modern World* (New York, 1957, pp. 55, 112, 128; Roderick A. McDonald, "The Williams Thesis: A Comment on the State of Scholarship," *Caribbean Quarterly*, 25 (1979), 63–68.

54 Denis M. Benn, "The Theory of Plantation Economy and Society: A Methodological Critique," *The Journal of Commonwealth and Comparative Politics*, 12 (1974), 249–260; George L. Beckford, "Toward Independent Economic Development for the Betterment of Caribbean Peoples," *The Massachusetts Review*, 15 (1974), 93–119; G. L. Beckford, *Persistent Poverty: Underdevelopment in Plantation Economies of the Third World* (New York, 1972).

oped countries from the standpoint of trade flows, flows of profits and dividends, and political and military influences. They contend that metropolitan or core regions exploit colonial and neocolonial peripheral regions through various mechanisms of unequal exchange, thus resulting in economic development in core regions and chronic underdevelopment in peripheral regions. Andre Gunder Frank is a leading theorist and historian of the dependency approach to the study of underdevelopment in Latin America and to a lesser extent Africa, the Middle East, and Asia. In his *World Accumulation 1492–1789,* he is concerned with the "historical process of capital accumulation, centered in Western Europe but increasingly encompassing other parts of the globe, beginning around 1500 and ending in 1789." He writes that by comparison with Adam Smith, Friedrich List, and Karl Marx, Eric Williams in his *Capitalism and Slavery* makes perhaps the most forceful argument regarding the connection between the expansion of colonial trade and the development of British industry.[55]

Michael Craton is a leading authority on the British West Indies in the era of slavery and sugar. In his book *Sinews of Empire* (New York, 1974), he addresses some of the issues raised by Eric Williams. Craton, like Fage and Hopkins, finds some merit in the views of both Coupland and Williams. He contends that abolition of the slave trade was owing, on the one hand, to the strength of the antislavery party, and, on the other hand, to the weakness of the defenders of the trade, at a time of fundamental changes in the course of empire. Craton analyzes the crucial question of profit in an able manner. "Of modern writers," he asserts, "Eric Williams in *Capitalism and Slavery* (1944) has given the most penetrating analysis of profits and tangential benefits and—more important still—has looked beyond the facade of figures into the *effects* of the sugar-slavery nexus." Overall, however, Craton adopts a cautious attitude concerning the Williams

---

55 Andre Gunder Frank, *World Accumulation 1492–1789* (New York and London, 1978), pp. 16–17, 229–231. Other scholars who are associated with the structuralist, dependency, and world economy school are Samir Amin, Giovanni Arrighi, Paul Baran, Fernando Cardosa, Theotonio Dos Santos, Arghiri Emmanuel, Celso Furtado, Raul Prebisch, and Immanuel Wallerstein. See Immanuel Wallerstein, *The Modern World System II: Mercantilism and the Consolidation of the European World-Economy, 1600–1750* (New York, 1980).

thesis, believing it is dangerously easy to overstate the direct influence of the Triangular Trade.[56]

In the first monograph-length critique of the Williams thesis, Seymour Drescher has investigated the "decline" thesis of British slavery. He attempts to show that, contrary to the Ragatz-Williams view, the slave system expanded down to the eve of abolition in 1807, and that the West Indies and Africa were among the most dynamic areas of British trade. Moreover, Drescher denies that the slave system was destroyed by the elites of trade and Parliament in the metropolis, or by the slaves who were exposed to the revolutionary ideology of the "Black Jacobins" of Saint-Domingue. Rather, he contends that the system was destroyed by the forces mobilized by the regional and local networks of social and religious life in the mother country.[57]

From his studies of the English outport trade, chiefly that of Bristol, Walter Minchinton has found reason to comment on certain aspects of the Williams thesis. He has investigated whether the Triangular Trade was indeed triangular in the sense of carrying cargoes on all three legs of the route. Despite the difficulties encountered in getting return cargoes from the Caribbean in the face of the growing shuttle trade between British ports and the slave-plantation colonies, Minchinton supplies evidence that slave traders did largely avoid returns in ballast. He has also found reasons for questioning the Drescher thesis in a paper that will be published in the near future.[58]

The two final studies I will attempt to summarize were written by cliometricians who employ mathematical models to test hypotheses involved in the debate on the Williams thesis. Barbara Solow has written a paper entitled "Caribbean Slavery and British Growth: The Eric Williams Hypothesis." She begins by noting that while the Williams thesis means different things to different people, it is her argument "that, properly understood,

56 Michael Craton, *Sinews of Empire: A Short History of British Slavery* (Garden City, N.Y., 1974), xxi, 109–110, 147–165, 239–240.
57 Seymour Drescher, *Econocide: British Slavery in the Era of Abolition* (Pittsburgh, 1977). According to Drescher, the West Indies became a leading source of raw cotton in the 1780s and 1790s. See P. J. Cain and A. G. Hopkins, "The Political Economy of British Expansion Overseas, 1750–1914," *Economic History Review*, 33 (1980), 473.
58 Walter E. Minchinton, "Williams and Drescher: Abolition and Emancipation," *Slavery and Abolition: A Journal of Comparative Studies*, 4 (1983), 81–105.

Capitalism and Slavery constituted a new and original reading of West Indian and British history. It was no mere restatement of Mercantilist fallacies, it demolished racial origin theories of slavery; it cast serious doubts upon the conventional interpretation of the anti-slavery movement." She then proceeds to clarify and lend support to Williams's argument relating the slave economies of the British West Indies to economic growth in Great Britain in the eighteenth century. In countering the critics of Williams, she concludes that the Williams hypothesis that slave labor provided the capital for financing British industrial development has neither been disproved because the profits were too small, nor because the colonies can be shown to have been a net loss to England. She praises Eric Williams for arguing that the growth of both the slave-plantation and temperate-zone colonies in America, as well as the British economy, was due in large part to the easy availability of slave labor. She believes that homage to Eric Williams is long overdue.[59]

William A. Darity, Jr., has woven together the works of Eric Williams, Walter Rodney, and C. L. R. James and shows how the vision of this "Caribbean School" provides a revision of history away from the interpretations offered by metropolitan historians. Whereas Williams concentrated on the central role of the Atlantic slave trade in the industrialization of Europe, Rodney advanced the proposition that simultaneously the Atlantic slave trade led to the underdevelopment of Africa. To Darity these two propositions potentially can be viewed as two sides of the same coin and when brought together they link two current phenomena, namely, European affluence and African poverty. C. L. R. James, the third member of the Caribbean School, by his pioneering research on the Haitian slave revolt, provided Eric Williams with his central thesis. It is Darity's contention that much of the recent criticism of *Capitalism and Slavery* is misplaced. Rather than the role of the Atlantic slave trade in providing finance capital for the Industrial Revolution, the core of the Williams thesis is the slave-plantation system which was central to an open-ended British mercantile strategy for economic development. Darity has developed a "least-likely" model which suggests "that the

59 Barbara Solow, "Caribbean Slavery and British Growth: The Eric Williams Hypothesis," *Journal of Development Economics,* 17 (1985), 99–115.

Williams-Rodney-James theory is quite robust as an explanation of the roots of European advance and African stagnation."[60]

From the above brief summaries, it is evident that the Williams thesis means different things to different people. It is also evident that the issues are so complex and imbued with such moral fervor that a resolution of the debate is unlikely in the foreseeable future. Supporters of Williams contend that *Capitalism and Slavery* constituted a new and original reading of West Indian and British history, that Williams sought to revise history away from the interpretations offered by metropolitan historians, that he gives a clear picture of the numerous benefits that Britain derived from trading and exploiting black slaves, and that his book sheds light on the forces making for persistent poverty in Africa and the West Indies. Critics of Williams and his thesis, on the other hand, contend that it is wrong to argue that the Triangular Trade made an enormous contribution to Britain's industrial development, that the Williams thesis has its taproot in the myth that capitalism was responsible for underdevelopment in Africa and the Caribbean, that the colonial system was an irrational drain on the metropolitan nations, that the Ragatz-Williams image of West Indian decline is ill-founded, and that principles of justice and humanity far overshadowed any economic factors in the campaign for abolition of the slave trade. Notwithstanding the failure to resolve the debate, progress has been made in defining the issues, new data sources have been uncovered, methods of analysis have been refined, and the debate has been broadened to include not only Europeans and North Americans, but also West Indians and Africans. Perhaps the most noteworthy development of the past decade has been the contribution of West Indian and African scholars to the debate on the Williams thesis. They have emphasized the negative impact of the slave trade and slavery upon the people of Africa and the Caribbean islands, an impact that has continued to the present day.

It should be emphasized that the debate on the Williams thesis is part of a larger debate on the causes and consequences of the

---

60   William A. Darity, Jr., "A General Equilibrium Model of the Eighteenth-Century Atlantic Slave Trade: A Least-Likely Test for the Caribbean School," Paul Uselding (ed.), *Research in Economic History* (Greenwich, Conn., 1982), Vol. 7, 287–325.

Industrial Revolution. The numerous causal factors have, according to one classification, been divided chiefly between those of an external or overseas origin and others of an internal, domestic, or home origin. One group of scholars believes that Europe developed economically through a succession of stages by drawing chiefly upon its own resources; the other group believes that the commercial revolution ushered in a new era of development largely from without inward, a process of interaction between the core states which concentrated on secondary and tertiary activities and the primary producing territories on the periphery. In this section I will look briefly at the rival claims of the home market advocates on the one hand, and those of foreign or overseas markets on the other hand.

In July 1960, the *Second Past and Present One-Day Conference* was held in London on the theme "The Origins of the Industrial Revolution." Among the numerous topics of discussion were population growth, markets, scientific discoveries, capital formation, entrepreneurship, and sources of raw materials. One participant questioned the usefulness of the notion of "takeoff," arguing that "it might be more helpful to consider the process of industrialisation as a sequence of several stages in the course of which society passed from a preindustrial to an industrial mode of life." On the other hand, it was suggested "that an adequate analysis of the Revolution would have to consider not just a single economy but a whole trading area of economic interactions within which one national economy managed to take the lead." Among the unresolved questions were the following: "What were the contributions respectively of overseas and home demand in providing the markets which made [Britain's] industrial innovations worth-while? In particular what was the real role of British colonial trade in the early eighteenth century?"[61]

The home market argument has long-established and respectable antecedents. It was Adam Smith who, in his attack on the mercantilists, asserted that it was the "inland or home trade" that was "the most important trade of all." By comparison with foreign trade, the inland or home trade was said to have afforded the greatest revenue to capital and created the greatest employ-

---

61 [Eric Hobsbawm], "The Origins of the Industrial Revolution: Conference Report," *Past and Present*, 17 (April 1960), 71–81.

ment to the people of the country.[62] Modern economic historians who give priority to the home market over foreign markets argue that the largest growth market was the home market, that foreign trade was unstable and still relatively small, and that Britain's full involvement in foreign commerce came after, rather than before, the Industrial Revolution. As M. W. Flinn argues, "Whatever influence is attributed to the growth of overseas demand, the fact remains that for most individual industries, and for all industries put together, home demand predominated, and was therefore able to exercise a more decisive influence on output." Similarly, Ralph Davis has argued that while there was an Atlantic economy, "it was subsidiary to, a modification and enhancement of, the economies of the individual countries of the Atlantic seaboard that took part in it."[63]

The first important break with the traditional home market emphasis in British economic history came in 1960 with the publication of a short article by Kenneth Berrill. He expressed a discontent with current theoretical models of economic growth in which demand played a passive role, and where the models were posed in terms of closed and homogeneous national economies and made no attempt to distinguish the separate roles of agriculture, transport, utilities, and particular staple crops or industries. He noted that, owing to water-linked trading areas, international trade is often much cheaper and easier than internal land-linked trade. Having gained greater command of seaborne trade than her rivals, Britain was able to expand her home and colonial markets and achieve rapid industrialization, particularly in cotton textiles which were both mass-produced and mass-consumed.[64]

---

62 Adam Smith, *The Wealth of Nations* (Modern Library edition, New York, 1937), 349–353, 403, 422.

63 M. W. Flinn, *Origins of the Industrial Revolution*, 62; R. M. Hartwell, *The Industrial Revolution and Economic Growth* (London, 1971), 151–152, 183; Ralph Davis, *The Rise of the Atlantic Economies* (Ithaca, N.Y. 1973), xiii; R. P. Thomas and D. N. McCloskey, "Overseas Trade and Empire 1700–1860," in Roderick Floud and Donald McCloskey (eds.), *The Economic History of Britain Since 1700. Vol. I: 1700–1860* (2 vols., Cambridge, 1981), 95–102; D. E. C. Eversley, "The Home Market and Economic Growth in England, 1750–1780," in E. L. Jones and G. E. Mingay (eds.), *Land, Labour and Population in the Industrial Revolution: Essays Presented to J. D. Chambers* (London, 1967), 206–259; Patrick O'Brien, "European Economic Development: The Contribution of the Periphery," *Economic History Review*, 2nd ser., 35 (1982), 1–18.

64 K. Berrill, "International Trade and the Rate of Economic Growth," *Economic History Review*, 2nd ser., 12 (1960), 351–359.

In their critique of W. W. Rostow's analysis of the takeoff stage in Britain, Phyllis Deane and H. J. Habakkuk present data and arguments that may be construed as indirectly supporting the Williams thesis. They call attention to the strong expansion of the volume of trade with the British West Indies and Asia, observing that such expansion was capable of having important multiplier effects on the British economy at the end of the eighteenth century. Overall, they claim that it was the international trade sector "which developed increasing returns by carrying the products of British industry to mass markets, which reaped the advantages of new resources and technical progress in primary producing countries and which created a world demand for new products."[65]

The role of Africa and the Caribbean slave-plantation colonies in European and British economic development is emphasized in the writings of Eric Hobsbawm. He claims that European expansion in the preindustrial era rested on three things:

> in Europe, the rise of a market for overseas products for everyday use, whose market could be expanded as they became available in larger quantities and more cheaply; and overseas the creation of economic systems for producing such goods (such as, for instance, slave-operated plantations) and the conquest of colonies designed to serve the economic advantage of their European owners.

Concerning the expansion of Great Britain, Hobsbawm contends that while home demand increased, foreign demand multiplied and served as a spark to ignite the cotton textile industry which was essentially tied to overseas trade.[66]

Hobsbawm has also shed considerable light on the Williams thesis in his analysis of the general crisis of the European economy in the seventeenth century. He contrasts the growth potential of the spice trade, which yielded high profits on a limited volume of business, with the sugar plantations, which

> turned out to be immensely stimulating to the economy in general, since they depended on a self-generated and constant expansion of

65 Phyllis Deane and H. J. Habakkuk, "The Take-Off in Britain," in W. W. Rostow (ed.), *The Economics of Take-off into Sustained Growth* (New York, 1965), 77–80.
66 E. J. Hobsbawm, *Industry and Empire: An Economic History of Britain since 1750* (London, 1968), 27–38.

markets all-round: more sugar sold at lower prices, more sales in Europe, more European goods sold in the colonies, more slaves needed for the plantations, more goods with which to buy slaves, and so on.

Indeed, Hobsbawm contends that "the new colonial system which emerged in the middle of the seventeenth century became one of the chief elements and it may be argued the decisive element, in the preparation of industrial revolution."[67]

F. J. Fisher, like Eric Hobsbawm, supplies data and analysis useful for an understanding of the Williams thesis. He looks at the factors that made London, in an important sense, the economic center of England in the seventeenth century. It is his argument that seventeenth-century English trade expansion became increasingly import-led, that London became "a vigorous market for the fruits, the cheap silks, the cheap spices, the cheap sugar, and such new commodities as tobacco and calicoes that flowed in gradually mounting quantities from Spain, the Mediterranean, Africa, America and the East and West Indies." Rather than stimulating the export industries, the rising tide of imports was paid for to a large extent by re-exports, and re-exporting was essentially the function of London merchants. Moreover, increased imports led to a movement for import substitution, but, for the most part,

> it took the form of substituting English colonies for foreign countries as sources of supply. Above all, it took the form of substituting the services of English ships and merchants for those of foreigners. The great import-substitution measures of the seventeenth century were not protective duties but the Navigation Acts. The competitor to be eliminated was not England's great industrial rival, which was France, but her commercial rival—the Netherlands.

In the course of the eighteenth century, as Fisher observes, foreign trade became export-led rather than import-led, so that the dynamic factor shifted to the manufacturing areas. Thus, Britain and other industrialized countries stimulated primary production

67   E. J. Hobsbawm, "The Seventeenth Century in the Development of Capitalism," *Science and Society*, Spring 1960, 97–112; E. J. Hobsbawm, "The General Crisis of the European Economy in the 17th Century," *Past and Present*, Numbers 5 and 6, May 1954, 33–53; November 1954, 44–65.

in other parts of the world in the earlier stages of their development, but in the course of time they developed import-substitution industries themselves.[68]

Born three years prior to the outbreak of World War I, in a colony that was an economic backwater of the British Empire, of poor parents who pushed their children to achieve intellectual excellence; winner of the island scholarship to Oxford University, author of a doctoral thesis that was revised and expanded into a highly controversial book, and longtime prime minister of his native island—the career and achievements of Eric Williams are awesome both in the breadth of his intellectual and political influence and the depth and penetration of his historical scholarship. His *Capitalism and Slavery* was a radical work of scholarship, highly original in its argument and liveliness of presentations, forcefully attacking the complacent school of imperial history that Williams encountered at Oxford in the 1930's. Conceived in the Depression years when British imperialism was under attack in the West Indies and elsewhere and published near the end of World War II, *Capitalism and Slavery* has in recent decades become a target of attack of certain scholars in the First World and a rallying cry for both intellectuals and politicans in the Third World. Interestingly enough, Williams wrote and later acted out as prime minister his own anticolonial manifesto, although he moderated his attitude and policies toward the North Atlantic metropolitan countries in the later years of his life. Eric Williams began his study with the origin of black slavery in a historical and international setting, with the doctrines and policies of the mercantilists, and with the seventeenth-century beginnings of the Caribbean sugar colonies and the African slave trade. He continued his historical analysis and interpretation, delineating the rise and decline of the Atlantic slave trade and slave-plantation economy and society, the age of the American Revolution, the abolition and emancipation movements, the repeal of the Corn Laws and Navigation Acts. It is still true today, as it was when the

---

68 F. J. Fisher, "London as an 'Engine of Economic Growth'," in J. S. Bromley and E. H. Kossmann (eds.), *Britain and the Netherlands. Volume IV. Metropolis, Dominion and Province: Papers Delivered to the Fourth Anglo-Dutch Historical Conference* (The Hague, 1971), 3–16.

dust-jacket summary of *Capitalism and Slavery* was written in 1944, that Williams's analysis of the causes and consequences of the Industrial Revolution and his account of the interplay of economic, social, and political forces make his book significant "for our own day."

Printed in the United States
25145LVS00002B/151-159